Thomas Hardy

State Trials for High Treason

Embellished with Portraits

Thomas Hardy

State Trials for High Treason
Embellished with Portraits

ISBN/EAN: 9783744726986

Printed in Europe, USA, Canada, Australia, Japan

Cover: Foto ©Suzi / pixelio.de

More available books at **www.hansebooks.com**

FOR

HIGH TREASON,

EMBELLISHED WITH PORTRAITS.

PART THE FIRST,

CONTAINING THE

TRIAL OF THOMAS HARDY,

REPORTED BY A STUDENT IN THE TEMPLE.

TO WHICH IS PREFIXED

.Lord Chief Justice Eyre's Charge to the
GRAND JURY.

WITH

I. Original Obfervations on the Charge and the Laws againſt High Treaſon.
II. Names of the Grand Jury.
III. Proceedings on finding the Bills of Indictment.
IV. Particulars of Mr. Holcroft's Surrender and Commitment, with attendant Obſervations.
V. Copy of the Bill of Indictment.
VI. Liſt of the Petty Jury.
VII. Witneſſes for the Crown.
VIII. Names of the principal Perſons ſubpœ aed by the Priſoners.
IX. Counſel for the Crown.
X. Counſel for the Priſoners.

WITH EVERY OTHER IMPORTANT OCCURRENCE RESPECTING THIS MOST INTERESTING SUBJECT OF PUBLIC CONCERN AND CURIOSITY.

LONDON:

Printed for B. Crosby, No. 4, Stationers Court, Ludgate Street; Lee, New Street, Covent Garden; Mason and White, Piccadilly; and all the Bookſellers under the Royal Exchange.

ADVERTISEMENT.

THE present trials for High Treason, being subjects of equal importance and curiosity to every native of the realm, this work is intended to contain the most minute and accurate detail of every proceeding, relative to the judicial enquiries into the truth or fallacy of the charges exhibited in the several bills of indictment found against the prisoners.

As thousands now existing, and yet unborn, may be implicated in the present decisions of the Law respecting High Treason, the strictest attention will be paid to the opinions of the court, the pleadings of the counsel, the reference to precedents, and the sanction of the great law authorities that may be adduced.

We shall be faithful to the discharge of such an important undertaking, as that of publishing essential information for every subject in so interesting a point as High Treason, in which the welfare of a nation is involved, and especially as individuals of the purest intentions may be endangered. Particular attention will be given to whatever relates to the existing laws, their application to the present circumstances, and the construction of the statutes respecting the crime.

In a word, whatever can tend to inform the mind, gratify the curiosity, and direct every subject in the knowledge of a law wherein the first of civilians have looked with awe, doubt, and perplexity, will be most carefully recorded in the series of our publications of the trials, as they happen in their destined order of succession.

OBSERVATIONS on HIGH TREASON.

LORD Chief Juſtice Eyre having, in his Charge to the Grand Jury, informed them that they were aſſembled under the authority of the King's commiſſion, iſſued for hearing and determining the offences of High Treaſon and miſpriſions of Treaſon againſt the *perſon and authority of the King*, induces us to ſtate a few preliminary obſervations on the exiſting law reſpecting this ſpecies of criminality.

According to the ſtatute of the 25th of Edw. III. which was expreſsly enacted to define what was High-Treaſon, ſo as to ſecure the ſubject from arbitrary deciſions, an overt act muſt be proved by two witneſſes, of compaſſing or imagining the death of the King.

Having ſtated that the ſubſtantiating the crime of High Treaſon depends on overt acts being proved, it is neceſſary to obſerve what conſtitutes an overt act. According to every principle of law, it muſt be an act determined or executed for the ſpecific purpoſe of compaſſing the death of the King. Without this can be proved, neither the deſign nor the fact can be deemed High Treaſon. No plans or operations that are not *provably* directed to effect the above purpoſe, are to be conſidered as overt acts of this atrocious crime. The moſt certain rule is, therefore, by the act of Edw. III. eſtabliſhed for directing the Jury in their deciſion on the charges of High Treaſon ſubmitted to their inquiry. Overt acts, however various in their nature, unleſs definite in their object, have no law to ſanction their being claſſed in the criminal liſts of treaſons. The deſign or " wicked imagination of the heart" muſt be obviouſly, and not conſtructively, tending to the atrocious purpoſe of compaſſing or imagining the death of the King. But, unhappily for the ſubject, arbitrary monarchs, ſervile judges, and dependant juries, have abuſed a ſtatute that every perſon ſhould admire for it's ſimplicity, humanity, and perſpicuity. In the reign of Charles II. one Gibbs was executed for High Treaſon, who had only heard treaſonable words ſpoken againſt the King, and had not diſcovered the perſon who uttered them. And although this happened from his ignorance of the law, and he had hazarded his life in defence of Charles II. againſt the fifth-monarchy men, yet ſuch was the vindictive perſecution of that reign, that he ſuffered equally with the moſt atrocious of traitors.

Such acts of tyrannical ſeverity could no but excite the greateſt
jealouſy

jealousy in the minds of the people respecting the investigation of charges for High Treason. Although it is a crime which must be abhorrent to the citizen of integrity and patriotism, yet it has since been considered as a subject of the most alarming import with regard to the abuse of it's prosecution.

We, therefore, cannot but agree with Mr. Justice Blackstone, who says, " as this is the highest civil crime, (considered as a member of the community) any man can possibly commit, it ought, therefore, to be precisely determined. For if the crime of treason be indeterminate, this alone (says the president Montesquieu) is sufficient to make any government degenerate into arbitrary power. And yet, by the ancient common law, there was a great latitude left in the breast of the judges, to determine what was treason, or not so: whereby the creatures of tyrannical Princes had opportunity to create abundance of *constructive* Treasons; that is, to raise by forced and arbitrary construction, offences into the crime and punishment of Treason, which were never suspected to be such.*

But to remedy such an abuse of jurisprudence, the act of Edward III. thus provides, " Because other like cases of Treason may happen in time to come, which cannot be thought of, nor declared at present; it is accorded, that *if any other case, supposed to be treason, which is not above specified*, doth happen before any judge, the judge shall tarry without going to the judgment of the treason, till the cause be shewed and declared before the King and his Parliament, whether it ought to be judged treason, or other felony." On this subject, Sir Matthew Hale has bestowed the most distinguished approbation. He praises the wisdom and care of the Parliament in thus keeping judges within the bounds and limits of the act; by not suffering them to establish constructive Treasons on the basis of their arbitrary motives, the Subject is secured from persecution, and the constitutional law is protected from violation.

Reserving cases not specified in the act of Edw. III. to the decision of Parliament, prevents, as Matthew Hale observes, Judges from running out upon their own opinions into constructive treasons. Well may, therefore, Justice Blackstone state, " This is a great security to the public, the judges, and even this sacred act itself, and leaves a weighty memento to judges to be careful, and not over-hasty in letting in treasons by construction and interpretation, especially in new cases that have not been resolved and settled."

Matthew Hale observes, that as the authoritative decision of these *casus omissi* is reserved to the King and Parliament, the decision

* Vol. iv. page 75. edit. 9. 1783.

sion of the law ought to be done by a new declarative act. And, therefore, as Blackstone states, "the opinion of any one, or of both Houses, though of very respectable weight, is not that solemn declaration referred to by this act, as the only criterion for judging of future treason."

To prove that forced and arbitrary constructions have punished individuals for treason which they never meditated, the incroaching or attempting to exercise royal power, which the great law commentator judiciously observe, is a very uncertain charge, was, in the 21st Edw. III. held to be treason in a knight of Hertfordshire. His crime was forcibly assaulting and detaining one of the King's subjects until he paid him 90l. although this crime deserved punishment, it was certainly no treason. There could be no compassing or meditating the King's death intended by such an assumed authority. The act was plainly directed to the sole purpose of obtaining payment of a debt due to the knight. And as there was no statute formed for the detention of the body until payment could be obtained, the person adopted this mode of violence as the dernier resort to which he could apply for the recovery of his due. Killing the King's father or mother, or even his messenger, or his judges on the bench, were deemed Treasons. On this, Blackstone says, with great propriety, that it was almost as tyrannical a doctrine as that by the imperial constitution of Arcadius and Honorius, which determines that any attempt or design against the ministers of the Prince shall be Treason. To prevent such abuses the statute of 25 Edward III. as before stated, was made. This statute must therefore be our text and guide in order to examine into the several species of High Treason.

The arbitrary stat. 21. Rich. II. c. 3, which made the bare purpose and intent of killing or deposing the King, without any overt act to demonstrate it, High Treason, did not preserve him from being deposed and murdered within two years afterwards. This evinces, that a King is never more exposed to danger, than when he has adopted the most arbitrary means for his security. But so insecure was held the life of the subject by this act, and so inadequate it was found to preserve the King from apprehended violence, that his successor Henry IV. with equal wisdom and magnanimity, passed an act which effected it's repeal, and every other extravagant and tyrannical imputation of treason adopted in the preceding reign. This act, in it's recital, contains the following memorable description of the uncertain tenure by which the subject could expect to preserve his life from ministerial vengeance. It states, "That no man knew how he ought to behave himself, to do, speak, or say, for doubt of such pains of

treason,

treason, and therefore it was awarded, that in no time to come, any treason be judged otherwise than was ordained by the statute of King Edward. III."

The following are "the new fangled treasons," which Blackstone states were abrogated by the statute, 1 Mar. c. 1. These were revived and invented from the reigns of Henry IV, until that of their extinction, when the statute of Edward was again made the standard of the crime. The treasons he mentions that were thus abrogated were clipping of money; breaking prison, or rescue; burning houses to extort money; stealing of cattle by Welshmen; counterfeiting foreign coin; wilful poisoning; execrations against the King; calling him opprobious names by public writing; counterfeiting the sign manual or signat; refusing to abjure the Pope; deflowering or marrying without the royal licence any of the king's children, sisters, aunts, nephews, or nieces; bare solicitation of the chastity of the queen or princess, or advances made by themselves; marrying with the king, by a woman not a virgin, without previously discovering to him such her unchaste life; judging or believing (manifested by any overt act) the king to have been lawfully married to Anne of Cleve; derogating from the King's royal stile and title; impugning his supremacy; and assembling riotously to the number of twelve, and not dispersing upon proclamation.

The act of assembling, therefore, and even riotously, is no longer a treason. The meetings of the societies, to which so much criminality has been endeavoured to be attached, cannot since the law of Mary be treasonable, when they are considered abstractedly as meetings or associations. To constitute them acts of treason, it is surely necessary to prove some overt act that evinces the compassing or meditating the death of the King.

Compassing or imagining the King's death must be proved to be the design, from overt acts of such meetings. As the terms *compassing* and *imagining* are held, in a legal sense, to be synonimous by Matthew Hale, Blackstone, and other judicial authorities, and that the word *compass* expressly signifies the purpose of the design of the mind, or will, and not, as commonly said, the carrying such design into effect. For an effect may be produced in which the will has no concern. Such was the case, as stated by Blackstone, of Sir William Tyrrel, who, by the command of King William Rufus, shooting at a hart, the arrow glanced against a tree, and killed the King upon the spot. Therefore this accidental stroke, which proved mortal to the sovereign, *per infortunium*, without any traitorous intent, cannot be treason. Nor can this compassing or imagination, from it's being an act of the mind, be subject to judicial cognizance, unless it be demonstrated by some open or *overt* act.

Were

Were such laws ever to be adopted, we might deem ourselves under such a system of oppression, as marked the tyranny of Dionysius, who executed a subject for merely dreaming that he killed him; this was held a sufficient proof of his having thought of the same act in his waking hours. But such not being the temper of the English law, an open or overt act of a more full, obvious, and explicit nature, must be proved, to convict any person of treason. This statute expressly states and requires, that the accused " be thereof upon sufficient proof attainted of some open act by men of his own condition." Thus the providing of weapons or ammunition for the purpose of killing the King would be held, according to the law institutes, a palpable overt act of treason, or imagining his death. But it must be proved, by certain open facts, that they were provided for that and no other purpose. It must be proved that, in the moment of alarm of an invading enemy, these arms were not provided as the means of defending themselves and their families from outrage; but, on the contrary, that they were meant for the sole purpose of killing the king.

Having thus stated the few observations that the limits of this number will admit, upon the law of treason, we shall conclude the introduction with the following short remark from Blackstone. By this it will appear that his idea of compassing, or meditating the King's death, is that of evidence being produced that weapons were provided to kill the King, conspiracies formed to imprison him, or some other acts adopted for rendering such treasonable purposes effective. " To conspire, to imprison the king by force, and move towards it by assembling company, is an overt act of compassing the king's death; for all force used to the person of the king, in it's consequence, may tend to his death, and is a strong presumption of something worse intended than the present force, by such as have so far thrown off their bounden duty to their sovereign; it being an old observation that there is generally but a short interval between the prisons and graves of princes. There is no question also but that taking any measures to render such treasonable purposes effectual, as assembling and consulting on means to kill the King, is a sufficient overt act of High Treason."

TRIALS OF THE STATE PRISONERS

FOR

HIGH TREASON.

AS several comments have been made upon the charge given by the Lord Chief Justice Eyre, to the Grand Jury, previous to their proceeding to find the bill of indictment against the persons committed on charges of High Treason, we beg leave to premise the following observations, previous to our insertion of the charge itself.

There is, perhaps, no part of a Judge's duty that requires more liberality, justice, humanity, and knowledge, than that of giving his charge to the Grand Jury, on all cases in which the life of the subject is so imminently concerned, as on bills of indictment for High Treason. In their zeal to preserve the King, or the State, from injury, mercy to the accused should not be forgotten. The law should be explained with precision and perspicuity; but it should not be interpreted so as to extend it's effect beyond it's original meaning. When exemplary punishments are necessary to preserve a King, or his people, from ruin, no bill of indictment should be found for crimes that were never meditated by the accused. Whatever he has positively committed, or whatever can be proved was his intention to commit, should be the only rule of sending him to be tried, for the same, by a jury of his equals.

On Thursday, October 2, the Special Commission for trying persons committed to the Tower, &c. charged with treasonable practices, was opened at the Sessions House, Clerkenwell Green, before Lord Chief Justice Eyre, the Lord Chief Baron, Baron Hotham, Mr. Justice Buller, Mr. Justice Grose, and Mr. Justice Lawrence, the Commissioners therein named.

GRAND JURY.

Benjamin Winthrop, Foreman,

John Snider,
Edward Ironsides,
Benjamin Kenton,
Robert H. Boddam,
John Aris,
W. H. Boddam,
John Perry,
John Hankey,
Samuel Cuff,
Thomas Winslowe,
Samuel Hawkins,
George Ward,
Thomas Boddam,
Joseph Lancaster,
Robert Wilkinson,
Thomas Cole,
George Galway Mills,
Henry Wright,
John Hatcher,
Robert Stephenson,
John Campbell, and
Tho. Everett, esqrs.

After they had been sworn in, Lord Chief Justice Eyre delivered the following charge:

Gentlemen of this Grand Inquest,

You are assembled under the authority of the King's Commission, which has been issued for the hearing and determining of the offences of High Treason, and Misprisions of Treason, against the person and authority of the King.

That which hath given occasion for this Commission is that which is declared by a late statute, namely, "That a traitorous and detestable conspiracy has been formed for subverting the existing laws and constitution, and for introducing the system of anarchy and confusion which has so lately prevailed in France;" a crime of that deep malignity which loudly calls upon the justice of the nation to interpose, "for the better preservation of his Majesty's sacred person, and for securing the peace, and the laws and liberties of this kingdom."

The first and effective step in this, as in the ordinary criminal proceedings, is, that a Grand Jury of the country should make public inquisition for the King, should diligently enquire, discover, and bring forward to the view of the criminal magistrate those offences which it is the object of this Special Commission to hear and to determine.

You are Jurors for our Sovereign Lord the King; you are so styled in every indictment which is presented; but let the true nature of this service be understood. The King commands you to enter upon this enquiry; but the royal authority in this, as in all it's other functions, is exerted, and operates ultimately for the benefit of his people. It is the King's object, his duty, to vindicate his peace, his crown and dignity, because *his peace, his crown and dignity*, are the *subjects' protection, their security, and their happiness.*

It is ultimately for them that the laws have thrown extraordinary fences around the person and authority of the King, and that all attempts against the one or the other are considered as the highest crimes which can be committed, and are punished with a severity which nothing but the *Salus Populi* can justify.

The business of this day calls upon me (in order that you may the better understand the subject which is to come before you) to open to you the nature of that offence, which I have before spoken of in general.

An ancient statute, 25 Edward III. has declared and defined it. I shall state to you so much of that declaration and definition as appears to me to have any probable relation to the business of this day.

By

By that statute it is declared to be High Treason " to compass " or imagine the death of the King," provided such compassing and imagination be manifested by some act or acts proved (by two witnesses) to have been done by the party accused in prosecution of that compassing and imagination; that is, from the moment that this wicked imagination of the heart is acted upon, that any steps are taken in any manner conducing to the bringing about and effecting the design, the intention becomes the crime, and the measure of it is full.

These acts or steps are technically denominated *overt acts;* and the forms of proceeding in cases of this nature require that these overt acts should be particularly set forth in every indictment of treason; and, from the nature of them, they must constitute the principal head of enquiry for the Grand Jury.

These overt acts involve in them two distinct considerations: 1st, The matter of fact of which they consist; in the next place, the relation of that fact to the design.

With respect to the mere matter of fact, it will be for the Grand Jury to enquire into the true state of it, and I can have very little to offer to your consideration respecting it; and with respect to the question, whether the fact has relation to the design so as to constitute an overt act of this species of treason, which involves considerations both of fact and of law, it is impossible that any certain rule should be laid down for your government: overt acts being, in their nature, all the possible means which may be used in the prosecution of the end proposed, they can be no otherwise defined, and must remain for ever infinitely various.

Thus far I can inform you, that occasions have unhappily but too frequently brought overt acts of this species of treason under consideration; in consequence of which we are furnished with judicial opinions upon many of them; and we are also furnished with opinions drawn from these sources by some of the wisest and most enlightened men of their time, whose integrity has been always considered as the most prominent feature of their character, and whose doctrines do now form great landmarks, by which posterity will be enabled to trace, with a great degree of certainty, the boundary lines between High Treason and offences of a lower order and degree.

It is a fortunate circumstance that we are thus assisted; for it is not to be dissembled, that though the crime of High Treason is " the greatest crime against faith, duty, and human society," and though " the public is deeply interested in every prosecution " of this kind well founded," there hath been, in the best times, a considerable degree of jealousy on the subject of prosecutions for High Treason; they are state prosecutions, and the consequences to the party accused are penal in the extreme.

Jurors and Judges ought to feel an extraordinary anxiety that prosecutions of this nature should proceed upon solid grounds. I can easily conceive therefore, that it must be a great relief to Jurors placed in the responsible situation in which you now stand, bound to do justice to their country and to the parties accused, and anxious to discharge this trust faithfully; sure I am that it is consolation and comfort to us, who have upon us the responsibility of declaring what the law is in cases in which the public and the individual are so deeply interested, to have such men as the great Sir Matthew Hale, and an eminent Judge of our own times, who, with the experience of a century, concurs with him in opinion, Sir Michael Foster, for our guides.

To proceed by steps—From these writers upon the law of Treason (who speak, as I have before observed, upon the authority of adjudged cases) we learn, that not only acts of *immediate and direct* attempt against the King's life are overt acts of compassing his death, but that all the *remoter steps* taken with a view to assist to bring about the actual attempt, are equally overt acts of this species of treason; even the meeting and the consulting what step should be taken in order to bring about the end proposed, has been always deemed to be an act done in prosecution of the design, and as such an overt act of this treason—This is our first step in the present enquiry. I proceed to observe, that the overt acts I have been now speaking of have reference, nearer or more remote, to a *direct* and *immediate* attempt upon the life of the King; but that the same authority informs us, that they who aim directly at the life of the King (such, for instance, as the persons who were concerned in the assassination plot in the reign of King William) are not the only persons who can be said to compass or imagine the death of the King. " The entering " into measures which, in the nature of things, or in the com" mon experience of mankind, do obviously tend to bring the life " of the King into danger, is also compassing and imagining " the death of the King;" and the measures which are taken will be at once evidence of the compassing, and overt acts of it.

The instances which are put by Sir Matthew Hale and Sir Michael Foster, (and upon which there have been adjudged cases) are of conspiracies to *depose* the King, *to imprison him, to get his person into the power of the conspirators, to procure an invasion of the kingdom.* The first of these, apparently the strongest case, and coming the nearest to the direct attempt against the life of the King; the last, the farthest removed from that direct attempt, but being a measure tending to destroy the public peace of the country, to introduce hostilities, and the necessity of resisting force by force, and where it is obvious that the conflict has an ultimate tendency to bring the person and life of the King into jeopardy;

it

it is taken to be a found conftruction of the ftatute 25 Edward III. and the clear law of the land, that this alfo is compalling and imagining the death of the King.

If a confpiracy to depofe or to imprifon the King, to get his perfon into the power of the confpirators, or to procure an invafion of the kingdom, involves in it the compaffing and imagining of his death, and if fteps taken in profecution of fuch a confpiracy are rightly deemed overt acts of the treafon of imagining and compaffing the King's death; need I add, that if it fhould appear that *it has entered into the heart of any man, who is a fubject of this country, to defign to overthrow the whole government of the country, to pull down and to fubvert from it's very foundations the Britifh monarchy, that glorious fabric which it has been the work of ages to erect, maintain, and fupport, which has been cemented with the beft blood of our anceftors; to defign fuch a horrible ruin and devaftation, which no King could furvive, a crime of fuch a magnitude that no lawgiver in this country hath ever ventured to contemplate in it's whole extent;* need I add, I fay, that the complication and the enormous extent of fuch a defign will not prevent it's being diftinctly feen, that " the compaffing and imagining the death of " the King is involved in it, is in truth of it's very effence."

This is too plain a cafe to require further illuftration from me. If any man of plain fenfe, but not converfant with fubjects of this nature, fhould feel himfelf difpofed to afk whether a confpiracy of this nature is to be reached by this medium only; whether it is a *fpecific* treafon to compafs and imagine the death of the King, and *not a fpecific* treafon to confpire to fubvert the monarchy itfelf; I anfwer, that the ftatute of Edward III. by which we are governed, hath not declared this (which in all juft theory of treafon is the greateft of all treafons) to be High Treafon.

I faid no lawgiver had ever ventured to contemplate it in it's whole extent. The *Seditio Regni*, fpoken of by fome of our ancient writers, comes the neareft to it, but falls far fhort of it. Perhaps if it were now a queftion whether fuch a confpiracy fhould be made a fpecific treafon, it might be argued to be unneceffary; that in fecuring the perfon and authority of the King from all danger, the monarchy, the religion and laws of our country are incidentally fecured; that the conftitution of our government is fo framed, that the imperial crown of the realm is the common center of the whole; that all traitorous attempts upon any part of it are inftantly communicated to that center, and felt there; and that, as upon every principle of public policy and juftice, they are punifhable as traitorous attempts againft the King's perfon or authority, and will, according to the particular nature of the traitorous attempt, fall within one or other of the

fpecific

specific treasons against the King, declared by the statute of 25 Edward III. this greatest of all treasons is sufficiently provided against by the law.

Gentlemen, I presume, I hardly need give you this caution, that though it has been expressly declared, by the highest authority, that there do exist in this country men capable of meditating the destruction of the constitution under which we live; that declaration, being extrajudicial, is not a ground upon which you ought to proceed.

In consequence of that declaration, it became a public and indispensable duty of His Majesty to institute this solemn proceeding, and to impose upon you the painful task of examining the accusations, which shall be brought before you; but it will be your duty to examine them in a regular judicial course, that is, by hearing the evidence, and forming your own judgment upon it.

And here, as I do not think it necessary to trouble you with observations upon the other branches of the statute 25 Edw. III. the charge to the Grand Inquest might conclude, had not the particular nature of the conspiracy, alledged to have been formed against the state, been disclosed, and made matter of public notoriety by the Reports of the two Houses of Parliament, now in every one's hands: but, that being the case, I am apprehensive that I shall not be thought to have fulfilled the duty, which the Judge owes to the Grand Jury, when questions in the criminal law arise on new and extraordinary cases of fact; if I did not plainly and distinctly state what I conceive the law to be, or what doubts I conceive may arise in law, upon the facts which are likely to be laid before you, according to the different points of view in which those facts may appear to you.

It is matter of public notoriety that there have been Associations formed in this country, and in other parts of the kingdom, the professed purpose of which has been a change in the Constitution of the Commons House of Parliament, and the obtaining of Annual Parliaments; and that to some of these Associations other purposes, hidden under this veil, purposes the most traitorous, have been imputed; and that some of these Associations have been supposed to have actually adopted measures of such a nature, and to have gone into such excesses, as will amount to the crime of High Treason.

If there be ground to consider the professed purpose of any of these Associations, "a Reform in Parliament," as mere colour, and as a pretext held out in order to cover deeper designs—designs against the whole Constitution, and Government of the country; the case of those embarked in such designs is that, which I have already considered. Whether this be so, or not, is mere matter of fact; as to which I shall only remind you, that an inquiry into a charge of this nature, which undertakes to make out that the ostensible purpose is a mere veil, under which is concealed a traitorous conspiracy, requires cool and deliberate examination, and the most attentive consideration; and that the result should be perfectly clear and satisfactory. In the affairs of common life, no man is justified in imputing to another a meaning contrary to what he himself expresses, but upon the fullest evidence. On the other hand, where the charge can be made out, it is adding to the crime meditated the deepest dissimulation and treachery, with respect to those individuals, who may be drawn in to embark in the ostensible purpose, as well as to the public, against which this dark mystery of wickedness is fabricated.

But if we suppose these Associations to adhere to the professed purpose, and to have no other primary object; it may be asked, is it possible, and (if it be possible) by what process is it, *" that an Association for the Reform of Parliament can work itself up to the crime of High Treason?"* All men may, nay, all men must, if they possess the faculty of thinking, reason upon every thing which sufficiently interests them to become objects of their attention; and among the objects of the attention of free men, the principles of Government, the constitution of particular Governments, and, above all, the Constitution of the Government under which they live, will naturally engage attention, and provoke speculation. The power of communication of thoughts and opinions is the gift of God, and the freedom of it is the source of all science, the first fruits and the ultimate happiness of society; and therefore it seems to follow, that human laws ought not to interpose, nay, cannot interpose, to prevent the communication of sentiments and opinions in voluntary assemblies of men; all which is true, with this single reservation, that *those Assemblies are to be so composed, and so conducted, as not to endanger the public peace and good order of the Government under which they live;* and I shall not state to you that associations and assemblies of men, for the purpose of obtaining a Reform in the interior Constitution of the British Parliament, are simply unlawful; but, on the other hand, I must state to you, that they may but too easily degenerate, and become unlawful, in the highest degree, even to the enormous extent of the crime of High Treason.

The process is very simple: Let us imagine to ourselves this case: A few well-meaning men conceive that they and their fellow subjects labour under some grievance; they assemble peaceably to deliberate on the means of obtaining redress; the numbers increase; the discussion grows animated, eager, and violent; a rash measure is proposed, adopted, and acted upon; who can
say

say where this shall stop, and that these men, who originally assembled peaceably, shall not finally, and suddenly too, involve themselves in the crime of High Treason? It is apparent how easily an impetuous man may precipitate such Assemblies into crimes of unforeseen magnitude, and danger to the state: but, let it be considered, that bad men may also find their way into such Assemblies, and use the innocent purposes of their association as the stalking horse to *their* purposes of a very different complexion. How easy for such men to practise upon the credulity and the enthusiasm of honest men, lovers of their country, loyal to their prince, but eagerly bent upon some speculative improvements in the frame, and internal mechanism of the Government? If we suppose bad men to have once gained an ascendancy in an Assembly of this description, popular in it's constitution, and having popular objects; how easy is it for such men to plunge such an assembly into the most criminal excesses? Thus far I am speaking in general, merely to illustrate the proposition, that men who assemble in order to procure a Reform of Parliament may involve themselves in the guilt of High Treason.

The notoriety to which I have alluded leads me to suppose, that the "project of a Convention" of the people, to be assembled under the advice and direction of some of these societies, or of delegations from them, will be the leading fact, which will be laid before you in evidence, respecting the conduct and measures of these Associations; a project, which perhaps, in better times, would have been hardly thought worthy of grave consideration; but, in these our days, having been attempted to be put in execution in a distant part of the united kingdoms, and, with the example of a neighbouring country before our eyes, is deservedly become an object of the jealousy of our laws: It will be your duty to examine the evidence on this head very carefully, and to sift it to the bottom; to consider every part of it in itself, and as it stands connected with other parts of it, and to draw the conclusion of fact, as to the existence, the nature, and the object of this project of a Convention, from the whole.

In the course of the evidence you will probably hear of "bodies " of men having been collected together, of violent resolutions " voted at these and at other meetings, of some preparation of " offensive weapons, and of the adoption of the language, and " manner of proceeding of those Conventions in France, which " have possessed themselves of the Government of that country:" I dwell not on these particulars, because I consider them, not as substantive Treasons, but as circumstances of evidence, tending to ascertain the true nature of the object, which these persons had in view, and also the true nature of this project of a Convention, and to be considered by you in the mass of that evidence; which

evidence

evidence it does not fall within the province of the charge to consider in detail; my present duty is, to inform you what the law is upon the matter of fact, which in your judgment shall be the result of the evidence.

I presume that I have sufficiently explained to you, that *a project to bring the people together in convention in imitation of those National Conventions which we have heard of in France in order to usurp the government of the country* and any one step taken towards bringing it about, such as for instance, "Consultations, forming of committees to consider of the means, acting in those committees," would be a case of no difficulty that it would be the *clearest High Treason;* it would be compassing and imagining the King's death, and not only his death, but the death and destruction of all order, religion, laws, all property, all security for the lives and liberties of the king's subjects.

That which remains to be considered is, "the project of a convention, having for it's sole object the effecting a change in the mode of representation of the people in Parliament, and the obtaining that Parliaments should be held annually;" and here there is room to distinguish. Such a project of a Convention, taking it to be criminal, may be criminal in different degrees, according to the case in evidence, from whence you are to collect the true nature and extent of the plan, and the manner in which it is intended to operate; and it will become a question of great importance, under what class of crimes it ought to be ranked.

In determing upon the complexion and quality of this project of a Convention, you will lay down to yourselves one principle which is never to be departed from; *That alterations in the representation of the people in Parliament, or in the law for holding parliaments, can only be effected by the authority of the King, Lords, and Commons, in Parliament assembled.* This being taken as a foundation, it seems to follow as a necessary consequence, that "a project of a Convention, which should have for it's object the obtaining a Parliamentary Reform without the authority of Parliament, and steps taken upon it, would be *High Treason* in all the actors in it;" for this is a conspiracy to overturn the Government. The Government cannot be said to exist, if the functions of Legislation are usurped for a moment; and it then becomes of little consequence indeed, that the original conspirators, perhaps, had only meditated a plan of moderate reform: it is, in the nature of things, that the power should go out of their hands, and be beyond the reach of their controul. A conspiracy of this nature is therefore, at best, a conspiracy to overturn the Government, in order to new model it, which is, in effect, to introduce anarchy, and that which anarchy may chance

[18]

to settle down into; after the King may have been brought to the scaffold, and after the country may have suffered all the miseries which discord, and civil war, shall have produced.

Whether " the project of a Convention, having for it's object " the collecting together a power, which should overawe the " Legislative Body, and extort a Parliamentary Reform from " it," if acted upon, will also amount to *High Treason*, and to the specific treason of compassing and imagining the King's death, is a more doubtful question. Thus far is clear; a force upon the Parliament must be immediately directed against the King, who is an integral part of it; it must reach the King, or it can have no effect at all. Laws are enacted in Parliament by the King's Majesty, by and with the advice of the Lords and Commons, in Parliament assembled. A force meditated against the Parliament, is therefore a force meditated against the King, and seems to fall within the case of a force meditated against the King, to compel him to alter the measures of his Government: but, in that case, it does not appear to me that I am warranted by the authorities to state to you, as clear law, that the mere conspiracy to raise such a force, and the entering into consultations respecting it, will alone, and without actually raising the force, constitute the crime of High Treason. What the law is in that case, and what will be the effect of the circumstance of the force being meditated against the King *in Parliament*, against the King in the exercise of the royal function in a point, which is of the very essence of his monarchy, will be fit to be solemnly considered, and determined when the case shall arise.

It may be stated to you as clear, That " the project of a " Convention, having for it's sole object a dutiful and peaceable " application to the wisdom of Parliament on the subject of a " wished-for Reform, which application should be entitled to " weight and credit from the universality of it, but should still " leave to the Parliament the freest exercise of it's discretion to " grant or to refuse the prayer of the petition," (great as the responsibility will be on the persons concerned in it, in respect of the many probable, and all the possible, bad consequences of collecting a great number of people together; with no specific legal powers to be exercised, and under no government but that of their own discretion,) " cannot in itself merit to be ranked " among that class of offences" which you are now assembled to hear and determine.

Upon this last statement of the fact of the case, I am not called upon, and therefore it would not be proper for me to say more.

Gentlemen, You will now proceed upon the several articles of enquiry which have been given you in charge: If you find

that

that the parties, who shall be accused before you, have been pursuing lawful ends by lawful means, or have been only indiscreet, or, at the worst, if criminal, that they have not been criminal to the extent of those treasons to which our enquiries are confined, then say, that the bills which shall be presented to you, *are not true Bills:* But, if any of the accused persons shall appear to you to have been engaged in that traitorous and detestable conspiracy described in the preamble of the late statute; or, if without any formed design to go the whole length of that conspiracy, they have yet acted upon the desperate imagination of bringing about alterations in the Constitution of the Commons House of Parliament, or in the manner of holding Parliaments, without the authority of Parliament, and, in defiance of it, by an usurped power, which should, in that instance, suspend the lawful authority of the King, Lords, and Commons, in Parliament assembled, and take upon itself the function of Legislation; (which imagination amounts to a conspiracy to subvert the existing laws and Constitution, differing from the former only in the extent of it's object,) *you will then do that which belongs to your office to do.*

In the third view of the case of the accused persons; that is, if you find them involved in, and proceeding upon, a design to collect the people together against the legislative authority of the country, for the purpose, not of usurping the functions of the Legislature, but of overawing the Parliament, and so compelling the King, Lords, and Commons, in Parliament assembled, to enact a law for new modelling the Commons House of Parliament, or for holding annual Parliaments; and that charges of High Treason are offered to be maintained against them upon this ground only; perhaps it may by fitting that, *in respect of the extraordinary nature and dangerous extent, and very criminal complexion of such a conspiracy,* that case, which I state to you as a new and a doubtful case, should be put into a judicial course of enquiry, that it may receive " a solemn adjudication, whether " it will, or will not, amount to *High Treason,*" in order to which the bills must be found to be true bills.

Gentlemen, I have not opened to you the law of *Misprision of Treason,* because I am not aware that there are any commitments for that offence; and therefore I have no reason to suppose that there will be any prosecution for that offence. It consists of *the concealment of treason committed by others,* (which undoubtedly it is every man's duty to disclose,) and the punishment is extremely severe; but the humanity of modern times hath usually interposed, and I trust, that the necessities of the present hour will not demand, that the law of Misprision of Treason should now be carried into execution.

Gentlemen, I dismiss you with confident expectation that your
judg

judgment will be directed to those conclusions, which *may clear innocent men from all suspicion of guilt, bring the guilty to condign punishment, preserve the life of our Gracious Sovereign, secure the stability of our government, and maintain the public peace, in which comprehensive term is included the welfare and happiness of the people under the protection of the laws and liberties of the kingdom.*

After this charge was delivered, the witnesses, who were to give evidence before the Grand Jury, were sworn in. No fewer than 36 witnesses were sworn to give evidence on one bill.

The Court then adjourned till next day, at ten o'clock.

COPY *of the* INDICTMENT *against the* PRISONERS *accused of* HIGH TREASON.

MIDDLESEX to wit, be it remembered that at a special session of Oyer and Terminer of our Sovereign Lord the King, of and for the county of Middlesex, holden at the Session-House on Clerkenwell Green in the said county, on Thursday the second day of October, in the thirty-fourth year of the reign of our Sovereign Lord George the Third, by the grace of God, of Great Britain, France, and Ireland, King, Defender of the Faith, and so forth; before the Right Honourable Sir James Eyre, Knight, Chief Justice of our said Lord the King, of his Court of Common Pleas; the Right Honourable Sir Archibald Macdonald, Knight, Chief Baron of our said Lord the King, of his Court of Exchequer; the Honourable Sir Beaumont Hotham, Knight, one of the Barons of our said Lord the King, of his said Court of Exchequer; the Honourable Sir Francis Buller, Baronet, one of the Justices of our said Lord the King, of his said Court of Common Pleas; the Honourable Sir Nash Grose, Knight, one of the Justices of our said Lord the King, assigned to hold Pleas before the King himself; the Honourable Sir Soulden Lawrence, Knight, one other of the Justices of our said Lord the King, assigned to hold Pleas before the King himself, and others their fellows, Justices, and Commissioners of our said Lord the King, assigned by Letters Patent of our said Lord the King under his Great Seal of Great Britain, made to them and others, and any three or more of them (of whom one of them the aforesaid Sir James Eyre, Sir Archibald Macdonald, Sir Beaumont Hotham, Sir Francis Buller, Sir Nash Grose, and Sir Soulden Lawrence, our said Lord the King willed should be one) to inquire by the oath of good and lawful men of the

County

County of Middlesex, of all high treasons, in compassing or imagining the death of our Lord the King, levying war against our Lord the King in his realm, or in adhering to the enemies of our said Lord the King in his realm, giving to them aid and comfort in his realm or elsewhere, and of all misprisions of such high treasons as aforesaid, or of any of them within the county aforesaid, (as well within liberties as without,) by whomsoever, and in what manner soever done, committed, or perpetrated, when, how, and after what manner, and of all other articles and circumstances concerning the premises, and every, or any of them, in any manner whatsoever, and the said treasons and misprisions of treasons according to the laws and customs of England for this time, to hear and determine by the oath of Benjamin Winthrop. Esquire, John Henry Schneider, Esquire, Edward Ironside, Esquire, Benjamin Kenton, Esquire, Rawson Hart Boddam, Esquire, John Aris, Esquire, William Pardoe Allet, Esquire, John Perry, Esquire, Henry Peter Kuff, Esquire, Thomas Winflowe, Esquire, Thome Cole, Esquire, Samuel Hawkins, Esquire, George Ward, Esquire, Thomas Boddam, Esquire, Joseph Lancaster, Esquire, Robert Wilkinson, Esquire, George Galway Mills, Esquire, Henry Wright, Esquire, John Hatchett, Esquire, Rowland Stephenson, Esquire, and John Campbell, Esquire, good and lawful men of the County aforesaid, now here sworn, and charged to inquire for our said Lord the King for the body of the said County touching and concerning the premises in the said Letters Patent mentioned. It is presented in manner and form as followeth, (that is to say)

MIDDLESEX to Wit, THE JURORS for our Sovereign Lord the King, upon their oath present, That Thomas Hardy, late of Westminster, in the County of Middlesex, shoemaker, John Horne Tooke, late of Wimbleton, in the County of Surrey, clerk, John Augustus Bonney, late of the parish of Saint Giles in the Fields, in the County of Middlesex aforesaid, gentleman, Stewart Kyd, late of London, Esquire, Jeremiah Joyce, late of the parish of Saint Mary-le-Bone, otherwise Marybone, in the County of Middlesex aforesaid, gentleman, Thomas Wardle, late of London, gentleman, Thomas Holcroft, late of the parish of Saint Mary-le-Bone, otherwise Marybone aforesaid, in the County of Middlesex aforesaid, gentleman, John Richter, late of Westminster, in the said County of Middlesex, gentleman, Matthew Moore, late of Westminster, in the County of Middlesex aforesaid, gentleman, John Thelwall, late of Westminster, in the County of Middlesex aforesaid, gentleman, Richard Hodgson, late of Westminster, in the County of Middlesex aforesaid, hatter, and John Baxter, late of the parish of Saint Leonard, Shoreditch, in the County of Middlesex aforesaid, labourer,

labourer, being subjects of our said Lord the King, not having the fear of God in their hearts, nor weighing the duty of their allegiance, but being moved and seduced by the instigation of the devil, as false Traitors against our said Lord the King, their supreme, true, lawful, and undoubted Lord, and wholly withdrawing the cordial love and true and due obedience which every true and faithful subject of our said Lord the King should, and of right ought to bear towards our said Lord the King, and contriving, and with all their strength intending, traitorously to break and disturb the peace and common tranquility of this kingdom of Great Britain, and to stir, move, and excite insurrection, rebellion, and war, against our said Lord the King within this kingdom, and to subvert and alter the legislature, rule, and government, now duly and happily established in this kingdom, and to depose our said Lord the King from the royal state, title, power, and government of this kingdom, and to bring and put our said Lord the King to death, on the first day of March, in the thirty-third year of the reign of our Sovereign Lord the now King, and on divers other days and times, as well before as after, at the parish of St. Giles aforesaid, in the County of Middlesex aforesaid, maliciously and traitorously, with force and arms, &c. did amongst themselves and together, with divers other false traitors, whose names are to the said Jurors unknown, conspire, compass, imagine, and intend to stir up, move, and excite insurrection, rebellion, and war, against our said Lord the King, within the kingdom of Great Britain, and to subvert and alter the Legislature, Rule, and Government, now duly and happily established within this kingdom of Great Britain, and to depose our said Lord the King from the royal state, title, power, and Government of this kingdom, and to bring and put our said Lord the King to death.

AND TO FULFIL, perfect, and bring to effect their most evil and wicked treason, and treasonable compassings and imaginations aforesaid, they the said Thomas Hardy, John Horne Tooke, John Augustus Bonney, Stewart Kyd, Jeremiah Joyce, Thomas Wardle, Thomas Holcroft, John Richter, Matthew Moore, John Thelwall, Richard Hodgson, and John Baxter, as such false traitors as aforesaid, with force and arms, on the said first day of March, in the thirty-third year aforesaid, and on divers other days and times, as well before as after, at the parish of Saint Giles aforesaid, in the county of Middlesex aforesaid, maliciously and traitorously did meet, conspire, consult, and agree among themselves, and together with divers other false traitors, whose names are to the said Jurors unknown, to cause and procure a Convention and Meeting of divers subjects of our said Lord the King, to be assembled and held within this kingdom,

with

with intent and in order that the persons to be assembled at such Convention and Meeting should and might wickedly and traitorously, without and in defiance of the authority and against the will of the Parliament of this kingdom, subvert and alter, and cause to be subverted and altered, the legislature, rule, and government, now duly and happily established in this kingdom, and depose, and cause to be deposed, our said Lord the King, from the royal state, title, power, and government thereof.

AND FURTHER TO FULFIL, perfect, and bring to effect their most evil and wicked treason and treasonable compassings and imaginations aforesaid, and in order the more readily and effectually to assemble such Convention and Meeting as aforesaid, for the traitorous purposes aforesaid, and thereby to accomplish the same purposes, they, the said Thomas Hardy, John Horne Tooke, John Augustus Bonney, Stewart Kyd, Jeremiah Joyce, Thomas Wardle, Thomas Holcroft, John Richter, Matthew Moore, John Thelwall, Richard Hodgson, and John Baxter, as such false traitors as aforesaid, together with divers other false traitors whose names are to the Jurors aforesaid unknown, on the said first day of March, in the thirty-third year aforesaid, and on divers other days and times, as well before as after, with force and arms, at the parish of Saint Giles aforesaid, in the county of Middlesex aforesaid, maliciously and traitorously did compose and write, and did then and there maliciously and traitorously cause to be composed and written divers books, pamphlets, letters, instructions, resolutions, orders, declarations, addresses, and writings, and did then and there maliciously and traitorously publish, and did then and there maliciously and traitorously cause to be published divers other books, pamphlets, letters, instructions, resolutions, orders, declarations, addresses and writings so respectively composed, written, published, and caused to be composed, written and published, purporting and containing therein, among other things, incitements, encouragements, and exhortations, to move, induce, and persuade the subjects of our said Lord the King to choose, depute, and send, and cause to be chosen, deputed, and sent, persons as delegates to compose and constitute such Convention and Meeting as aforesaid, to be so holden as aforesaid, for the traitorous purposes aforesaid.

AND FURTHER TO FULFIL, perfect, and bring to effect their most evil and wicked treason and treasonable compassings and imaginations aforesaid, and in order the more readily and effectually to assemble such Convention and Meeting as aforesaid, for the traitorous purposes aforesaid, and thereby to accomplish the same purposes, they the said Thomas Hardy, John Horne Tooke, John Augustus Bonney, Stewart Kyd, Jeremiah

miah Joyce, Thomas Wardle, Thomas Holcroft, John Richter, Matthew Moore, John Thelwall, Richard Hodgson, and John Baxter, as such false traitors as aforesaid, on the said first day of March, in the thirty-third year aforesaid, and on divers other days and times, as well before as after, with force and arms, at the parish of Saint Giles aforesaid, in the county of Middlesex aforesaid, did meet, consult, and deliberate among themselves, and together with divers other false traitors whose names are to the said Jurors unknown, of and concerning the calling and assembling such Convention and Meeting as aforesaid, for the traitorous purposes aforesaid, and how, when, and where such Convention and Meeting should be assembled and held, and by what means the subjects of our said Lord the King should and might be induced and moved to send persons as delegates to compose and constitute the same.

AND FURTHER TO FULFIL, perfect, and bring to effect their most evil and wicked treason and treasonable compassings and imaginations aforesaid, and in order the more readily and effectually to assemble such Convention and Meeting as aforesaid, for the traitorous purposes aforesaid, and thereby to accomplish the same purposes, they, the said Thomas Hardy, John Horne Tooke, John Augustus Bonney, Stewart Kyd, Jeremiah Joyce, Thomas Wardle, Thomas Holcroft, John Richter, Matthew Moore, John Thelwall, Richard Hodgson, and John Baxter, as such false traitors as aforesaid, together with divers other false traitors whose names are to the Jurors aforesaid unknown, on the first day of March, in the thirty-third year aforesaid, and on divers other days and times, as well before as after, with force and arms, at the parish of Saint Giles aforesaid, in the county of Middlesex aforesaid, maliciously and traitorously did consent and agree that the said Jeremiah Joyce, John Augustus Bonney, John Horne Tooke, Thomas Wardle, Matthew Moore, John Thelwall, John Baxter, Richard Hodgson, one John Lovett, one William Sharp, and one John Pearson, should meet, confer, and co-operate among themselves, and together with divers other false traitors whose names are to the said Jurors unknown, for and towards the calling and assembling such Convention and Meeting as aforesaid, for the traitorous purposes aforesaid.

AND FURTHER TO FULFIL, perfect, and bring to effect their most evil and wicked treason and treasonable compassings and imaginations aforesaid, they, the said Thomas Hardy, John Horne Tooke, John Augustus Bonney, Stewart Kyd, Jeremiah Joyce, Thomas Wardle, Thomas Holcroft, John Richter, Matthew Moore, John Thelwall, Richard Hodgson, and John Baxter, as such false traitors as aforesaid, together

with

with divers other false traitors whose names are to the Jurors aforesaid unknown, on the said first day of March, in the thirty-third year aforesaid, and on divers other days and times as well before as after, with force and arms, at the parish of Saint Giles aforesaid, in the county of Middlesex aforesaid, maliciously and traitorously did cause and procure to be made and provided, and did then and there maliciously and traitorously consent and agree to the making and providing of divers arms and offensive weapons, to wit, guns, musquets, pikes, and axes, for the purpose of arming divers subjects of our said Lord the King, in order and to the intent that the same subjects should and might unlawfully, forcibly, and traitorously oppose and withstand our said Lord the King in the due and lawful exercise of his royal power and authority in the execution of the laws and statutes of this realm, and should and might unlawfully, forcibly, and traitorously subvert and alter, and aid and assist in subverting and altering, without and in defiance of the authority and against the will of the Parliament of this kingdom, the Legislature, Rule, and Government now duly and happily established in this kingdom, and depose, and aid and assist in deposing our said Lord the King from the royal state, title, power, and government of this kingdom.

AND FURTHER TO FULFILL, perfect, and bring to effect their most evil and wicked treason and treasonable compassings and imaginations aforesaid, they, the said Thomas Hardy, John Horne Tooke, John Augustus Bonney, Stewart Kyd, Jeremiah Joyce, Thomas Wardle, Thomas Holcroft, John Richter, Matthew Moore, John Thelwall, Richard Hodgson, and John Baxter, as such false traitors as aforesaid, with force and arms, on the said first day of March, in the thirty-third year aforesaid, and on divers other days and times, as well before as after, at the parish of Saint Giles aforesaid, in the county of Middlesex aforesaid, maliciously and traitorously did meet, conspire, consult, and agree among themselves, and with divers other false traitors, whose names are to the said Jurors unknown, to raise, levy, and make Insurrection, Rebellion, and War within this kingdom of Great Britain, against our said Lord the King.

AND FURTHER TO FULFILL, perfect, and bring to effect their most evil and wicked treason and treasonable compassings and imaginations aforesaid, they, the said Thomas Hardy, John Horne Tooke, John Augustus Bonney, Stewart Kyd, Jeremiah Joyce, Thomas Wardle, Thomas Holcroft, John Richter, Matthew Moore, John Thelwall, Richard Hodgson, and John Baxter, as such false traitors as aforesaid, on the said first day of March, in the thirty-third year aforesaid, and on divers other days and times, as well before as after, at the parish of

Saint Giles aforesaid, in the county of Middlesex aforesaid, with force and arms, maliciously and traitorously did meet, conspire, consult, and agree amongst themselves, and together with divers other false traitors, whose names are to the said Jurors unknown, unlawfully, wickedly, and traitorously to subvert and alter, and cause to be subverted and altered, the Legislature, Rule, and Government now duly and happily established in this kingdom, and to depose, and cause to be deposed, our said Lord the King from the royal state, title, power, and government of this kingdom.

AND FURTHER TO FULFILL, perfect, and bring to effect their most evil and wicked treason, and treasonable compassings and imaginations aforesaid, and in order the more readily and effectually to bring about such subversion, alteration, and deposition as last aforesaid, they, the said Thomas Hardy, John Horne Tooke, John Augustus Bonney, Stewart Kyd, Jeremiah Joyce, Thomas Wardle, Thomas Holcroft, John Richter, Matthew Moore, John Thelwall, Richard Hodgson, and John Baxter, as such false traitors as aforesaid, together with divers other false traitors, whose names are to the Jurors aforesaid unknown, on the said first day of March, in the thirty-third year aforesaid, and on divers other days and times, as well before as after, at the parish of Saint Giles aforesaid, in the county of Middlesex aforesaid, with force and arms maliciously and traitorously did prepare and compose, and did then and there maliciously and traitorously cause and procure to be prepared and composed, divers books, pamphlets, letters, declarations, instructions, resolutions, orders, addresses, and writings, and did then and there maliciously and traitorously publish and disperse, and did then and there maliciously and traitorously cause and procure to be published and dispersed divers other books, pamphlets, letters, declarations, instructions, resolutions, orders, addresses, and writings, the said several books, pamphlets, letters, declarations, instructions, resolutions, orders, addresses, and writings, so respectively prepared, composed, published, dispersed, and caused to be prepared, composed, published, and dispersed as last aforesaid, purporting and containing therein (amongst other things) incitements, encouragements, and exhortations, to move, induce, and persuade the subjects of our said Lord the King, to aid and assist in carrying into effect such traitorous subversion, alteration, and deposition as last aforesaid, and also containing therein, amongst other things, information, instructions, and directions to the subjects of our said Lord the King, how, when, and upon what occasions the traitorous purposes last aforesaid should and might be carried into effect.

AND FURTHER TO FULFILL, perfect, and bring to effect

effect their most evil and wicked treason, and treasonable compassings and imaginations aforesaid, they, the said Thomas Hardy, John Horne Tooke, John Augustus Bonney, Stewart Kyd, Jeremiah Joyce, Thomas Wardle, Thomas Holcroft, John Richter, Matthew Moore, John Thelwall, Richard Hodgson, and John Baxter, as such false traitors as aforesaid, together with divers other false traitors, whose names are to the Jurors aforesaid unknown, on the said first day of March, in the thirty-third year aforesaid, and on divers other days and times, as well before as after, at the parish of St. Giles aforesaid, in the county of Middlesex aforesaid, with force and arms maliciously and traitorously did procure and provide, and did then and there maliciously and traitorously cause and procure to be provided, and did then and there maliciously and traitorously consent and agree to the procuring and providing arms and offensive weapons (to wit) guns, musquets, pikes, and axes, therewith to levy and wage war, insurrection, and rebellion against our said Lord the King within this kingdom, against the duty of the allegiance of them the said Thomas Hardy, John Horne Tooke, John Augustus Bonney, Stewart Kyd, Jeremiah Joyce, Thomas Wardle, Thomas Holcroft, John Richter, Matthew Moore, John Thelwall, Richard Hodgson, and John Baxter, against the peace of our said Lord the now King, his crown and dignity, and against the form of the statute in that case made and provided.

Sessions-house, Clerkenwell, Monday, October 6.

The court sat, pursuant to adjournment. At two o'clock, the gentlemen of the Grand Jury made their first presentment.

Names of the Persons against whom true Bills are found for High Treason.

Thomas Hardy,
John Horne Tooke,
John Augustus Bonney,
Stewart Kyd,
Jeremiah Joyce,
Thomas Wardle,
Thomas Holcroft,
John Richter,
Matthew Moore,
John Thelwall,
Richard Hodgson, and
John Baxter.

Not found against John Lovat.

All these persons are included in one Bill, which was presented to the Grand Jury. Three of them, viz. Thomas Wardle, Matthew Moore, and R. Hodgson, are still at large.

The Right Hon. Sir *James Eyre* observed, that the gentlemen of the Grand Jury had been engaged in a very arduous duty; that being the fourth day of their attendance. His Lordship asked

asked them, if they meant to proceed any further in their enquiries that day?

The Foreman replied, that they did, as there was one Bill before them.

His Lordship asked them, about what time they thought they would be ready with it?

The Foreman hoped they should hear all the evidence on it next day, at ten o'clock.

His Lordship informed them, he should certainly be there to-morrow at that hour.

The Foreman said, he had been desired by all the other gentlemen of the Grand Jury, to request of his Lordship, that he would order the very excellent charge he had delivered to them to be printed.

His Lordship said, the gentlemen of the Grand Jury did him great honour; and as he had not delivered that charge entirely without notes, he hoped to be able to comply with their request.

The learned Judge then asked the Attorney General, when the Bills would be ready, as they must be delivered to the prisoners ten days before the trials commenced.

The *Attorney General* said, he did not know, but hoped to be able to give his Lordship an answer to-morrow.

By 7 ann. c. 21. All persons indicted for High Treason, and Misprision of Treason, shall have not only a copy of the indictment, but a list of all the witnesses to be produced, and of the Jurors empannelled, with their professions, and places of abode, delivered to them ten days before the trial, and in the presence of two witnesses, the better to enable them to make their challenges and their defence.

His Lordship said, he did not know whether there were any gentlemen present, who were concerned as Attornies or Agents for the persons against whom bills had been found. If there were, his Lordship wished it to be understood, that upon any application that is made, either to that court, or to the court at the Old Bailey, or to either of the Justices of either of those courts, by the Attornies or Agents of any of the persons indicted, that counsel would be assigned to them; and that they, their Attornies, and Agents, would have proper access to them. This his Lordship wished to be understood once for all, without calling for the personal attendance of those who were now in custody, until arraignment. His Lordship said, his reason for saying this was, that it might be harrassing to the persons, now in confinement, to be brought there, to be told that indictments had been found against them, and that they would have a copy of them, &c. His Lordship, therefore, begged that intimation might some how or other be given to those now in custody..

The court then ajourned, until next day, at ten o'clock.

LIST

LIST of the PETTY JURORS summoned.

Acton. Thomas Buck, esq.
Back-lane. John Warner, gent.
Baker-street, Portman-square. Thomas Skipp Dyott Bucknell, esq.
Barnet. Benjamin Bradbury, Fryer's-lane, Fryer's-barnet, gent.
Bedford-square. Joseph Shrimpton, Esq.
Bethnal-green. Josiah Boydell, gent.
Bow. Thomas Sayer, esq. and distiller; Edward Gordon, esq. and brewer; Mark Hudson, esq. and brewer.
Brentford. Hugh Ronalds, esq. and nursery-man; David Roberts, distiller.
Broad-street, St. George's in the East. Joseph Ainslie, coal-merhant.
Bromley. Nathaniel Stonard, brewer; Charles Smith, distiller; Christopher Metcalf, esq. and distiller.
Brompton. Thomas Hammersly, esq. and banker; Hanbury Potter, Old Brompton, esq.
Buckingham-street. Archibald Paxton, wine-merchant.
Bur-street, East-smithfield. Thomas Allen, brewer; Rice Davies, esq.
Chancery-lane. Richard Masters, esq. and banker; Thomas Druce, stationer.
Charing-cross. Charles Fourdrinier, stationer; James Shepnell, silversmith.
Charlotte-street, Rathbone-place. Edward Campion, esq. and wine-merchant; Isaac Mark, gent.
Charterhouse-square. Lacy Primatt, esq. and chemist.
Cheny-street, Bedford-square. John Peavey, cooper.
Chiswick. Thomas Laurence, Strand on the Green, esq. John Thompson, brewer; Thomas Beach, Strand on the Green, esq.
Clerkenwell. Apsley Pellatt, St. John's-street, ironmonger; John Guest, ditto, esq. and potter; George Fillingham, ditto, hopfactor; David Dean, ditto, cheesemonger; John Wright, Red Lion-street, watch case-maker.
Cockspur-street. James Oliphant, hatter; James Crompton, paper hanging-maker.
Colnbrook. Henry Bullock, this side of Colnbrook, esq.
Dalton. Cecil Pitt, esq.
Downing-street, Westminster. Thomas Maude, esq. and army agent.
Duke-street, Westminster. Calvert Clapham, gent.
Ealing. Thomas Wood, Hanging-hill, esq. and coal-merchant; Richard Meux, esq. and brewer; Robert Winn, Lower-side, esq. Richard Hunt, Windmill-lane, esq. Sampson Bowles, esq. and haberdasher; John Baker, esq. James Smith, esq. and perfumer; Robert Vincent, esq. Thomas Smith, Upper-side, esq. and distiller; Edward Roberts, esq. Thomas Cheap, esq.
Edgware. Thomas Cockington, gent.
Edmonton. Daniel Goffeu, esq. and broker; John Blackburn, esq. and merchant; Thomas Lewis, South-street, esq. and Irish-factor.

Elstree.

Elstree. Samuel Rudge, esq John Rudge, esq.
Enfield. Matthias Dupont, of the Chace-side, gent. wine and brandy-merchant; George Capes, esq. and warehouseman; Richard Gough, Forty-hill, esq. William Emerson, Bush-hill, esq. John Horsley, Bull's-cross, esq. Henry Purrier, Chace-side, esq. George Ellward, ditto, esq. and upholder; Christopher Strothoff, Bull's-cross, esq. and merchant.
Finchley. Thomas Allen, East-end, esq. William Hamerton, esq. Thomas Gildart, Nether-street, esq. and merchant.
Frith-street, Soho. Alexander Trotter, esq. and upholder.
Fulham. Robert Lewis, North-end, esq. John James, esq.
Goodman's-fields. Major Rhode, Lemon-street, esq. and sugar-baker.
Goswell-street. Robert Hawkins, coal-merchant.
Gray's-inn-lane. Thomas Harrison, Cowkeeper.
Great George-street, Westminster. Francis Jenks, gent.
Greek-street. Josiah Wedgwood, potter.
Green-street, Grosvenor-square. George Brooks, esq. and banker; James Fisher, the elder, esq.
Hackney. Thomas Boddington, esq. Charles Digby, Mare-street, esq.
Hammersmith. James Dorville, esq. Simon Lesage, esq. Bryan Marshall, gent. Benjamin Goodison, esq. James Keene, grocer; Henry Osbaldiston, esq.
Hampstead. Philip Godsall, gent. and coachmaker; John Peter Blaquire, esq. and merchant; Thomas Rhodes, Hampstead-road, cowkeeper.
Hampton. Thomas Chadwick, esq. John Hillman, esq.
Hanwell. William Harwood, esq.
Hartesdown-hill, near *Harrow.* William Nichol, farmer.
Hatton-garden. Nathaniel Wright, surveyor.
Hayes. John Blencowe, esq.
Hendon. Michael Collinson, esq. Edward Hill, gent.
Highgate. Edward Hale, gent. Samuel Provey, esq. and weaver.
High-street, Mary-le-bone. James Sheridine, esq.
Hillington. Samuel Marsh, esq. William Perry, esq. and doctor of physic; James Cook, esq.
Holborn. Robert Mairis, near Great Turnstile, gent.
Hornsey. David Duveluz, esq. and merchant, John Mayhew, esq. and upholder.
Islington. Samuel Pullen, gent.
Kensington. James Wheble, gentleman and tallow-chandler; John Walker, Square, esq. Thomas Ayliffe, esq. Samuel Palmer, esq. Edw. Helme, Parson's-yard, esq. Jeffery Holmes, Young-street, esq. Alexander Baxter, esq. Edward Green, Square, esq. Edmund Jennings, Young-street, esq. Stephen Aisley, esq. Robt. Willson, Square, esq. Thomas Sanders, Fillimore-place, esq. John Mason, esq. John Battye, esq. Thomas Burnett, Parson's-yard, esq. John Robinson, esq. Isaac Lucas, esq. and oilman; John Jenkinson, esq. Thomas Robin-

Robinson, Church-lane, esq. and gardener; John Butts, esq. and ironmonger.

Knightsbridge. Sir Joseph Andrews, bart.

Limehouse. Robert Batson, ship-builder; Robert Mellish, ship-builder; James Mitchel, rope-maker; Adam Steinmetz, biscuit-baker; Jeremiah Blakeman, timber-merchant; Thomas Bird, distiller; Charles Turner, sail-maker; Thomas Draine, brewer; Emanuel Goodheart, sugar-refiner; Christopher Richardson, timber-merchant, Norrison Coverdale, rope-maker; Anthony Calvert, merchant.

Lisson-green. James Stephens, esq.

London-street, Tottenham-court-road. George Sewell, gent.

Marlborough-street, (Great). John Harrop, gent.

Mile-end. John Charrington, esq. and brewer; John Liptrap, esq. and distiller; Ralph Keddey, esq. and merchant.

Mimms (South). Francis Baroneau, esq.

Moorfields. Samuel Mills, weaver.

Newington (Stoke). George Rigby, esq. and Irish-factor; Jonathan Eade, esq. and ship-chandler.

New-road, Tottenham-court-road. Joshua Brooks, dealer in birds; John White, esq. and builder; Cam Farmer, gent.

Northumberland-street. Henry Capel, gent.

Old-street. Richard Child, distiller.

Ormond-street, (New). Thomas Nixon, esq. and merchant; William Cooke, esq.

Paddington-street, St. Mary-le-bone. Richard Carter, esq.

Pall-mall. Richard Croft, esq. and Banker.

Percy-street, Rathbone-place. Thomas Elmsley, esq.

Pimlico. George Shakespear, esq. and builder.

Poplar. John Powsey, carpenter and surveyor.

Portman-square. William Atwick, esq.

Potter's-bar, near Northam. Francis Hammond, esq.

Princes-street, Red-lion-square. John Lovett, gent.

Queen-square, Bloomsbury. William Fraser, esq. William Moffatt, esq. and merchant; William Arnold, esq.

Queen-street, (Great), Lincoln's-inn-fields. Robert Kilby Cox, esq. and brewer.

Ratcliff. Charles Bowles, Glass-house-yard, Sun-tavern-fields, glass-manufacturer; Joseph Bird, Cock-hill, esq. and sail-maker; John Thompson, Sun-tavern-fields, rope-maker.

Rathbone-place. Hugh French, esq. and apothecary.

Russel-place. Sir John Crofts, bart. Charles Bishop, esq. and proctor.

St. Catherine's. William Mashiter, wharfinger; Henry Goodwyn, esq. and brewer.

St. James's-street, Piccadilly. James Crane, esq.

Seymour-street (Upper), Mary-le-bone. William Phillimore, esq.

Shadwell. Newell Connop, distiller; Arthur Shakespear, Stepney-causeway, esq. and rope-maker; Matthew Whiting, ditto, sugar-refiner.

Shore-

Shoreditch. Thomas Proctor, Hollywell-street, esq. and brewer; John Marshall, ditto, esq.

Smithfield, (East). William Down, wharfinger; Rawson Aislabie, wine-merchant and soap-boiler.

Somer's-town. John Harrison, Duke's-row, gent.

Southampton-place, New-road. James Haygarth, esq. and builder; John Mandell, gent. Thomas Matthews, gent.

Southampton-row, Bloomsbury. George Wade, Stockbroker.

South Molton-street. John Pratt, gent.

Spring-gardens. Edmund Antrobus, New-street, esq. and banker.

Stanmore. Samuel Dickenson, esq. Charles Wiggin, esq.

Strand. George Jefferys, jeweller and silversmith.

Sunbury. Roger Boehm, esq. and merchant; Dicker Saunders, esq. James Shergold, esq. William Parker, esq.

Teddington. William Sandby, esq. and banker.

Tottenham. Thomas Powell, High-cross, esq. and merchant, William Row, ditto, esq. and broker; Charles Pratt, miller.

Tottenham-street. John Leader, gent. Joseph Mawley, gent.

Turnham-green. James Payne, esq.

Turnmill-street, Cow-cross. Philip Booth, distiller.

Twickenham. John Davenport, esq. and woollen-draper; George Gosling, esq. and banker; Benjamin Green, esq. and register in Chancery; Edmund Hill, Whilton, esq. and gunpowder merchant.

Uxbridge. John Mercer, mealman; Daniel Cock, distiller.

Wapping. Thomas Martin, King Edward-stairs, oilman; John Rixon, Hermitage-street, cooper; Daniel Martin, Red Lion-street, esq. Andrew Burt, Charlotte-street, esq. Michael Henley, coal-merchant; Nathaniel Allen, Wapping-wall, ship-chandler.

Wellclose-square. Theophilus Pritzler, sugar-refiner; Casten Rohde, esq. and sugar-refiner.

Whitechapel. Henry Bullock, High-street, brewer.

Wilsden. Joseph Nicoll, Neasdown, gentleman-farmer; Edward Franklin, farmer.

Wimbley-green. Richard Page, esq.

A LIST *of the* WITNESSES SUBPŒNAED.

MIDDLESEX.

The King against Thomas Hardy, John Horne Tooke John Augustus Bonney, Stuart Kyd, Jeremiah Joyce, Thomas Wardle, Thomas Holcroft, John Richter, Matthew Moore, John Thelwall, Richard Hodgson, and John Baxter.

Upon an Indictment for High Treason.

Alexander Aitchison, student of medicine, residing in Cannongate, of Edinburgh, in the parish of Cannongate, in the county of Edinburgh, a prisoner in the Tolbooth of Edinburgh.

Henry

Henry Alexander, abiding at the Rose-tavern, Fleet-market, in the City of London, Linen-draper.

Daniel Adams, of Took's-court, Cursitor-street, in the county of Middlesex, gentleman.

George Allen, of Turner's-court, Bedford-Bury, in the county of Middlesex, one of the constables attending the Public-office in Bow-street, Covent-garden, in the said county.

John Armstrong, of Kingsland-road, in the parish of St. Leonard, Shoreditch, in the county of Middlesex, one of the constables attending the Police-office, in Worship-street, in the said county.

James Agar, of Hare-court, in the Temple, barrister at law.

Joseph Butterworth, of Fleet-street, London, bookseller.

John Bullock, of Church-yard-court, in the Inner-temple, London, stationer to the Board of Ordnance.

William Broomhead, of Watson's-walk, Sheffield, in the county of York, cutler and scissar finisher, now in custody, at the house of Mrs. Mary Parkinson, in Little Charles-street, Westminster, in the county of Middlesex.

Grant Broughton, one of his Majesty's messengers in ordinary, abiding at the house of the Right Honourable the Marquis of Salisbury, in Arlington-street, in the county of Middlesex.

Bernard Bayley, of Union-crescent, Kent-road, in the county of Surry, gentleman, one of the clerks of the Police-office, in Lambeth-street, Whitechapel, in the county of Middlesex.

Joseph Burchell, of the Sheriff's-office, in Took's-court, and residing in great James-street, Bedford-row, in the county of Middlesex, attorney at law.

George Cheek Barnes, of Noble-street, Goswel-street, in the county of Middlesex, printer.

John Boult, of Red-lion-court, Charter-house-lane, London, newsman and ticket porter.

Thomas Blackburne, of Craven-street, City-road, in the county of Middlesex, paper hanger and undertaker.

William Black, of York-street, Westminster, in the county of Middlesex, green grocer, and one of the constables attending the Public-office in Bow-street, Covent-garden, in the said county.

Robert Beresford, residing at the corner of Bennet's-court, Drury-lane, in the county of Middlesex, taylor and green grocer, and one of the constables attending the Public-office in Bow-street, Covent-garden, in the said county.

Arthur Blake, of Devonshire-street, Portland-place, in the county of Middlesex, esq.

Richard Bennet, of Redman's-row, Bethnal-green, in the county of Middlesex, warehouseman.

William Barclay, of Duke's-court, St. Martin's-lane, in the county of Middlesex, shoemaker.

Nathaniel Birch, of Vine-street, in the parish of St. John, Westminster, in the county of Middlesex, labourer, one of the patroles attending the Public-office in Bow-street, Covent-garden, in the said county.

Anthony Beck, of Oxford-ftreet, in the county of Middlefex, fadler.

John Burfey, of Blackman-ftreet, in the Borough of Southwark, in the county of Surrey, one of the clerks in the Auditor's-office, Somerfet-place.

John Bone, of Wefton-ftreet, Snow's-fields, Southwark, in the county of Surrey, muflin clearer.

William Camage, of Fargate-ftreet, Sheffield, in the county of York, inkbottle maker, now in cuftody at the houfe of Mrs. Mary Parkinfon, in Little Charles-ftreet, Weftminfter, in the county of Middlefex.

John Child, of Crown-ftreet, Weftminfter, in the county of Middlefex, one of his Majefty's meffengers in ordinary.

John Coates, a foldier, in the Birmingham Volunteers, late of China-walk, Lambeth, in the county of Surrey, apprentice to John Philip Francklow, taylor, and now refiding with his father, Chriftopher Coates, of Little College-ftreet, Weftminfter, in the county of Middlefex.

Stephen Cottrell, of Grofvenor-place, in the county of Middlefex, efq. one of the clerks of his Majefty's moft Hon. Privy Council.

William Carter, of Angel-alley, Long-acre, in the county of Middlefex, bill fticker.

Patrick Colquhoun, of Charles-fquare, Hoxton, in the county of Middlefex, efq. one of the Juftices of the Police-office, in Worfhip-ftreet, Shoreditch, in the faid county.

Thomas Chapman, of Fleet-ftreet, London, bookfeller.

John Combes, of Oakham, in the county of Rutland, attorney at law.

Chriftopher Cridland, of Kemp's-court, Berwick-ftreet, Soho, in the county of Middlefex, fhoemaker, and one of the conftables attending the Public-office in Bow-ftreet, Covent-garden, in the faid county.

Thomas Carpmeal, of Bow-ftreet, Covent-garden, in the county of Middlefex, victualler, and one of the conftables attending the Public-office in Bow-ftreet, aforefaid.

Henry Croker, of Tottenham-court-road, in the county of Middlefex, broker, and one of the conftables attending the Public-office in Bow-ftreet, Covent-garden, in the faid county.

John Chapman, of Dean-ftreet, Fetter-lane, London, labourer.

Alexander Corney, of Red-lion-court, Watling-ftreet, in the city of London, fhoe-factor.

James Clark, efq. fheriff deputy, of the county of Edinburgh, refiding in George-fquare, in the parifh of St. Cuthbert's, in the faid county.

John Chatfield, of Back-hill, Hatton-garden, in the county of Middlefex, timber merchant.

Bernard Cobbe, of Walnut-tree-walk, Lambeth, in the county of Surry, one of the clerks in the Auditor's office, Somerfet-place.

William Clarke, of Mount-row, Lambeth, in the county of Surry, meffenger to the folicitor for the affairs of his Majefty's treafury.

Henry

Henry Dealtry, of Essex-street, in the county of Middlesex, clerk of the rules, on the crown side of his Majesty's court of King's-bench.

Richard Davison, of Sheffield, in the county of York, printer.

James Davidson, of Russel-place, Russel-street, Covent-garden, in the county of Middlesex, printer.

William Dakin, of Downing-street, Westminster, door porter at the office of Lord Grenville, one of his Majesty's principal secretaries of state, situate in Downing-street aforesaid.

Joseph Deboffe, of Gerard-street, Soho, in the county of Middlesex, bookseller.

Joseph Edwards, the younger, of Jewin-street, London, silversmith, now in custody at the house of William Needham, in Cork-street, Hanover-square, in the county of Middlesex, one of his Majesty's messengers in ordinary.

Daniel Isaac Eaton, of Newgate-street, London, bookseller.

Henry Eaton, of Newgate-street, London, the son of Daniel Isaac Eaton, of the same place, bookseller.

Evan Evans, late a prisoner in the custody of the Marshal of the Marshalsea, of the Court of King's-bench, grocer, now residing at the house of Samuel Giles, at Newington-causeway, in the county of Surry.

Ann, the wife of the above-named Evan Evans, now residing at the house of Samuel Giles, at Newington-causeway, in the county of Surry.

Samuel Edwards, of Beaufort-buildings, in the Strand, in the county of Middlesex, wine merchant.

John Frost, late of Spring-garden, Westminster, but now of Pinner, in the county of Middlesex, gentleman, late an attorney of the court of King's-bench.

Richard Ford, of Sloan-street, in the county of Middlesex, esq. one of the Justices at the Public-office in Bow-street, Covent-garden, in the said county.

William Fawkener, of South-street, Park-lane, in the parish of St. George, Hanover square, in the county of Middlesex, esq. one of the clerks of his Majesty's most Hon. Privy-council.

Edward Fugion, of the Pleasant-retreat, Palmer's-village, Tothill-fields, in the county of Middlesex, shoemaker, and one of the officers of the Public-office in Bow-street, Covent-garden, in the said county.

William Henry Fallofield, of Inner-Scotland-yard, in the county of Middlesex, attorney at law.

William Fitzgerald, of the Middle-temple, London, barrister at law.

John Fairley, of Broughton, in the parish of St. Cuthbert's, in the county of Edinburgh, wright, a prisoner in the Castle of Edinburgh.

Isaac Fawcett, the younger, of Camomile-street, Bishopsgate-street, in the city of London, attorney at law.

Thomas Furmage, of Windmill-street, Tottenham-court-road,

in the county of Middlesex, collector of the rate for paving, &c. within the parish of Saint Pancras, in the said county.

William Fletcher, of Lincoln's-Inn, in the county of Middlesex, barrister at law.

Duncan Grant, of Strutton-ground, Westminster, in the county of Middlesex, one of the constables attending the Public-office in Bow-street, Covent-garden, in the said county.

Edward Gosling, late of Hoxton, in the parish of Saint Leonard, Shoreditch, in the county of Middlesex, but now residing at the house of James Bisset, Upper-broker-row, Moorfields, in the said county, and clerk to William Wickham, esq. one of the Justices at the Police-office in Lambeth-street, Whitechapel, in the said county.

John Gurnell, of King-street, Westminster, in the county of Middlesex, one of his Majesty's messengers in ordinary.

Richard Gay, of Hopkins-street, Saint James's, in the county of Middlesex, drug and perfume grinder, a prisoner in the custody of the Marshal of the Marshalsea, of the court of King's-bench, in the King's-bench-prison, in Saint George's-Fields, in the county of Surry.

Thomas Green, of Orange-street, Leicester-fields, in the county of Middlesex, perfumer.

John Gurney, of Essex-court, in the Middle-temple, barrister at law.

Alexander Grant, of Wardour-street, Soho, in the county of Middlesex, printer.

William Gotobed, of Hosier-lane, West-smithfield, London, newsman.

Roger Gastrell, of Hemlock-court, Cary-street, in the county of Middlesex, taylor, and green-grocer, and one of the constables attending the Public-office in Bow-street, Covent-garden, in the said county.

Arthur Gliddon, of Great Ormond-street, Queen's-square, in the county of Middlesex, attorney at law.

John Griffiths, of Plumber's-row, Mile-end-old-town, in the county of Middlesex, carpenter and joiner, and one of the constables attending the Police-office in Lambeth-street, Whitechapel, in the said county.

Thomas Griffiths, of Fashion-street, Spitalfields, sawyer, and assistant constable at the Police-office in Lambeth-street, Whitechapel, in the county of Middlesex.

Thomas Glegg, No. 60, Charing-cross, Westminster, in the county of Middlesex, gentleman, clerk to Mr. White, of No. 6, Lincoln's-inn.

John Groves, of Crown-court, Russel-street, Covent-garden, in the county of Middlesex, gentleman.

Richard Hayward, of Friendly-place, Shoreditch, in the county of Middlesex, wax-chandler, now a prisoner in his Majesty's gaol of Newgate.

George Higgins, of South-street, in the parish of Saint George,

Hanover-square, in the county of Middlesex, one of his Majesty's messengers in ordinary.

Christopher Hull, of Chancery-lane, attorney at law.

Edward Hodson, of Bell-yard, near Temple-bar, printer.

Henry Hill, of Fargate-street, in Sheffield, in the county of York, cutler, now in custody at the house of Mrs. Mary Parkinson, in Little Charles-street, Westminster, in the county of Middlesex.

John Hancock, of Chichester-rents, in Chancery-lane, in the county of Middlesex, gentleman, clerk to Mr. White, of No. 6, Lincoln's-Inn.

William Huskisson, of Pall-mall, in the county of Middlesex, esq. chief clerk in the office of the Rt. Hon. Henry Dundas, one of his Majesty's principal secretaries of state.

Edward Harvey, of Lamb-street, Spital-square, in the county of Middlesex, warehouseman.

John Hollingworth, of Threadneedle-street, London, banker.

John Hillier, of Bishopsgate-street, London, bookseller, now a prisoner in his Majesty's gaol of Newgate.

Jeremiah Samuel Jordan, of Fleet-street, in the city of London, bookseller.

Joseph Johnson, of St. Paul's Church-yard, in the city of London, bookseller.

Joseph Clayton Jennings, of Hart-street, Bloomsbury, in the county of Middlesex, barrister at law.

Charles Jealous, of Brownlow-street, Drury-lane, in the county of Middlesex, sadler, and one of the constables attending the Public-office in Bow-street, Covent-garden, in the said county.

Joshua Joyce, of Essex-street, in the Strand, in the county of Middlesex, tallow-chandler.

Thomas Jones, of Milford-lane, in the Strand, in the county of Middlesex, labourer and one of the constables attending the Public-office in Bow-street, Covent-garden, in the said county.

William Jones, esq. of St. George's-fields, in the county of Surrey, marshal of the Marshalsea, of the court of King's-bench.

David George Jacmar, of Frith-street, Soho, in the county of Middlesex, one of the clerks in the Auditor's-office, in Somerset-place.

William Johnson, of the Inner-temple, London, attorney at law.

John King, of Queen-street, Queen's-square, Westminster, in the county of Middlesex, esq. one of his Majesty's under secretaries of state.

John Kirby, keeper of his Majesty's gaol of Newgate, residing there.

Christopher Kennedy, of Cross-court, Broad-court, Long-acre, in the county of Middlesex, carpenter, and one of the constables attending the Public-office in Bow-street, Covent-garden, in the said county.

William Knight, of Windmill-street, Piccadilly, in the county of Middlesex, shoemaker.

David Kinghorn, gentleman, gaoler of his Majesty's Tower of London, abiding there.

William Lowndes, of the Middle-temple, London, barrister at law.

Edward Lauzun, of Little George-street, Westminster, in the county of Middlesex, one of his Majesty's messengers extraordinary.

James Lyon, messenger at arms, residing at the house of James Cooper, in Advocate's-close, in the city of Edinburgh.

George Lynam, of Walbrook, London, ironmonger.

Edward Lavender, of Drury-lane, in the county of Middlesex, attorney at law, and chief clerk of the Public-office in Bow-street, Covent-garden, in the said county.

Arnold Langley, of Gloucester-street, Queen's-square, in the county of Middlesex, gentleman, clerk to Mr. White, No. 6, Lincoln's-inn.

William Lockhart, sheriff clerk depute of the county of Edinburgh, residing at Newhaven, in the parish of St. Cuthbert's, in the county of Edinburgh aforesaid.

David Lloyd, of York-street, Westminster, in the county of Middlesex, footman to Mrs. Campbell, of Bury-street, St. James's, in the same county.

Robert Moody, of China-square, Sheffield, in the county of York, carpenter and joiner, now in custody at the house of Mrs. Mary Parkinson, in Little-Charles-street, Westminster, in the county of Middlesex.

Thomas Maclean, of Whitehall, in the county of Middlesex, one of his Majesty's messengers in ordinary.

John Moore, of Gray's-inn, in the county of Middlesex, attorney at law.

—— *Merry*, of Ramsgate, in the county of Kent, doctor of physic.

William Mainwaring, of Hanover-square, in the county of Middlesex, esq. one of the prothonotaries of the court of common pleas.

George Munro, of George-street, Manchester-square, in the county of Middlesex, esq. a captain in the army.

William Metcalfe, of Dowgate-hill, in the city of London, attorney at law.

Patrick Macmanus, of Stanhope-street, Clare-market, in the county of Middlesex, hatter, and one of the constables attending the Public-office in Bow-street, Covent-garden, in the said county.

Andrew Milne, of Great Russel-street, Bloomsbury, in the county of Middlesex, shopman to Mr. Jordan, bookseller, in Fleet-street, London.

Joseph Mack, clerk in the Sheriff-clerk's office in Edinburgh, residing in Castle Wynd, in the city of Edinburgh.

William M'Cubbin, writer, residing in the house of John Donaldson, smith and room-setter, in Todderick's Wynd, in the city of Edinburgh.

Alexander Mitchell, linen manufacturer, residing at Strathaven, in the parish of Strathaven, in the county of Lanark.

Arthur

Arthur M'Ewan, of the Water of Leith, in the parish of Saint Cuthbert's, in the county of Edinburgh, weaver, a prisoner in the Tolbooth of Cannongate, of Edinburgh.

Walter Miller, wright and merchant, of the High-street of Perth, in the parish of Perth, in the county of Perth, a prisoner in the Tolbooth of Edinburgh.

John Miller, of Duke's-court, Bow-street, Covent-garden, in the county of Middlesex, one of the constables attending the Public-office in Bow-street aforesaid.

Stephen Henry Murrell, of Ray-street, Cold-bath-fields, in the county of Middlesex, auctioneer.

William Middleton, one of the Sheriff's officers of the county of Edinburgh, residing in Warriston's-close, in the city of Edinburgh.

Joseph Milner, of Aldermanbury, London, warehouseman.

William Needham, of Cork-street, in the parish of St. George, Hanover-square, in the county of Middlesex, one of his Majesty's messengers in ordinary.

Frederick Polydore Nodder, of Brewer-street, Golden-square, in the county of Middlesex, botanic painter.

John Nost, residing at the Lord Chamberlain's-office, in St. James's-palace, in the county of Middlesex, one of his Majesty's messengers extraordinary.

Evan Nepean, of Scotland-yard, Whitehall, in the county of Middlesex, esquire, one of his Majesty's under secretaries of State.

Randle Norris, of Hare-court, in the Temple, clerk to Mr. Spinks, under treasurer of the society of the Inner-temple.

Arthur Onslow, of Craven-street, in the Strand, in the county of Middlesex, barrister at law.

Robert Orrock, of Dean, in the parish of St. Cuthbert's in the county of Edinburgh, blacksmith, a prisoner in the castle of Edinburgh.

George Orr, of Camberwell, in the county of Surry, taylor.

Jane Partridge, of Nottingham, spinster, the daughter Mr. Partridge, of Nottingham aforesaid, apothecary.

William Pope, of Little Mary-le-bone-street, in the county of Middlesex, blacking ball maker, and one of the patroles attending the Public-office in Bow-street, Covent-garden, in the said county.

John Pearson, of Lincoln's-inn, in the county of Middlesex, student at law.

James Parkinson, of Hoxton-square, in the county of Middlesex, surgeon and apothecary.

John Pearson, of Fig-tree-court, in the Temple, gentleman.

William Ross, of Crown-street, Westminster, in the county of Middlesex, one of his Majesty's messengers in ordinary.

John Reeves, of Cecil-street, in the Strand, in the county of Middlesex, barrister at law.

George Ross, clerk, or late clerk in the Gazetteer-office at Edinburgh, of South-bridge, of Edinburgh, a prisoner in the Tolbooth of Edinbugh.

Archibald Ruthven, of Rodney-row, Newington-butts, in the county of Surry, baker, one of the patroles attending the Public-office in Bow-ftreet, Covent-garden, in the county of Middlefex.

James Ridgway, of York-ftreet, St. James's-fquare, in the county of Middlefex, bookfeller, now a prifoner in his Majefty's gaol of Newgate.

Thomas Clio Rickman, of Upper Mary-le-bone-ftreet, in the county of Middlefex, bookfeller, and Jane his wife, of the fame place.

Samuel Reece, of Carthufian-ftreet, Charter-houfe-fquare, in the county of Middlefex, ftationer.

Ifaac Saint, of the city of Norwich, victualler, now in cuftody at the houfe of Thomas Wagftaffe, in South-ftreet, in the parifh of St. George, Hanover-fquare, in the county of Middlefex, one of his Majefty's meffengers in ordinary.

John Thomas Slack, of Buckle-ftreet, Goodman's-fields, White-chapel, in the county of Middlefex, ftaymaker.

Henry Delahay Symonds, of Paternofter-row, London, bookfeller, now a prifoner in his Majefty's gaol of Newgate.

William Sharp, of Charles-ftreet, Middlefex-hofpital, in the county of Middlefex, engraver.

John Schaw, of Eaton-ftreet, Pimlico, in the county of Middlefex, one of his Majefty's meffengers in ordinary.

Thomas Symonds, of Crown-office-row, Inner-temple, London, ftudent at law.

Matthew Swift, of Gould's-buildings, near the New Church in the Strand, in the county of Middlefex, fhoemaker, and one of the conftables attending the Police-office in Great Marlborough-ftreet, in the faid county.

George Sanderfon, of the bunch of grapes, in Butcher-row, Temple-bar, in the county of Middlefex, victualler.

Ifaac Clayton Smith, of Artichoke-yard, Lambeth-marfh, in the county of Surrey, meffenger in the office of the Rt. Hon. Henry Dundas, one of his Majefty's principal fecretaries of ftate.

Thomas Shelton, of the feffion-houfe in the Old-bailey, in the Suburbs of the City of London, attorney at law.

William Scot, folicitor at law, refiding in Merchant-ftreet, in the city of Edinburgh.

Daniel Stuart, of Frith-ftreet, Soho, in the county of Middlefex, gentleman.

Thomas Stiff, of Paternofter-row, in the city of London, hair-dreffer.

John Shallard, of Charlton-ftreet, Somers-town, in the county of Middlefex, paftry-cook, and one of the patroles attending the Public-office in Bow-ftreet, Covent-garden, in the faid county.

John Shelmerdine, of the Grove, Southwark, in the county of Surry, hatter.

James Savage, of Maiden-lane, Wood-ftreet, London, ware-houfeman.

William Sturch, of Stanhope-ftreet, Clare-market, in the county of Middlefex, ironmonger.

John Taylor, of Fleet-street, London, gent. now a prisoner in his Majesty's gaol of Newgate.

William Tims, of Crown-street, Westminster, in the county of Middlesex, one of his Majesty's messengers in ordinary.

James Thornton, of Weymouth-street, Cavendish-square, in the county of Middlesex, clerk at the Police-office in Great Marlborough-street, in the said county.

Thomas Thomson, of Shrub's-hill, near Bagshot, in the county of Berks, esq.

Thomas Tourle, late a prisoner in the custody of the Marshal of the Marshalsea, of the court of King's-bench, dealer in timber and coals, now residing at the house of Samuel Giles, at Newington-causeway, in the county of Surry.

Joseph Towers, of St. John's-square, Clerkenwell, in the county of Middlesex, dissenting minister.

James Templeton, messenger at arms, residing in President's-stairs, in Parliament-close, in the city of Edinburgh.

John Thompson, of Oakham, in the county of Rutland, gardener.

Mary Thompson, the wife of John Thompson, of Oakham, in the county of Rutland, gardener.

Mary Thompson, the wife of George Thompson, of Oakham, in the county of Rutland, gardener.

John Townsend, of Duke's-row, Pimlico, in the county of Middlesex, labourer, and one of the constables attending the Public-office in Bow-street, Covent-garden, in the said county.

Thomas Ting, of King's-road, Chelsea, in the county of Middlesex, stage-coachman, and one of the patroles attending the Public-office in Bow-street, Covent-garden, in the said county.

John Taylor, of St. George's, Norwich, surgeon.

John Thompson, near the turnpike, in the New-road, St. George's in the East, in the county of Middlesex, assistant clerk at the Public-office in Lambeth-street, Whitechapel, in the said county.

John Taplin, of Mulberry-street, Mile-end Old-town, in the county of Middlesex, gardener, one of the constables attending the Police-office in Lambeth-street, Whitechapel, in the said county.

William Taylor, of Bridge-street, Westminster, in the county of Middlesex, esq. one of the clerks in the office of the Rt. Hon. Lord Grenville, one of his Majesty's principal secretaries of state.

Felix Vaughan, of Crown-office-row, Inner-temple, London, barrister at law.

John Vellam, of Oakham, in the county of Rutland, butcher and grazier.

Thomas John Upton, of Bell-yard, near Temple-bar, watch-maker, and machinist, now a prisoner in the New Prison, Clerkenwell, in the county of Middlesex.

Alexander Willis, of Harley-street, in the county of Middlesex, dancing-master.

Samuel Williams, now in custody at the house of Mr. Fordham, in Lambeth-street, Whitechapel, in the county of Middlesex, coach-

coach-master, apprentice to and late abiding with Joseph Whitton, at Tower-stairs, Tower-dock, London, gun engraver.

John Williams, of Leicester-fields, in the county of Middlesex, wine-merchant.

George Williams, of West-smithfield, London, leather-seller.

Thomas Wagstaffe, of South-street, in the parish of St. George, Hanover-square, in the county of Middlesex, one of his Majesty's messengers in ordinary.

William Wickham, of St. James's-place, in the county of Middlesex, esq. one of the justices of the Police-office in Lambeth-street, Whitechapel, in the said county.

John Wharton, of Skelton-castle, in the county of York, esq.

Joseph White, of Essex-court, Middle-temple, and of Lincoln's-inn, in the county of Middlesex, attorney at law, and solicitor for the affairs of his Majesty's treasury.

William Walker, of Buckingham-street, in the Strand, in the county of Middlesex, attorney at law.

James Walsh, late of the Strand, in the county of Middlesex, but now abiding at Hatfield, in the county of Hertford, gent.

William Woodfall, of Salisbury-square, Fleet-street, London, printer.

Henry Sampson Woodfall, late of No. 1, the corner of Ivey-lane, Paternoster-row, printer, but now of Chelsea, in the county of Middlesex, gent.

George Williamson, messenger at arms, residing in President-stairs, in Parliament-close, in the city of Edinburgh.

John Watts, of Rosemary-lane, Whitechapel, in the county of Middlesex, dyer.

Thomas Whitehorn, abiding at the house of Mr. John King, in Cumberland-street, Tottenham-court-road, in the county of Middlesex, and shopman to Mr. Baxter, near Cecil-street, in the Strand, in the said county, bookseller.

George Widdison, of Fargate-street, Sheffield, in the county of York, hair-dresser, now in custody at the house of Mrs. Mary Parkinson, in Little Charles-street, Westminster, in the county of Middlesex.

Thomas Wiffin, of Fludyer-street, Westminster, in the county of Middlesex, one of his Majesty's messengers in ordinary.

Thomas Wood, of Red-lion-street, Holborn, in the parish of St. George the Martyr, in the county of Middlesex, lottery-inspector.

William Worship, of Ball-alley, Lombard-street, London, engraver.

Richard Williams, of Oakham, in the county of Rutland, clerk.

Richard White, of Piccadilly, in the parish of St. James, Westminster, in the county of Middlesex, oilman.

George Willington, of the Inner-temple, London, attorney at law.

John Wigglesworth, of Somerset-place, in the county of Middlesex, esq. one of the inspectors general of accounts in the Auditor's office there.

John York, of his Majesty's Tower of London, and deputy lieutenant thereof.

Matthew Yatman, of Percy-street, Rathbone-place, in the county of Middlesex, apothecary.

The

The following persons have been summoned as evidences on behalf of the state prisoners.

Mr. Pitt,	Mr. Rose, Secretary of State,
Duke of Richmond,	Mr. Ford,
Duke of Portland,	Mr. W. Fawkener,
Mr. Dundas, Secretary for the home department,	Mr. Reeves,
	Mr. Cottrell, &c.
Mr. Nepean, under Secretary of State,	Mr. Johnson, Bookseller, St. Paul's Church Yard.

The summonses served on several of the ministry, to attend the ensuing trials for High Treason, have given them, it is said, no little uneasiness. Neither Mr. Pitt, Mr. Dundas, or the Duke of Richmond, ever imagined they should *be brought* to the *Old Bailey.*

When Mr. Pitt was served with his subpœna, he said that he should attend with the greatest pleasure.

Sessions-House, Clerkenwell. Tuesday, October 7.

The Court, composed of the Right Hon. Sir *James Eyre,* Lord President of the Special Commission, and of *William Mainwaring,* Esq. sat at ten o'clock.

The gentlemen of the Grand Jury attended at the same time, when their Foreman returned a true Bill against John Martin, Attorney, for High Treason.

The *President* then asked, if there was any thing more ready for the Grand Jury?

The Foreman said, the Jury would be glad to adjourn to some day when there would be business sufficient to engage them the whole day.

Mr. *White* said, if it was convenient for the gentlemen of the Grand Jury, he should be glad they would adjourn to Thursday, as he hoped against that day to have all the Bills that were to be returned.

The Foreman replied, that the gentlemen of the Jury had no objection to Thursday.

The *President* said, that being the case, after the business of the day was over, he should adjourn the Court until Thursday at ten o'clock.

At this moment, appeared in Court Mr. Holcroft, who addressed the Court to the following effect:

" My Lord,

" Being informed that a Bill for High Treason has been preferred against me, Thomas Holcroft, by his Majesty's Attorney General, and returned a true bill by a Grand Jury of these realms, I come to surrender myself to this Court, and my country, to be put upon my trial; that, if I am a guilty man, the whole

whole extent of my guilt may become notorious; and, if innocent, that the rectitude of my principles and conduct may be no lefs public. And I hope, my Lord, there is no appearance of vaunting in affuring your Lordfhip, this Court, and my country, that, after the misfortune of having been fufpected as an enemy to the peace and happinefs of mankind, there is nothing on earth, after which, as an individual, I more ardently afpire than a full, fair, and public examination.

"I have further to requeft that your lordfhip will inform me, if it be not the practice, in thefe cafes, to affign counfel, and to fuffer the accufed to fpeak in his own defence? Likewife, whether free egrefs and regrefs be not allowed for fuch perfons, books, and papers, as the accufed, or his counfel, fhall deem neceffary for juftification?"

Chief Juftice.—"With regard to the firft, Sir, it will be the duty of the Court to affign you Counfel, and alfo to order that fuch Counfel fhall have free accefs to you at all proper hours—with refpect, Sir, to the liberty of fpeaking for yourfelf, the accufed will be fully heard by himfelf, as well as by his Counfel; but with regard to papers, books, and other things of that kind, it is impoffible for me to fay any thing precifely, with regard to them, until the thing required be afked. However, Sir, you may depend upon it, every thing will be granted to the party accufed, fo as to enable him to make his defence. If I underftand you rightly, you now admit that you are the perfon ftanding indicted by the name of Thomas Holcroft?"

Mr. Holcroft.—"Yes, my Lord."

Chief Juftice.—"You come here to furrender yourfelf, and I can only accept of that furrender on the fuppofition that you are the perfon fo indicted. You know the confequence, Sir, of being indicted for High Treafon. I fhall be under the neceffity of ordering you into cuftody. I would not wifh to take any advantage of your coming forward in perfon, indifcreetly, in this manner, without being called upon by the ordinary procefs of the law. You fhould have a moment to confider whether you furrender yourfelf as that perfon."

Mr. Holcroft.—"It is certainly not my wifh, either to inflict upon myfelf unneceffary punifhment, or to appear to put myfelf forward on this occafion. I come only as Thomas Holcroft, of Newman-ftreet, in the county of Middlefex, and I certainly do not wifh to ftand more forward, than any other man ought to ftand."

Chief Juftice.—"I cannot enter into this point. If you admit yourfelf to be the perfon indicted, the confequence muft be, that I muft order you to be taken into cuftody to anfwer this charge. I do not know whether you are, or are not, Thomas
Hol-

Holcroft. I do not know you, and therefore it is impossible for me to know whether you are the person stated in the indictment."

Mr. Holcroft.—" It is equally impossible for me, my Lord."

Chief Justice.—" Why then, Sir, I think you had better sit still.——Is there any thing moved on the part of the Crown with respect to this gentleman ?"

Solicitor General.—" My Lord, as I consider him to be the person against whom a true bill is found, I move that he be committed."

Chief Justice.—" I do not know how many persons there may be of the name of Thomas Holcroft: it would be rather extraordinary to commit a person on this charge, if we do not know him."

Mr. Knapp, one of the Counsel for the Crown, contended, that from what the prisoner had said at first in Court, he admitted himself to be the person."

Chief Justice.—" That does not signify. Does the Counsel for the Crown think fit that this gentleman should be committed ?"

Solicitor General.—" I move that he now be taken into custody."

Chief Justice.—" Sir, you must now stand committed."

A sheriff's officer now took Mr. Holcroft into custody.

Chief Justice to the prisoner.—" Are you prepared to name your Counsel ?"

His Solicitor immediately named Mr. Erskine and Mr. Gibbs, whom the Court assigned in the usual form.

The same learned advocates were named for Mr. Thelwall and Mr. Baxter.

John Pearce stated to the Court, that he was an articled clerk to Mr. Martin, against whom the Grand Jury had found a bill. He requested that he might be permitted to attend Mr. Martin, as, without his assistance, he did not think Mr. Martin would be able to proceed to his trial.

The *Solicitor General* objected to this application, because there might be a charge against Mr. Pearce himself.

The *Judge* observed, that until some charge was preferred, he could not refuse this application.

Mr. White, the Solicitor, desired that the order might be postponed until Friday, which the Judge consented to, on condition that a copy of the indictment was not preferred till that time. The Chief Justice then ordered the officer to adjourn the Court.

Mr. Holcroft begged that his servant might be permitted to have access to him.

The

The *Chief Justice* said, that was a sort of thing that was quite new, and he did not know that he could grant it, unless something was stated by Mr. Holcroft, with respect to his health, to make it requisite.

Mr. *Holcroft* said, there was nothing of that sort; that he did not know it to be unusual, or he should not have asked it. The reason for his asking it, was, that his servant was his amanuensis; it had been his habit to dictate to this man, and therefore it would be extremely convenient for him to be indulged in this particular, if that was not contrary to custom.

The *Chief Justice* said, he was afraid it was, and he thought it would be proper for Mr. Holcroft to apply to another quarter, which could better grant indulgence than he could, sitting in that Court.

Mr. *Holcroft* said, he wished to have no indulgence; he only wished for justice.

The *Chief Justice* said, "Then, Sir, I cannot make the order."

The Court then immediately adjourned to Thursday, at ten o'clock in the morning.

Session-House, Clerkenwell, Thursday Oct. 9th.

At ten o'clock, the Court met again, when the Grand Jury presented a true bill for High Treason against *John Hillier.* After which the Court adjourned to Thursday the sixteenth of October.

Session-House, Clerkenwell, Thursday, Oct. 16th.

The Grand Jury returned a true bill against *John Philip Frankloe* for High Treason. And the Court adjourned to Tuesday, the 21st of October.

Tuesday, October 21st.

THE Court met, when the Grand Jury found a true bill against *Thomas Spence* for High Treason.

A bill against *John Ashley*, for the same crime, was not found. Adjourned to Saturday the 25th of October.

Removal of the State Prisoners.

Friday, at eight in the morning, the sheriffs, in their cariages, attended by the under sheriffs, the city marshals on horseback, and the marshals men, together with a strong party of sheriffs officers and constables, proceeded from Guildhall to the

Tower,

Tower, and having stopped at the outer gate, sheriff Eamer sent a message to the commander of the guard, desiring his attendance; to whom he produced an order of the privy-council to deliver into the sheriff's charge the following state prisoners: Thomas Hardy, John Horne Tooke, John Augustus Bonney, Stewart Kyd, Rev. Jeremiah Joyce, John Richter, and John Thelwall.

In about half an hour, the prisoners were brought out, under the escort of a captain's guard; and upon their delivery, the sheriffs gave a formal receipt to the Lieutenant of the Tower, or his Deputy, for their bodies.

They were placed in three coaches, one of the sheriff's carriages leading the procession, the prisoners following, and the other sheriff and his train closing. The sheriff's officers were on horseback, and had their hangers drawn.

About ten, they arrived at Newgate, where the prisoners were safely lodged under the care of Mr. Kirby, the keeper, who conducted them to the state side of the prison, and placed them in seven different rooms, which had been previously prepared for their reception.

The lord-mayor and sheriffs have ordered the different avenues to the Sessions-house to be incircled with strong barricadoes, and a bar to each, with a superscription, containing the names of persons who are to be admitted at that particular avenue.

The officers have a peremptory order, that no others are to be admitted under any pretext whatever.

The seats for the Jury will contain one hundred and eighty-seven. The cushions for them were sent in on Friday night by Mr. Phillips, and every precaution is taken to preserve a due solemnity upon this awful occasion.

The voluntary surrender of Mr. Holcroft, to the decision of the laws of his country, respecting the Bill of Indictment found against him for High Treason, having considerably prepossessed the public with opinions of his innocence, we cannot resist this opportunity of submitting a few observations upon the subject. His anxiety to avow himself in court, is a great indication of conscious innocence. Instead of agreeing with Mr. Knapp, counsel for the crown, who said that his acknowledging himself in court was an admission of his being the person against whom the indictment was found, the reverse seems to us the most rational conclusion. Had he been sensible of his having committed any acts that could afford the least pretence for a bill of indictment of such an atrocious nature being found against him, he would surely have had more sense than to have braved the awful justice of his country with such a premature avowal of

his

his guilt. He would not have condemned himself before the laws had substantiated his criminality. Such a conduct would have been equally censurable for it's indecency and rashness. But from what we have heard of Mr. Holcroft, and read of his writings, we have such an opinion of his understanding as to be convinced, it would have restrained him from an obtrusive and premature offering of himself as a victim to unavoidable infamy and the most terrible of punishments. To be daring, without design or object to attain, is the weakest act of temerity that can possibly be committed. Were he guilty, he would surely have known that his, thus, impatiently resigning himself to justice, could afford him no restoration of impeached character, nor protection from impending punishment. He could have, therefore, nothing to expect but a name consigned to disgrace, and an existence ended by the most horrid executions. It is, therefore, contrary to every principle of reason or reflection to imagine he has committed any act that he knew would subject him to the charge of High Treason. Surely the Solicitor General ought to have recognized his person before he had moved for his being taken into custody. And when he confessed that he did not know Mr. Holcroft, personally, it was the strongest of all possible pleas to have secured him from being sent to prison, until every evidence had been produced of his being the identical individual against whom the bill had been found. Supposing him innocent, what reparation can be made for his being imprisoned, and arraigned for such a crime, against the security of his fellow-citizens? For, in this sense, the enormity of High Treason is chiefly to be considered. The preservation of the Sovereign's life is rendered sacred by his being the bond in which all the ties of social safety unite. Every person, who meditates a design inimical to the life of a lawful, reigning King, commits the greatest of violences against the community, of which he is a member. Whether he be impelled by personal resentment, inordinate ambition, factious turbulence, or erroneous prejudices, he equally hazards the welfare and organization of his country. To be unjustly committed, and tried for such a dreadful act of incivism, is an injury that no concession can repair, or gratuity recompence; for such are the illiberal prejudices of mankind, that innocence, once arraigned, is never restored to it's ancient purity.

But what is still more lamentable and dreadful, with regard to the trial of innocence for capital offences, is their safety or danger too frequently depending on the balance of the pleaders' powers being for or against him. However the laws may be founded in justice, the proceedings impartially conducted, or the jury disinterested, yet such is the irresistible force of superior eloquence, that it confounds reason, perverts truth, and temporizes justice, while the innocent falls beneath the general wreck of equity and

pro—

propriety. Every man, therefore, who goes into a court of juſtice, however right or innocent, ought to enter it with awe, and not with an unqualified confidence. No laws, as a general code, were ever founded with more wiſdom, equity, or humanity, than thoſe of England; but, with all their perfections, the innocent are ſometimes ſacrificed, while the guilty triumph. And as this is one of thoſe irremediable evils attending every human inſtitution, the greateſt caution ſhould be exerted by Grand Juries, leſt they ſubject the lives, properties, and characters, of their fellow-citizens, to a danger againſt which innocence itſelf cannot always find protection.

Seſſions-Houſe, Clerkenwell, Saturday, Oct. 25.

After the Court had adjourned at the Old Bailey, it ſat at Clerkenwell, at one o'clock, when Lord Chief Juſtice *Eyre* aſked who attended on the part of the Crown.

Mr. *White* immediately came into Court, and on being aſked whether there were any more bills ready to be preferred to the Grand Jury, anſwered in the negative, and that he did not know when any more would be ready.

Lord Chief Juſtice *Eyre*.—"Gentlemen of the Grand Jury, I find on enquiry that there are no more bills at preſent ready to be preſented, and that there is an uncertainty whether there are any more to be preferred to you. Under theſe circumſtances, I am ſure the Court are bound to take the earlieſt opportunity of giving you all the relief they can, with reſpect to any further attendance on this very arduous ſervice.

"Before I diſmiſs you for the preſent under this uncertainty of meeting you again, it is my duty to expreſs my own ſenſe, and the ſenſe of the whole Court, with reſpect to the obligations which the country owes you for the punctual attendance you have given, for the great ſacrifice you have made of your time, and perſonal convenience, to a laborious inveſtigation of the many complicated facts that have been laid before you.

"Gentlemen, I ſhall now diſmiſs you for this time, formally enjoining you to give your attendance if you receive new notice to attend on a particular day. At the ſame time, I am not without hopes, that this is the laſt time I ſhall have the honour of addreſſing you in the character of Grand Jurymen."

Foreman.—"My Lord, I am deſired by the Gentlemen of the Grand Jury, to expreſs their thanks to your Lordſhip, for your obliging condeſcenſion, in publiſhing your charge at their requeſt. I am alſo deſired by them to thank the Sheriffs for their kind indulgence, and attention to our accommodation."

The Court then adjourned to Monday ſe'nnight.

Old-Bailey, Saturday, Oct. 25.

For the trials of the prisoners, the Commission consisted of the following

JUDGES:

Sir JAMES EYRE, Lord President,
Chief Baron Macdonald, | Judge Buller,
Baron Hotham, | Judge Grose, &c. &c.

At ten o'clock the Lord President, accompanied by the other Judges, the Lord-mayor, the Recorder, and six Aldermen, took their seats on the Bench.

After the usual proclamation, Mr. *Kirby*, the keeper of Newgate, was ordered to bring to the bar the following prisoners in his custody, against whom the *Grand Jury* had found their

FIRST BILL OF INDICTMENT.

Thomas Hardy, late of Westminster, in the County of Middlesex, shoemaker.

John Horne Tooke, late of Wimbledon, in the County of Surrey, clerk.

John Augustus Bonney, late of the Parish of St. Giles in the Fields, in the County of Middlesex aforesaid, gentleman.

Stewart Kyd, late of London, Esq.

Jeremiah Joyce, of the Parish of St. Mary-le-bone, otherwise Marybone, in the County of Middlesex aforesaid, gentleman.

Thomas Holcroft, late of the Parish of St. Mary-le-bone, otherwise Marybone, in the County of Middlesex aforesaid, gentleman.

John Richter, late of Westminster, in the said County of Middlesex, gentleman.

John Thelwall, late of Westminster, in the County of Middlesex aforesaid, gentleman.

John Baxter, late of the parish of St. Leonard, Shoreditch, in the County of Middlesex aforesaid, labourer.

The Court, immediately on their appearance, wished to know, whether the prisoners' Counsel attended in pursuance to their nomination and appointment?

Mr. *Gurney* replied, that in addition to his learned friends present, who had been retained, he expected Mr. *Erskine*, Mr. *Gibbs*, and Mr. *F. Vaughan*, who had been nominated by the Court.

The Court condescended to wait a few minutes.

The windows which are behind the bar, where the prisoners were, having been previously let down by the *Lord President's* orders, so as to admit a strong current of air, the following observations were made by

Mr. *Horne Tooke*.—" My Lord, I beg leave to represent to the Court, that we have just come out of a very confined and close

close hole, and the windows now opened at our backs, expose us to so much cold air, that our health, particularly my own, will be considerably endangered, and most probably we shall lose our voices before we leave the place. I shall, therefore, request of the Court to be dismissed as soon as their convenience will permit."

The *Lord President* of the Commission.—" If you are prepared to plead, Sir, you may be dismissed almost immediately. We were waiting for your Counsel, that you might have the benefit of their assistance."

Mr. *H. Tooke.*—" My Lord, in a great measure am I prevented from being now able to say any thing on the subject of the indictment, from the circumstance of our not having had the ten clear days allowed by Act of Parliament, to persons in our situation. By the change of custody a whole day has been completely lost to us; in consequence, we have not had an opportunity of conversing with our Counsel. Mr. *Erskine* and Mr. *Gibbs* had engaged themselves to dine with me on Friday, for the purpose of conferring together on the business of this day. Notice was given me as late as nine or ten on Thursday night only, of my intended removal; I was removed by eight o'clock the next morning: it was perfectly impossible for me, therefore, to take the advantage of my Counsel's advice, as our arrangements were thus completely destroyed, and all my papers, which I had collected and arranged in the Tower, thrown into disorder and confusion. Your Lordship—who never was a prisoner—can have but a very imperfect idea of the change of custody."

The *Lord President*.—" The Court is inclined to make every allowance that can be expected, and is willing to wait the arrival of your Counsel."

Mr. *Tooke.*—" Rather than catch cold, I should chuse to plead at present. I ask no indulgence, but desire substantial justice. When I mentioned the circumstance of the day's loss, I did not, by any means, wish to cause delay. It is undoubtedly clear, that the Act, which says, that *not less* than ten days should be allowed, by no means meant to preclude the accused from having the advantage of *more* than ten days, if necessary for the preparation of materials requisite for their defence. I hope that no inconvenience will arise to us from the shifting of custody:—but we certainly have not had the indulgence which that law intended us. I am, however, ready to plead, though deprived of the advantage of my papers, and the benefit of advice. We have been six months in close confinement, without being able yet to imagine what was the nature of the charges to be brought against us, nor have we been able to discover it from the indictment found against us."

Mr. *Thelwall.*—" My Lord, I think it my duty, and an act of justice to myself and my country, to mention, in this public manner, the hardships which we have suffered. Not to mention the loss of a day, I myself have to complain of a circumstance very detrimental indeed to me. I have been deprived of the benefit of my books and papers, which I had collected together, and arranged in the Tower. When we were removed from the Tower, the sheriffs thought proper not to allow me time sufficient to take them with me; I do not mean to attach any blame to them, when I mention this, for with great politeness they promised I should have them sent me.—Afterwards, when I had an opportunity of sending for them through the medium of a friend who was sending to the Tower for some things he wanted, I was refused, and received an evasive answer. I was informed, that they could not send what I wanted, as I had a number of other things there, and they must be sent for together, as it would be necessary to have a separate coach for them. This morning I received a second evasive answer. I mention this circumstance not with any view of delay, for I am as anxious, as any man can be for any thing, to meet the justice of my country."

The Indictment was then read by the Clerk of the Arraigns. It charged the Prisoners, that they being subjects of the King, not having the fear of God in their hearts, nor weighing the duty of their allegiance, but being moved and seduced by the instigation of the Devil, withdrawing their affection and allegiance from the King, did, on the first of March last, contrive, in concert with other persons, to disturb the peace of the Kingdom, to subvert the Government, to depose the King, and to put him to death.

The Indictment then proceeded to specify, and set forth in nine different counts, the overt acts of the above compassings and imaginations.

The Prisoners were then severally asked the usual questions, *" Guilty or not guilty?"*—*" How will you be tried?"*

Mr. *Hardy.*—*" Not guilty."*—*" By God and my country."*

Mr. *Tooke.*—*" Not guilty."* On being asked how he would be tried, he eyed the Court for some seconds with an air of significancy, which few men are so well able to assume, and, shaking his head, emphatically answered—*" I* WOULD *be tried by God and my country. But*——"

The others answered in the usual manner—*" Not guilty."*— *" By God and my country."*

Mr. *Bonney* was about to make some remarks, when he was interrupted by

The

The *Lord President.*—" Tooke having complained of the coldness of the air, may withdraw."

Mr. Tooke then withdrew.

John Augustus Bonney.—" My Lord, there is an *error* in this indictment, which intitles me to plead in abatement. I am described late of the parish of *St. Giles in the Fields*, whereas I ought to have been described of the parish of *St. Pancras*. I never did reside in the parish of St. Giles. But, my Lord, I am also charged by this indictment with having committed treason in the parish of St. Giles; and as my description is just as true and correct as this assertion, I am content to take my trial upon the indictment in it's present form; for I look forward with earnest and anxious expectation for the day when a Jury of my country shall justify me from the aspersions thrown on my character by this indictment: I therefore wave my objection, and plead generally, that *I am not guilty.*"

Mr. *Thelwall.*—" There is a circumstance, my Lord, which my Counsel have informed me would entirely quash this indictment as far as regards me, if I were inclined to take advantage of it. My description is not right: I am described as an inhabitant of *Westminster*, whereas I reside in the *Liberties* of the *Dutchy* of *Lancaster*. Anxious as I am to have my conduct examined into by my country, I despise the idea of availing myself of any paltry subterfuge. I feel perfectly convinced, that when the long expected day shall come, no *honest* Jury can say otherwise than I do now,—*Not guilty.*"

Mr. *Bonney* then said, "I beg that your Lordships will allow me a few words before we quit the bar. I assure you, if I had been arraigned for any known and certain treason, for murder, or for felony, I would ask no favour of your Lordships; but when I stand before you upon a case, in which (and I believe I have your Lordships' opinion in my favour on the subject) if the facts charged against us should be proved, there would still be very great doubt upon the law, I trust I do not make an improper request when I solicit your Lordships, that we may be allowed as many of the little comforts and conveniences of life (to which we have been accustomed) as may be consistent with the security of our persons. Your Lordships, I am sure, will agree with me, that a situation in which a man can neither sleep by night, nor cast his eye on a ray of comfort by day, is not much adapted to prepare his mind for so important a trial as mine—and yet, my Lords, such is my situation.

" I beg to be understood not to intend the smallest insinuation against the Sheriffs; their language and their countenances, when they visited me yesterday in my cell, sufficiently convinced me of the concern they felt at not being able to afford me better accommodation.

modation. My requeſt, therefore, to your Lordſhips is, that we may be remanded to the cuſtody of the Governor of the Tower, where we have been treated, for two and twenty weeks, with the greateſt humanity and attention."

Mr. *Richter* and Mr. *Baxter* alſo complained of the want of accommodation in the places where they were confined.

The *Lord Preſident.*—" I muſt repeat, that the Court can only refer you to the diſcretion and humanity of the Sheriffs, who have already undertaken to pay attention to your complaints."

Mr. *Attorney General.*—" My Lord, as the Priſoners have ſignified their deſire to be tried ſeparately, I move that Mr. Hardy be tried firſt ; and that the warrants, made neceſſary by a late Act of Parliament, for conſtituting the commiſſion, be recorded."

Mr. Erſkine, who, together with Mr. Gibbs and Mr. Vaughan, Counſel for the Priſoners, had come into Court during the reading of the Indictment by the Clerk of the Crown, apologized to the Court for their momentary abſence, as not expecting the buſineſs of the Court to begin ſo early. He underſtood that Mr. *Horne Tooke* had ſtated, and truly, to the Court, the total want of communication between him and his Counſel, owing to his unexpected removal. He therefore confided in the diſcretion and humanity of the Court, that they would, in ſome degree, remedy this evil, by not proceeding to trial till Tueſday next at the ſooneſt, in order to afford an interval for ſuch communication between the Priſoners and Counſel as was neceſſary for their ſafety.

The *Attorney General* ſaid, the Priſoners were duly apprized of their being to be arraigned as on this day. Their removal from the Tower to Newgate was arranged to take place as late as poſſible, in order to prevent their being embarraſſed by interruption in their communication with their Friends and Counſel. Of the preſent objection he had heard nothing till the preſent moment, which he was convinced was unpremeditated, elſe he was ſatisfied that the Counſel would not have concealed it from him. As the great object, however, he had in view was, that a Jury of the Country ſhould ultimately decide whether or not thoſe charges were well or ill founded, which a Grand Jury had already declared were not totally deſtitute of foundation, he was ready to aſſent to the delay propoſed, and therefore had no objection, if the Court ſo willed it, that the trial of Mr. Hardy ſhould ſtand over till Tueſday.

The Court accordingly decided to poſtpone the commencement of the trials till Tueſday next. The Attorney General ſuggeſted to the Court, either that they muſt meet on Monday next, for which day the Petit Jury were ſummoned, or elſe they muſt be ſummoned afreſh for Tueſday.

The

The Court directed that the Sheriff should give notice to the Gentlemen of the Jury, that their presence would not be necessary till Tuesday; and that the Court would meet on Monday morning *pro forma*, and so adjourn over to the following day, then to proceed to business.

The Court was then adjourned till Monday next at eight o'clock in the morning.

The above Prisoners Indicted for High Treason, having appeared to their Arraignments, with such firm and decent manliness, excite the greatest assurance of their innocence. Those who, under such severe charges, meet the laws of their country with fortitude, excite respect for their behaviour, and hopes of their being restored to the confidence of their fellow citizens, by their honourable acquitment; it is therefore to be presumed, our anxious expectations will be fulfilled by the result of these trials, proving that the King and Constitution have no such causes for alarm, as have been lately entertained.

STATE TRIALS
FOR
HIGH TREASON.

THE FIRST PART,

CONTAINING

THE TRIAL OF THOMAS HARDY,

COMMENCED

TUESDAY, Oct. 28, 1794.

THE Right Hon. the Lord Mayor, the Lord Chief Juftice Eyre, Lord Chief Baron M'Donald, Mr. Baron Hotham, Mr. Juftice Buller, and Mr. Juftice Grofe, met purfuant to their adjournment, precifely at eight o'clock in the morning.

The arrival of their Lordfhips was anticipated a few minutes by the Counfel for the crown, who confifted of the Attorney and Solicitor General, Meffrs. Serjeant Adair, Bearcroft, Plomer, Garrow, Law, Anftruther, Wood, and Fielding. The Counfel for the prifoner confifted of Meffrs. Erfkine, Gibbs, and Vaughan.

Their Lordfhips having taken their places on the Bench, Mr. Hardy was ordered to the Bar. He was decently dreffed in mourning for his lately deceafed wife. Confidering his fituation, with regard to the lofs of his dearest relation, his deportment feemed to be that which could only be founded upon the moft firm refignation to the fevere viciffitudes, to which human life is liable.

The peremptory challenge was made by Mr. Erfkine to the legal number of five and thirty Jurors. The Crown alfo excepted to a few, and concurred in the exception againft one perfon, whom therefore we do not name.

At length by Ten o'clock, the nomination had been gone through, and the following Twelve Gentlemen were impanneled to try the caufe at iffue, between our Sovereign Lord the King, and the prifoner Thomas Hardy.

Thomas

Thomas Buck, Esq. *Back-lane, Acton.*
Thomas Wood, Esq. Coal Merchant, *Ealing.*
William Frazer, Esq. *Queen's-square, Bloomsbury.*
Adam Stainmitz, Esq. Biscuit Baker, *Lime-house.*
Newall Connop, Esq. Distiller, *Shadwell.*
John Mercer, Esq. Mealman.
Thomas Sayer, Esq. Distiller, *Bow.*
Richard Carter, Esq. *Paddington-street.*
Nathaniel Stonard, Esq. Brewer, *Bromley.*
Joseph Nicol, Esq. Gentleman farmer, *Wilsdon.*
John Charrington, Esq. Brewer, *Mile-end.*
Joseph Ainsley, Esq. Coal Merchant, *St. George's in the East.*

The Cryer then pronounced the accustomed Oyes, and the Clerk read the indictment. Mr. Wood, Solicitor for the Treasury, briefly recapitulated the counts of the indictment; after which the Attorney General rose to open the prosecution on behalf of the Crown.—Sir J. Scott, delivered himself in substance as follows:

He observed, amongst many things, that in the course of stating to the court and Jury what he should have the honour to submit to their most serious attention in this great, important and weighty instance, affecting the dearest interests of the accused, and affecting also the dearest interests of the public, affecting indeed every thing that could be valuable to the prisoner, and to the state, he should have occasion to call the anxious attention of the Jury to the different parts of the indictments which had just been opened to them; many of these parts he forbore now to mention, because it was fit that they should be given in another part of what he had to state upon this subject. The Prisoner stood indicted generally, with others, for that they had been guilty of the offence of encompassing the King's death. That in consequence of charges that were made against him, and many circumstances of suspicion of his guilt, the Prisoner was committed by his Majesty's most Honourable Privy Council, at the same time that charges were laid against others whose names did not occur upon this indictment; this, however, was a proceeding of some notoriety, and the general impression which it made, occasioned the passing of an act of Parliament to enable his Majesty to secure and detain such persons as he suspected to be conspiring against his person and government; by this act, it was expressed to be the opinion of the two branches of the legislature, that there did exist in this country a traitorous conspiracy for the purpose of introducing into this country a system of anarchy, which had so fatally prevailed in France. This act was an act of emergency, to authorize his Majesty to detain such persons as he might suspect to be conspiring against his person and government.

ment. This measure did not suspend the *Habeas Corpus* act, as had been commonly said; it was only an act to enable the King to secure for a time certain suspected persons. It was a measure never adopted but in cases in which the emergency of affairs called for it; a measure which encroached on the Rights of the Subject, and never adopted but in cases of necessity; and in such cases it had been repeatedly tried and put in force, for it had always been thought by the nation at large in these cases, that it was wise to give up a little of our liberty for a while, that it might not lose the whole of it's liberty for ever. In appearing before the Jury this day, he did only a duty which he was commanded to execute, and the Jury would collect from the facts that would be laid before them, that he was called upon to execute this duty; and he was ready to say, that if the crime did not appear to the extent stated in the indictment, the Prisoner would be entitled to his acquittal. He had brought it forward, and his Majesty was called upon to cause this inquiry to be made as the great conservator of the public peace; in consequence of that character with which his Majesty was clothed, he was pleased to order the present commission, under the authority of which the court was now proceeding, and the question now to be decided was, whether the conspiracy had existed as a Grand Jury of this country had declared. In all, however, they had done, nothing more was said, than that there was ground of charge against the person now standing at the Bar of the Court; they had only said that enough had appeared before them to put the Prisoner upon his trial for High Treason, that of encompassing or imagining the death of his Majesty.

He had stated these circumstances to the Jury, in order that he might the better convey to them this observation, that as the proceedings of the act of Parliament he had already alluded to, ought not, so he was persuaded it had not, the least influence on the judicial proceedings of the Grand Inquest, nor ought that proceeding to induce the present Jury to determine on their mode of judging, in any other way than from their own conviction. If no circumstance of the proceedings of Parliament ought to influence the Grand Inquest, it was to be observed, that the genuine principles of the constitution of this country forbad another Jury from suffering themselves to be biassed by the decision of a Grand Jury, who had had the case in part before them. They would, therefore, consider the prisoner as standing before them in full possession of an absolute right, of a presumption of innocence, completely, except the simple fact, that he stood accused by a Grand Jury of his country: but before he concluded on this, they would permit him to say, that if there had been any act or thing done, or any thing published improperly with a view to

pre-

pre-occupy the opinion of the Jury, however well or ill executed that might be, if any thing had been done to work in their minds either against the prisoner or on his behalf, he was perfectly sure they would not regard it, they would proceed with due regard to the security of the public; and on the other hand he was equally sure, he need not ask an English Jury whether they would permit any thing to operate against a Prisoner that might be supposed to follow from an ill-executed attempt to serve him.

In order for the Jury to understand the law of treason, he should take the liberty of stating to them, that the law of treason was made for the protection of his Majesty's person. The constitution of this country said, that the power of making law resided in his Majesty, by and with the advice of his lords and commons in Parliament assembled. The enforcing the execution of such laws when made, devolved to his Majesty himself. The laws, the constitution declared, were enacted by the King and the Lords and Commons in Parliament assembled, according to the custom of England. To execute the law thus made, was the duty of his Majesty as the conservator of the public peace, and it was one condition on which his Majesty received the sovereignty of these realms; any law therefore, or any attempt at making one independent of his authority and of this form, his Majesty was bound to resist; he pledged himself to resist it by his coronation oath. He would therefore now say, that an attempt to create such a power as that which his Majesty was called upon to resist, was treason according to the statute of the 25th of Edward III. In the King was vested the executive power of the State, this power was to be executed according to the laws and the custom of this realm. To him we owed allegiance on condition of the protection which we derived from him by his thus executing these laws, and those who conspired against his person, his crown, or his dignity, were guilty of treason; according to the statute, a breach of this allegiance was High Treason, and the executing of the laws as enacted by the King's Majesty, by and with the advice of Lords and Commons in Parliament assembled, was one of the rights, and the security of the subject, on the due observance of which by his Majesty was founded the just claim he had upon us for our allegiance. All these were secured to us as rights. The crown which his Majesty wore by hereditary authority, the limitation of which was one of the rights of the subject, all were secured to us by the statute on which the law of treason was formed, for it protected both. The law that settled the hereditary right of the crown also ascertained his duty, which it was incumbent on him to execute: in consideration of this, his character was clothed with dignity.

dignity. The duty of the King to execute the law made by the King's Majesty, by and with the advice of the Lords, temporal and spiritual, in Parliament assembled, and according to the custom of this Realm, was as well known and understood as the allegiance of the subject; in the oath which the King took at his coronation, he swore to excute the law as thus described; for it was expressly declared by that oath, that he shall cause justice to be done, and that he shall maintain the law and the established religion. The learned Counsel then proceeded to quote the opinions of Mr. Justice Foster on the law of treason, which he took to be, he said, a solemn recognition, not only of the duty of the King, but also of the rights of the People: it imposes on him the duty of governing according to the laws and customs of this Kingdom, and no other. In a situation, therefore, of this kind, we could not suppose it to be possible for the King, consistently with his own oath, either to act of his own will, or permit others to act, contrary to such laws. Now, no laws could be made but by the King's Majesty, with the advice of his Lords and Commons in Parliament assembled: it seemed, therefore, as a necessary conclusion, that those who conspire to drive the King out of that mode of governing, must drive him out of the government altogether; for they could not divide him from the Parliament. In endeavouring to alter any of the laws so made, persons so endeavouring must necessarily be resisted by the King: he must—he is bound to resist such an attempt; that resistance, if he does not succeed, must necessarily lead to his deposition. The law and the constitution had assigned to his Majesty very grave council, and responsible persons, as his advisers, and it was to the support of civil liberty; and also, by a fiction of law, we say, that he never ceases to exist. In form he was the author of law. He was the fountain of honour, the conservator of the public peace, the distributor of justice, and the protector of our religion. All these were the rights of his subjects, and they were due to his people. He was also the governor of domestic peace, and our protector in public danger; these were the duties of the King, and it was the interest we had in these things that formed the duty of our allegiance; and it was on account of these things that such extraordinary fences were cast around his person; it was on this account that the encompassing or imagining his death was attended with such severe penalties.

Mr. Justice Hale said on treason, that it was against the person and Government of the King, and he could not state a better authority: the language also of the Counsel of Lord George Gordon admitted on that trial, that any attempt against the Government of the King was the same thing as an attempt against
the

the King himself; that the Government of the King and the life of the King were so interwoven together, that an attempt upon the one was an attempt against the other. And Mr. Justice Foster said that the utmost rigour of the law was thought necessary in the case of treason, because when the King's life was in danger, it could not happen without involving the whole nation in tumult and confusion; a level at him was against public tranquillity; but he must put the Jury in mind also on the other hand, that the same learned Judge said, that High Treason should not be determined according to construction of law, not warranted by the law itself. It had been long ago said, that prosecutions for treason were so common, that a man knew not how to act or to speak for fear of the penalties of treason. He admitted that might have been the case before the statute of Edward III. was made; the security of the subject was not then sufficiently defined; he therefore admitted that the prisoner was entitled to his acquittal, if nothing could be brought forward as law against him, but a construction on the statute which the statute itself did not intend; but unless an offence of this kind was to be punished when clearly made out, no Government could subsist. No Government could last an hour unless there was an established power somewhere, and the sovereignty of that power was the sovereignty of society itself. A breach of some points of law did not necessarily involve the destruction of all law, because, in ordinary cases, the law was sufficient to support itself, such as the protection of personal rights; but not so with treason; that crime, unless guarded against in an extraordinary manner, would be the end of all law at once. Thus said Judge Hale upon that subject. The severity of punishment for this crime, is for this reason, because the tranquillity of the kingdom is highly concerned in it, and therefore the law of the kingdom has given extraordinary security to the person of the Sovereign. When they enacted the Act, they formed the precise definition of the crime, when the common law was thought insufficient for the protection of the person and the honour of the Sovereign, and security for the execution of the law. In addressing in this place, he said, he would dare to say, that there had not been committed any offence, if that was not described by the statute. If the statute should not appear adequate for the security of the Sovereign, and for the due execution of the law, it was, nevertheless, all the security which the law had authorised them to go upon. On the other hand, if the law had been violated, and the facts were proved by such evidence as the law required, in form as well as in substance, then they were bound to go the length of severity which that law required; and he would not hesitate to say, that men of honour and conscience, acting under the sanc-

tion.

tion of the oaths they had taken, muſt come to one concluſion in ſuch a caſe as this, unleſs they ſhould differ on the facts; for on the trial of the Author of the Rights of Man, it was admitted, that the crime was made out as ſtated, to the minds of the Jury; no man could have the audacity to ſay, they would not come to the concluſion the law called for upon the facts.

The ſtatute of the 25th of Edw. III. defined what was treaſon. The encompaſſing the King's death, or the death of his eldeſt ſon—levying war againſt the King, giving to his enemies aid and comfort, &c. and many other like caſes of treaſon, had been ſtated by the ableſt lawyer to be included; theſe were called ſuppoſed caſes of treaſon, but it was declared by the act, that they ſhould not be deemed treaſon, until it ſhould go before the King and his Parliament: he deſired the Jury to mark the diſtinction and the anxiety which thoſe had who framed the Act of Parliament, for it was ſtated by the learned Judge, he had already quoted, that they ſhould not truſt a ſubject in the hands of a Court of Juſtice; he marked this, becauſe it went to ſhew the authority of the learned Judge who made it. It did not appear to him that Hale and Foſter had expounded the ſtatute, by any unfavourable reaſoning againſt the accuſed; but on the contrary, that they had given proofs of the candour of their expoſition, and he thought he could not do better than by giving the ideas of Hale ſtill further. He ſaid, though the crime of High Treaſon was againſt good faith, and the greateſt breach of duty in human ſociety, and brings with it the moſt fatal danger to ſociety itſelf, and brings on the moſt juſt penalty, yet inſtances ſhew how dangerous it is to introduce conſtruction where the law will not make any; after having ſtated what was within the act, he ſays, the great wiſdom of Parliament kept Judges within the act, and kept them from making conſtructions of their own; this is a great ſecurity to Judges themſelves, &c. The queſtion, therefore, before them now was, whether the defendant was guilty of the treaſon ſpecified in the ſtatute, and whether the evidence would amount to what the charge ſpecified, in the minds of the Jury, judging under the obligation of an oath, and that the Priſoner might be attainted in the manner which the act ſpecified? The indictment charged the defendant with the crime of encompaſſing and imagining the King's death, and with having taken meaſures for that purpoſe. He ſaid he ſhould not enter into diſtinctions on the law of treaſon, however clear or manifeſt, that did not ſeem to him to bear on the caſe before them. Depoſing the King, or entering into meaſures for the purpoſe of depoſing him, and doing an Act to manifeſt ſuch a purpoſe, agreeing with foreigners to invade the kingdom, giving any aſſiſtance to procure an invaſion, raiſing inſurrection to dethrone the King,

taking

taking measures to compel him to alter the form of his Government, or to change his Counsellors, were all of them within the statute, and clearly were treason. The law was this: He that did any thing that might endanger the life of the King, if in the ordinary course of things that was fairly to be apprehended from the act, was guilty of treason. This was the opinion of Hale and Foster, and it would be very extraordinary if these two Judges had misinterpreted the Law: he believed they would both have suffered death before they would have said or done any thing injurious to the liberty of the subject. The question was simply this: Whether the Jury would be in their conscience satisfied that any of the acts of the prisoner were to be fairly deemed, according to the experience of mankind in the world, overt acts, for imagining or encompassing the death of the King, as specified in the indictment?

There were many acts that might be called constructive treasons—levying war against the King, without declaring it to be a war against his person, was constructive treason; to pull down prisons was constructive treason too. These acts being against the Royal Majesty of the King, were just as much against the law as if they had been against his person. These were all constructive treasons; they were not specified in the act, but were the decisions of Judges of the highest character, and in these decisions Parliament had uniformly acquiesced, and many had been convicted on them; execution had followed, and no one had ever doubted either the law or the justice of these determinations.—Deposing the King, says Foster, or to conspire to imprison him without any actual attempt to put him to death, is treason. Why? Because his life may be in danger, and therefore this is an act of treason; for, says he, experience has shewn to us that between the prison and the grave of a King, the distance is very small; and experience had lately shewn to us that this was not a false idea.

He then proceeded to consider the indictment, and he said he should not go one iota beyond what the law warranted. The defendants wished to be tried separately; this they had a right to if they chused it, notwithstanding their being included in one indictment, and he had no inclination to oppose it. The indictment stated that a Convention was to be held, in defiance of the authority of Parliament, and to depose the King, and for having formed resolutions, orders, writings, &c. If they should not be satisfied that the calling together the Convention, was in itself an act to encompass or imagine the death of the King, yet they would have evidence enough of a conspiracy to depose the King. Having stated to the Jury, that a conspiracy to depose the King is an overt act of treason, what would be the crime of

sub-

subverting the whole monarchy, including in that the whole existence of the state, in which the King was necessarily embodied? Read as they were in the history of the country, they would have no difficulty in saying, that a conspiracy to depose King William, to restore King James, would without any doubt be treason. If a Convention was formed to alter the Legislature, otherwise than by the legally constituted authorities of the realm, that must be in effect to depose the King, because the King was bound to resist that, for he was sworn by law to govern according to law. There could not be two sovereign powers in any state; there might be two numbers, making and constituting a sovereign power. If there had been a Convention, as was intended, to compel the Legislature to alter the law, either one or the other must fall; either the King and his Parliament must be obedient to the meeting, or the meeting be obedient to the King and his Parliament. He thought they would find that the whole of the plan of the Convention was to alter the whole form of the goverment of this country, and to establish a form of government founded on the unaiterable and imperscriptible rights of man, together with Universal Suffrage, Annual Parliaments, &c. The indictment stated, that this Convention was meant to carry every thing by force; and the fact was, that the application to Parliament was intended only as a colourable thing, and done with a view of having the application rejected; there was a certain use to be made of that circumstance. To compel the King in the exercise of the highest and most essential act of his function, surely was treason, if any thing could be so; it was encompassing his death, for his death was almost sure to follow his refusal, if the party opposing him had the power; but whether they had the power or not, was a matter of no importance in the discussion, for the intention constituted the guilt after an overt act was proved to manifest that intention. The Jury might possibly reason in this way:—When the indictment stated that a few individuals had formed an idea of deposing a Monarch, reigning in the hearts of a great majority of his subjects—what was the evidence of the probability of success? The question was not here, whether their means were adequate to their end, and whether they had reason to think so, but what their intention was. If the Jury should be satisfied that they had that end in view, and attempted to carry it into effect, then they must be found guilty of Treason. He then took notice of the progress of the French revolution and the cause of it, in the course of which he maintained that the different societies of the kingdom were connected with affiliated societies in France, and that the addresses, penned chiefly, he said, by Mr. Tooke,

Tooke, with whom the Prisoner, Mr. Hardy, was connected, and adopted by the different societies, had some effect in producing the decree of Fraternization in the French Convention, and by which they declared war against every state that would not adopt their principles, and called on the subjects to rebel against their lawful sovereigns, to depose and murder them as the French had done their Monarch. He then proceeded to read the different papers of the society, and maintained that they proved from the vote of approbation of Mr. Paine's Rights of Man, the First and Second Part, and above all the Address to the Addressers, the publishing of which he considered to be High Treason of itself, but as others doubted it, the book was only treated as a libel. He then went through the whole history of the London Corresponding Society; the Society for Constitutional Information; the Sheffield, Manchester, and other Societies mentioned in the Reports of both Houses of Parliament, by the Committees of Secrecy. He read almost all the papers of these societies, and maintained that from the tenor of them, the intention of the members who composed and published them was nothing less than what the indictment imputed to them, that of altering the government of the country, and to encompass the death of the King.

The Attorney General then proceeded to the history of the Scotch Convention. What he first remarked were the instructions given by their societies to their respective delegates. By these instructions they were directed to contend for the adoption of annual Parliaments and universal suffrage, and to act on the same principle of resistance to the great majority of the nation, which had already discovered itself in their former proceedings. That principle of resistance, it appeared from the subsequent conduct of the delegates, that they had carried even farther than they were warranted by their instructions. But the responsibility of the persons concerned in those societies, rested not merely on the instructions which they had originally given, since they had afterwards, from time to time, communication with their delegates, in which they highly approved of all the proceedings, and thus made them, as it were, their own acts. This was particularly the case with respect to the prisoner at the bar, who, at different times, wrote to the delegates, as secretary of the London Corresponding Society. In confirmation of these remarks, he read several letters from the societies in England, addressed to the Convention at Edinburgh.—He then proceeded to notice more particularly the circumstances in which that Convention met, and the manner in which they had conducted themselves. Mr. Skirving sent a circular letter to the societies in England, inviting them to send delegates. After they had met, one of their firſt meaſures was to ſtile themſelves the Britiſh Convention of the Delegates of the People, for the purpoſe of obtaining Annual Parliaments and Univerſal Suffrage. Thus they were not content with ſtiling themſelves the delegates of their own ſocieties, but aſſumed to themſelves the title of the delegates of the people; thus concentering in themſelves the functions, and arrogating the authority of repreſentatives of the nation. In the exerciſe of their newly uſurped authority, they propoſed an act of union, not between their own reſpective ſocieties, but between the two nations, England and Scotland. They immediately, in order to ſhew their temper, began with adopting French practices. They divided their ſocieties into ſections, the nation into departments; they had their patriotic gifts, their committee of ſecrecy, &c. They came to a reſolution, that in caſe of a Convention Bill, ſimilar to what had paſſed in Ireland, being propoſed in this country, or of foreign troops being landed, or in the event of an invaſion, they ſhould immediately repair to the place that the Convention ſhould appoint; that the firſt ſeven members ſhould declare the ſitting permanent, and that twenty-one ſhould proceed to buſineſs. Thus they were not to wait till a Convention bill ſhould be paſſed, but to conſider even the circumſtance of Parliament proceeding to agitate ſuch a meaſure as a ſignal for open reſiſtance. And when they talked of aſſembling in the event of an invaſion—coupling this reſolution with their former expreſſions, of their deſire to co-operate with the French in the cauſe of freedom, with hands, violence, and troops; what interpretation could the Jury put upon their conduct? But there was another circumſtance on this head that required to be attended to, and which certainly appeared of a nature extremely ſuſpicious. They mentioned that there were ſome of their reſolutions, which in the circumſtances of the time it might not be ſafe or prudent to publiſh. Accordingly, in the letter which they ſent to Mr. Hardy, giving him an account of their tranſactions, no mention was made of that part of their reſolution to aſſemble in the event of any invaſion; this was a circumſtance which they certainly might be apt to ſuppoſe that they could not ſafely publiſh. The violent and illegal proceedings of the Convention at Edinburgh, at laſt called for the interference of the magiſtrates; and the members on that occaſion had certainly been treated with a much leſs degree of ſeverity, than in his opinion had been fully warranted by their conduct. Their diſperſion did not, however, induce the ſociety to lay aſide their object. They were ſenſible, that if they were deſirous to carry their views, it was neceſſary that they ſhould again undertake the ſame work at the ſame hazard. Accordingly they began to concert the means of aſſembling a Convention

tion in this country. But firſt, in order to put in a more ſtrong light what their views were, he would read ſome of their own letters. He then read two letters of Margarot to Hardy, in which he ſtates, that the cauſe is in great forwardneſs in Scotland, that nothing but ſufficient ſupplies of money are wanting, in order to avow their views with ſucceſs, and that a very ſhort time indeed will be ſufficient to put things in ſuch a train as will completely exclude the poſſibility of a failure. In another, he talks of Sinclair having gone to Perth on very urgent buſineſs. The Attorney General called the attention of the Jury to another circumſtance, of Sinclair having come to town, from Scotland, juſt at the time, when it was ſtated in their letters, that there were ſome things which might be improper to commit to paper, and who, of conſequence, might be inferred to have been ſent for the purpoſe of communicating this ſecret intelligence. He then read a letter of Hardy, in which he mentions a report of fifty ſail of French ſhips having been ſeen at ſea with a number of tranſports; and infers from the circumſtance, the probability of an intended deſcent: he concludes the letter, with an exhortation to freſh ardour and perſeverance in the cauſe of freedom. How comes it, ſaid the Attorney General, that this mention of a French deſcent is ſo cloſely followed by an exhortation of this nature? Is it to be inferred that the two ideas were connected in the mind of the writer, and that the proſpect of a French deſcent gave them additional ſpirits, and taught them to look to a more ſpeedy accompliſhment of their views? Having brought forward ſo many written documents, he would only ſtate to the Jury, that they would find in the evidence which would be given, a ſufficient confirmation of all that he had read, and from that evidence, would be able ſtill more fully to form their own judgment upon the whole of the facts. At the commencement of 1794, the views of theſe ſocieties began ſtill more to develope themſelves, and to aſſume an air of greater boldneſs. He then went into a long recital of the proceedings at the dinner at the Globe Tavern, and of the meeting at Chalk Farm. He adverted to the circumſtance of Margarot having written a letter to Hardy, in which he tells him that ſome ſtrong reſolutions were wanted. This deſideratum was quickly ſupplied; the dinner at the Globe-Tavern produced ſome ſtrong reſolutions indeed! In theſe reſolutions they treat the government of the country as plunderers, enemies, and oppreſſors, to whom it would be in vain to apply, and from whom they have no redreſs to expect. Indeed the reaſoning upon the paper is ſo entire, it's expreſſions of hoſtility to the Conſtitution are ſo decided, that it is impoſſible for any ingenuity to ſurmount it's contents. Of this paper they ordered 100,000 copies to be printed and diftributed. The toafts which they adopted upon this occafion breathe the fame fpirit with the refolutions to which they are attached. Among others he enumerated the fentiment of " Succefs to the Arms of Freedom, againft whomfoever directed." The application of this phrafe was obvious with refpect to his Majefty. Their previous declaration to the French "that if ever the Elector of Hanover fhould forget that he was King of England, they would know what conduct to purfue," was not to be forgotten on this occafion. At this dinner alfo they expreffed their approbation of a character who had fo far fatisfied the juftice of his country, as he had already fuffered the punifhment inflicted for his offence againft it—he alluded to Mr. Froft, whofe health was drunk, and drunk, no doubt, from an approbation of the fentiments he had expreffed, " No King, no Parliament; Liberty, Equality." He then read the letter from Martin, who was chairman, giving an account of what had paffed at this dinner. It was in vain that they continually affected to make ufe of the phrafes Legal and Conftitutional, while the things which they did, as well as the manner in which they were done, were clearly illegal and unconftitutional. In all the tranfactions of thefe focieties which he had ocfion to mention, it would afterwards appear from the evidence, that the prifoner at the bar had been the moft zealous and active.

Gentlemen of the Jury, continued he, if I fucceed in proving this—that means have been taken by one meeting to concert another, in order to fuperfede the functions of the Legiflature, even though I fhould ftop, I have proved here enough for my purpofe. In fuch a cafe the King is bound to profecute by the oath which he takes at his coronation; by the duty which he owes to his fubjects; by his regard to the ftability of his own throne. In fact, the queftion is neither more nor lefs than whether he fhall himfelf continue to reign, as the exiftence of his power is effentially involved in a confpiracy, which ftrikes at the very root of the conftitution, and threatens equally extermination to all it's branches. The meeting at Chalk Farm was evidently only a ftep preparatory to the affembling the propofed Convention. It was intended to found the temper of the people, and afcertain how far they were prepared to enter cordially into the views of thefe focieties. It is of extreme importance to attend to the meafures that preceded this meeting, and the circumftances with which it was accompanied. They carry with them an air of concert and preparation, which could only be the effect of deliberation and time. On the fame day, meetings in the open air took place at Leeds, Wakefield, Newcaftle upon Tyne, &c.

The

The Prisoner sent a circular letter for the purpose of calling together these Conventions. In this letter he assumes a tone of greater boldness than before he had been accustomed to employ. The critical moment, he affirms, is at last arrived; formerly they had agreed to meet only on the eve of passing a Convention Bill, but now that moment is anticipated.

He states that there is a central situation in view for the purpose of holding the general Convention, but he forbears to mention the spot till he has consulted the Societies. Was this then a Convention of the People, or was it a Convention in which the particular object to be studied, was the convenience of those Societies? Thus it is, that while they hold themselves out as for the People, we find them always acting from themselves. He recommends to them to adopt an example of the Corresponding Society, in appointing a Secret Committee to consult upon all matters relating to this Convention. There remained only one other point, and on that he would but slightly touch, as it would be better established by particular proof—he meant whatever related to the subject of actual military preparations that had been made by these Societies. And it was surely rather a singular fact, that in different parts of the Kingdom, London, Sheffield and Edinburgh, there should have been found arms of a peculiar construction, and which of late years had been heard of only in France. It seemed probable that in consequence of the dispersion of the British Convention, perceiving they could no longer trust to the effect of naked numbers, they deemed it necessary to have recourse to arms. There were some circumstances from which indeed the charge received a high degree of probability. Could a supposition of this kind be too harsh, when there appeared on the secret records of the Corresponding Society, a resolution for guillotining George's head in a basket!—thus shewing a disposition to strike at the sacred person of Majesty. Mr. Thelwall, after the meeting at Chalk-Farm, took up a pot of porter, and cutting off the froth with a knife, said, "Thus would I serve all Kings." Mr. Yorke stated, "That he was going to Belgium in order to bring to this country the true Defenders of Liberty." We find, indeed, the Society at Sheffield pursuing the same objects by the same means as the Corresponding Society, with an exactness which cannot but appear to be the effect of concert. We find the most active members of both Societies directing and superintending the fabrication of Pikes. We find the Society at Lambeth practising military exercise, and ordering a plate, representing the different positions and manœuvres, to be actually engraved for their own use. The Prisoner at the Bar gave directions for guns and pikes to be made for these Societies, and previously stipulated that

the

the person who was employed to make them, should become a member of the Society. I wished only to give this general idea of the subject, because it is of that nature which will be much better substantiated by particular proof. But if you, Gentlemen, find persons of a lower order talking of seizing august personages, if you find them talking in a stile of the most contemptuous rudeness of the characters of respectable Members of the Legislature, and of having the means of watching and controuling their motions, you must then draw your inferences for yourselves. With respect to the witnesses, whom I shall have occasion to call, some of them are persons who were Members of these Societies; others, I must confess, were employed by government for the purpose of mingling with Members of those Societies, and watching over their operations. Indeed I should have considered it as an instance of neglect equally dangerous and criminal on the part of government, if knowing that there existed such Societies, who were actuated with such designs, they had not taken some means of precaution in order to defeat their mischievous intentions. It is the great province of a British Jury to sift out the truth by every possible means of investigation; to dismiss all prejudice —but at the same time to be on their guard against imposition. In this point of view the character of the witness is certainly of some importance with respect to the credit to be given to his testimony; you will of course listen with some degree of suspicion to the evidence of the persons employed for the purpose of discovering the designs of these Societies; and in proportion as you find it corroborated, by similar evidence from those whose character affords no such ground for distrust or prepossession, you will be able to appreciate the weight which it ought to have in influencing your decision. There is one circumstance which I forgot to mention, that previous to the steps taken to prevent the designs of those Societies from being productive of further mischief, and bringing to trial their most active Members, in order the better to promote their views, they were engaged in forming for themselves a new Constitution. Of the necessity to preserve the respect due to public justice, I need not remind you; miserable indeed would be the situation of the country, if that respect were either weakened or lost. If you shall find that the facts charged against the prisoner, and substantiated by evidence, amount to the crime of High Treason, you will then, no doubt, by your verdict, discharge what you owe to your country, your posterity, and yourselves; but if, after the case being fully stated, and attempted to be proved, you shall be inclined to form a contrary judgment, I have discharged my duty, and have only to join in the prayer, "God send the prisoner a good deliverance!"

After

After the Attorney-General had concluded his speech, which took him up eight hours and fifty minutes in the delivery, an intermission of rest took place for about twenty minutes, during which period the prisoner was accommodated with some refreshment, from the humane attention of Mr. Sheriff Eamer.

At half past seven o'clock the Court was resumed, and the evidence commenced: Thomas M'Lean, John Gurnell, and Edward Harpur, King's messengers, deposed as to the facts of apprehending the prisoner, and the seizure of his papers, which were identified.

Mr. Law, for the Crown, proceeded to examine evidence.

Thomas M'Lean, a King's messenger.

Q. Did you at any time seize any papers from the prisoner?
A. Yes; on the 12th of May last I seized several books and papers at the house of Mr. Thomas Adams, in Took's-court.
Look at the letter.
A. It is one of the papers which I seized.
Alexander Grant.—Q. Do you know the prisoner?
A. Yes.
Q. Have you ever seen him write?
A. I have.
Q. Look at the letter. Is it the prisoner's hand-writing?
A. I cannot swear to it.
Q. Do you believe it is?
A. I again say, I cannot swear to it.
Q. I only ask, do you believe it to be so?
A. I think it is.

Mr. Shelton read the letter, March 22, 1794, signed T. Hardy, Secretary, directed to Mr. Thomas Adams, Secretary to the Constitutional Society. It conveys the strong resolutions entered into by the Corresponding Society, and has this passage in the letter: "*The moment is now arrived* whether we shall abandon our cause, or pursue our purpose of a radical Reform, by immediately assembling a Convention."

John Gurnell, a King's messenger, proved, that he went to the house of the prisoner on the 12th of May, 1794, in consequence of a warrant which he received at the Secretary of State's Office, and seized several papers which he found there in a back room. The witness marked all the papers.——Papers read.

"A Meeting of the Delegates from the two Societies being held, they came to the following Resolutions.

"Resolved,

"First, That it appears to this Committee very desirable, that a Convention or General Meeting of the Friends of Liberty should
be

be called, for the purpose of taking into consideration the proper methods of obtaining a full and fair Representation of the People.

"Second, That it be recommended to the Society for Constitutional Information, and London Corresponding Society, to institute a regular and pressing correspondence with all those parts of the country where such measures may be likely to be promoted, not only to instigate the Societies already formed, but to endeavour also to produce such other associations as may further the general object.

"Third, That it appears to this Committee, that the general object would be promoted if a standing Committee of Co-operation between the two Societies were established, for the purpose of holding personal communication with such Members of similar Societies in other parts of the country, as may occasionally be in London, and who may be authorized by their respective Societies to act with such Committee."

"The above Resolutions being reported to the Society for Constitutional Information, it was by them resolved that the same should be entered on their books as part of the proceedings of the Society; and the Committee of Correspondence was appointed to co-operate with the London Corresponding Society, in conformity with the third Resolution."

It further appears, from correspondence of a recent date between different Societies in the country, and the Secretary of the Corresponding Society, that some time in the course of a few weeks past, circular letters had actually been sent to different parts of the kingdom, on the subject of assembling a Convention, and a printed paper to this effect has been found in the custody of the Secretary to the Society; which is here inserted, and which your Committee have good reason to believe is a copy of the circular letter referred to.

[The following is a Copy of the said printed Paper.]

"Citizens!

"The critical moment is arrived, and Britons must either assert with zeal and firmness their claims to Liberty, or yield without resistance to the chains that ministerial usurpation is forging for them. Will you co-operate with us in the only peaceable measure that now presents itself with any prospect of success? We need not intimate to you, that, notwithstanding the unparalleled audacity of a corrupt and overbearing faction, which at present tramples on the Rights and Liberties of the People, our Meetings cannot

cannot in England be interrupted without the previous adoption of a Convention Bill; a measure it is our duty to anticipate, that the ties of union may be more firmly drawn, and the sentiments and views of the different Societies throughout the Nation be compared, while it is yet in our power, so as to guide and direct the future operations of the Friends of Freedom. Rouse then to one exertion more; and let us shew our consciousness of this important truth—" If we are beaten down with threats, prosecutions, and illegal sentences, we are unworthy—we are incapable of liberty." We must, however, be expeditious. Hessians and Austrians are already among us; and, if we tamely submit, a cloud of these armed Barbarians may shortly be poured in upon us. Let us form, then, another British Convention. We have a central situation in our view, which we believe would be the most convenient for the whole Island, but which we forbear to mention, (entreating your confidence in this particular) till we have the answer of the Societies with which we are in correspondence. Let us have your answer, then, by the 20th at farthest, (earlier if possible) whether you approve of the measure, and how many Delegates you can send, with the number also, if possible, of your Societies.

"We remain yours, in Civic Affection,
"*The London Corresponding Society.*
"T. HARDY, *Secretary*.

" For the management of this business we have appointed a secret committee; you will judge how far it is necessary for you to do the same."

Mr. Grant again called.—*Q.* Do you believe that paper to be the prisoner's writing?

A. I cannot swear so, but I believe it.—That will do.

The paper was then put in and read. It ran thus:

" CITIZEN, *March* 27, 1704.

" I am directed by the London Corresponding Society to transmit the following Resolutions to the Society for Constitutional Information, and to request the sentiments of that Society respecting the important measures which the present juncture of affairs seems to require.

" The London Corresponding Society conceives that the moment is arrived, when a full and explicit declaration is necessary from all the friends of Freedom—whether the late illegal and unheard of prosecutions and sentences shall determine us to abandon our cause, or shall excite us to pursue a radical Reform, with an ardour proportioned to the magnitude of the object, and with a zeal as distinguished on our parts, as the treachery of others,

K in

in the fame glorious caufe, is notorious. The Society for Conftitutional information is therefore required to determine whether or no they will be ready, when called upon, to act in conjunction with this and other Societies, to obtain a fair Reprefentation of the People—Whether they concur with us in feeing the neceffity of a fpeedy Convention, for the purpofe of obtaining in a Conftitutional and Legal method, a redrefs of thofe grievances under which we at prefent labour, and which can only be effectually removed by a full and fair reprefentation of the People of Great Britain.

The London Correfponding Society cannot but remind their friends, that the prefent crifis demands all the prudence, unanimity, and vigour, that ever may or can be exerted by Men and Britons; nor do they doubt that manly firmnefs and confiftency will finally, and they believe, fhortly terminate in the full accomplifhment of all their wifhes.

I am, Fellow Citizen,
(In my humble meafure)
A Friend to the Rights of Man,
(Signed) ————, Secretary.

Refolved unanimoufly, 1ft. That dear as Juftice and Liberty are to Britons, yet the value of them is comparatively fmall without a dependance on their permanency; and there can be no fecurity for the continuance of any right but in Equal Laws.

2d. That equal laws can never be expected but by a full and fair reprefentation of the people; to obtain which, in the way pointed out by the Conftitution, has been, and is, the fole object of this Society. For this we are ready to hazard every thing, and never, but with our lives, will we relinquifh an object which involves the happinefs or even the political exiftence of ourfelves and pofterity.

3d. That it is the decided opinion of this Society, that to fecure ourfelves from future illegal and fcandalous profecutions, and to prevent a repetition of wicked and unjuft fentences, and to recall thofe wife and wholefome laws that have been wrefted from us, and of which fcarcely a veftige remains, there ought to be immediately a Convention of the People, by Delegates deputed for that purpofe from the different Societies of the Friends of Freedom affembled in various parts of this nation. And we pledge ourfelves to the Public to purfue every legal method fpeedily to accomplifh fo defirable a purpofe.

P. S. I have to inform you that a General Meeting of the Society will be holden the 14th of April, the place to be announced by public advertifement.

Refolved, That it is fit and proper, and the duty of this Society,

Society, to send an answer to the London Corresponding Society.

Ordered, That the Secretary acquaint the London Corresponding Society, that we have received their communication, and heartily concur with them in the objects they have in view: and that, for the purpose of a more speedy and effectual co-operation, we invite them to send to this Society next Friday evening a delegation of some of their Members."

Mr. Maclean produced another paper, dated April, 10, 1794, a letter to Citizen Adams, approving of the Resolution to assemble a Convention, and appointing Citizens Thelwall, Lovett, and two others, to meet the Convention in behalf of the Society.

Another paper was next sworn to, with a plan of a Reform, of Universal Suffrage, and Annual Election. This paper states that a great majority of the people are not represented. The majority of the Commons are chosen by about 12,000 voters. Birmingham, Sheffield, Leeds, Halifax, and other large towns, have no Members. It also contains the foundation of the Society, which was called the Corresponding Society, with the forms of admission, &c. and that they were to pay one penny per week.

William Woodfall was called, but did not answer.

Mr. Erskine observed, that it was impossible to take all the contents of the papers down as the clerk read them, and therefore proposed that there might be copies, that they might have access to them. This proposition was acceded to.

Edward Lazun, an extra messenger.—On the 12th of May last, he seized some papers; the first shewn to him was one of them.

Grant swore that he believed it to be Hardy's writing. It was dated August 20, 1792, directed to Mr. Buchanan, at Edinburgh, and contains the resolutions of the Corresponding Society to effect a Parliamentary Reform. The prisoner, in that letter, endeavours to promote a union between the societies—" A threefold cord is not easily broken."

A second paper, dated September 4, 1792, is a letter to the secretary of the Manchester society, containing thanks for that society's letter, and inclosing twelve copies of an address to the people of England. The letter and address recommended a reform in very strong terms.

August 13, 1792. A letter to Richard Cartwright, chairman to the Constitutional society, containing a copy of the address to the people, to persuade them to a parliamentary reform. This letter is signed Maurice Margarot, chairman, and Thomas Hardy, secretary.

The address was now read, and the resolutions, all of them setting forth the inequality and corruption of the present state of representation; the address contains a minute description of the Boroughs, which, with very few electors, viz. some *three, four, five,* and *six* electors, return *two* members each, whilst large and populous towns send no members; states a long list of evils and grievances which the nation was obliged to suffer on that account. The opinions of Mr. Pitt, the Duke of Richmond, &c. &c. are quoted—" That the nation would never regain it's ancient constitutional rights, until a fair and equal representation in parliament was effected." Also a very long catalogue of evils and enormities, which are stated to flow like a torrent upon the people through that corrupted source. It is dated London, August 26, 1792. This piece took half an hour in the reading.

A fourth paper was produced, which Mr. Grant did not believe to be the writing of the prisoner; but it being found in the Prisoner's own possession, with the others which were read, the Court admitted it in evidence. This was a letter containing two copies of Paine's Rights of Man, together with copies of the foregoing addresses, directed to Stockton.

The next paper was a letter of thanks from that town, directed to the prisoner, in which they say that they need all their assistance.—Mr. Lauzun found it in the prisoner's possession.

The next head of evidence was an address to the French Nation, written by Mr. Horne Tooke.

Mr. William Woodfall, examined by Mr. Wood, proved the hand-writing; and Maclean proved that he found it in Mr. Hardy's custody. It was a letter to Mr. Adams, signed by Mr. Hardy, dated October 11, 1792, and inclosed in it an address to the French National Assembly, which was in the hand-writing of Mr. Tooke. The answer of Mr. Adams followed, acknowledging the receipt of the Address. This was proved to be found in the Prisoner's custody by the Messenger, Lauzun.

The next document was a letter to Mr. Thomas Walker, Chairman of the Manchester Constitutional Society, and inclosing another copy of the intended Address to the French National Assembly.

Another letter, dated October 11, 1792, acknowledging the receipt of a letter from Norwich, and inclosing in return another copy of address to the French.

October 18, 1792, a similar letter to the Society at Derby. —October 18, 1792, a similar letter, with an Address—A letter, dated November 11, 1792, from Mr. Baxter, Chairman to the Norwich Society, to the Prisoner, and containing a desire that three of their members might be incorporated with the Corresponding Society, in order to further the views of the Society; and

desiring

desiring to know whether it was their design. "*'to root up Aristocracy* by the roots, and place *Democracy* in it's room? or whether to follow the plan of the Duke of Richmond?"

November 26, 1792, contains an answer from the Prisoner to Mr. Baxter; but in which he cautiously avoided answering that question, but strongly recommends a reform, &c. upon legal and constitutional principles; and states to the Society the great acquisition of strength which the Society was daily acquiring.

An address was then read from a Society in the country to the London Corresponding Society, in which they thanked the latter for their kind advice in recommending it to them to preserve order and obedience to the laws.—Another paper was an agreement, in conjunction with other Societies, to present an address to the National Convention of France. It said, that it was congenial to the heart of a Briton to wish success to the cause of Freedom, and expressed great abhorrence to the Duke of Brunswick's Manifesto, which, it is said, aimed not only at the liberties of France, but of the whole world. Two more letters were read; one written in February, 1793, from the *Friends of the People*, in answer to one from the Corresponding Society; and the other an answer to that again, supposed to be written by Mr. Margarot.

Mr. Grant, the printer, was again called as a witness, to prove that a certain paper, in the form of a posting bill, was printed by him. He said, he had been made a member of the London Corresponding Society in the beginning of the year 1792, the first division of which then met in Exeter-street, at a public house, the master of which was a member. He then saw Mr. Margarot, Mr. Hardy, Mr. Richter, &c. He had attended the division but seldom. In November of the same year he was applied to by Mr. Richter to print the posting bill in question, which he accordingly did, to the number of 500 copies, which were given to one Carter, a bill-sticker, who he heard was apprehended for sticking them up. This paper was an address from the London Corresponding Society to all the other Societies in Great Britain, associated for the purpose of obtaining a reform. It denied the charges of Republicanism and Levelling, applied to it by Mr. Reeves's association: it denied that they had any other object in view than that of obtaining a reform in Parliament. They wanted to destroy no property but what had been raised on the ruins of their liberties.

Several other papers were read, consisting of correspondence between the above Society and several others in Sheffield, Norwich, Edinburgh, &c. some relative to petitioning Parliament for a Reform, and others complaining of grievances.

About half past eleven o'clock, Mr. Erskine, as counsel for Mr.

Mr. Hardy, expreſſed a wiſh to know whether it was the intention of the Court to continue ſitting or to adjourn. He did not conceive it poſſible for human nature to be able to hold out without reſt or intermiſſion until that immenſe volume of evidence ſhould be gone through. For his own part, he had no objection to ſit there any length of time; but he conſidered the ſituation of their Lordſhips and the Jury, whoſe duty was more arduous and important than his.

The Chief Juſtice ſaid, there was a poſitive rule in law that no adjourment could take place during a trial, particularly a criminal one; and from that rule he would not depart, unleſs ſome extreme neceſſity occured which muſt juſtify ſuch a deviation; that neceſſity, he thought, did then exiſt, inaſmuch as it would be impoſſible to keep the attention of the Jury alive, ſhould the trial be continued without intermiſſion. For that reaſon, he was inclined to enter into the conſideration of the queſtion, how far the adjournment, in the preſent inſtance, might be juſtified. An adjournment once took place in the caſe of a miſdemeanor, and the Jury ſeparated; but that was different from the preſent, for which there was no precedent, except one mentioned in the year-book (if it could be called a precedent), being a caſe in which the Jury were ſeparated, and the Court obliged to adjourn by means of a terrible ſtorm. The queſtion, however, never was decided. Notwithſtanding, if counſel then made an application on the ground of it's being neceſſary to the priſoner, and if the proſecuter conſented, he ſhould have no objection to adjourn, provided the Jury could be kept together. His Lordſhip did not then ſee how that could be done. Before his coming into Court, he had made ſome enquiry on that ſubject, foreſeeing the neceſſity there would be to deviate from the ſtrict rules of law. The Sheriffs ſaid, that the Jury could either be accommodated in the houſe where they then ſat, or in their own houſes, after having given their words of honour not to have any communication with any perſon. Whatever ſhould be done in the preſent inſtance, he, with all his heart, would take his ſhare of the riſk.

Mr. Erſkine made ſome obſervations on the delicate ſituation in which he ſtood. He thought it would be perfectly ſafe to permit the gentlemen of the Jury to go to their own houſes; for he entertained not the leaſt doubt but that gentlemen of their character would ſtrictly adhere to their word of honour; and the priſoner, he was ſure, would aſſent to ſuch a meaſure.

The Chief Juſtice obſerved, that it was not the conſent, but the requeſt of the priſoner, that ſhould be made in ſuch a caſe.

The Chief Baron thought an adjournment muſt neceſſarily take place, if juſtice could not be done without ſuch a deviation;

ſome

some regard should be had to the prisoner. The Court had heard the charge of the Attorney General when it was fresh to receive it. His defence ought to be heard in a similar situation. Yet this deviation should be made as little as possible; and he thought it better that the gentlemen of the Jury should not go to their own houses.

One of the Jury stood up, and said, he was an invalid, and would rather go home.

The Chief Justice told the Jury they could be accommodated where they were. They said they wished to go home.

Mr. Baron Hotham was against their going to their own houses.

Mr. Justice Buller said there was an Alderman then on the Bench, who once knew an instance of a Jury going home.

This Alderman, whose name we learned was Mr. Newnham declared that to be the case.

Mr. Justice Buller asked the Sheriff whether there were any accommodations there for the Jury? Who replied, that beds and mattrasses had been provided, as well as every other possible accommodation.

The Chief Justice then said, that as it was visible to all mankind that the strict rule of law could not be adhered to, the Court had only to desire the Sheriffs to give what accommodations they could, to request the Jury to submit to those difficulties which were unavoidable; and as they might require something more than ordinary refreshments, their attendance would not be required until eight o'clock next morning.

Mr. Erskine informed the Court, that he had not been able to procure from the Privy Council copies of the several papers which were to be read in evidence against Mr. Hardy. He expected to know what was contained in that huge mass: and it was impossible for that to take place during the reading of them in Court. He should, therefore, when he came to the prisoner's defence, beg a little time of the Court. He mentioned the circumstance then, that the Court might not be thought to have a sudden application made to it. He had not, however, any the remotest intention of trespassing on the time of the Court.

The Lord Chief Baron thought the general rule against separation was very wisely adopted. The Jury, in that case, gave their verdict with a full and undisturbed impression of the evidence. When however this rule superinduced a failure of justice, an exception became necessary. But in his opinion, the exception should be no greater than the necessity required. If, therefore, the Jury could be accommodated in the house, that accommodation would remedy the evil, and depart least from the general rule.

Baron Hotham coincided with the Lord Chief Baron, and
conceived

conceived the case novel, and pregnant with very serious consequences, unless the rule was departed from with the greatest caution.

Judge Buller asked the Sheriff if he could accommodate all the Jury.

The Sheriff answered, "Yes, either with beds or mattrasses."

The Lord President concurred with the distinction, and the Jury had such accommodation prepared as the Sheriffs could procure.

The Court adjourned at 12 o'clock, until seven o'clock, Wednesday morning.

Old Bailey, Wednesday, Oct. 29.

The Court met at eight o'clock this morning, when Mr. Wood proceeded to examine the witnesses for the Crown.

A letter was produced, signed T. Hardy, and addressed to Mr. Skirving, Edinburgh, which Grant proved to be the hand writing of Hardy. The purport of this letter was to return thanks for two copies of Mr. Muir's trial; to assure Skirving that the society looked on Muir and Palmer as Martyrs to the cause of liberty, and to express their warmest hopes that the oppressors of mankind might be ashamed or afraid of carrying their revengeful malice into execution. It is also declared, that Hardy had no doubt the society would, with pleasure, accept the invitation of sending a deputation to the Convention.

The next document produced, was a letter of Oct. 22, 1793, signed by Skirving, Secretary to the Scotch Convention, mentioning their meeting, and their full determination to procure Annual Parliaments, and Universal Suffrage, with their resolution respecting the delegates. This paper was proved to be found among Hardy's papers, by Maclean. Mr. Grant proved that an indorsement on the back of it was Hardy's writing.

The next paper was an answer to the former, signed by Hardy, declaring the nomination of Margarot and Gerald, as delegates from the Corresponding Society. This document Scott declared was one, among others, signed at Skirving's, which he saw taken out of a sealed bag, at the Sheriff's office in Edinburgh, while Skirving was present. The writing was proved by Grant, as before.

The article of instruction from the Constitutional Society to Gerald and Margarot, as their delegates to the Convention, were next identified. They were as follow;--1st, That they should on no account depart from the original object and principles of the society, viz. Annual Parliaments, and Universal Suffrage, *by peaceable and lawful methods.* 2d. That they should support the opinion, that representatives of the people should be paid. 3d. That the election of sheriffs should be by the people. 4th. That Jurors should be chosen by lot. 5th. And that Jurors should be instructed. 6th. They were to maintain the liberty of the press. 7th. And the right of resistance against any act of parliament contrary to the liberty of the

the People. 8th. That the society consider all party names as contrary to the general happiness.

Another letter was produced, signed by Hodgson and Hardy, dated Nov. 1, 1793, addressed to Margarot and Gerald, expressing their approbation of the number and zeal of the friends of liberty in the north.

Three other letters were read from Hardy to Margarot and Gerald, bearing date Nov. 15, 22, and 29, 1793, of similar import with the former.

Gurnell, one of the King's messengers, was brought forward as an evidence of the seizure of some papers at Hardy's; the first of which was a letter from Gerald and Margarot, in Edinburgh, dated Dec. 2, 1793, stating the line of conduct the Convention meant to pursue, in opposition to administration, if the Habeas Corpus act were suspended, foreign troops landed, a Convention bill passed, &c.

Then followed the correspondence between Mr. Hardy, as secretary to the Corresponding Society, and Mr. Gerald and Mr. Margarot, two of the delegates at the Convention in Edinburgh; most of these papers were printed also in the appendix to the report of the committee of secrecy; they were produced by a witness of the name of Gurnell. These papers being all read by the officer of the Court, Mr. Bower said, " My Lords, we now propose, on the part of the Crown, to read the proceedings of the Convention itself."

Mr. Erskine.—" I am not very anxious, I confess, to shut out any of the evidence which the learned gentlemen for the Crown have yet offered for the consideration of the Jury. As the case stands at present, I am entitled to say, that although this Society has been formed, the object of it's formation has not yet been heard of by evidence, so as to entitle the Crown to call upon the Jury to put upon it any construction that would make it our duty to explain. They appoint two delegates for the Convention, and the character of that Convention is not the thing complained of on this record. This record did not complain of that Convention, it only imputed guilt to the defendant now at the Bar, for being one of those who assembled to concert measures for calling afterwards another Convention of the people. We have evidence that those two Gentlemen were delegates to the first Convention, and that they had instructions given to them; these instructions instructed these delegates, as the Court has heard, to pursue closely the rule and institutions of those by whom they were appointed; the rules and institutions of this Society, and which have already a long time been made public. If therefore it should turn out in the course of this proceeding, that the delegates ordered to act under the rules and institutions of this society, did what many honest men may do, and what many honest men have done, in the moment of heat and irritation, say something that in their cooler moments they could not approve—if Mr. Margarot had said or done any thing of this kind, and went beyond the letter and the spirit of his instructions, I maintain that you cannot by such an Act affect the prisoner at the bar, of which, however, there is no evidence; nor can there in this way be any evidence fairly brought against him, for it is not the thing complained of in the record. Your Lordships will give me leave to call this point to your recollection: the defendant now at your bar, is charged with no act of the Convention of Edinburgh. He is charged with that of which I cannot think him guilty; if I thought him so, as I am his counsel, I must have gone through my duty unquestionably in defending him; but I should then have done it in a manner very different from that which I shall adopt for his defence. He is charged with having encompassed the death of the King, whose life is dear to us all; to prove that he had that wicked intention, the evidence should be clear, and refer to the act itself, but no act can be given in evidence, that does not go to shew that the prisoner had that wicked encompassing in his own breast at the time the act was committed. If they can shew that any instructions were given to the two men who attended this convention, and that evidence demonstrated a wicked intention, which was manifested afterwards, on the part of the prisoner, in the way which this indictment imputes to him, or any thing that approached towards it; then the counsel for the Crown will be right. My Lord, I do not make this objection from any apprehension of the importance of the present question: I have no desire to make captious objections; I think we have already given proofs that we have no wish for such a practice.—My friend, Mr. Gibbs, and myself, have sat here silent enough, while many of these papers have been read in evidence. I do not mean to give to the Court any unnecessary trouble; all that I wish is that nothing of this sort should pass, so that just rules of evidence may be done away. As to that which is now proposed, I do not know what it is, very probably I am wasting my own breath upon nothing, for that the thing itself conveys no intelligence; but I speak from another motive, I speak in defence of the rules of evidence in a Court of Justice. I am now engaged in defending the life of Mr. Hardy only; but I ought to consider that if the rules of law and justice are broken in upon, I may soon have to defend my own life. I must take care that the rules of evidence are preserved inviolate—All that I mean to say is, that if Mr. Hardy knew of the proceedings of this convention in Edinburgh, then my objection falls to the ground in this respect."

The Lord President agreed, that the evidence proposed could not be adduced immediately against the prisoner. He observed, however, that it might be let in: but that the application of it was another thing. At all events, the prisoner might afterwards object that the Delegates had exceeded their commission, and that objection would be valid so far.

Mr. Bower. Yes, my Lord, we mean to shew, in many instances, the prisoner's subsequent approbation of the proceedings of the British Convention.

The Lord President. That declaration is enough to let in the evidence; the application of it will depend on what will further
appear-

appear. If the Deputies exceeded the limits of their mission, it will be matter for observation to the Jury.

The Solicitor General. The Deputies must be regarded, I apprehend, as agents to the prisoner; and if he did not disclaim their conduct when he became acquainted with it, he of course becomes a party.

Mr. Templar, Clerk of the Rules in the King's Bench, now proceeded to read the Minutes of the British Convention, after Mr. Scot had proved the seizure of them.

Mr. Gibbs. I beg your Lordship's pardon, but we have not yet found the place in our copy to follow the reading.

The Lord President. You need not apologize; we shall think no delay misplaced by which you become enabled to make the most complete defence for the prisoner that his case will admit.

The Proceedings of the General Committee at Edinburgh, of the 6th November, 1793, were then read through.

The first Sitting of the Convention at Edinburgh, of the 1st November, 1793, was also read through.

Read also the following Resolutions of the Convention, entered into on the 28th November, 1793.

"That this Convention, considering the calamitous consequences of any act of the Legislature which may tend to deprive the whole or any part of the People of their undoubted right to meet, either by themselves or by delegation, to discuss any matter relative to their common interest, whether of a public or private nature, and holding the same to be totally inconsistent with the first principles and safety of society, and also subversive of our known and acknowledged Constitutional Liberties, do hereby declare, before God and the World, that we shall follow the wholesome example of former times, by paying no regard to any act which shall militate against the Constitution of our Country, and shall continue to assemble and consider of the best means by which we can accomplish a real Representation of the People, and Annual Elections, until compelled to desist by superior force.

"And we do resolve, That the first notice given for the introduction of a Convention Bill, or any Bill of a similar tendency to that passed in Ireland in the last Session of their Parliament;

"Or any Bill for the Suspension of the Habeas Corpus Act, or the Act for preventing Wrongous Imprisonment, and against undue Delays in Trial in North Britain;

"Or in case of an Invasion; or the admission of any Foreign Troops whatsoever in Great Britain or Ireland;

"All or any one of these calamitous circumstances, shall be a signal to the several Delegates to repair to such place as the Secret Committee of this Convention shall appoint; and the first seven Members shall have power to declare the *sittings permanent*, shall constitute a Convention, and twenty-one proceed to business.

"The Convention doth therefore resolve, that each Delegate, immediately on his return home, to convene his Constituents, and explain to them the necessity of electing a Delegate or Delegates, gnd eſtabliſhing a fund, without delay, againſt any of theſe emergencies, for his or their expence; and that they do inſtruct the ſaid Delegate or Delegates to hold themſelves ready to depart at one hour's warning."

Letter dated 8th December, 1793, at Edinburgh.

Letter dated 19th December, 1793, at Edinburgh, ſigned Maurice Margarot to Thomas Hardy, read.

Mr. Garrow, for the proſecution, then called James Daviſon, who being ſworn, ſaid he was a printer—was employed to print the paper now preſented to him—believes that that happened on the 20th of February laſt. Thelwall brought him the copy or manuſcript, from which he printed it. There was alſo another perſon along with Thelwall, but does not know who he was—it was not Hardy.

Here Mr. Erſkine, on the part of the priſoner, objected to the further proceeding in this part of the evidence, as it appeared that Hardy was not concerned in it.

Mr. Garrow contended for the propriety of the evidence. He ſaid that the connection of Thelwall with Hardy had been already ſo fully proved, that this being an act of Thelwall's, attached alſo upon Hardy; beſides, the priſoner having paid for the printing, ſtrengthened the application of it to him.

Mr. Erſkine ſaid, that no doubt, in indictments for conſpiracy, when one perſon is connected with another, the act of one, if it be to one and the ſame purpoſe, even from one and the ſame crime as that for which they are convicted, attaches upon the other; but this, he contended, was totally different, and therefore inadmiſſible. Thelwall gives papers to be printed; that naked fact could by no means criminate the priſoner; and as to his paying for them, that was not in proof, and could not be taken into conſideration. Suppoſe this paper contained crime, would the Court, he demanded, faſten it on the priſoner? In criminal caſes the Court would not ſtretch the rules of evidence.

The Lord Preſident ſaid, that he thought the inſiſting on one ſide, and objection on the other, were both premature. It muſt be firſt known what the paper contains, before the Court can determine, or the Counſel contend, on the admiſſibility of it as evidence.

Mr. Garrow ſaid that this was a paper of incitement to the people to riſe in furtherance of the general conſpiracy, and an inſtrument to carry it into effect.

The Lord Preſident. " In order to judge of it, it will be neceſſary to open that point of the writing; I have caſt my eyes over it, and ſaw ſomething applying to the general charge."

Mr. Garrow then read the paper, and continued the examination of Daviſon, who depoſed that he printed, by Thelwall's order, 2000 copies of it. Did not print the whole that day; printed 200 only; carried them to the Globe tavern; met Hardy on the ſtairs; was a member of the Correſponding Society; had been at ſome of their meetings; ſaw Hardy at them; knew he was Secretary; told Hardy

that

that he had brought the 200 copies, but Hardy defired him to take them back, and not diftribute them; brought them back accordingly, and returned to the Globe tavern to dinner. On that day the Refolutions were paffed. Being queftioned as to the time of the day, faid he faw Thelwall at one or two o'clock, at four or five carried the copies to the Globe tavern, and came again to it about fix; was not prefent when the Refolutions were propofed. Had the copy given to him on the 18th, and delivered them on the 20th—had no doubt about it. The dinners on thofe occafions were public; each man paid for his ticket of admittance. Believes there was a chairman, but cannot pofitively fay who; imagines that Thelwall was the man, but is not fure—the prifoner Hardy was there. Some one afterwards fent to him for fome of the copies to the Globe tavern, and they were brought to the meeting: he himfelf faw only one there, which was handed round. There were three hundred people prefent. Stayed there till about ten o'clock. Afterwards, in the fame week, he printed a thoufand more, in purfuance of the original order given him by Thelwall; gave many of them to Hardy, members of the fociety often came for more. Printed fix thoufand more at other times; and Hardy ordered him to go on printing until defired to ftop. Thinks that it was in March he was defired to ftop. Printed eight thoufand in all. Has not been paid for them yet: no one promifed to pay for them: had no communication about the payment with Hardy, but put the printing down to the account of the fociety, and made them his debtors for them: on other occafions printed for them, and Hardy paid. —Knows John Martin a little; cannot fay whether he was or was not a member of the Correfponding Society: was at the meeting held at the Globe tavern when he went there.

Here a paper containing the Addrefs and Refolutions of 20th of January, together with the toafts drank on that day, were read.

The witnefs being afked whether he knew if any perfons not being members of the fociety were admitted, anfwered that he did not know; but being preffed by one of the Jury, faid that there were, at dinners. Spoke of the toafts with Martin; to whom he faid, that he thought there were fome hard words in them; but Martin faid, No, they were conftitutional—there was no danger. This happened on the 21ft or 22d.

Richard Williams was then fworn, to prove the hand-writing of Mr. Thelwall.

Mr. Garrow. We have fhewn Thelwall to be a party in the confpiracy, and an agent for printing the works of the fociety. Any act of his, therefore, in purfuance of the grand object of the deftruction of all rank, and the eftablifhed order, is evidence againft the prifoner. The mode he adopted was, that of writing fongs to expofe and vilify the eftablifhed orders, to prepare the minds of low and ignorant people for their ultimate deftruction. We mean to produce in evidence an account of thefe fongs, as given by Thelwall.

Mr.

Mr. Erskine. If these songs had been sung at the society, it would have been evidence; but Thelwall's account that such songs had been sung is not. What an agent does, binds the principal, but not what he says he does. The account is given to a stranger, unconnected with the society.

Mr. Gibbs. We can have no anxiety to resist this kind of evidence, but the consideration, that if it be frequently admitted, there is no knowing where it may end.

The defendant is charged, 1st, With compassing the King's death; 2d, With endeavouring to effect that object by means of an insurrection, or with inciting the insurrection with that settled design. All evidence, therefore, must apply to one of these points of the indictment: the present letter applies to neither.

Mr. Garrow. The whole objection applies to the effect and tendency of the letter, which is applicable only to the Jury. Now, we say, that the letter being in furtherance of the general conspiracy, all the collateral parts involve every one concerned, provided they do not diverge into separate and distinct offences.

The Lord President. I have great doubts on this point of evidence. Every part of a general conspiracy should be admitted as imputable to all; but this is only a private letter: and though good against Thelwall, in my opinion, should not be received against the prisoner. It is not similar to a fact done by Thelwall; it is only an account given by him like a declaration and confession.

The Lord Chief Baron and Baron Hotham were silent.

Judge Buller. I think this evidence is admissible. The indictment, in the present case, involves two distinct points, which, if kept separate, the evidence will apply: 1st, The existence of a traitorous conspiracy; 2d, How far the prisoner is concerned in it. The first point should be established, and then the second enquired into. Suppose the case stood thus: Thelwall had spoken words to the same effect; the evidence might have been received as establishing the first point of the existence of a conspiracy. This was done in Dameray and Purchale's case; and recently in Lord George Gordon's, evidence was received of what the mob said, although his Lordship was not present at the time. It shewed what design was on foot. The other point involving the prisoner must afterwards be made out; but Thelwall's letter or words make of the fact a conspiracy.

Judge Grose. There are doubts on this subject, but I cannot think that the evidence should be rejected. Both are parties to one plot, and it is very material to hear what either says concerning it; for that shews the *animus* and object. I am therefore for it's admission.

The Lord Chief Baron. There certainly is great doubt on the subject; but it does not appear to me that the letter meets the definition of furthering the conspiracy. I therefore am for rejecting the evidence.

Baron Hotham. It does not appear to be part of the plan, but
a simple

a simple narration, which should not be received against the prisoner.

The Lord President. I retain my opinion, and see a wide distinction between *words* and *actions*. The cry of a mob in Lord George Gordon's case was a part of the action and a fact.

Three Judges being against the evidence, and two for it, the evidence was rejected.

Mr. Garrow wished to produce a letter from Martin, a member of the London Corresponding Society, to Margaro', while at Edinburgh, as a Delegate to the British Convention.

Mr. Erskine objected, as Martin was not included in the indictment, nor any way known but as a member of the London Corresponding Society. If his letter were to affect the defendant, he saw no end to evidence, as any letter of any of the numerous members might be produced in the same way, and he wished to know if in that case he should be allowed to rebut the evidence by the same kind; namely, evidence of innocent or meritorious intention.

Mr. Gibbs regarded this case as similar to the last. It was a relation and not a fact.

Mr. Garrow observed, that the letter was an excitation to insurrection in direct terms.

The Solicitor General said, the objection appeared to him to have no weight, and not at all connected with the question which the Court had decided.—That decision he was bound in duty to submit to; but in contending for the admissibility of the present evidence, he should not be obliged to controvert what had fallen from the Bench. It appeared to him a clear proposition, that where a conspiracy was proved to exist, a conversation among a part of the conspirators might be adduced in evidence against any other of the conspirators, though he might not have been present at the conversation. The distinction between the present question and that which had been just decided, was very obvious; for this was a letter from a person charged with being in the conspiracy to another standing in the same predicament, and therefore ought, upon every principle of evidence, to be read as a proof of the intentions of the parties, and the object of the Conspiracy.

In the case of Lord Stafford, much of the evidence was of the general nature, such as the conversation between Anderton and two other conspirators, at which Lord Stafford was not present.

In the case of Lord Lovat, the same doctrine was laid down by the Solicitor General of that day, and the same species of evidence admitted.—In contending for the admission of the evidence, he did not mean it as a positive proof of the *quo animo* with which Hardy acted, but merely as a means, by which to ascertain the general views of the conspirators.

Serjeant Adair was extremely anxious that this point should be decided, not only from it's importance in the present case, but that it might serve as a rule for posterity.—It was necessary to state exactly the grounds upon which the evidence was tendered; he did

not

not mean to contend, that the idle converfations of Martin were pofitive proof of guilt againft Hardy; but as the letter offered to be read, was from one confpirator to another, ftating a fact which had occurred in furtherance of their plan, it certainly ought to be read, as tending to fhew the views of the parties. The charge againft the prifoner was, that of confpiring againft the King, with an intent to depofe him and take away his life; but this plan was to be effected under the cloak of a parliamentary reform. The latter might, under circumftances, be innocent; but among people acting in this manner, there muft of courfe have been ufed many equivocal expreffions, which it would be impoffible to develope, if fuch an evidence as this were not to be admitted.—The letter itfelf, if read, would not prove perhaps any great degree of guilt againft the prifoner, but the principle was fo extremely important, that he felt anxious for it's being eftablifhed by the admiffion of this evidence.

Mr. Bearcroft faid, he would not apologize for troubling the Court upon fo important a cafe; there were two things which he would, in the courfe of what he had to fay, cautioufly avoid; he would not break in upon the determination which the Court had lately given, nor would he repeat one word which had been faid by his learned friends who had preceded him. He thought he might lay it down as a pofition clearly acknowledged, that the general rules of evidence, acted upon in cafes of a fmaller magnitude, were equally applicable in a cafe of High Treafon. In every trial for a Confpiracy, the fact of the confpiring having been proved, the declarations or acts of one of the confpirators were always admitted as evidence againft the others. It had already been proved, that Margarot, Martin, and the Prifoner, were connected together in this plan, and the letter of one of them was admiffible againft the others, whether it proved much or little.

Mr. Bearcroft, Mr. Bower, and Mr. Law, made feveral obfervations on the admiffibility of this letter.

Mr. Erfkine in reply declared, that it never was his intention to oppofe the reading of any document relative to this bufinefs, but it was to prevent a dangerous precedent being eftablifhed. It was not a matter of flight importance. He ftood there as counfel for the innocent man at the bar, for the Country, and for the Conftitution, and he would fuffer no precedent to be adopted that was incompatible with their fafety.

Mr. Solicitor General fmiled.

The learned Counfel obferved, that the folemnity of the occafion ought to infpire emotions of a very different nature. If he was miftaken in point of law, he was open to correction, but it was not to *him* that he would apply for information on the fubject.

The Lord Prefident faid, a confiderable portion of time had been taken up in the difcuffion of this point.—He did not throw any blame any where, as the point certainly was of much importance. He confeffed he did not think this evidence could be diftinguifhed from that which the Court had refufed to admit.

This

This letter was not proved to come to the hands of Margarot, and therefore might merely have been written by Martin, and never sent. Suppose four persons are accused of a conspiracy, and three of them acknowledge the conspiracy, that would not be evidence against the other. The case of Lord Stafford did not apply to this, because in that case all the parties were engaged in conversation proved. His Lordship therefore thought the evidence ought not to be admitted.

The Lord Chief Baron thought there was a material distinction between the former case and the present, for this was a complete act in one of the conspirators, and in his opinion good evidence against the rest.

Baron Hotham retained his opinion upon the former case, but thought it very distinguishable from the present, and therefore was of opinion that the evidence ought to be admitted.

Mr. Justice Buller and Mr. Justice Grose were of the same opinion; and the letter was read, the hand writing of Martin was proved by William Walker.——It was dated Richmond-buildings, Jan. 22, 1794; and directed to Mr. Margarot, Edinburgh.

The following papers found in Hardy's house, were then read:

A letter from the Bristol Society for constitutional information, dated the 24th Jan. 1794, and addressed to the prisoner.

Some circular letters, dated 9th of April.

A letter from the Norwich Society to the prisoner.

A letter, purporting to be an answer to the last, but not signed by the prisoner, or in his hand-writing.

A letter, dated Bristol, 24 April, 1794, from the Bristol Society.

A letter from the Norwich Society, dated 29th April 1794.

A letter from the Hereford Society, dated 12th April 1794.

The answer to the above, signed T. Hardy.

A letter from the Halifax Society, May 11, 1794.

A letter dated Edinburgh, Oct. 1793, addressed to the prisoner.

A letter from the Society for Constitutional Information, dated 14th June, 1792.

A letter from Hardy to the Society for Constitutional Information.

A letter from a society at Sheffield, addressed to the prisoner, but found amongst J. Thelwall's papers, was next produced.

Mr. Erskine contended, that this paper was not matter of evidence against Hardy. There was no proof that he had ever seen the paper, nor that the Sheffield Society, from which it came, was that with which his client had been in the habit of corresponding.

Mr. Garrow said, that as Thelwall was a subordinate agent of the society, and acted in conjunction with Hardy, the address was a sufficient proof that the latter was acquainted with it's contents.

The Lord President *(Eyre)* agreed with the Counsel for the prosecution. He added, that the act of any one man engaged in such a conspiracy, was sufficient to criminate those with whom he co-operated.

The letter was then read. It stated the increase of their numbers in defpite of the ariftocracy, by which they were furrounded, and their determination not to abate in their efforts until a reform was accomplifhed.

Daniel Adams, late fecretary to the Society for Conftitutional Information, was then fworn. He identified the books of that fociety, which were feized at his houfe. Thefe books, he faid, were always open to the infpection of the members, and lay on the table at their meetings. This privilege was however ufed but feldom, as the minutes of the former were always read before they proceeded to bufinefs at the fubfequent meeting.

The minutes of the meeting of the Conftitutional Society, held at the Crown and Anchor on the 18th of Auguft 1792, and the fubfequent days, were then read. Thefe related to the admiffion of fix members from the London Correfponding Society; their thanks to Mr. Paine for his works; their declining his offer of a thoufand pounds from the profits of the fale of the Rights of Man, to be applied to fuch purpofes as the Society may think proper. The ground on which they declined this offer was, that the principal fource of his enjoyment they faid muft arife from his own confcioufnefs of the good which his labours had rendered to mankind; yet they did not think it right, that he fhould be deprived of the profits fairly refulting from thofe labours.

As much ftrefs was laid by the Counfel for the profecution on the fanction and adoption thus given to the works of Mr. Paine, we fubjoin a lift of the members prefent at thofe meetings.

Mr. Froft	Mr. J. H. Tooke
Mr. Edwards	Mr. Bonney
Mr. J. Williams	Mr. Payne
Dr. Maxwell	Mr. Hull
Mr. Sharpe	Mr. Pierfon
Dr. Kentifh	Mr. Sturch
Mr. G. Williams	Mr. Conftable
Mr. Rivington	Capt. Harwood
Mr. Bufhe, fen.	Mr. Bufhe, jun.
Mr. Tuffnell	Mr. Maillow
Mr. Hinde	Lord Sempill
Mr. Fitzgerald	Mr. Barbelow
Mr. Jennings	Mr. Allen
Mr. Chapman	Mr. Afpinhall
Mr. Hardy	Mr. Grant
Capt. Perry	Dr. Towers
Mr. Gerald	Mr. Littlejohn
Mr. Rutt	Mr. Sutton
Mr. Moore	Mr. Martin
Mr. Gough	Mr. Simmons
Mr. Joyce	Mr. Walfh, &c.

Mr. Jordan, bookfeller, in Fleet-ftreet, was then called, to identify the work of Mr. Thomas Paine, and to prove his hand-writing. Mr. Jordan had never feen Mr. Paine write. He had received

feveral

several notes from him, but never, as far as he can recollect, had a conversation with him afterwards on the subject of those notes. He had published the works of Mr. Paine, but he could not swear that the copy presented to him was one of his publication.

[Here appeared a temporary chasm in the evidence, as the man was dead who had bought the Rights of Man at Mr. Jordan's by direction of Mr. White, the solicitor of the treasury. Mr. Chapman, the printer of the book, was called, but did not appear. The Lord President said, that as there was no appearance of the written evidence approaching to a conclusion, the Jury may avail themselves of this interval to take some refreshment. The court adjourned at half past three o'clock for an hour.]

The court being resumed, Mr. Lauzun, the messenger, was called in, and proved his signature to a copy of the cheap edition of the Rights of Man, found in the prisoner's house.

A letter was then read from Mr. Paine to the people of France, dated Sept. 25, 1792; in this letter he returns them thanks for having elected him a French Citizen, and a member of the Convention, and on having broken the line, which limited patriotism, like vegetation, to the soil. Their's, he said, was not the paltry cause of kings, but the great cause of mankind. He should therefore chearfully join their cause, and embrace their hazards. He congratulated himself on the share which he had taken in the American Revolution, and the more as it now appeared that the Old World had been regenerated as it were by the efforts of the New. He observes that it is impossible to conquer a nation determined to be free; but that Kings, accustomed to make war only on each other, had no idea of the resources of an armed nation. The latter were always found at their height when they were expected to be at an end, &c.

Mr. Chapman, bookseller, of Fleet-street, was then called. He proved the printing of the first part of the Rights of Man, and the second part as far as page 128, by the direction of Mr. Paine. The copy on the table he believed to have been printed by him. This Mr. Garrow said was sufficient for his purpose, and the chasm in the evidence being thus supplied, he directed the following extracts to be read by the Clerk at the table.

[As on these extracts, and the sanction given by the two societies in question to the *antimonarchical* principles of Mr. Paine, the treasonable charge of aiming to subvert the monarchy of this country appears chiefly to hinge; we have felt it our duty, though the task is accompanied by a considerable share of reluctance, to give them literally to our readers.]

RIGHTS OF MAN, PART I.

Page 54.—" Can then Mr. Burke produce the English constitution? If he cannot, we may fairly conclude, that though it has been so much talked about, no such thing as a constitution exists, or ever did exist, and consequently that the people have yet a constitution to form.

" Mr. Burke will not, I presume, deny the position I have already

already advanced; namely, that governments arise either out of the people or over the people. The English government is one of those which arose out of a conquest, and not out of society, and consequently it arose over the people; and though it has been much modified from the opportunity of circumstances since the time of William the Conqueror, the country has never yet regenerated itself, and is therefore without a constitution."

Page 55.—" A government on the principles on which constitutional governments arising out of society are established, cannot have the right of altering itself. If it had, it would be arbitrary. It might make itself what it please; and wherever such a right is set up, it shews there is no constitution. The act by which the English parliament empowered itself to sit seven years, shews there is no constitution in England. It might, by the same self authority, have sat any greater number of years, or for life. The bill which the present Mr. Pitt brought into parliament some years ago, to reform parliament, was on the same erroneous principle. The right of reform is in the nation in it's original character, and the constitutional method would be by a general convention elected for the purpose."

Page 60.—" Much is to be learned from the French Constitution. Conquest and tyranny transplanted themselves with William the Conqueror from Normandy into England, and the country is still disfigured with the marks. May then the example of all France contribute to regenerate the freedom which a province of it destroyed."

Page 152.—" The two modes of Government which prevail in the world, are, first, Government by election and representation: Secondly, Government by hereditary succession. The former is generally known by the name of republic; the latter by that of monarchy and aristocracy.

Those two distinct and opposite forms erect themselves on the two distinct and opposite bases of Reason and Ignorance.—As the exercise of Government requires talents and abilities, and as talents and abilities cannot have hereditary descent, it is evident that hereditary succession requires a belief from man, to which his reason cannot subscribe, and which can only be established upon his ignorance; and the more ignorant any country is, the better it is fitted for this species of Government."

Page 156—" From the Revolutions of America and France, and the symptoms that have appeared in other countries, it is evident that the opinion of the world is changing with respect to systems of government, and that revolutions are not within the compass of political calculations. The progress of time and circumstances, which men assign to the accomplishment of great changes, is too mechanical to measure the force of the mind, and the rapidity of reflection, by which revolutions are generated: All the old governments have received a shock from those that already appear, and which were once more improbable, and are a greater
subject

subject of wonder, than a general revolution in Europe would be now.

"When we survey the wretched condition of man under the monarchical and hereditary systems of government, and dragged from his home by one power, or driven by another, and impoverished by taxes more than by enemies, it becomes evident that those systems are bad, and that a general revolution in the principle and construction of Government is necessary.

"What is Government more than the management of the affairs of a nation? It is not, and from it's nature cannot be, the property of any particular man or family, but of the whole community, at whose expence it is supported; and though by force or contrivance it has been usurped into an inheritance, the usurpation cannot alter the right of things. Sovereignty, as a matter of right, appertains to the nation only, and not to any individual; and a nation has at all times an inherent indefeasible right to abolish any form of Government it finds inconvenient, and establish such as accords with it's interest, disposition, and happiness. The romantic and barbarous distinction of men into Kings and subjects, though it may suit the condition of courtiers, cannot that of citizens; and is exploded by the principle upon which Governments are now founded. Every citizen is a member of the sovereignty, and, as such, can acknowledge no personal subjection; and his obedience can be only to the laws.

"When men think of what Government is, they must necessarily suppose it to possess a knowledge of all the objects and matters upon which it's authority is to be exercised. In this view of Government, the Republican system, as established by America and France, operates to embrace the whole of a nation; and the knowledge necessary to the interest of all the parts, is to be found in the center, which the parts by representation form: but the old Governments are on a construction that excludes knowledge as well as happiness; Government by Monks, who know nothing of the world beyond the walls of a Convent, is as consistent as government by Kings.

"What were formerly called Revolutions, were little more than a change of persons, or an alteration of local circumstances. They rose and fell like things of course, and had nothing in their existence or their fate that could influence beyond the spot that produced them. But what we now see in the world, from the Revolutions of America and France, are a renovation of the natural order of things, a system of principles as universal as truth and the existence of man, and combining moral with political happiness and national prosperity."

Page 161.—"As it is not difficult to perceive, from the enlightened state of mankind, that hereditary Governments are verging to their decline, and that revolutions on the broad basis of national sovereignty, and Government by representation, are

makin

making their way in Europe, it would be an act of wisdom to anticipate their approach, and produce revolutions by reason and accommodation, rather than commit them to the issue of convulsions.

"From what we now see, nothing of reform in the political world ought to be held improbable. It is an age of revolutions, in which every thing may be looked for. The intrigue of Courts, by which the system of war is kept up, may provoke a confederation of nations to abolish it: and a European Congress, to patronize the progress of free Government, and promote the civilization of nations with each other, is an event nearer in probability, than once were the revolutions and alliance of France and America."

PART SECOND.

Page 21.—"All hereditary government is in it's nature tyranny. An heritable crown, or an heritable throne, or by what other fanciful name such things may be called, have no other significant explanation than that mankind are heritable property. To inherit a government, is to inherit the people, as if they were flocks and herds."

Page 27.—"How irrational then is the hereditary system which establishes channels of power, in company with which wisdom refuses to flow! By continuing this absurdity, man is perpetually in contradiction with himself; he accepts, for a king, or a chief magistrate, or a legislator, a person whom he would not elect for a constable."

Page 47.—"This convention met at Philadelphia in May 1787, of which General Washington was elected president. He was not at that time connected with any of the state governments, or with congress. He delivered up his commission when the war ended, and since then had lived a private citizen.

"The convention went deeply into all the subjects; and having, after a variety of debate and investigation, agreed among themselves upon the several parts of a federal constitution, the next question was, the manner of giving it authority and practice.

"For this purpose, they did not, like a cabal of courtiers, send for a Dutch Stadtholder, or a German Elector; but they referred the whole matter to the sense and interest of the country.

"They first directed, that the proposed constitution should elect a convention, expressly for the purpose of taking it into consideration, and of ratifying, and ratification of any nine states should be given, that those states should proceed to the election of their proportion of members to the new federal government; and that the operation of it should then begin, and the former federal government cease."

Page

Page 52.—" The history of the *Edwards* and the *Henries*, and up to the commencement of the *Stuarts*, exhibits as many instances of tyranny as could be acted within the limits to which the nation has restricted it. The Stuarts endeavoured to pass those limits, and their fate is well known. In all those instances we see nothing of a constitution, but only of restrictions on assumed power.

" After this, another William, descended from the same stock, and claiming from the same origin, gained possession; and of the two evils, *James* and *William*, the nation preferred what it thought the least; since, from circumstances, it must take one. The act, called the Bill of Rights, comes here into view. What is it, but a bargain, which the parts of the government made with each other to divide powers, profits, and privileges? You shall have so much, and I will have the rest; and with respect to the nation, it is said, for *your shares you shall have the right of petitioning*. This being the bill of rights, is more properly a bill of wrongs and of insult. As to what is called the Convention Parliament, it was a thing that made itself, and then made the authority by which it acted. A few persons got together, and called themselves by that name. Several of them had never been elected, and none of them for the purpose.

" From the time of William, a species of government arose, issuing out of this coalition bill of rights; and more so, since the corruption introduced at the Hanover succession, by the agency of Walpole; that can be described by no other name than a despotic legislation.

" Though the parts may embarrass each other, the whole has no bounds; and the only right it acknowledges out of itself, is the right of petitioning. Where then is the constitution either that gives or that restrains power?

" It is not because a part of the government is elective, that makes it less a despotism, if the persons so elected, possess afterwards, as a parliament, unlimited powers. Election; in this case, becomes separated from representation, and the candidates are candidates for despotism.

" I cannot believe that any nation, reasoning on it's own rights, would have thought of calling those things a constitution, if the cry of constitution had not been set up by the government."

Page 63.—" With respect to the two houses, of which the English Parliament is composed, they appear to be effectually influenced into one, and, as a legislature, to have no temper of it's own. The Minister, whoever he at any time may be, touches it as with an opium wand, and it sleeps obedience.

" But if we look at the distinct abilities of the two houses, the difference will appear so great, as to shew the inconsistency

of

of placing power where there can be no certainty of the judgment to use it. Wretched as the state of representation is in England, it is manhood compared with what is called the house of Lords; and so little is this nick-named house regarded, that the people scarcely inquire at any time what it is doing. It appears also to be most under influence, and the furthest removed from the general interest of the nation. In the debate on engaging in the Russian and Turkish war, the majority in the house of Peers in favour of it was upwards of ninety, when in the other house, which is more than double it's numbers, the majority was sixty-three."

Page 65.—" But in whatever manner the separate parts of a constitution may be arranged, there is *one* general principle that distinguishes freedom from slavery, which is, that all *hereditary government over a people is to them a species of slavery, and representative government is freedom.*"

Page 107.—" Having thus glanced at some of the defects of the two houses of Parliament, I proceed to what is called the Crown, upon which I shall be very concise.

" It signifies a nominal office of a million sterling a year, the business of which consists in receiving the money. Whether the person be wise or foolish, sane or insane, a native or a foreigner, matters not. Every Ministry acts upon the same idea that Mr. Burke writes, namely, that the people must be hood-winked, and held in superstitious ignorance by some bugbear or other; and what is called the Crown answers this purpose, and therefore it answers all the purposes to be expected from it. This is more than can be said of the other two branches."

Page 161.—" The fraud, hypocrisy, and imposition of governments, are now beginning to be too well understood to promise them any long career. The farce of monarchy and aristocracy, in all countries, is following that of chivalry, and Mr. Burke is dressing for the funeral. Let it then pass quietly to the tomb of all other follies, and the mourners be comforted.

" The time is not very distant when England will laugh at itself for sending to Holland, Hanover, Zell, or Brunswick, for men, at the expence of a million a year, who understand neither her laws, her language, nor her interest, and whose capacities would scarcely have fitted them for the office of a parish constable. If government could be trusted to such hands, it must be some easy and simple thing indeed, and materials fit for all the purposes may be found in every town and village in England."

The Preface and Dedication of the second Part to the Marquis de la Fayette were also read.

A minute of the proceeding of the Constitutional Society, dated

Sept.

Sept. 28, was next read. It contained the thanks of the Society to *Joel Barlow*, Esq. for his pamphlet, entitled "Advice to the National Convention."

Mr. Johnson, bookseller of St. Paul's Church-yard, was called to prove the publication of this work. Of this pamphlet about 5 or 600 had been sold. He was asked how many of Mr. Paine's book had been circulated? Mr. Johnson admitted that he had sold the Rights of Man, but it was before it had been declared by the verdict of a Jury to be a libel. He appealed to the Court, when pressed on this subject, and the question was over-ruled. He admitted in reply to a more general question from Mr. Garrow, that the sale of Mr. Paine's book has been very considerable

On being asked whether he had sold any of Paine's letters to Mr. Dundas, he replied in the negative. He had forwarded some in a parcel to the country, but he could not say from what quarter they had been received.

The Clerk then proceeded to read several Extracts from Mr. Barlow's pamphlet, addressed to the National Convention, on the defects of the Constitution of 1791.

A variety of other Letters of Correspondence and Papers were produced and read in evidence. Among them was a pamphlet written by Joel Barlow.

Mr. Johnson was called, who proved that about one thousand of these pamphlets were printed and published, and that it underwent three editions.

Of this pamphlet several passages were read, which purported to be an answer to Mr. Burke. In one of the passages, Kings were represented to be inimical to a popular and free government. Others contained a strong panegyric on the Revolution of France and republican principles. This pamphlet was found in the possession of the prisoner.

Mr. Johnson also proved the publication of Paine's Letter, entitled the Address to the Addressers, found also in the prisoner's possession.

A book of the London Corresponding Society was then produced, from which a minute was read. By this minute it appeared, that an Address of Congratulation was sent to the National Convention of France, signed by Margarot, as Chairman, and the prisoner as Secretary.

Minutes of a meeting of the 26th of October, held at the Crown and Anchor Tavern, of the Constitutional Society, were also read in evidence.

At this meeting it was resolved, that the secretary should procure copies of several manifestos that had issued.

The minutes of the proceedings at several other meetings of the Constitutional Society were read. At some of these meetings it was refolved, that the letters from the Sheffield and other focieties be referred to the Committee of Correfpondence.

An addrefs to the National Convention of France was alfo at one of thefe meetings produced and approved of, and Paine's Rights of Man ftrongly recommended.

It was agreed, that this addrefs fhould be prefented at the bar of the National Convention, by Mr. Froft and Mr. Barlow.

All thefe papers were found alfo in the prifoner's poffeffion.

The anfwer of Meffieurs Froft and Barlow, who prefented the addrefs to the National Convention, was read. They faid, they received the fraternal kifs from the prefident, and that the addrefs was received with the greateft pleafure and fatisfaction.

Mr. Herfkiffell was called, to prove the correct tranflation of a letter from a fociety in France, directed to the Conftitutional Society. It recommended the people of England " to follow the example of France, and to lift themfelves up againft the perfidious Court of St. James's, whofe infernal policy had made fo many victims between the two nations, and difunited the people for the purpofe of tyrannizing over them. It concludes by an offer of bayonets and pikes." This letter, addreffed the Conftitutional Society by the ftile of " Generous Republicans."

Another letter from the fame French Society, to the Conftitutional Society, and which was found among D. Adams's papers, was alfo read. It contained a warm eulogium on the tranfactions in France, on the memorable tenth of Auguft 1792, reprobated royalty, and fpoke in high terms of liberty and equality. It alfo expreffed a grateful fenfe of " the intention of the Conftitutional Society to contribute to the fuccefs of the French arms."

A letter from Mr. Froft was likewife read, dated at Paris, a fhort time prior to the execution of the French King, giving an account of the proceedings in France.

Mr. Herfkiffell was then examined, to prove what the tranfactions were, that happened on the 10th of Auguft 1792, alluded to in the letter before ftated. He accordingly detailed the notorious circumftances that took place on that memorable day.

Mr. Woodfall was called, to prove the hand-writing of Mr. Horne Tooke, to a draft of a letter he fent to Petion, in his character of prefident of the National Convention.

In this letter, he fays, you are in no want of friends in England. We can now begin the patriotic gift of 1000l. and it will, no doubt, in time, amount to many thoufands.

A letter, figned Petion, directed to Mr. Horne Tooke, was then read. It mentions thefe words, " You have the glorious advantage of being hated by your Government." It defcribes the caufe of liberty, in England and France, to be the fame. It alludes to pecuniary aid, and mentions a fum of 3000 livres.

An

An anfwer of Mr. Horne Tooke, to Petion, was alfo read, in which he mentions his having inclofed 3000 livres, for the promotion of the caufe of liberty.

The proceedings, as entered in the book of the Conftitutional Society, were then read. They contained a great variety of refolutions, tending to manifeft their difapprobation of the prefent war, their attachment to the Revolution in France, their wifhes for a parliamentary reform, and the extenfion of liberty and equality all over the world.

J. Du Bœuf, a Frenchman, was next called. He faid, he fold French newfpapers, which he received, by means of Meffrs. Minett and Fector, from France. Among thefe, was the French Univerfal Gazette, or *Moniteur*.

The Attorney General faid, he produced three of thefe French papers, to prove, that they contained the fpeeches of Citizens Barrere and Saint Andre, which had become the fubject of a refolution of the Conftitutional Society.

The fpeeches contained in thefe newfpapers were accordingly read. They contained many ftrong expreffions againft kings, who were ftiled tyrants and defpots. The people were defcribed to be " the fovereign ;" and a Convention was faid to be the only means by which the people could effectually emancipate themfelves from the flavery of kingly government, and exercife their fovereignty.

The minute of the meeting of the 15th of February, 1793, of the Conftitutional Society, was then read. It expreffed a firm refolution to perfevere in the caufe in which they had fet out, and to obtain, by all legal and peaceable means, a reform in the reprefentation of the people.

An addrefs from the United Political Societies of Norwich, directed to Mr. D. Adams, as fecretary to the Conftitutional Society, was read. It ftated, that their worthy London Correfponding Society had fubmitted to their confideration three propofitions, namely: " Whether to petition Parliament, addrefs the King, or have a general Convention, for the purpofe of obtaining a parliamentary reform." They wifhed to refer the matter to the fuperior judgment of the Conftitutional Society; but, they added, that they wifhed the day was arrived when a Convention of the people fhould take place.

The Conftitutional Society deferred the confideration of his addrefs, and afterwards directed Mr. John Froft to prepare an anfwer to it.

Another proceeding of the Conftitutional Society was read, in which they refolved to thank Mr. Simon Butler and Mr. Hamilton Rowan, Efq. for their patriotic conduct, and declared that their fentences were, in their opinions, unjuft and illegal.

At ten o'clock at night Mr. Erskine suggested to the Court, that his learned coadjutor, Mr. Gibbs, was so extremely fatigued with the laborious duty of the day, as to render his retiring very desirable to him. It was then past ten o'clock, and the fatigue, inseparable from the business of the day, was easy to be conceived. It was to be noticed, that the prisoner's counsel had a harder duty to perform than the counsel for the crown, because the number of the latter being so great, one could be occasionally absent for a whole day, but there being only two for the prisoner, neither of them could be spared. Mr. Erskine said, that from the early hour the Court met in the morning, and the late period at which it adjourned at night, he saw no day-light till the business commenced.

The Chief Justice said, that he should certainly do every thing in his power, to accommodate the prisoner's counsel. His Lordship admitted the force of the remark made by Mr. Erskine, respecting the different situation, in point of accommodation, between the counsel for the crown and for the prisoner. The learned Judge thought Mr. Gibbs might retire for that night, and still the business go on.

Mr. Erskine said, he hoped that after the great chaos of evidence on the part of the crown was finished, he should have some time allowed to consider it, before he was called upon to address the Jury.

The Court said, that every accommodation would be granted, to both the prisoner's counsel that public justice would admit.

The trial then proceeded.

Mr. Daniel Adams, the secretary to the Constitutional Society, was called, to prove some original papers, intended to be entered by him in the Books of the Society.

The counsel for the crown, by the instruction and proceedings of the Constitutional Society, intend to avow the connection between the two societies, and that they combined to promote the same object.

A resolution of the Constitutional Society was read, appointing a delegation to hold a conference with the London corresponding society.

A resolution for holding a convention of the people for the purpose, as it stated, of producing a fair and full representation of the people, was also read in evidence.

The Court at half past twelve o'clock adjourned to next morning at seven o'clock.

The Lord President lamented, that at the close of a second day, the labour of the Jury was so far from being at an end.

The Jury complained of the coldness of the room appropriated for their purpose; and said it was impossible for them to get rest,

A long

A long conversation then took place, between the Court, the Bar, and the Jury, upon the best mode of accommodating the Jury. It was proposed to send them to the London Coffee-house, if twelve beds could be got there for them; upon enquiry, it appeared that beds could not be procured. The Hummums was then mentioned, and agreed to, and the Jury were sent there in three coaches, attended by three bailiffs and a servant, who were sworn to attend them.

The Court then adjourned to eleven o'clock the next day, on the request of Mr. Erskine, who wished for a little time to examine and collate the evidence.

Thursday Oct. 30.

The Court did not assemble this day until twelve o'clock.

Mr. Gurnell deposed, that he found a paper in the prisoner's possession, dated April 30, which mentioned the election of Maurice Margarot, he being appointed delegate of the division, No. 7, of the London Corresponding Society, for three months, James Sheriff in the chair.

Another paper was also put in and read, which was sworn to have been found in the possession of Mr. Hardy, mentioning the appointment of David Rowland as a delegate, at the Blue Posts, in the Haymarket. Margarot Sec. and M'Neil in the chair.

Mr. Gurnell swore to another paper found in Mr. Hardy's possession, stating that the sixteenth division of the London Corresponding Society had appointed John Baxter a delegate to the standing committee. ——— Grey, Secretary.

The next paper put in and received, found in Mr. Hardy's possession, mentioned that John Richter was appointed a delegate by the London Corresponding Society, to establish a sixteenth division of the society, at the Friend's Hand, Knightsbridge. This paper was also proved to be found in the prisoner's possession by Mr. Lauzun.

The next paper put in and read was found in Mr. Hardy's house by Gurnell, dated the 7th of May, 1792, which mentioned that he, Mr. Hardy, was appointed a delegate from the London Corresponding Society, to a meeting held in Exeter-street, Strand, for the purpose of forming a constitutional code of laws, for the government of the Constitutional Society. Signed Thomas Boyd.

The next paper put in on the deposition of Mr. Gurnell, signed T. Hardy, was for the purpose of delegating Mr. Vaughan, from a division of the society, and authorising him to be present at the meeting at the Bell, Exeter-street, to assist the committee appointed to form the constitutional code of laws for the government of the society.

The

The Attorney General followed this paper by another found in the poſſeſſion of the priſoner by Mr. Gurnell; it was ſigned T. Hardy, and directed to Mr. Wharton, M. P. It began by informing Mr. W. "That it was an original paper worthy of his peruſal, and if he ſaw any thing in the preamble worthy his approbation, or adopting, he may uſe it accordingly. In all it's parts it poſſeſſed many ſweets, and it expreſſed a hope that he would, like the bee, extract a little from each. It pointed out the preſent ſtate of repreſentation, and lamented the many who were deprived of having voices for members to ſerve in Parliament. It had been read in the ſociety, and excited univerſal diſguſt;—the evils in the repreſentation it ſtated to be of the moſt glaring kind, and could not be made too public."

A letter from the Conſtitutional Society, at Sheffield, in Yorkſhire, to Mr. Hardy, was ſhewn Mr. Gurnell, which he ſaid he found among the priſoner's papers. It was as follows:

"Sheffield, April 24, 1794.

"Fellow Citizens,

"The barefaced ariſtocracy of the preſent adminiſtration has made it neceſſary that we ſhould be prepared to act on the defenſive againſt any attack they command their newly-armed minions to make upon us. A plan has been hit upon; and if encouraged ſufficiently will, no doubt, have the effect of furniſhing a quantity of pikes to the patriots; great enough to make them formidable. The blades are made of ſteel, tempered and poliſhed after an improved form. They may be fixed into any ſhafts, but fir ones are recommended, of the girth of the accompanying hoops at the top end, and about an inch more at the bottom. The blades and hoops, more than which cannot be properly ſent to any great diſtance, will be charged one ſhilling, money to be ſent by the order. As the inſtitution is in it's infancy, immediate encouragement is neceſſary.

Struck through in the original.

"Orders may be ſent to the Secretary of the Sheffield Conſtitutional Society."

Signed

"To prevent poſt ſuſpicion, direct to Mr. Robert Moody, at Sheffield."

Another was produced, directed to the ſecretary of the Norwich Patriotic Society, and incloſed in the above. It was as follows:

"Fellow citizen,

"The barefaced ariſtocracy of the preſent adminiſtration has made it neceſſary to prepare to act upon the defenſive, in caſe of any attack upon the patriots.

"A plan

"A plan has been formed for the carrying into effect this necessary business. Pike blades are made with hoops for the shafts to fit the top ends; the bottom end of the shafts should be about an inch thicker; and fir is recommended for the shafts, selected by persons who are judges of wood. The blades and hoops will be sold at the rate of one shilling, properly tempered and polished. The money sent with the orders.

"Signed.

"Direct to Mr. Robert Moody at Sheffield."

Mr. Lauzun deposed having found a paper in the possession of Mr. Hardy, entitled, "The Report of the Committee of Constitution of the London Corresponding Society, printed for the use of the members, and sold by Thomas Spence." This paper stated,

First, That all men are by nature free.

Secondly, That though a man, who enjoys the advantages of society, must relinquish a part of his liberty for the general benefit, yet he should not surrender more than necessity absolutely required.

Thirdly, That the majority, however great, cannot deprive the minority of the whole of their civil rights.

Fourthly, That the people should have an equality of voices, in the election of persons, by whom the laws were administered, and that the people had a right to the free exercise of public opinion, and should be suffered to enjoy religious freedom.

This paper next adverted to the hardship of the Game Laws, which subjected the people to those bashaws, Country Justices, and encouraged a system of spies and informers repugnant to the English constitution. It took a general view of politics, and urged, that every person arrived at the years of discretion, not disqualified by any mental derangement, should have a voice for a representation in parliament. It mentioned that no name should be used in the society calculated to make party distinctions, and recommended the use of the word citizen, as being what was used during the republics of Greece and Rome.

It entered into a definition of the phrases, Aristocrats, Royalists, Republicans, Democrats, &c. and mentioned, that when any division of the society amounted to thirty, books should be kept, and all members admitted above that number should be entered as supernumeraries, and when they amounted to sixteen, they should be formed into a division, &c.

Jane Rickman, wife of Clio Rickman, bookseller, was examined on the part of the crown.

She deposed, that two books presented to her were written by Thomas Paine, and published at her house. She knew Mr. Paine;

Paine: her husband was a bookseller. Paine had lodged in her house, but when one of the books was printed, her husband was not in England. She saw the book in sheets, which were brought to her house. The large book was published during the absence of the author from England. She said, that Paine was at the house when the small one was published, the Address to the Addressers, and was to have profits from the large book, but not, she believed, from the other.

Mr. Erskine asked her, if she had ever read the books shewn her, and if she had not, how could she presume to say, that they were not written and published by some person else; and was it not possible that some other person might have written a book with the same title, and have affixed her husband's name to it?

She said, she was positive as to the books.

Mr. Erskine to the Court.—" I trust, my Lords, that whenever this society, or that is mentioned, that we shall not have looser proof allowed, than what is required in case of libel."

Mr. Attorney General.—" I shall not admit any proposition to the extent you say."

Mr. *Clio Rickman* examined on oath.

Q. Have you published those books? (shewing him the two pamphlets).

A. They were published with my name without my knowledge.

Q. How did you know they were published?

A. I heard it in the country, where I went early in September 1792.

Q. Who was to have the profits?

A. Never heard from my wife on that subject during my absence.

Q. Whose hand-writing is on this book? (shewing it to the witness).

A. Not mine, it is my wife's.

Q. Look at the matter of the book; did you, in the common course of your profession, ever see any other book, entitled, The Address to the Addressers?

A. Never read any other book, under that title, but these.

Q. You have been a member of the Constitutional Society?

A. I have, but not for some time.

Q. Are these the books sold at your shop?

A. They are something like, but I cannot swear positively.

Jane Rickman swore, that she put her name on the books sold in her shop.

Mr. Erskine observed, that the publication in question, was entitled, " The Address to the Addressers." What he wished

to

to know was, how it could be admitted as evidence in this cause; He was aware that the book entitled, "The Rights of Man," could be admitted, because it was proved in evidence on a former occasion, by members of two societies that came to resolutions to circulate it, that Thomas Paine was the author of the work; but in the present case no evidence of that kind was before the court.

The Attorney-General, in reply, said, that it had been proved in evidence that Thomas Paine was the author of the first part of The Rights of Man, and of a Letter addressed to Mr. Dundas. It was proved that Thomas Paine was a member of the Constitutional Society; and it was in evidence that Clio Rickman was a member also. Thus, from both being members of the same society, he submitted, that the witness might know that Mr. Paine was the author of the Pamphlet in question.

The Lord President. "This is perfectly a distinct matter."

The Attorney-General. "Then I shall not trouble you, my Lord, to hear this paper read."

Mr. Gurnell proved that he found two papers in the possession of the prisoner. The one was dated Sheffield, April 24, 1794, signed "Richard Davidson," and addressed to "T. Hardy." It began with these words: "The barefaced aristocracy of the present administration, &c." The other was directed to the Secretary of the Norwich Society, and signed "Richard Davidson." These papers contained several observations on the grievances of the people, and alluded to a model for pikes. They both concluded with the advice, that in case any answers should be sent, no letters should be directed to "Richard Davidson," but addressed, to prevent the suspicion of the Post-master, to "Robert Moody, China-square, Sheffield."

The Attorney-General now proposed to prove, that there was a person of the name of Richard Davidson connected with the Sheffield Society.

William Cammage was therefore called, and said, that he was a member of the society for constitutional information at Sheffield, of which he was secretary, till the latter end of May, 1793. He signed letters, but a committee managed the affairs of the society, composed of David Martin, John Holcroft, George Widdeson, and Matthew Campbel Brown. The avowed object was first a parliamentary reform, and it so continued. He remained a member after he ceased to be secretary. They had a delegate to the Scotch Convention, who was Brown. He himself too went to that meeting, and carried Brown a supply of cash; 10l. from Sheffield, and 10l. from Leeds. Gailes, a printer at Sheffield, he knew, and Henry York. The latter used to exhort at the meetings of the society. Arms, he never heard him mention in public. At first they thought of applying to Parliament for a parliamentary reform; but no specific plan was ever pointed out to obtain it. In private, he had heard York say, that the society should be armed to protect itself, which he understood to allude to the threats, that the people of Sheffield meant to disperse the society when it met. He had seen the blade of a pike made by one Hill, which was approved of by York, for the purpose of arming. Others had been shewn him, which he did not approve of. In all he had seen about three dozen of these. He knew Widdeson, and had seen handles for the pikes. They met to talk about this business, and see the instruments at night, and it was always at private apartments.

He recollected, that at the meeting on Castle-hill near Sheffield, York strongly recommended in his address not to petition Parliament for a reform, in consequence of which, a resolution was come to by the society to that effect. York, at that time, recommended an address to the nation, and after the meeting was over was drawn home in a carriage by the populace. He, the witness, had never heard him talk of a Convention, but had heard him disapprove of the Scotch Convention, assigning, as a reason, that the people were unprepared for it. They should first, he said, have brought out an Address to the People. The two letters to Hardy and the Norwich Society, he, the witness, had seen in Davison's possession, who came from Leeds to Sheffield. Robert Moody was the man who put handles to the pike blades, and was a carpenter by trade. The blades were ten inches long; the handles seven feet; the former were like a bayonet, fluted and sharp at the point. Davison and Gailes absconded from Sheffield before the witness was apprehended. He had seen the model of a night-cat, and had been told that it was to use against cavalry, having three sharp blades by five or six inches long to lame them as they trod.

On being cross-examined by Mr. Erskine, he said, that a Parliamentary Reform was his only object in belonging to the society, of which he was secretary from it's first institution in 1791, till May 1793. By that reform he meant a more equal representation of the people in the House of Commons. He had no intention whatever against the King or House of Lords, and had no reason to think that the society had. The change was sought for without any specific plan to obtain it. Had he had any idea of force being used, he would not have been a member, or have continued so after that plan had been discovered. He had no conception that the society or it's objects affected the safety or honour of his Majesty, or that the Scotch Convention meant to assume the power of the King or Parliament, but that they meant to petition by numbers for a reform, thinking that it would be more effectual than the petition of a few. He professed himself a friend to the English Constitution in it's purity, and that he had no wish to introduce the misery and desolation of France into this kingdom, or to bring down ruin on our Royal Family. He was afraid, and the Society, of the persecution of the people of Sheffield, who were averse to them. He considered all they did as legal, and the pikes and cats he never thought intended against the King or

Govern-

Government. By the Bill of Rights, he conceived, he had a right to have arms individually and collectively for their defence.

The Attorney General. Who told you that the Bill of Rights permitted you to have arms?

A. Mr. York. I never conceived that they were to support a convention; but that what I contended for would make the King's title more secure.

Q. Why were pikes chosen?
A. For cheapness.
Q. Did you ever hear of night-cats being used?
A. Yes; at Newcastle many years ago.
Q. You say you expected to oppose the people of Sheffield only. Why, therefore, were the arms provided for London, as Davison's letter mentions?
A. Davison might think them necessary for the society in London as well as here.
Q. If meant only to oppose the opposite party of town's people, what signification had the words *barefaced aristocracy of Ministers* in the letter?
A. It alluded to the opposite party.
Q. Were night-cats too, to be used against the opposite party, in that sense town's people?
A. I know of none that were made.

William Broomhead was next called, and examined by Mr. Garrow.

Q. Where do you reside, Mr. Broomhead?
A. I live at Sheffield.
Q. What are you by profession?
A. I am a carpenter by business.
Q. Did you at any time, and when, become a member of the Constitutional Society at Sheffield?
A. I became a member of the Sheffield Constitutional Society when it was first formed in the year 1791.
Q. Did you at any time become a member of the Society of Twelar at Sheffield, that was associated with the Constitutional Society in London?
A. I never knew of any such Society.
Q. Do you not know of your own knowledge, Sir, that the Sheffield Society was associated with the Constitutional Society in London?
A. I understood that both the Societies acted in conjunction, but I know nothing further of the junction of the Societies, than that they corresponded by letter.
Q. Do you happen to know what the object of the Society was?
A. The professed object of the Society was the effecting a Parliamentary Reform.
Q. In what manner was a reform to be effected?
A. It was to be effected by meetings.
Q. How by meetings?

A. By

A. By means of those meetings the minds of the lower order of people were to be enlightened, knowledge to be diffused, and the nation at large made acquainted with it's grievances, and with the necessity of a reform.

Q. Was the mode of obtaining reform ever discussed in your Society?

A. No; it never was.

Q. Do you know that your Society ever had for it's object universal suffrage?

A. No; it never had.

Q. Whom did your Society send as delegate to the Edinburgh Convention?

A. They sent a person of the name of Matthew Campbell Brown.

Q. Do you happen to know a person of the name of Henry Yorke?

A. Yes, I know a gentleman of the name of Henry Yorke.

Q. Do you know that he went by any other name?

A. Yes; he went by the name of Henry Redhead.

Q. Did Yorke reside at Sheffield?

A. No, but he has frequently visited the town.

Q. How long have you known Yorke stay at Sheffield at a time?

A. For the space of six, seven, or eight weeks.

Q. Did he frequent your meetings?

A. He did, and was very much respected whenever he made his appearance.

Q. On what account was he respected?

A. Because he was a great Orator, and a man of splendid talents.

Q. Were there not meetings held every week, and was there not a Committee?

Q. There were weekly Meetings held, but regularly speaking, there were no Committees.

Q. Did Yorke write any work when he was at Sheffield?

A. Yes, Mr. Yorke wrote several Pamphlets while he was there; as well as I can recollect, I believe he brought a great part, if not the whole of the manuscript copy to the different meetings, to be read previous to their being printed.

Q. Where were those meetings held?

A. They were held at my house.

Q. In a large and commodious room I suppose?

A. Yes, the room was commodious.

Q. Was there any particular elevation appointed for the person who was to address the meeting, and what was it called?

A. Yes, there was an elevation, which some called the pulpit, and some the tribune, but it was never regularly *christened*?

Q. Do you remember any of the speeches that Yorke made at those meetings?

A. Yes, but I cannot charge my memory with any particular part at present. I recollect Mr. Yorke at one of those meetings, held a book written by Locke, in his hand, and read extracts from it.

it. He expatiated upon the Conſtitution, and he informed the People, that there was a great deviation from the Conſtitution as it was originally formed.

Q. Can you remember any particular paſſages in his ſpeech?

A. Why, I cannot ſay I do. I know he was peculiarly energetic, and in ſome parts very warm, and in others very ſtrong.

Q. Strive to recollect ſome paſſages of his ſpeech?

A. Why, I do not think he ſaid any thing detrimental to the Conſtitution.

Q. Do you recollect any propoſition that Yorke ever made to you?

A. Yes; I remember that Mr. Yorke and Mr. Gales both propoſed that I ſhould make a motion at the meeting at Caſtle-hill, for a reform in the repreſentation of the People.

Q. Why you in particular?

A. In order that it might be over-ruled, and for the purpoſe of making another motion in it's ſtead.

Q. And did you make this motion?

A. Yes, I did, and it was objected to either by Mr. Yorke or Mr. Gales.

Q. Was there any elevation at the meeting at the Caſtle-hill, from whence the Orators ſpoke?

A. Yes, there was what was called the pulpit.

Q. Was this meeting very numerous?

A. Yes, there were ſeveral thouſand people aſſembled in the open air.

Q. And what was the conſequence of this meeting; were there any reſolutions drawn up?

A. Yes, the motion which I made to petition the Houſe of Commons was rejected, and another motion made to petition his Majeſty to redreſs the grievances of the people.

Q. Was that motion carried?

A. Yes, and drawn up upon parchment.

Q. Where was the petition left?

A. It was left at my houſe for ſignatures.

Q. Did Mr. Yorke make a ſpeech to the multitude upon this occaſion?

A. Mr. Yorke addreſſed the meeting in an eloquent ſpeech.

Q. What became afterwards of the petition?

A. It was ſent up to Lord Stanhope, in order that his Lordſhip might preſent it to his Majeſty.

Q. And did he?

A. No, his Lordſhip would not preſent it in that form.

Q. Do you happen to know that Yorke's ſpeech upon that occaſion was ever printed?

A. I remember that Mr. Yorke agreed to have his ſpeech printed, and it was printed accordingly.

Q. Did you ſee it in print?

A. Yes,

A. Yes, I saw it after it was printed, and I believe it contained the substance of what Mr. Yorke said.

[Here Mr. Garrow handed the Witness a pamphlet, which he desired him to look at, and to tell the Court and Jury whether he thought it was the same pamphlet that he saw at Sheffield. This question the Witness answered in the affirmative.]

Q. Did you receive any copies of this pamphlet, and from whom?

A. Yes, I received a number at Gales's shop, in consequence of resolutions of the society.

Q. What did you do with those books?

A. I packed them up in 24 different packages, addressed them to different persons, put them all into one box, and, to the best of my recollection, sent them to Thomas Hardy.

Q. Who applied to you to send those books?

A. A person of the name of John Allcock.

Q. Why did you become secretary to the society?

A. In order to increase my means, as the War had destroyed my business.

Q. Do you know that there were arms prepared before the meeting at Castle-hill?

A. I believe there were a few pikes, but this circumstance demands a very full illustration.

Q. We shall be particularly thankful to you, Sir, for an illustration.

A. Two days before the meeting, when it was understood that it was the Right of Englishmen to take arms in their own defence, a spurious hand-bill was circulated, spurious I say, because it was not signed by any magistrate. But how do you think it was circulated? Not as one would be led to suppose, in the open day, no, it was scattered about the town in the very dead of night, in the dark, in order to excite us to the commitment of some desperate and unjustifiable act. But this was not the case, and the hand-bill completely failed.

Q. What species of arms were talked of at this time?

A. The arms that were talked of were pikes.

Q. Did you see the model of a night-cat, as it was called?

A. Yes, I saw a thing that was called a night-cat, but it was only a play-thing for a child.

Q. Where did you see this model?

A. I saw it at the house of one Benjamin Dunn.

Q. Who produced it there?

A. One Charles Rose.

Q. Was it examined?

A. Yes, the model was then thrown upon the floor in order to be examined. I recollect it was then called a cat.

Q. What was the nature of the conversation that was held about it's use?

A. I never heard any conversation about it's use, but a mere
trifling

trifling and defultory converfation, an irregular difcourfe. It was fhewn as the production of a boy.

Q. Were you prefent at any other meetings where Yorke made any particular fpeeches?

A. Yes, I have heard Mr. Yorke when he did not fpeak fo cautioufly as he did at the meeting at Caftle-hill.

Q. Be fo good as to defcribe in what manner he fpoke.

A. He was certainly very warm at fome of the fubfequent meetings, and his warmth confifted in his drawing a very able comparifon between the grievances that Englifhmen now labour under, and the ineftimable privileges they formerly enjoyed.

Q. Go on, Sir.

A. Mr. Yorke faid, that Englifhmen were now reduced to a low, pitiful, and defpicable fituation, and that fooner than fubmit to it any longer, he would go up with them (meaning the people then prefent) to London.

Q. When was this fpeech delivered?

A. It was made before the fubject of arming came upon the carpet.

Q. Was not this fpeech delivered from the Tribune?

A. I believe it was.

Q. How did that declaration of Mr. Yorke's affect you; I mean when he faid—Sooner than fubmit to it any longer, he would go up with them to London?

A. I muft confefs that declaration gave me fome pain.

Q. Why?

A. Becaufe I fear God, and honour the King.

Q. Did you ever fee this pamphlet? [Shewing him a pamphlet.]

A. O yes, I think I have feen a copy of it.

Q. Do you remember the proclamation for a general faft?

A. I believe I do.

Q. How was it received at Caftle-hill?

A. The bufinefs relating to the proclamation was not tranfacted at Caftle-hill, but in the open air at Weftgate.

Q. Were there many people affembled upon that occafion?

A. There were fome thoufands.

Q. Of what number did your fociety confift?

A. It confifted of 600 perfons.

Q. How do you happen to know the number fo exactly?

A. I know it by the number of diftrict books that were fent to each member of the fociety.

Q. How were the diftrict meetings attended?

A. The diftrict meetings were not attended fo well as the general meetings.

[The examination of this witnefs was here interrupted by Mr. Lauzun, who was called up to prove that he found the two papers, which had been fhewn the witnefs in the courfe of his examination, in the poffeflion of Mr. Hardy.]

Q. Do

Q. Do you recollect any hymn that was composed for the purpose of celebrating the fast-day?
A. Yes, there was a hymn composed, and printed too, by Mr. Gales.
Q. Do you recollect whether any lecture was read?
A. Yes.
Q. By whom was the lecture read?
A. By a gentleman from Halifax.
Q. Was there any prayer upon the occasion?
A. Yes, I composed a prayer for that occasion.
Q. By whom was it delivered?
A. By myself, before a private meeting of several members of the society.
Q. Did you ever happen to hear the name of John Paine?
A. Yes.
Q. Was he a member of your society?
A. He was.
Q. Were Joseph Gales and David Martin members also?
A. They were.

[The clerk of arraigns was here directed to read the proceedings of a meeting held at Sheffield on the 7th of April, 1794; which he did accordingly. The proceedings were contained in the two pamphlets already alluded to.]

William Broomhead cross-examined by Mr. Gibbs.

Mr. Gibbs. Attend to me, Mr. Broomhead.—I think you said, if I understood you right, that there was a spurious hand-bill circulated at the time that the pikes were talked of?
A. There was, Sir.
Q. What was the tendency of this hand-bill?
A. It advised the measure of taking up arms, in order to guard against foreign invaders and domestic enemies. It had a most flagitious tendency, for the body of it contained these words: " We never can do any thing, till we have ourselves caused a riot."— This was evidently done with a view to throw us off our guard, and to incite us to commit some unjustifiable act.
Q. What was the first occasion of your speaking of arms?
A. This spurious hand-bill, which was circulated without the sanction of any magistrate.
Q. What idea had you, Sir, about the people taking up arms then?
A. The only idea that I entertained of the people taking up arms was, not that they might be prepared to make any attack, but that they might be ready to oppose any illegal force, and to maintain the law of the land.
Q. How were these *pikes* that you talk about to be used?
A. They were to be used as instruments of defence only.
Q. Had you, Sir, or do you think the society had, any idea of attack-

attacking the King and Parliament, or of meddling with the Constitution?

A. O no, Sir: I think if they had they would deserve to be sent to Bedlam!

Q. Had you yourself any such idea?

A. No more than I have the idea this moment *of flying to the sun!*

Q. What did you understand the object of the society was?

A. What I understood the object of the society was, is this, that they would use their endeavours to have the grievances which had been stated to have existed, redressed in a legal and constitutional manner. Such grievances I say as these—*where a man works fourteen or fifteen hours in the day, and after all is not able to support his family.*

Q. Would you, Sir, have continued in the society a moment, if you were aware that they entertained the least notion of attacking the King, Lords, and Commons?

A. Most assuredly not.

Q. Do you think there was a man in the whole society so wicked as to harbour such an idea?

A. I do not think there was so wicked a man among them all.

Q. The object of the society was not to meddle with the King or Lords, but to endeavour to effect a Reform in the Commons House of Parliament?

A. Most certainly that was their object.

Q. Did they not think, Sir, that the King and Lords with the Commons so reformed, would immediately redress the grievances that were complained of?

A. They assuredly did.

Q. Was it not their object to obtain this peaceably?

A. Most certainly.

Q. You have no reason to think that those persons, who might be sent as delegates to a convention, would not act in a peaceable manner?

A. None in the least.

Q. When a reform was talked about, did you not understand that by that was meant a reform in the Commons House of Parliament?

A. I certainly did.

Examined again by Mr. Garrow.

Q. If a convention had been called, you could not take upon yourself to answer for the conduct of evil disposed persons?

A. I should think it enough to answer for myself.

Q. Do you not know, Sir, that the measure of discarding the society of the Friends of the people, from the Sheffield Society, was discussed in the district meetings?

A. I believe it was.

Q. Do you not know, that the Constitutional Society at Sheffield,

field, discarded the society of the Friends of the people, because they would not go the same lengths with them?

A. I know of no such thing.

Q. Was it not the object of the mischievous hand-bill, that you have mentioned, to excite the people to take up arms against foreign invaders and domestic enemies?

A. It was. But when the subject of arms had been talked of, we were afraid that illegal force might be employed against us, as was the case in Birmingham and Manchester.

Q. You did not then, in consequence of this hand-bill, apply to the civil power for protection, but immediately came to the resolution of arming?

A. These resolutions were come to, though not with any mischievous intention.

Q. Do you happen to know who proposed these resolutions?

A. They were proposed by Mr. Yorke and Mr. Gales, and winked at by the society.

Q. Do you not know, that plans of arming were communicated by the Sheffield Society to the other different societies?

A. If such a thing was done, I was not informed of it.

A printed paper was next put in and read, containing minutes of the meeting at Sheffield on the fast-day on the 28th of February; the lecture read on the occasion, together with the resolutions entered into at the said meeting, expressive of the disapprobation of those present, upon the war, the landing the Hessian troops, and the universal construction of barracks throughout the kingdom.

Henry Alexander, examined by Mr. Wood, said, he was a member of the London Corresponding Society; that he became so in the latter end of November, 1793; that the society of which he became a member met at Robin's Coffee-house, in Shire-lane. He thought he was the 95th member then admitted. He knew Mr. Yorke; he came in while he was there. He remembered him, and was with him there in the year 1793, at about the end of it. There might be between 60 and 100 people in the room when he went there, for it was quite full. On the last night Mr. York was there, he took leave of the company in a long speech. He said he was going, the witness said, to Belgium, (laying the accent broadly on the letter i) for that he had received a letter from a friend of his; he said they would be ripe for a revolution there, and he was going to be at the head of them. He said he was afterwards coming to England, and that he was in hopes he should be at the head of them.

Juryman. "Look this way; where was he to come to?"

Witness. "To London. He made a very long speech. He said in that speech, in substance, that he had received a letter, that he had the honour of being a member of the National Convention of France, and that he had hopes of coming over here, and that he should see them all ready to join him; and Mr. Pitt's, with the different members that he meant, and the King's head, should be
on

on Temple-bar, and that that society would join him. Mr. Pitt's, meaning the Minister, and the King's head, would be on Temple-bar."

Juryman. "Mention the time."

Witness. "The time was the 5th of November, 1793. He made many observations on the King and Queen of France."

Counsel. "This was the substance."

Chief Justice. "Put the witness in mind of the subject, but not what he is to say."

Witness. "I cannot recollect the words he used. It was that they had met with what they deserved. I do not recollect he said any thing to us about the war. He said something of the *Sans-Cullottes*. That they were a set of brave fellows, I believe. He said a deal about them, but I do not recollect what. He said something to us about arms. That when he came home he should find them all ready to join, and that when the time came he hoped he should not shrink from what he professed. He said it was impossible to do any thing without bloodshed. This was in the society. He said there could not be good done without bloodshed. He said there was a set of brave men at Sheffield. I cannot tell that he said how they were brave. He did not say where the blood was to be shed. He said nothing about bread and cheese, but a person came from Sheffield and said something about pikes, and said it would be good for them as they had nothing but bread and cheese. Mr. Yorke's speech was well received, and he spoke very loudly. They were all unanimous, and got up and shook hands with him as he got up to leave the room. I saw no more of Mr. Yorke—I do not know where he went. I went after that to Mr. Dundas, and likewise to the Lord Mayor, Sir."

"I went to the Lord Mayor and Mr. Dundas, because I thought they were not going on properly. At first I was asked to go to the society. When I went in I saw Mr. Smith. He asked me to become a Member. I did not know what it was. I had a ticket, but I have not it here, for I gave it to Mr. Dundas's secretary. I think it is seven times I was there.

Cross-examined by Mr Erskine.

I am a linen-draper, I live at the Rose, in Fleet-market: the time I went into the society was in the latter end of the year 1793; I did not go for the purpose of being a member, though I became one. A friend of mine of the name of Whitcombe asked me to a club; I went for nothing but curiosity. Mr. Yorke was not there the first night, Smith was there, and Ashley was there. I do not know who else. I cannot say the month. I did not hear any thing that was said to me that night. They sat until 12 o'clock. They had papers which I think Mr. Smith read. I became that night a member. There was nothing said but making a member.

Mr. Erskine. In plain English you are a spy!

Witness.

Witness. After I found what they were, I became a spy, I did not wish for a parliamentary reform.

Mr. Erskine. Why did you become a member, if it was not for the purpose of becoming a spy?

Witness. I did not know what they meant by it.

Mr. Erskine. Did you wish any parliamentary reform when you became a member, upon your oath, Sir? Look to the Jury, look at these Gentlemen. You need not look at me, Sir, I shall hear you.

No answer for some time.

Mr. Erskine. Are you acquainted with Dunn of Manchester?

Witness. No, Sir.

Mr. Erskine. I should have thought you was.

Chief Justice. Why don't you answer, Sir?

Witness. I do not understand you, Sir.

Mr. Erskine. I am sorry for it, Sir. I believe you are the only one in Court who does not.

Witness. I never wished any thing of the kind.

Mr. Erskine. Why did you become a member of that society?

Witness. Smith said to me, be a member—One man then got up and read something, but what he read I did not understand. What they read or said afterwards that night I do not know. I do not know what I heard that night, but I heard it before I came back again. I did not approve of it. I related it to two or three of my friends, and they did not approve of it; they were of the same opinion as myself. I went a second time to see what they were upon. I had not been desired to go a second time.

Mr. Erskine. You wished to be serviceable to the Public? You went there a second time as a spy?

Witness. So it proved, at least, Sir; I went there to see the real grounds then acted upon.

Mr. Erskine. Did you take any notes of what you heard?

Witness. No; they would not suffer me to take any notes; they would not suffer me to take down any thing. They sat every week.

Mr. Erskine. What time, what month was this?

Witness. I do not recollect.

Mr. Erskine. Was it in the summer or in the winter?

Witness. I cannot say, Sir; I attended twice after I had been with Mr. Dundas.

Mr. Erskine. Mr. Yorke said he was going to Belgium.

Witness. He said something of Belgium, or Belgiam.

Mr. Erskine. You went there as a lover of your country?

Witness. Nothing less, Sir; I went voluntarily: there were three of my friends said I was very right.

Mr. Erskine. Who are they? name them.

Witness. One, whose name is Broughton; another, Mrs. Gresfell,

Mr. Erskine. You are a master linen-draper, I take it for granted?

Witness. I am not in business for myself.

Mr. Erskine. You are a journeyman, then?

Witness. No, Sir; I am not in a situation, myself.

Mr. Erskine. Yes, indeed, you are, Sir, in a very singular situation, Sir!

The witness then proceeded to give an account of himself; he said he was out of employment now. He said he lived with Mr. Gallaway, in Moorfields, who was a linen-draper then, but who is now in the tayloring business. He came to him in December, and left him in May; that he lived with Mr. Faulding, a linen-draper, on Holborn-bridge; he lived there two years; that he had been applying for business to several people; that he had applied at Tynham and James's, in Holborn, and to another person in Holborn, facing Gray's-Inn-lane. That he had lost his business by his attendance upon this business, according to his subpœna. He agreed with the persons he served last by the year; they were to give him 25l. a year; this was some time before his master opened his shop, which was on the 22d of the last month; he could not say how long before he opened his shop he entered into this agreement with him: it was, he believed, the latter end of July, or the beginning of August last. He told his master, the day he had the subpœna, he must leave him. Mr. Wood subpœnaed him. He did not know it would be necessary for him to leave his situation. He did not apply to the Solicitor of the Treasury, to know whether he must leave his employment, in order to give his evidence at the Old Bailey. He had no other reason for leaving his employment than that of attending to give his evidence. He did not apply to his master, to inform him, that he was subpœnaed, or to know whether he would consent to his coming here. He kept himself out of employment, without knowing whether his master would allow him to do so. He told his master that he was going out of town—first to York, then to Sheffield, as soon as this trial was over; but that was all out of his own imagination: the reason of his thinking so was, that he was informed by Mr. White, that he was to go down to York after this should be over. He had not looked out for any employment since.

Juryman. "Look across the Court."

The witness then proceeded on Mr. Erskine's interrogation to give an account of himself. He said he lived with Mr. Smith, of Cheapside; between four and five years ago he was with him, he believed 18 months; he afterwards went into the country, and staid their for 11 months, to his friends, who lived at Whiteford, six miles from Salisbury; he went to his aunt there, whose name is Alexander. He was afterwards with another aunt, on the other side of Moorfields, but he could not say how long; he was there a considerable while; he was there until he went to Mr. Faulding's. He left Mr. Smith because he had some words with him.

Mr.

: Mr. Erskine asked him what words; what was the cause of their quarrel?

The Chief Justice. "Why don't you answer, Sir."

He hesitated again.

Chief Justice. "Do you recollect?—If you do, have you an objection to answer?"

Witness. "No, my Lord."

Mr. Erskine then again asked him what was the cause of the quarrel.

The Witness then said that he quarrelled first with the other shopman, he believed they might have fought, and that afterwards made him quarrel with his master. He then came again to the business of the Club in Shire-lane. He said he was sure it was at the latter end of the year 1793, that he went there about 8, and staid until 11 or 12. He heard some conversation about the pikes; but he did not recollect any thing of what was done, except Mr. Yorke's speech on the third night. On the fourth night he did not recollect any thing at all that passed; he went the fifth night and staid until they broke up; he did not recollect that Mr. Yorke said much about the pikes, but a person from Sheffield said, they ought to have something instead of bread and cheese at 6d. a day; he could not tell whether that was or was not the seventh night he attended.

Mr. Erskine. "I have done with you, Sir."

Thomas Whiteall sworn.

He was shopman to a bookseller; he had lived with Mr. Owen, and went from him to Mr. Baxter, at No. 81, in the Strand. He became a member of the society at the latter end of the year 1793; he went the first time with Alexander; saw Yorke but once, and went himself once or twice; after which he discontinued it, as it interfered with his business, and was inconvenient on account of situation—never conversed with Alexander upon the subject, and became acquainted with him at Holborn-bridge. Yorke, he said, seemed to be very well known at the society. He went away, and left him speaking; but knows nothing of the substance of his speech.

George Widdison.

He said he was a member of the Constitutional Society at Sheffield, before they were classed into divisions. He had left them some time. He knew Mr. Yorke—he saw him first about a twelvemonth ago. He saw him at several meetings of the society—he was generally chairman of them when present.

[The Counsel for the Crown was about to examine the witness to what was said by Mr. Yorke at one meeting, but upon his stating that he (Mr. Yorke) was rather intoxicated, he desisted.]

He remembered the meeting at the Castle-hill, in April, 1793, as also the meeting this year, in March. The witness was hair-dresser to Mr. Yorke while at Sheffield. He remembered conversing with him on the subject of arms—it was in April—they talked of such being making. The witness himself made a dozen and half of shafts for pikes; they were seized in his house, and taken away by Mr. Wilkinson, the magistrate. It was generally understood among the society, that those pikes were intended for use only in self-defence. Mr. Yorke explained to him, that the reform to be looked for was the extension of the elective franchise to *universal suffrage*. He himself, and the society, as far as ever he knew, so understood and pursued their object. In progress of time he changed his opinion upon the propriety and expediency of such a measure; he told Mr. Yorke his idea upon the subject, declaring that, such a plan of reform was, in his opinion, impracticable, and carrying things too far; he said he would no longer subscribe to such a measure: to which Mr. Yorke replied, he must then give it up. He remembered the meeting in April last, in the open air; Mr. Yorke was there, and spoke at considerable length. He was not paid for the pike-shafts he had made; he expected to be paid for them only by those who took them of him.

Upon his cross-examination, he said, he was at first in favour of universal suffrage. At that time, he was firmly attached to the King and Queen too. He believed that all those with whom he acted loved the King; he certainly would not have remained of their society otherwise. He neither then nor now considered universal suffrage as containing principles adverse to the Crown. The famous plan of the Duke of Richmond was that which was adopted by the society. Among the many publications, his Grace's letter to Colonel Sharman was read at the society, and adopted by them. A well-known passage out of the letter was read to him by Mr. Erskine, in which his Grace states, that after long and mature deliberation, he was decidedly of opinion, that universal suffrage, together with annual parliaments, is the only radical and effectual cure for the evils crept into our constitution. This, the witness said, was precisely the sentiment borrowed from his Grace by the society; and he firmly believed, as far as he could dive into the hearts of men, that this was their only object. He never understood that force or violence was intended: He quitted the Society not from any idea or apprehension of this kind, but solely from his dissent upon the question of universal suffrage, as being of opinion that the minds of the people were not as yet sufficiently enlightened or prepared for it. He was not present when the society chose a delegate for the British Convention held at Edinburgh; but if he had been, he would have consented thereto, as approving of the measure at the time. He never understood the object of holding that Convention to be any thing else than petitioning for reform. From any thing that passed there, he by no means supposed them as intending to assume the functions of Parliament. He then, and now, considered the majority of the society as firmly attached to the King. It was then their general idea, that the safety of the monarch and the liberties of the subject were inseparable. He never heard any thing said of using arms for the intent and purpose of attacking the King, and putting

putting down the Government. He himself made the pikes for the purpose of defending himself, if neceſſary. He did ſo becauſe there was not a good underſtanding between the two parties; this he explained as alluding to thoſe who were eager for univerſal ſuffrage, and thoſe adverſe to that meaſure. It was intended to defend themſelves, not againſt the magiſtrates of the country, and the legal force.

He had himſelf been threatened ſeveral times in company. The Ariſtocrats had ſaid publicly, that if the French invaded the country, they would firſt put to death their domeſtic enemies.

He, nor he believed the ſociety, had entertained no intentions inimical to the Houſe of Lords. The only book he had ever ſeen upon that ſubjeƈt was that written by Major Cartwright. On the whole, he declared himſelf to be, and believed the ſociety to have been firmly attached to the King and Conſtitution of the Country. He repeated that he ſaw Mr. Yorke at ſeveral meetings, who always behaved with great moderation, except at the time when he was intoxicated.

Henry Hill.

He was a member of the Conſtitutional Society at Sheffield from the beginning; he was the ſecond or third member. Mr. Yorke viſited them in 1792; he was alſo at the meeting on the Caſtle-hill in 1794. The witneſs, a blackſmith by trade, made a pike from a pattern given him by Davidſon, which was approved of by him. He alſo ſhewed it to Mr. Yorke. He made about one hundred and thirty of them. The iron was procured upon Davidſon's credit. He had three-pence a piece allowed him for making them. Davidſon ſaid to him, the pikes might be wanted in London as well as Sheffield; by this he underſtood him to mean, as againſt thoſe who might unlawfully attack them. Davidſon left Sheffield about the beginning of May.

Croſs-examination.

He never had in view, on becoming a member of the ſociety, the oppoſing the King; nor did he believe that others of the ſociety ever entertained ſuch an idea. They adopted and followed the plan ſo ably ſuggeſted and promulgated by the Duke of Richmond: He had always heard them ſay ſo.

The preparation of the pikes was occaſioned by the threats of the oppoſite party. They had carried thoſe threats ſo far, as to come to the houſe where he lodged, and which they called the Jacobin Houſe, on account of the club having ſometimes met there, and threaten to pull it down, and burn it. They had alſo paraded the ſtreets with arms, and fired into ſeveral houſes. This conduƈt of the Ariſtocrats of the town, and no other, he ſwore poſitively was the reaſon of their deeming it neceſſary to provide arms; not for rebellion, but ſelf-defence.

Thomas

Thomas Moody.

He had been a regular member of the Conſtitutional Society of Sheffield for the laſt twelve months—he had been occaſionally ſo before that time. Beſide their general meetings, they were ſubdivided into diſtrict meetings.

He knew Mr. Yorke, who acted as orator, chairman, &c. at different times, particularly at the meeting at the Caſtle-hill. There were ten thouſand men preſent. Mr. Yorke ſpoke there, but he did not hear what he ſaid, as he was at too great a diſtance. A carriage was brought for him when the meeting broke up; but the populace took off the horſes, and drew him home.

Gamage brought ſome pike-blades, and beſpoke three dozen handles for them; the remainder of the blades were afterwards ſent and fitted. He always underſtood they were intended for ſelf-defence. There had been rumours, that the oppoſite party intended, and had threatened to diſperſe their meetings, either without or with the aſſiſtance of a magiſtrate, whom it would not be difficult to procure; and they were reſolved to reſiſt ſuch force.

He ſaw in Gamage's ſhop a model of an inſtrument called a cat; but at the Privy Council he heard it called a night-cap. He aſked what it was for, and was informed it was an inſtrument which might be thrown into the ſtreet, in order to prevent a horſe from paſſing.

A pike was here produced, which the witneſs ſaid was ſuch as he had made.

He remembered Davidſon aſking his permiſſion to have his letters directed to his houſe, which he conſented to; none, however, came ſo directed.

Croſs-examination.

The cat he ſpoke of was about an inch long, and was merely a model—none were ever made from it. It was lying open in the ſhop, to the view and obſervation of every paſſer by.

He never heard any expreſſions made uſe of in the ſociety diſreſpectful to the King perſonally; nor did he ever hear mention made of pikes, till the threats thrown out by the Ariſtocrats. If he himſelf had an idea that any intent had ever been entertained of uſing thoſe pikes againſt the King or the Government, he would never have been concerned in making them.

[Here the Court adjourned for refreſhment, it being near ſeven o'clock.]

John Edwards depoſed, that a plan had been formed to make pikes and blades at Sheffield, to be uſed by the London Correſponding Society; and that a meeting had been appointed at the Parrot, in a court in the Old Bailey, to conſider of a ſubſcription for that purpoſe; that it had, at the meeting of a diviſion in the Borough, been propoſed to the Society to learn the uſe of the muſquet; that a diviſion of the London Correſponding Society met at the houſe of one Franklow in regimentals, and Franklow appeared in those regimentals at the Globe tavern. There was no proposal for instructing Franklow's association in the use of arms; neither was any such proposition made at any other division.

It was suspected that one Lynam had given information, and therefore the Secret Committee had been dissolved, and a new one appointed to meet in private, to communicate with the society occasionally. The General Committee of Delegates met at Compton-street. A Committee of Correspondence had been appointed between the London Corresponding Society and the Constitutional Society.

He knew of a meeting at Chalk Farm, and was present at it. There were two thousand people assembled there. Several persons of the Corresponding Society were there. Mr. Hardy was in the long room all the time; he did not know what passed there, the business was transacted in another room from that in which the witness was.—He received a paper from Baxter, dated the 29th of April, which was read.—The same day with the meeting at Chalk Farm he supped in Compton-street. There was an anniversary dinner on the 9th of May, at which he was present.

On Hardy's apprehension, there was a proposal to fine a shilling a-piece to buy blades for pikes, one of which he had, but it was afterwards destroyed. The pikes were only bought for self-defence.

They were reading the Address of Mr. Pitt and the Duke of Richmond, when the Society was assailed by two police officers.

The idea of having a military association was rejected.

Hardy was always a quiet man, and never spoke improperly. He always was against having arms, or pikes. There was no connection between the order for making pikes, and the landing of Hessian troops. The societies had met for two years without interruption.

Samuel Williams proved the existence of an association at Lambeth, instituted by one Franklow, a member of the London Corresponding Society; and that he, Williams, was employed to teach such association the manual exercise.

At eight o'clock the proceedings were resumed, when Mr. Garrow called upon

John Edwards, a member of the London Corresponding Society. The witness said, that he knew the prisoner Thomas Hardy; that he recollects certain orders for Sheffield respecting pikes in April last; that hearing a letter was about to be sent thither, he wished to inclose a few lines to know who would undertake to forge the blades of pikes; that he remembers afterwards reading a letter to Mr. Hardy, which letter the witness had received from Sheffield, explanatory of a plan formed there for pikes; that he had also communicated the particulars of that plan to Spence, Barks, Hillier, and others; that he had propos-

ed

ed the adoption of a similar one in London; that each member who wished to have a pike, was to pay one shilling for it.

Mr. Garrow. Do you recollect of any place in the Borough occupied to learn the use of the musket, &c.?

John Edwards answered, that he had heard of such a place, but did not know the particular spot; that he knew of no subscription for the furnishing of fire-arms; that he had been acquainted with Higgins and Goodwin, who were members; that he believed the society in the Borough had been initiated in the use of muskets, but that he never had attended any of their meetings; that he did not know Bandy Legged Walk (which Mr. Garrow mentioned as the place of their meeting); that he believed Franklow was a member of the London Corresponding Society, but that he did not belong to his division; and that he himself remained a member till taken into custody.

Mr. Erskine objected, at this time, to what might be stated as having fallen from Higgins, Goodwin, or Franklow.

Mr. Garrow persisted in his interrogatories, to which the Court acquiesced.

Edwards, the witness, then proceeded by saying, that he understood there was a corps called the Lambeth Loyal Association, for the purpose of acquiring the use of the musket; that he could not tell what Franklow's association was for; that they wore uniforms which consisted of a Blue Coat and a Red Collar, white Breeches and Waistcoat; that he saw Franklow in that dress at the anniversary dinner, at the Globe Tavern on the 20th of January last; that he knew the division number 20, which met at the Three Tuns, Snow-hill; that at one of the meetings, which consisted of sixteen persons, he, the witness, proposed to form a corps similar to that of the Sheffield Association, which was unanimously refused; that this was long before the anniversary dinner now mentioned; that he afterwards suggested the formation of a society like that of Franklow's, but that no person would support or join him; that some time after the Secret Committee was dissolved by consent; that Martin (attorney), Thelwall, Hodgson, and others, were members of the Secret Committee; that they met at their own houses; that the committee was instituted to receive and answer letters; and that these communications were kept a secret from the society at large.

On being farther interrogated, Edwards answered, that he was a member of the Committee of Delegates, Compton-street; that the meeting was transferred to Mr. Thelwall's, No. 2, Beaufort-buildings; that he understood the Constitutional Society had deputed six persons, and the Corresponding Society deputed

deputed five; that the society to which he belonged added one; that thus six and six met to deliberate on particular measures; that he remembered a meeting for the purpose of presenting medals to the Jury who had acquitted Eaton; that he was present at the meeting at Chalk-Farm, which consisted of 2000 persons; that he first went to Store-street, that he had cards of admission at the committee, Compton-street; that the reason of his going first to Store-street, was because a room had been there advertised for the meeting; that when he arrived at the latter place, he understood that Justice Addington had been there; that there was no other ceremony at Chalk-Farm, but the transfer of the ticket; that one half of it was given to the person at the door, and that the other half was put in his hat; that Thelwall, Lovet, Moore, Richter, Blackman, and most members were there; that Mr. Lovet took the chair; that he did not see Hardy, the prisoner, there; that he was in the long-room with the ladies; that he knew Robins's Coffee-house, Shire-lane, where division, No. 29, used to meet; that he had been there frequently; that he knew the matter of the paper now presented; and that what he had seen was a different sized paper, and of a different date.

[Here a very short conversation took place between the counsel respecting the propriety of such evidence.]

The paper now alluded to was read in court, and, among other expressions, contained the subsequent words:—

On the 30th of January, 1794, will be presented,

A DRAMATIC ENTERTAINMENT,
Called
THE GUILLOTINE,
OR
GEORGE's HEAD IN A BASKET!
To which will ne added,
THE PRINCE OF LEEKS!
Among other Actors, were
Mr. FOX, Mr. GREY,
Mr. SHERIDAN, Mr. ERSKINE.
(Loud Laugh)
Chancellor of the Exchequer,
BILLY TAX LIGHT!
Between the Acts, a Song,
TWENTY MORE! KILL THEM!
To conclude with
GOD SHAVE GREAT GEORGE OUR
Vive la Liberté! Vive la République.

On being further interrogated, Edwards affirmed, that he read this bill of entertainment in October, three months before the time

time appointed for the performance ; that after the meeting at Chalk-Farm the witness went to Compton-street, where he supped ; that Mr. Thelwall was there ; that he never received any information farther than what he has related respecting arming ; that he knew Ashley, but never heard any thing from him detrimental to the prisoner; that he was at the meeting at the Crown and Anchor on the 2d of May last ; that he received his ticket from Mr. Joyce ; that after the other dinner at the Globe Tavern, the address read in the morning was circulated in a printed handbill ; that he recollects nothing started there respecting the Hessian troops ; that he saw no political paper there about the *ins* and *outs*, but that he read one at the Three Tuns, Snow-hill ; that he never received any paper on that subject from Hodgson ; that he had attended Thelwall's lecture ; that the price of the pike was one shilling a blade, as he had already stated ; that the Friday previously to Hardy's being apprehended, there was to have been a meeting at Green-arbour-court, in the Old-Bailey, which was postponed ; that while waiting, they first learnt that Hardy was apprehended ; that each member summoned was to have deposited a shilling for his pike-blade ; that the only blade at the meeting was that of the witness; that the shaft now in his hand (here the witness examined it) was that on which his blade had been fixed ; that he had destroyed the blade, fearful lest it should be discovered in his possession ; that he believed Hillier also had a pike similar to that which he had now described ; and that he recollected a handbill for another dramatic entertainment, which he himself had suggested, called the Taking of the Bastille, &c.

Mr. Erskine cross-examined the witness, who answered, that he was by trade a silversmith ; that he had made a pike for himself ; that the only design which he had in the use of that instrument was to resist any allegal dispersion of their meeting ; that Mr. Yorke of Sheffield first communicated the idea of a pike ; that this was at the same time when the Hessian troops had landed in this country, without the consent of parliament ; and the witness solemnly declared, that neither he nor his associates had the most distant idea either of aiding or abetting a rebellion, or of exciting the people to oppose the government.

Edwards further recapitulated, that the sole purpose of the pikes was to repel any attempt at an illegal dispersion of their society, and that he was well grounded in apprehending such an attemp, tbecause the societies had been several times harrassed by the police officers ; that once when the society to which he belonged was assailed by the officers, he well remembered that they were busily engaged in reading the Address of the Duke of

Rich-

Richmond and Mr. Pitt in favour of Parliamentary Reform; and that he in his confcience knew thefe to be fo many truths.

Mr. Erfkine. " I wifh it to be underftood that I am no advocate for the Duke of Richmond's or Mr. Pitt's Confcience!"

The Lord Prefident.—" I think this levity unbecoming the dignity of the Court."

Mr. Erfkine feemingly affented to what had paffed from the learned Lord Prefident; but waxed warm and indignant on hearing

The Attorney General fay, " I cannot fit in filence when the Court is harraffed by fuch frivolous or flippant obfervations."

Mr. Erfkine. " I muft tell the learned gentleman, that he ufes language here, which he dare not avow in any other place."

The Attorney General. " The change of place or fituation will never make me fhrink from what I have advanced."

The Lord Prefident. " I lament the intemperate language which has been ufed; and I am forry to remark, that Mr. Erfkine has betrayed an inclination to inflame, rather than to conciliate, the gentlemen employed in the profecution for the Crown. I hope, however, that all the learned gentlemen will perceive how neceffary it is for the difpatch of bufinefs, to have a proper underftanding on the occafion."

Edwards, the witnefs, being interrogated, faid, that he was convinced no perfon meant to make any other ufe of the pikes, than what he had ftated as his own defigns; that the Lambeth Loyal Affociation had been incorporated for that purpofe; that he had always underftood that Hardy, the prifoner, had conducted himfelf in a very peaceable manner; that he never heard him make ufe of any improper expreffions; that he never heard him mention any thing about pikes; and that he had always underftood that Hardy was an enemy to every kind of violence.

Mr. Erfkine. " From whom did you firft receive the *ridiculous* play-bill now brought forward?"

The Lord Prefident. " *Ridiculous* play-bill! I think it is an *infamous* play-bill."

Mr. Erfkine. " I agree cordially with your Lordfhip. It is a very *infamous* bill! From whom did you receive it?"

Edwards. I faw it firft in the poffeffion of Baxter, whom I requefted to procure me a copy.

Mr. Erfkine. " Do you believe that Hardy, the prifoner, would have approved of fuch an infamous bill?"

Edwards. " From what I know of Hardy, I am convinced that he would by no means approve, or encourage, the circulation of fuch a bill."

Mr. Garrow. Were not the pikes formed to oppofe the landing

landing of the *Hessian Butchers*, as they were called by certain men?

Edwards. No.

Mr. Garrow. Upon your oath, was your pike begun before that time, and for what purpose?

Edwards. All the allusion which I made to the Hessians was, that I had begun or finished my pike, just at the time when the Hessians had landed in this country without the consent of Parliament; and that this instrument had been formed to prevent any illegal dispersion of our Society.

Samuel *Williams* deposed, that he knew Hardy, the prisoner, to whom he applied for a ticket for the constitutional dinner, but was refused, not being a member. He then went to him and bespoke a pair of shoes, and afterwards a pair of boots, and by the introduction of a Mr. Franklow, was admitted a member of the society. He was soon appointed to instruct some five or six members in the manual exercise, at Spence's house in Turnstile, by candle-light, up two pair of stairs. Hardy told him, that Franklow intended to raise an armed society, and had the post of serjeant major, teaching his men himself their exercise at Lambeth. Williams supplied them with seven stand of arms, for which he was paid by Franklow. He said, that the armed society at Lambeth was composed of different persons from those he saw at Spence's, and that they were to have 60 rammers and bayonets complete.

The clerk then read the regulations by which they were to be organized. There was to be 1 Captain, 1 Lieutenant, 1 Ensign, a Serjeant Major, and 60 rank and file, a Fifer, Drummer, &c. &c.

He said, that Franklow appeared in the society with his military uniform; and that it was their avowed intention to obtain a reform by force of arms, if not by fair means.

Mr. Gibbs submitted, that this evidence did not apply in the least to the prisoner, Hardy. Where a set of men were joined in a conspiracy, all the parties were accountable for the conduct of any one of them, as far as regarded that same conspiracy; but here was a man, Franklow, who, though belonging to the Corresponding Society, was instituting another society himself, unconnected, as far as the evidence went, with the matter of this charge. He did not alledge that Hardy either employed him or paid him in this transaction.

The Lord President said, that in this case some species of evidence may be admissible, which had no immediate relation to the prisoner.

Williams then proceeded to swear, that a Parliamentary Reform was not the general topic of conversation in their meeting;
and

and that in Hardy's shop, and in his presence, he was consulted about drilling 1000 men, which he declined undertaking.

The Lord President observing, that there was nothing applicable to the present case in the evidence of this witness, he was ordered to stand down.

—— Saunders examined.

On the 2d of April last, he went to Shelmedy's in the Borough, where there were seven or eight stand of arms, and twenty-seven or twenty-eight men of the Corresponding Society, as he thinks, but knows that many of them were of that description. From the 11th of April to the 1st of May, he attended at St. James's, and the *shed* at Westminster, where he was drilled with others, by *Williams, Franklow,* and *Augh.*

On the 2d of April, he heard some members declare, that a Parliamentary Reform must be carried at the point of the bayonet. In a division which met on May last, in Shire-lane, he heard a member say, mysteriously, that Pitt went over the bridge at twelve o'clock, but did not know what bridge was meant by it. Another announced the defeat of the British army as a piece of good news; and on hearing that one of the King's messengers was killed, a third declared that he would rejoice in his fate, were it his own father or his brother.

In his cross-examination, he acknowledged that he was a spy, but said he was led into the society by means of a bet. He did not then know who used the expression of carrying reform at the point of the bayonet. It happened in general conversation.

Edward Gosling examined.

He became a member of the London Corresponding Society in April 1794, in consequence of some seditious publications which he saw by them, and after a conversation upon the subject with Mr. Wickham, a magistrate. When he was admitted on the 15th of April, at Clerkenwell, there were about 30 members present. It was the day after the meeting at Chalk Farm. The members talked much of the fate of Charles I. and being, as he supposed, elated after the meeting, they also declared that the British Convention, like that of France, must be supported by arms. He went afterwards, with Hillier, to visit Dr. Hodgson in Newgate, with whom he was before unacquainted, and there were a number of persons present. Hodgson asked him, if he had seen the New Constitution of the Corresponding Society? and he replied, that he had not, as he was a very young member. Lloyd, one of the prisoners then in Newgate, was of the party. One of the toasts given, was,

"The world a republic or a desart."

Hodgson

Hodgson said, amongst other things, that he hoped soon to see a revolutionary tribunal established in this country.

The same evening, April 25, he went to meet the 11th division, where Wright, the delegate, said, that he was provided with his arms, and so should the other members. Gordon, the secretary, who is since gone to America, assured the society that he was sorry to leave them at a time that they were about to act as well as think, and to regenerate their country.

He accompanied Hillier to his own house, where he shewed him, and others, the drawings of pikes, knives, &c. which he said were the instruments soon to be made use of. He added, that the principal dependance of the society was in seizing upon the persons of the Royal Family, and the members of both Houses of Parliament, after which, nothing was to be apprehended from the army, as they would have no leaders to refer to, and that they could not fail to be allured by the additional pay of eighteen-pence a-day, instead of sixpence. One of the parties in this conversation was very much in liquor, but the rest were all perfectly sober.

At Hillier's house, on the 9th of May, he met with Hill, Bennet, and Baxter. The last said, that he had been with Mr. Joyce, Chaplain to Lord Stanhope, who assured him, that though the ministers had taken up Stone, he was a man of sufficient firmness to remove all apprehension. Baxter also said, that the committee of correspondence and co-operation was drawing up an address to the armies, accompanied by some strong resolutions; that a person, of the name of Moore, was particularly active and successful in gaining over the military; that of the old soldiers in Westminster, one third was already gained, and the other two wou'd not act against them. Baxter said, he saw an officer, lately introduced to the Queen, who, in speaking of Her Majesty, used language which the witness could not repeat, and demanded why they did not send the whole family to the devil, or words to that effect.

One of them asked the witness if he would buy a pike? He answered that he would, if he knew how to make use of it. He then desired him to go to the sign of the Parrot, in Green Arbour-court, in the Old Bailey, and, using his name, ask for Mr. Edwards, who would come out, and not only furnish him with a pike, but also have him instructed in the use of it. He asked if a Reform could not be effected without coming to blows? Baxter replied, there is not a man in the Society who believes that a Parliamentary Reform is all we want; and without having recourse to the sanguinary measures of the French Revolution, may be brought about in a few hours. He did not wish the King or any of the Royal Family to be killed. They may be sent to

R Hanover;

Hanover; but at the same time some blood must unavoidably be shed, on account of the insults offered to the people, which human nature could not bear.

He said that the heads of many thousand pikes were manufacturing at Sheffield, but that the stocks would be made in town. That silence, however, should be observed in the divisions until the new constitution should be established, as there were spies amongst them. A part of the plan was to set the French prisoners of war at liberty, and if the emigrants made any opposition, they should share the same fate, that the Swiss did in Paris. Mr. Pitt, Mr. Dundas, and Mr. Reeves, were mentioned amongst the enemies of the people, whom it would be necessary to secure. The purport of the address to the army was to sow jealousies between the British troops and the French emigrants, to explain to them the severity of their treatment, and propose, on the part of the societies, more lenient usage, and to have their pay increased to 1s. 6d. per day.

On May the 14th, he attended another meeting at Hillier's, but as that was subsequent to Hardy's being taken up, Mr. Garrow did not think the present was the properest time for offering it in evidence.

Cross Examined.

Is by profession in this business of an informer, and in the writing way; was a dealer in naval stores, but did say the direct contrary of this to Mr. Worship. Never said he lived by cheating the King; did not always go by his name; went by the name of Douglas ten years since, and was in that name a hair-dresser seven years in Petty-France, No. 3; took the name from pride, his father being in the wig and shaving way, who kept several journeymen. *Played* the part of Douglas seven years; knew Mr. Lincoln, borrowed money of him (a twenty pound note) four or five years ago; and gave him a note in the name of G. Douglas, and paid part by himself and part by his wife.

Here the cross examination was interrupted by Mr. Garrow, who seeing or fancying that he saw Mr. Macnamara, who sat not far distant from the prisoner, using some gestures to embarrass the witness, requested that he may be accommodated with a seat upon the bench if he could not be quiet.

Mr. Macnamara wished to know in what he was not quiet.

Mr. Garrow explained, that as he appeared to be communicating with the Counsel against the prosecution, it was right that he should do so in the full face of the Court, as the witness was already sufficiently agitated by the nature of the examination, without the intervention of a gentleman of so much consideration, and once a Member of Parliament.

The

The witness then proceeded to state, that he told Worship he was a dealer in naval stores, becouse he told him if he was a Clerk he would not give him what he wanted, but did not speak against the King, or use inflammatory expressions in the societies; swears positively that he never said, why do not you arm? He knew a Mrs. Colman, who rented a shop of him, died at his house, and he buried her; she left a will, leaving her property to Burrows and Leech; don't know Mrs. Biffin; he hesitated to answer whether there was a complaint made against him respecting that will; Leech was a hair-dresser, and Burrows a relation; he (the witness) made the will; never heard that he was charged with having forged that will; knew Mr. Cox, a cheesemonger, with whom he dealt, for a shop his wife kept; never dealt in naval stores, though he did in paper stuff; did not say that he got things for a fifth of their value, by feeing the keeper to under-sell them; did not tell Hillier that he was in the habit of stealing; but whatever he told him was for the purpose of extracting information from him.

The points of character being discussed, Mr. Erskine, though he exerted great ingenuity, was not able to extract from him any observable variation in his first testimony.

Mr. Garrow, to explain the circumstances relative to the affair of Mr. Macnamara.—The prisoner gave the following account: He gave a note to Mr. Lincoln for 10l. or ten guineas, of which there remained about four guineas due, and no demand was made upon him till the present prosecution was instituted. Mr. Macnamara met him at the London Coffee-house, told him he was a man of considerable property, and a friend to the Constitution; but that he would see justice done, and the debt owing to him would be spoken of in Court.

The witness said, that he was a stranger to Mr. Macnamara, and that they were in an improper place for entering upon explanations. Mr. Macnamara used no other threat.

Mr. Garrow then asked him if he had been under any prosecution for the forgery of the will to which Mr. Erskine alluded? The prisoner answered in the negative.

Here the business concluded, the Jury again remitted to sleep at the Hummums, and at Two o'clock in the morning the Court adjourned to Eight.

Friday, October 31.

The Court met at nine o'clock, and Mr. Hardy being placed at the bar,

Mr. Attorney General produced two papers found at the prisoner's house, dated July, 1792, and addressed to a Mr. Rouffel (now in Newgate) as a Member of the Constitutional Society. It would appear, that these papers were produced merely to prove that Rouffel was implicated in the alledged conspiracy.

Bernard Bailey proved the seizure of two papers at Rouffel's apartments. One of them was a small pamphlet, containing directions for learning the manual exercise. It was intended as a glossary to the engraving that was produced last night, describing the different positions in platoon firing.

The other was a song, which, without any imputation of blame to the Counsel on either side, happened to be read before the Court perceived that it was not legal evidence, inasmuch as it had been seized subsequent to the apprehension of Mr. Hardy.

The Court and the learned Counsel regretted this circumstance exceedingly, and hoped the Jury would endeavour to expunge it from their minds. As to the book, it appeared by the title-page to have been printed previous to the arrest of the prisoner, and it was thought proper evidence.

Several papers, found on Mess. Thelwall and Martin, after the prisoner had been taken up, were produced. They were judged good evidence, because they related to the business at Chalk Farm, and appeared to have been prepared for that meeting in April last.

Mr. Gibbs begged to state the question, whether, in the present instance, it came within the rules of evidence, to bring forward papers, bearing date the 19th of May, as Hardy, the prisoner, was taken up on the 12th of that month.

Chief Justice Eyre said, that certainly the paper which had been read, might have been printed after the Prisoner was in custody, and the circumstance of it's having been found was no proof that it had existed before the period of his apprehension, except evidence could be brought to prove that it was then in existence.

John Groves was then called, who deposed, that he was present at a meeting of the Corresponding Society, on the 20th of January, 1794; that he was afterwards desired, by a particular gentleman, to become a member, which accordingly he did. The name of this gentleman he had no objection to mention, but was told by the Counsel for the prosecution that there was no occasion. At the meeting where he first attended, *Martin* was in the chair, an Address was read, and a great many toasts given, which he did not now recollect.

Q. Do you remember any part of the conversation in the first meeting, at which you were present?

A. There

A. There was a general talk of Univerſal Suffrage and Annual Parliaments.

Q. After you became a member of the Society, what was publicly profeſſed to be their object?

A. A Reform of Parliament.

Q. What were the means by which they propoſed to attain that object?

A. By enlightening the minds of the lower claſſes, in order that they might arrive at the knowledge of their natural freedom.

Q. What particular means did they take in order to enlighten the people?

A. Chiefly by diſtributing pamphlets ſuited to their capacities.

Q. Do you not recollect the names of ſome of the perſons, who were ſo loud in the cauſe of Univerſal Suffrage and Annual Parliaments?

A. I canot mention their names: it was the general voice of the Society.

Q. Did you never hear any thing ſtarted on the ſubject of arms?

A. I never did.

Q. Were you preſent at any of Thelwall's Lectures?

A. Yes, I was two or three times preſent.

Q. What was the ſubject of theſe Lectures?

A. A general abuſe of Adminiſtration.

Q. Did he not touch on the branches of the Legiſlature? how did he ſpeak of the King?

A. In terms of contempt.

Q. Do you recollect any of thoſe terms?

A. He called him a Solomon.

Q. How did he expreſs himſelf of the other branches of the Legiſlature?

A. As entirely corrupt.

Q. Did he ſay then that they ought to be deſtroyed?

A. No, but they ought to be new modelled.

Q. What means did he recommend for that purpoſe?

A. Annual Parliaments and Univerſal Suffrage.—The witneſs then proceeded to ſtate, that he was preſent at the meeting of the Correſponding Society at Chalk Farm, on the 14th of February. Lovatt was in the chair; a letter was read from the Friends of the People, and an Addreſs propoſed; ſome printed papers were delivered to the perſons preſent. He was aſked if he had any of theſe printed papers about him, and upon anſwering in the affirmative, was required to produce them. The printed account of the proceedings at Chalk Farm was then read.

Q. How was the letter from the Society of the Friends of the People received?

A. With univerſal ſilence and hiſſing.

Q. Did you go to Chalk-farm in company with any perſon?
A. Yes, with Mr. Thelwall.
Q. Where was the meeting firſt to have taken place?
A. It was propoſed to have taken place at Store-ſtreet.
Q. Why was it afterwards changed?
A. I was told by Mr. Thewall it was only to be given out that it was to take place at Store-ſtreet, becauſe they were afraid that the magiſtrates might interfere; accordingly at the door of the houſe, there was a notice ſtuck up that it was to be held at Chalk-Farm.
Q. Who were the principal perſons who ſpoke and acted at the meeting?
A. Lovatt, Thelwall, Richter, Hodſon.
Q. Do you recollect any thing being ſaid about ſpies?
A. Yes, Thelwall ſaid that he would permit all ſpies to be preſent at that meeting, for the account they would have to carry home of the numbers of the Correſponding Society, would be no very agreeable news to their employers.
Q. Do you recollect in any reſolution that paſſed on that occaſion, the phraſe Britiſh ſenate being objected to?
A. Yes.
Q. Do you recollect any thing that Hardy ſaid at the meeting?
A. I recollect him only to have uttered three words.
Q. What were theſe?
A. While Richter was reading the reſolutions, he ſtopt to make ſome remark of his own, when Hardy ſaid, "Read without comment."
Q. After the meeting was over, where did you adjourn to ſpend your evening?
A. I adjourned along with Thelwall, to the public-houſe in Compton-ſtreet, where the diviſion met, and there indeed I heard ſomething that much aſtoniſhed me; for Thelwall taking up a pot of porter, and cutting off the head, ſaid, "Thus would I have all Kings ſerved," or "Thus I would ſerve all Kings," I cannot exactly recollect which of theſe expreſſions he uſed.
Q. Was there any particular toaſt afterwards given?
A. Yes; Thelwall gave, "The Lamp iron at the end of Parliament-ſtreet; and called upon another perſon to cover it, who gave, "And at the Treaſury Bench."
Q. Do you know a perſon of the name of Green, or recollect any particular expreſſions which he uſed?
A. Yes; he once ſaid, "That the pretexts of annual Parliaments and univerſal ſuffrage were only ladders to gain their ends."
Q. Did Green ever ſhew you a knife of a particular conſtruction?
A. At the meeting at Chalk-farm, I was ſitting in a box, about ten, and was rather ſurpriſed at remarking that five or ſix of them produced out of their pockets, ſmall inſtruments exactly correſponding with each other. Theſe reſemble what the French call *couteau ſecret*; opening with a ſpring, and not apt to fly back. One of

of the company remarked that thefe were bread and cheefe knives, at which I could obferve a fmile upon their countenances. I was told that I might have one at Mr. Green's fhop, Orange-ftreet, Leicefter-fields; I went there about a week after, he told me that he had fold about two or three hundred of thefe knives, and, the parlour door being open, defired me to fpeak very low, " For," faid he, " *My Wife is a damned Ariftocrat.*"

Upon being afked whether he recollected any thing further of the proceedings of the fociety, he faid, that at one meeting at which he was prefent, an application was made to grant fome relief to Dr. Hodfon, then confined in Newgate, but was refufed, and the reafon affigned, was, on account of his extreme violence, and he believed, it was alfo mentioned that he was no member of the Correfponding Society. He was prefent at the dinner of the Society for Conftitutional Information, held at the Crown and Anchor, on the fecond of May laft. He ftated, that Hardy brought him a ticket for that dinner; he put his hand into his pocket, but was told that there was nothing to be paid for it. Previous to the company having affembled to dine, fome very bad news had arrived from the Continent, and feemed to diffufe an air of general fatisfaction. A copy of a fong was delivered to every individual of the company, and there was likewife a paper laid on each plate, but it's contents he did not recollect.

Q. Who was in the chair?
A. Horne Tooke.

The Counfel defired him to recollect himfelf, and that he faid he believed the chairman was not Horne Tooke, but Mr. Wharton, Member of Parliament.

Q. Had you any mufic?
A. The moment the company entered the dinner-room, the air of ça-ira ftruck up, and continued to be playing during the whole time of dinner, being repeatedly encored; it was followed by the Marfeilles march, and the Carmagnole.

Q. What effect did thefe airs produce upon the Company?
A. They called forth an univerfal peal of approbation; the clapping continued fo loud and fo long that hands fmarted, and ears ached.

Q. What took place after dinner?
A. Horne Tooke got up; he faid that there were in the room fome government fpies, and thofe he wifhed in the firft place to addrefs. To this I particularly attended.—He defired the company to remark that he was not in a ftate of inebriation, for having fomething to fay, he had taken care to refrain from the indulgence of his glafs. He then proceeded: he called the Treafury Bench a fcoundrel fink of corruption; and the oppofition, a fcoundrel fink of oppofition; he faid there was a junction between thefe two parties for the purpofe of deftroying the Rights and Liberties of the Nation. He then, fpeaking of the hereditary nobility, afked, whether that fkip-jack Jenkinfon could be confidered as one of the hereditary Nobility.

Q. What

Q. What did he say of the House of Lords?

A. If my memory serves me right, he paid them much the same sort of compliment, which he had already paid the House of Commons.

Chief Justice Eyre.—"Sir, in giving evidence, do not use that language, in talking of the same sort of compliment; confine yourself to facts and expressions which actually were made use of."

Q. How did he express himself of the king?

A. He called the King *a poor man*, but whether to amuse or abuse I know not.

Q. How was his speech received?

A. With great applause.

Q. Was there any song sung upon the occasion?

A. Yes; there was a song to the tune of "God save the King," but I do not recollect whether it was sung by Horne Tooke, or whether he only added a verse, which he said had been forgotten. This was the song of which a copy was handed about to each of the company, previous to dinner.

The Attorney General. This was the song, a copy of which was read in evidence in the proceedings of yesterday.

Cross-examined by Mr. Gibbs.

Q. Mr. Groves, what are you?

A. I have been a conveyancer for these two or three and twenty years?

Q. Are you a solicitor?

A. I am not a solicitor in chancery.

Q. I did not ask whether you were a solicitor in chancery, but whether you were a solicitor. You do not answer; do you not understand the meaning of the question? Are you not a solicitor at the Old Bailey?

A. I am; I did not indeed at first understand the meaning of your question.

Q. What, you forgot then that you were a solicitor at the Old Bailey, and thought it a satisfactory answer to my question to tell me that you were not a solicitor in chancery?

A. I intended to give a direct answer.

Q. I have no doubt that your ignorance was involuntary; it was very natural that you should forget your profession in the court where you practise; but when did you first attend the meetings of the Corresponding Society?

A. In the month of January.

Q. You were sent, you say, by a gentleman?

A. Yes, I was employed to attend by a gentleman high in office, for the purpose of procuring information. At the same time I must remark that I was not desired by that gentleman to conceal his name.

Q. What is his name?

Witness (addressing the Chief Justice). "My Lord, is it a proper question?—If it is, I am ready to answer it."

Mr.

Mr. Gibbs—"If it was an improper question, I would not have asked it."

Chief Justice Eyre.—"Mr. Gibbs, he has admitted all that is necessary for your purpose, by saying that he was sent to these meetings to procure information. I conceive that it would not be expedient to answer your question, as he has confessed that he was employed by a person high in office, and to require from him the name of his employer, might lead to a sort of discussion, which has nothing to do with the present trial."

Q. How arose your connection with your employer?

A. I have had the honour of being personally known to him for these ten years, during which, I have enjoyed his confidence. That gentleman would not employ me on any thing dishonourable; he made use of me in order to procure necessary information, and I have very different ideas of the nature of that engagement, from what are generally entertained.

Q. I dare say that the gentleman would employ you on nothing which you conceived to be dishonourable, as well as that your ideas on the subject are very different from those which are generally entertained. But from the amount of all you have said, I am to understand that you never were present at any of the meetings, except in the character of a spy?

A. If to be employed to procure necessary information deserves the appellation, I must be content to bear it.

Q. Then you confess that as a Spy——

Chief Justice Eyre. "Mr. Gibbs, he has admitted that his object was to disclose information, I must object to any name of that sort being applied to a witness."

Q. You went then to pick up information, and carry it to your employer?

A. I did.

Q. You say that there was a large company at the first meeting that you attended?

A. So very numerous that the floor broke down, and we were obliged to remove to another room.

Q. And how happened it, Sir, that you, going there as you did to collect information in order that you might afterwards be able to bring it forward in evidence against individuals, made yourself master of no particular fact, of no expression which can be made the ground of a direct personal charge? Did you conceive it sufficient for the purpose of individual examination that you should bring such evidence, as, that there was a general clamour for universal suffrage, and annual parliaments?—

Chief Justice Eyre. "Mr. Gibbs, you go beyond the bounds of cross-examination. You are only to probe into all facts, and to endeavour to bring forward such as have not come out in the course of the examination. You ought not to introduce such a periphrasis as you have just now done."

Mr. Erskine. "I do not conceive that my learned friend has exceeded the usual limits of cross-examination. What he addressed to the witness may be taken as a question. "How do you, having been employed for the express purpose of procuring information, account for being so deficient in your knowledge of particular facts?" I have now practised these seventeen years, and I recollect an instance when a learned Judge (Buller), now on the bench, presided, Mr. Garrow, who was then introduced to the bar, at which he now ranks so high; put a question to a witness, to which I objected; it turned out to be in the course of cross-examination, and the laugh was raised against me."

Judge Buller. "I confess, that a greater latitude has been introduced into cross-examination than, perhaps, is proper. It has, in some degree, been sanctioned by practice. It is allowable to lead the evidence to the point to which counsel may wish to bring him; but certainly not to put words into his mouth which make directly against himself."

Chief Justice Eyre. "In all these cases my judgment is, that it is the business of counsel to get at the particular. Any remarks on the nature of the evidence ought to be reserved to their proper place, in the reply."

Mr. Gibbs. "I am happy to find myself supported by the authority of my learned friend, with respect to the practice; though, I confess, my Lord, that I feel myself considerably mortified, to have incurred any remark from you, with respect to my mode of conducting the examination."

Chief Justice Eyre and the Attorney General took an opportunity to profess the highest esteem and respect for Mr. Gibbs, in his professional capacity; and the cross-examination proceeded.

Q. You are then employed in the law?
A. I have not practised these six months.
Q. You do not mean to say that you have declined practice, but that no business was brought to you?
A. Such has been the case.
Q. So indeed I supposed. How happened it at the meeting at the Globe Tavern, of which you have given an account, you do not recollect any of the expressions used by particular persons?
A. When I first went there, I was a stranger to almost every person in the company, and could not, therefore, discriminate the particular speakers.
Q. You went afterwards, you say, to Chalk Farm?
A. Yes.
Q. On that occasion, you seem to have fixed yourself on Thelwall?
A. No; he fixed himself on me—we met at the door of the house in Store-street, where the meeting, which afterwards they thought proper to adjourn to Chalk Farm, was originally proposed to have been held, and Thelwall seeing me there with a view to attend, said, "come along."
Q. Was there not at that meeting a great cry against spies?
A. Yes.
Q. I suppose then that you joined in that cry?

A. I certainly did.
Q. Did you fee any perfon whom you knew?
A. Yes.
Q. What was his name?
A. Walſh.
Q. Was an enquiry made to you refpecting your knowledge of him?
A. Yes; I was afked who he was, and I anfwered I knew him to be a perfon employed by government.
Q. And you told him that he had come there to procure information?
A. I did.
Q. So you admitted that he was a fpy?
A. I did.
Q. You conceived him on that occafion to be there in the fame capacity with yourfelf; for the purpofe of making difcoveries?
A. I did.
Q. You faid that you knew he was a perfon employed by government, and a fpy?
A. I was carried acrofs the garden by fome of the members who fufpected him, for the purpofe of telling who he was; befides, he had the words *King and Conſtitution* infcribed on his buttons.
Q. So you admitted a perfon in the fame fituation with yourfelf employed by government, and with the words King and Conftitution infcribed on his buttons, to be a fpy. Was you not afraid by this declaration to expofe your friend to the hazard of being torn in pieces, by the perfons, at whofe expence he came to make difcoveries?
A. Had I not made the declaration, I might have been myfelf fufpected.
Q. Oh! it was only a fetch of cunning in order to conceal your own character; and I think you told us before, that Mr. Thelwall had faid, he wifhed all fpies to be admitted. What might be the number prefent?
A. I fuppofe about two or three thoufand, of whom however only about eight or nine hundred belonged to the Conftitutional Society. The others were drawn there by curiofity.
Q. At that meeting you faw fome knives of a particular defcription employed by the company in eating bread and cheefe. Had not you often feen fuch knives before?
A. I certainly had.
Q. Did not you know that they were exceedingly common?
A. Certainly I did.
Q. You were afterwards, you fay, prefent at the Crown and Anchor, on the 2d of May?
A. I was, and was very much aftonifhed to find, on entering the room, fo great a number of refpectable gentlemen affembled.
Q. I have no doubt you was; but how did you contrive to get into their company?

A. I have

A. I have mentioned that I had been presented with a ticket for the dinner by Mr. Hardy.

Q. You are not certain who was in the Chair?

A. I now recollect that it was Mr. Wharton.

Q. Did Mr. Horne Tooke, in the speech which he made on that occasion, and of which you gave some account, speak highly of the antient hereditary nobility?

A. Yes; he paid them every compliment.

Q. Did he not also remark that the antient nobility had lost their due influence in the country, in consequence of the new nobility (I do not wish to make any offensive allusion to individuals) introduced by those upon whose conduct he had been adverting in the House of Commons?

A. I now recollect he did.

Q. Did he not also speak highly of the office of the King in the Constitution?

A. I am clear he did, for he lamented the circumstance of the new nobility, in conjunction with a corrupt House of Commons, continuing, as he expressed it, to amuse that poor man, the King.

Q. Did he make any other complaint then against the Constitution, except that persons were introduced into the House of Commons, and by this means into the House of Peers, who restrained the due privileges of the crown, and deprived the King of his proper weight in the Constitution?

A. I perfectly recollect that he made use of those expressions.

Mr. Gurnell was next examined. He proved that a paper, which was put into his hand, was found in the possession of the prisoner at the bar. On that paper was written a song to the tune of "The Vicar of Bray."

After this song was read,

Mr. Erskine observed, that it was sent to Mr. Hardy by somebody or other in a letter.

John Thompson produced a pike, which he said he found in the possession of one Hillier on the 18th of May last. The handle was about six or seven feet, and the blade about 10 inches or a foot.

Camage, who had been before examined, was again called. He had seen Margarot in the Tolbooth of Edinburgh, and on his table he perceived a knife with a spring similar to those which Mr. Groves saw at Chalk-farm. It appeared to be a knife that opened with a spring, nine or ten inches in length. It was very hard to shut after it was once open.

On cross-examination by Mr. Erskine, the witness said he never saw a knife of that kind before. It lay on the table, and Mr. Margarot eat his dinner with it. It was in no way concealed; and there were six or seven people present. It did not strike the witness that there was any thing wrong in it. It was a curious knife, and Margarot shewed it to him.

George Lynam deposed, that he became a member of the division, No. 12, at the sign of the Mansion-house. He received rules of the Society, and an address; did not know the date, but believed it was in March, 1792. The division of the society adjourned from thence, in consequence of intimation given to the landlord, to the Crown in Newgate-street.

[This witness gave a very day and tedious evidence, from several books which he had filled with memorandums of the proceedings at the different meetings and divisions.]

The next meeting was at the Unicorn, Covent-garden: the room was full, and from seventy to eighty persons were present. Hardy was there, whom he understood to be the secretary. This was a meeting of division No. 2. There was brought forward Tom Paine's address to the French people, which was reported and ordered to be printed, and delivered out to the divisions of the society. It was also ordered that a paper, entitled The Rights and Duty of Man, should be continued weekly. He next read an extract from his notes, describing the mode in which the society and divisions did their business. The next meeting was on the 31st of October, at the Crown, Newgate-street, where the address to the French Convention was reported and agreed to. A letter was read from the editor of the Sheffield paper, at the division No. 2, at the Boar, which stated, that it would be good to send down delegates to teach the farmers politics. A delegate from division No. 11, made a report that the society at Stockport approved of the different proceedings of the meetings of the Corresponding Society.

Lauzun, the messenger, proved the finding a paper in the prisoner's house, signed "Hardy," dated Monday May 1, 1792, appointing him a delegate to one of the divisions, in which office he was to continue three months.

Alexander Grant proved the hand writing.

Lynam continued his evidence by adverting to what passed at the meeting of the Crown, Newgate-street, at which nothing material occurred.

He was interrupted by Mr. Bower, as to what passed at division No. 2.

A. An inflammatory letter was read from Joel Barlow to the National Convention, and loudly applauded, and the report was made from the committee of delegates. It was also reported, that the London Corresponding Society amounted to nine thousand in number; and that the division No. 14, Spitalfields, was increasing, and was in number equal to any other division. The first meeting of the society, he said, was at R. Boyd's, Exeter-street, when a letter was read from Major Johnson, that he did not approve of the letter to the Convention, but that he would prepare one. It was reported by a delegate, that the address of the society was approved by the National Convention, and ordered to be sent to the eighty-five departments. At this meeting there was much talk about Judge Ashhurst's charge to the Grand Jury. He was himself a delegate,

and

and it was recommended to him to state that it was necessary to publish that the society were not levellers, on account of the magistrates interfering with the publicans, and threatening to take away their licences.

The witness stated the proceedings of the general committee of delegates from the several divisions of the Corresponding Society, at their meetings during the year 1792; but nothing material turning on them, we forbear to repeat them. At the meeting of the delegates in Compton-street, on the 10th of January, 1793, a letter was read from the Friends of the People, addressed to the society, in which they recommend to the society, to abstain from foreign parties and correspondence, and to confine themselves to attending to domestic concerns; by which means they would avoid the imputation of being considered as levellers. On this it was resolved by the society to put an end to all further correspondence and communication with the Friends of the People. On the debate on this question, Mr. Bell said, their address to the National Convention of France evinced their intention of adopting the laws of that country; to which Mr. Margarot added, No doubt.

Meeting 14th Jan. The prisoner acquainted the society he had sent 30 copies of their address, together with 12 copies of M. Kiersant's speech in the National Convention, into the country to be dispersed.

Meeting 31st Jan. Mr. Baxter made a motion, that out of each person's quarterly subscription, six pence should be applied to the use of the division to which he belonged, and seven-pence for the defraying the charge of rent for the rooms where the poorer societies met. This, it was remarked by a member, was a good plan for the support and encouragement of the poorer divisions, such as Spitalfields, Moorfields, who were very numerous, and it was absolutely necessary, in case of resistance, to encourage and support them. This the witness stated not from his notes, but from recollection. These divisions were, he said, as many in number as all the other divisions put together. At another meeting it was moved and resolved, that the surplus of their subscriptions in hand should be applied to the discharge of the rent of the meeting-room of the above division, (Spitalfields) and the same reason assigned at the time, their poverty, and in case of war they would be serviceable. Being called on to explain what he meant by the word *war*, he said, it was understood at the meeting to mean a rising in the country.

Feb. 14. At this meeting the measure of a petition to Parliament was agreed to upon the subject of reform. The delegates from the Borough, and the Friends of the People, were not for going so far. The Holborn society were for republicanism. There were three objects under consideration of this meeting—to petition the King, to petition the House of Commons, or to call a Convention.

Feb. 19. The petition to Parliament was further discussed.

Feb. 21. It was stated, that if their petition to Parliament for reform was rejected, then they might petition the King. A letter was

was read from the Friends of the People, dated 15th of February, and addreſſed to the ſociety, in anſwer to one from them of the firſt of February. It ſtated, that their plan would ſoon come forward. Their object was to create an organ which ſhould ſpeak to the legiſlature:—it ſtated the reſolutions of the ſociety not to give up it's power of action to any other ſociety—the time of action may not be very far diſtant.

Feb. 28. Thanks voted to Mr. Fox, and the minority of 44, in the Houſe of Commons—as alſo to Lord Lauderdale—for their ſpirited exertions in the cauſe of the people.

March 14. The meeting reſolved, that the petition to Parliament ſhould be drawn up on parchment, one for each delegate, for the purpoſe of trying what coffee-houſe would take it in, in order to procure ſignatures to it.

March 21. There was a notice communicated to the ſociety, expreſſive of an apprehenſion that they would be taken up. A letter was read from a ſociety from Birmingham, dated March 15, requeſting to correſpond with the ſociety, and urging them to perſiſt in their petition to Parliament. A motion was made by Mr. Margarot, to print the addreſs written by Mr. Friend, accompanied by remarks and comments on particular paſſages.

March 28. A ſelect committee was appointed to draw up laws for the guidance of the ſociety: the committee were to ſubmit thoſe laws, when digeſted, to the conſideration of the ſeveral diviſions, for their approbation. A reſolution was entered into to write to all the ſocieties throughout the kingdom, requeſting their co-operation in the general cauſe. It was alſo determined, that bills ſhould be ſtuck up in various parts of the town, during the night, requeſting ſignatures to the petition to Parliament. It was likewiſe reſolved, that application be made to Mr. Francis to preſent the ſaid petition.

April 29. The anniverſary dinner of the ſociety was held at the Crown and Anchor tavern, in the Strand. The Witneſs was preſent at it. There were many who talked very boldly. They ſeemed aſſured that a revolution would ſoon take place. Several toaſts were given, which the witneſs read, but which have been long in poſſeſſion of the public.

May 2. At the meeting of the delegates at their uſual place in Compton-ſtreet, a letter was read from Mr. Francis, in which he ſtates, that by radical reform, the term uſed in their intended petition, was generally underſtood univerſal ſuffrage—a meaſure to which he was certainly no friend. He however conſented to preſent their petition.

The witneſs was here aſked, and ſtated, that a new election of delegates from the ſeveral diviſions of the London Correſponding Society had taken place in the preceding March.

Lauzun, the meſſenger, was called to identify a paper found by him in the poſſeſſion of the priſoner, among his other papers. It was a letter ſigned C. J. Fox, in anſwer to an application from the ſociety, in which he ſtated, that having never refuſed to preſent a petition

petition from any of his constituents, he would present their's, although repugnant to his ideas, as he conceived that by radical reform was generally understood universal suffrage, to which he declared himself adverse.

[Here the Court adjourned from four o'clock to half past five.]

Upon the resumption of the Court, *Lynam* proceeded in the detail of his evidence out of his written documents.

May 16. At the next meeting of the delegates, an anonymous letter, addressed to Mr. Hardy, as secretary to the society, was read, expressing his patriotic zeal, his good wishes for the society, apprehensions for their safety, and exhortations to spirited but prudent conduct. A motion was made for drawing up a remonstrance against the war. It was urged, that if a petition appeared against the war, it would serve to refute the idea of it's being a popular one.

May 23. A proposition was made for calling a general meeting. An address to the public was likewise proposed. Le Brun's Letters to Lord Grenville were spoken of as proper for publication; but the matter was postponed, lest it should appear as if they held communication with France.

May 30. At this meeting Mr. Hardy proposed to the society to break up for three months. This proposition was negatived.

June 6. A public meeting was talked of, to be advertised. There was to be no dinner. The meeting to be called for five, and proceed to business at six in the evening. Thanks were voted to Mr. Wharton, for his speech in Parliament upon reform, and ordered to be printed four times: the speech itself was also ordered to be printed, together with comments thereon, and a committee appointed to draw them up. A letter from a society at Leeds was read, requesting to correspond with the society, and stating the object of their association to be for the purpose of instructing their neighbours.

June 15. A letter was read from Mr. Stone, exhorting the society to persevere in their endeavours to restore the constitution to it's primitive purity, as established in 1688—endeavours that must ultimately prove successful; in spite of the contemptuous silence of the majority of the country. Upon this it was resolved by the society, that they will give their decided support to every measure brought forward tending to restore the rights of the people, as established in 1688. Thanks were voted to the 112 members of the House of Commons, together with Mr. Wharton, for their exertions. Ten thousand copies of his speech were ordered to be printed, and distributed by the society.

About this time the witness ceased to be a delegate from his division to the meeting.

Sept. 25. He was present at the meeting of his division, No. 23, which met in a court near Bunhill-row.

It was stated there that a new Society was forming near Moorfields, and was increasing very fast; also that a new division of the Corresponding

responding Society, who appeared very violent, was formed at the Grove in Bandy-legged-walk. A report was presented from the division at Walworth by one of it's members, the same who wrote the bill of the farce of the Guillotine. He was supposed to be employed by the National Convention in France. The address intended to be presented to the King having been reported to be pronounced treasonable by Mr. Vaughan, whose professional opinion was taken on it, another was ordered to be prepared October 7. At the next meeting a letter was read from a member, stating that he was going to Ireland, where he would open a correspondence between the societies there and the Corresponding Society.

The witness was also present at a meeting of the society, held at Hackney, Mr. Hodgson president, when Messrs. Margarot and Gerald were elected delegates, to attend the British Convention to be holden at Edinburgh.

Nov. 5. Meeting of the division, No. 23. It was stated, that Messrs. Gerald and Margarot had set off for Scotland—and that the funds of the society were very low. A new society, formed at Bristol. Messrs. St. Clair and M'Cleod, gone to Edinburgh to the Convention from the Constitutional Society. They were informed that associations were forming at Lambeth for the purpose of learning their exercise; and that similar ones were about to be established all over London.

Nov. 12. Division Meeting. Read a letter from a society at Norwich, approving of the Convention at Edinburgh, and requesting correspondence. It was stated that the funds of the society were very low, and a second subscription proposed, for the purpose of defraying the expences of their delegates at Edinburgh. There was a letter to their delegates, instructing them to visit the several societies in Scotland. It was said there was going to be a second general meeting in Edinburgh, but changed to Glasgow.

The witness was about this time re-elected delegate from his division to the general meeting of delegates from the several divisions of the Corresponding Society.

Jan. 2, 1794. Attended the general meeting for the first time. Mr. Hardy was re-elected secretary. They had changed the place of meeting from Old Compton-street, to No. 3, New Compton-street. It was resolved, that no person could be a delegate but those who have been at least three months a member of the division from which he was delegated. A hand-bill was adopted, approving of the conduct of the British Convention at Edinburgh, and passing a censure upon the magistrates of that city. Ten thousand copies of it were ordered to be printed and sent down immediately to be dispersed in Edinburgh. A letter was read, addressed from a meeting held at Sheffield, at which two thousand persons were present, recommending to the society to adopt spirited resolutions, and to support their delegates at Edinburgh.

January 9. It was resolved that a general meeting be held on the 20th instant, at the Globe Tavern in the Strand, to receive their late delegate to Edinburgh, Mr. Gerald. The meeting to be held at one one o'clock in the forenoon; dinner at five. Stewards appointed, Messrs. Thelwall, Agar, Kyd, Harrison, Stiff, Franklow, Harris, St. Clair, Powell, Williams, Mitcham, Pearce, Moore, Moffatt, and Martin. An address to the public upon innovated rights by the magistrates, was read and adopted. It was also resolved to discuss the conduct of Mr. Secretary Dundas upon the above occasion.

The Witness was here called upon by Mr. Bower, the Counsel for the Crown, who was examining him to explain the reason of his ceasing to be a delegate for some time. He said he had been accused by one of the London Corresponding Society of being a spy; and was thereupon suspended. He was tried by a committee appointed for that purpose, and after hearing evidence against him, he was *honourably* acquitted. He was in consequence of his purgation re-elected.

Jan. 20. He was present at the meeting at the Globe Tavern in the Strand. Mr. Martin was president at the meeting before dinner. He went early, before many members had assembled, and he stayed till all was over. They assembled before dinner in a room upon the first floor. They were alarmed with the floor giving way. They removed to the ball room upon the second floor. The President, with a few others, were placed in the music gallery. An Address to the Nation was read and carried. At the dinner Mr. Thelwall was in the chair.

January 23. Meeting of Delegates. It was recommended that a hand-bill be stuck up at night in various quarters of the town, representing our grievances, and demanding that they be redressed. A subscription also was adopted in support of their delegates in Scotland. It was proposed to publish the names of those who gave evidence against the delegates at Edinburgh; but this was opposed by Mr. Thelwall, as a measure which, by resentment, might lead to bloodshed and massacres. It was proposed to appoint two members, whose business it should be to be present at, and watch over the proceedings in the House of Commons.

January 30. A measure was brought forward for dividing the metropolis into divisions, and to open those. This he explained thus:—That houses were to be appointed in the various quarters of the town, to collect those in the different neighbourhoods round about them. It was resolved to advertise for subscriptions from persons, not being members, in support of the delegates in Edinburgh.

A permanent committee was appointed to consider of such measures as it should be necessary to pursue during the present posture of affairs—the same to be a secret committee. They were to have a discretionary power—and to report to the general committee of delegates at pleasure; but the general committee of delegates might dissolve them at pleasure. Messrs. Martin, Baxter, Williams, Thelwall and Moore, were unanimously elected upon this committee. The sub-committee of three, to consider of subscriptions for the delegates in Edinburgh—referred to the secret committee.

Feb.

Feb. 6. The Secret Committee above-named stated, that they wished to decline the trust reposed in them, as there was a danger to be apprehended of their being taken up. They proposed that a Secret Committee should be appointed, the names of whose members might not be disclosed. This was accordingly adopted.

Here this witness closed his evidence from his minutes. To the questions put to him by Mr. Bower, he stated himself to have been bred an ironmonger. He became a member of the London Corresponding Society by accident. Being at a public house where one of the divisions met, he saw a printed paper, containing some resolutions; he warned the landlord against these societies, which had for their object to overturn the Constitution; and if he suffered them to continue to meet in his house, he would have his licence taken from him. He afterwards introduced himself among them, for the purpose of observing them, and became a member.

On cross-examination by Mr. Erskine, he said he had been engaged in the commission line, for several years, for captains in the service of the East-India company. He had been first induced to become a member of the London Corresponding Society, from a conviction that traitorous designs against the Government were entertained by it's members, and that it was his duty, as a good subject, to assist in procuring the overthrow of their plans. Soon after his admission into the society, he became the object of suspicion to some of the members of which it was composed, and was tried and honourably acquitted of such a charge.

He was then asked by Mr. Erskine, whether he had communicated the memorandums he occasionally made to any person whatever. To which he answered, that he had communicated them to one who, he was well assured, would convey the intelligence to Government. He was then asked if such person was a magistrate, and if he was not, who he was? To both of which questions,

The Attorney General objected, stating as to the first, that it was obvious to all, that on the greatest principles of public justice and utility, the Executive Government ought to meet with every degree of assistance, in the discharge of the important functions entrusted to it, and consequently every Magistrate ought to be protected in the doing of these acts, which he imagined he was performing for the good of the community at large. Such was the indisputable rule as to the case of the magistrate himself, and upon the assumption of it's truth, he would rest the decision of the first object of enquiry before the Court; with respect to the second object of investigation he humbly submitted to the Court, that if (as appeared from the oath of the witness) the communication was made with the design of being given to the magistrate, and that design was afterwards carried into effect, it came within the principle which he had laid down, and consequently the same rule of construction ought to be adopted. In support of these abstract positions, he assimilated the present case to that of an information filed in the Exchequer, according to the practice of which, any man might be deprived of the whole of his fortune without any possibility of his knowing through what channel the informer against him obtained his intelligence.

Mr. Erskine on the other side contended, that it was not his wish in pressing the right he had to put the present question to infringe upon the principles of abstract justice, which had been laid on the other side. To preserve those principles from violation, to protect the Laws and Constitution of his country from violation, and in doing both, to save the life of his unfortunate client, were the great and important objects which he now had in view. In conformity to those objects, he submitted to the Court that he might put this question, as it did not appear that this communication was made to a magistrate, nor with the certainty that it would ever be communicated to one; though therefore he might be disposed to concede the first point, yet as it was premature to enter upon the discussion of it till he had obtained an answer to the last, he would at present content himself with insisting upon it's propriety.

Mr. Gibbs, on the same side, stated the same distinction between a communication to a magistrate, and one to a third person who might inform that magistrate, contending, that the adoption of the latter principle might involve every transaction of social life, and bring every thought, word, and action, under the controul of Executive Government, contrary to the purposes for which it was introduced, and the limits which natural justice had set to it.

Lord Chief Justice Eyre, Mr. Baron Hotham, and Mr. Justice Grose, were of opinion that the evidence was admissible, as the communication was made with the express design of being given to the magistrate; and as they could not distinguish it from the case in the court of Exchequer, cited by the Attorney General, *contra* the Lord Chief Baron, and Mr. Justice Buller, who acceded to the propriety of the distinction of the prisoner's counsel.

The question was accordingly rejected, and the witness was at last ordered to attend to-morrow with his notes separate, which were then so intermixed with the memoranda of his private affairs, that they could not be examined by the counsel for the prisoner.

John Coates, late of the Birmingham Volunteers, acknowledged that he had been a servant or apprentice to P. Franklow, taylor, No. 1, China-row, Lambeth; that in the one pair of stairs his master and several others used in the evening to be taught the use of fire-arms; that he never heard of any circumstance which induced him to believe that those who met there conspired against the King; that so far as he understood, their principal aim was a Reform in Parliament, and that he had seen his master in his uniforms of blue coat and red collar, with white waistcoat and breeches.

James Walsh's evidence followed. He stated his having been at the Chalk Farm Meeting. He heard something mentioned respecting a Convention. The resolutions were read in his presence. One hundred thousand copies were ordered to be printed; and, if necessary, it was said, that the number might be increased

creased to 200,000. He remembered having heard Thelwall speak on the occasion; but does not recollect any part of his speech. He was convinced, that there was no proposition, nor one word uttered, relative to arms. There was one man there from Ireland, which he knew by his brogue. Cannot charge his memory with any further particulars.

Thomas Green, of Orange-street, Leicester-fields, was then sworn. He declared, that he had dealt in knives and forks ever since he had been in business. Of three dozen of spring knives which he had received from Sheffield, he had sold fourteen. He had sometimes disposed of single knives. The prisoner, Hardy, had purchased some in packages, which consisted of six, sometimes seven in the package. Green sold one to Billington, and another to Groves; but said that he had got most of those taken by Hardy on account, returned to him when the prisoner was apprehended. The witness remembered having been one evening at supper in Compton-street, where he cut his food with a knife of this description, which received the approbation of the company.

Mr. Erskine cross-examined Green.

The Witness answered, that he had dealt in those knives for several years.

Mr. Erskine. "Did you ever understand that these dreadful knives were for the purpose of throat-cutting?"

Green. "Never."

Mr. Erskine. "Were they of a new or an old construction? Were they considered as secret knives for terrible designs?"

Green. "They were neither new nor secret. They always lay in my window for common sale, and I dealt in them for more than seven years."

Mr. Erskine. "I suppose all cutlers sell such knives?"

Green. "I never knew any cutler without them."

Mr. Erskine. "When Groves wished to purchase a knife, did you desire him to speak in a low tone of voice, because your wife was a damned Aristocrat, and might hear what he said, from the parlour?"

Green. "I never said my wife was a damned Aristocrat; nor did I ever advise Groves to speak in a low tone of voice."

Mr. Erskine. "Upon your oath, you did not?"

Green. "I swear positive, I did not call my wife a damned Aristocrat."

Attorney General. "No, Mr. Green, I dare say you could not be so unpolite to your wife."

Mr. Erskine. "Groves has sworn to it."

Edward Hodson was next sworn. He said that he was a member of the London Corresponding Society about three months.
Believed

Believed that there was no other object in view than a Parliamentary Reform. That the change which they wished to effect was that in the Commons House of Parliament; that it was no part of their plan to attack the King, but that they entertained very different objects; that [they] designed no diminution of his power; that they never intended to displace or overthrow the Lords; and that the witness left the Society when he learnt that Hardy and Adams had been apprehended.

Mr. Gibbs. - Had the Society ever any idea of taking upon themselves the legislation of the country?

Hodson. "No."

Mr. Gibbs. "Did you believe that from their conduct they ever meant to introduce the anarchy of France?"

Hodson. "Never."

George Ross lives in Edinburgh, entered a member of the Society of the Friends of the People at the end of the year 1792, was a member of the British Convention, as delegate from his Society in 1793. At the end of November or beginning of December, attended several of their meetings. There were several delegates from England. Was not a member of the London Corresponding Society. Received amongst other letters in number about half a dozen, one from Mr. Stock in Edinburgh, the same with that which was then given into his hands. Sent several of the letters he received from Stock into the country. Sent one to Strathaven, one to Paisley, and some to other places. Took some of the minutes of the Convention, acting occasionally as secretary. Recollects the dispersion of the second Convention.

Cross-Examination.

The object of this Society was a Reform in the House of Commons, and no further. There was, to his knowledge, no intention in the Association to attack the King's Majesty. The Convention did not consider themselves as the British Parliament, nor attempt to usurp the functions of the Magistracy. Made no laws to bind the people. Their only object was to gain a Reform by means of a petition. The Convention consisted of about two hundred persons, unprovided with arms, and yielded to the authority of the Magistrates when they came against them. The Convention consisted of all ranks, poor and rich, many of them reputable people, and chiefly of sober morals.

Mr. Garrow, in re-examination, asked him if he was present when the Convention declared they would continue to assemble until compelled to resist by superior force?

He does not know that such a resolution had passed, or at least does not recollect that he was present at the time of such a proposition,

position, as he had not an opportunity of attending every hour in the day. Was present when a Convention Bill, &c. was to have been a signal for their assembling.

Speaking of the morality of the Members, he denied that Watt was a Member of the Convention, but acknowledged that Downie was.

The Lord President interrupted this kind of examination as irregular.

Mr. Erskine. What were they to do when assembled in consequence of such signal?

He said it was to forward their petition; but if their petition was rejected they would not desist.

Arthur M'Nell, of the Water of Leath, was a Delegate, in the Edinburgh Convention, and attended their Meetings sometimes. After the Convention was dispersed, there was a Committee of Union formed, some of them of the Committee of which Watt was a Member. There was a Committee of Ways and Means appointed afterwards, Mr. Holt, Mr. Burke, Mr. Richardson, Mr. Watt, Mr. Downie, and himself.

In that Committee, which was held in the month of April, the original object was to defray the expences of Mr. Skirving.

Watt read a plan, proposing to seize the Lord Justice Clerk and the rest of the Lords of Council and Sessions, and the Lord Provost of Edinburgh; to kindle a fire in the Excise Office of the New Town, and there was to be a party stationed.

Mr. Erskine wished to know the relevancy of this evidence.

The Attorney General rested the applicability upon letters of correspondence between Skirving and the prisoner Hardy, in which he endeavoured to shew that they understood, and were in concert with each other. The documents which he brought forward on this occasion, were exceedingly numerous and complicated. From their concert, union, and correspondence, he inferred that they were all parties in the same design. They were both preparing pikes, and preparing plans of resistance to Government, going on at the same time in both countries, and similar circumstances were deemed a conspiracy in the case of Lord Lovat.

Mr. Erskine said, that having scarcely the time allowed him which nature demanded for rest, he was hardly prepared to answer the Attorney General in all the references to which he had recourse; but as far as the prisoner was implicated in the proceedings of the Scotch Convention.

The President recommended to let the examination go on.

The examination being resumed, the witness said, that a party was to be stationed at Lochin Brach, and a party in another part of Edinburgh. The fire was to draw the military from the
Castle.

Caftle. The two parties were to take them in front and rear. Different parties were to feize the different banking houfes in Edinburgh, and commiffioners were appointed to collect the cafh of the banks. When Watt read this firft plan, were prefent Mr. Stock, himfelf, Watt, Downie, and an another, being five out of the nine of which the Committee was compofed. The prifoner objected to any thing that would tend to fhed the blood of his country, in which Downie agreed with him.

On one of the laft nights he attended, Watt read another plan in the prefence of the fame Committee, in form of a proclamation, prohibiting all farmers or dealers in corn, grain, or hay, to remove the fame from their dwellings, under pain of death: alfo that no gentleman fhould go above three miles from their refpective habitations, under pain of death.

On the other fide of the paper was an addrefs to his Majefty, ordering him to difmifs his prefent Minifters, and put an end to the prefent war, or abide by the confequences.

The addrefs was to be fent to his Majefty the morning after the attack. This plan he conceives was to ftrengthen the former one.

The witnefs told Watt thofe things did not belong to a Parliamentary Reform, and he would have nothing to do with him.

Watt called upon him, and afked him to take a walk to Orrock's, whom he afked to make fome pikes, which Orrock fketched out upon a board or plate. Watt defired him to be bufy and work, as he had 4000 to fend to Perth, befide what he was to diftribute about Edinburgh.

He met Stock at the Committee, who faid he was going to London or Briftol; and that he would wait upon Mr. Hardy, the prifoner. Watt offered him a letter to the prifoner, to form a correfpondence with Mr. Hardy and him in a fafe manner.

Crofs-Examination.

Does not know whether Hardy defired fuch correfpondence, or whether any took place. The object of his Society, confifting of twenty, was a Parliamentary Reform. Attended the Convention, and never heard fuch converfation as that he heard from Watt. As far as he could underftand, they meant, by a petition, to obtain a Parliamentary Reform. The very night they had been difperfed, they were to have confidered of a Petition to Parliament, or the King. Never faw any arms amongft them, nor was any propofitions for an armament made. He fpoke in general well of the moral characters of the Members, and gave the fame defcription of their object as the former witnefs. He fwore, that he did not know that the Convention had agreed not to feparate, except compelled by force, and as to the other latter, refolutions,

tions, which were considered as violent, he only knew of them by report.

Mr. Garrow was examining why he did not give information to the Magistrates of Watt's first plan, when he was interrupted by the Lord President, who said he was leading himself to make a confession of High Treason, and expressed his regret for suffering it to proceed so far.

William Middleton said he had on the 15th of May searched the house of Watt.

This evidence was objected to by the Court, as being subsequent to the time when Hardy was taken into custody.

Mr. Erskine then said, that the evidence on behalf of the Crown being now in a great measure closed, he must represent to their Lordships that Mr. Gibbs and himself, being the Counsel, appointed by the Court, for the prisoner, had been so continually occupied, as to allow them insufficient time even for that rest which nature required; but none at all for consulting upon the manner of conducting his defence. For himself, he was so much indisposed as to be unable to avail himself of the few hours granted on a former day, and he yet remained so ill that nothing but an imperious sense of duty could induce him to attend any longer. Notwithstanding this he was far from wishing to trespass on the time or convenience of the Court; but, as much time would be saved by suffering him to proceed according to the arrangement he wished to make, he hoped the Court would indulge him in some time to make the necessary preparations.

The Lord President observed that this was a very new and unprecedented situation. The Court felt for the difficulty of his situation, and he could assure him that, as far as depended on himself, the Lord Chief Baron, and the other Judges, any personal inconveniance to them should not deprive him of any necessary accommodation. But that was not all—the Jury were in the discharge of a more severe duty than any he had heard of, and they bore it in a manner that did them very great honor. Besides, it was a matter of notoriety that great part of this evidence had been for a long time in print, and it was not to be supposed that it had not been duly weighed and examined. There was one alternative which suggested itself, which may be of general accommodation, which was, that Mr. Erskine should go on to examine his witnesses to-morrow, for, though he did not wish to name Sunday expressly, he must inform him that the Court meant to sit very late on Saturday night.

Mr. Erskine said, that the Attorney General having opened up so copiously, and with so many comments, the evidence on behalf of the Crown, he could not venture a thing so unprecedented in the history of our jurisprudence, as to suffer that evidence to go in such a state before the Jury, and the impressions which the cross-examination might have made to be worn off without entering fully upon the defence, and explaining the nature of the exculpatory evidence.

U

evidence. He meant not to afk any time for preparing his addrefs; but fimply to make fuch arrangements in the evidence as would expedite the proceedings, and for this I require only a few hours.

Mr. Gibbs alfo remarked, that they could not hazard fo novel a proceeding, as to enter upon the exculpatory evidence without addrefling the Jury, left any imputation may lie upon them, fhould the event be adverfe to the prifoner.

The Prefident faid, that confideration was perfonal to themfelves, but not effential to the adminiftration of juftice. The Court, he faid, was afraid to hear Mr. Erfkine's explanation of what he meant by a few hours, and was defirous to know what time he demanded.

Mr. Erfkine declined the appearance of prefcribing to the Court, and would be contented with what time they fhould think proper to afford him.

The Attorney General being afked what further witneffes he meant to produce? faid there were only two, and thofe to points given in evidence before, which may not take above twenty minutes.

Mr. Erfkine was afked whether he intended to call witneffes, or reft the defence on the evidence already adduced?

He anfwered, that he intended to call witneffes.

Judge Buller faid, that he neither accepted their expedient, nor would mention precifely the delay he wifhed to obtain.

Mr. Erfkine reminded them that the Attorney General had taken upwards of nine hours in opening the profecution, and it would be but juft to allow an equal, or if neceffary a longer fpace of time for making the defence; but if he was fuffered to make fuch arrangements and felection, inftead of reading that part at full length of the evidence upon which he fhould have occafion to obferve, he need not occupy half the time that was taken by the Attorney General. He therefore propofed an adjournment till twelve o'clock to-morrow.

The Prefident then offered to adjourn till eleven o'clock.

Mr. Erfkine begged earneftly for another hour, and afked the Jury, whether they would agree to accommodate him in that manner?

The Jury with one voice declared that they would agree to any thing which would accommodate them.

The Lord Prefident faid, if the Jury begged it for him, he would not refufe him.

The Court then, at half paft One o'clock, adjourned till Twelve.

Saturday, November 1.

The Court met at twelve o'clock, purfuant to adjournment, and the ufual forms of opening being gone through,

George Lynam was called in, and finifhed his crofs-examination. He produced his books and papers. The moft material part of his evidence was, that he never heard the prifoner propofe any other

mode

mode of reform than by a peaceable and conftitutional application.

The Attorney General then produced two papers, which were found in the poffeffion of Thelwall, and in the hand writing of Martin, after Hardy was in cuftody. They were brought forward to prove that they exifted before the apprehenfion of the prifoner. They were the refolutions of the Chalk Farm meeting, and were proved by Shaw, the meffenger, to have been found in Thelwall's houfe fince the apprehenfion of Mr. Hardy.

Mr. Gibbs thought this an informal mode of proceeding. He conceived that the papers could not in the leaft attach to Hardy, fince found fubfequent to his being taken into cuftody. After fome converfation between the counfel for the crown and prifoner, the papers were admitted.

William Walker, of the Adelphi, fwore to the hand writing of Martin.

Evan Evans fwore that he had been confined for debt in the King's Bench prifon about two years; that he was liberated from thence on the 31ft of July laft. From Martin having been confined for debt in the fame prifon, he became acquainted with him, and he there faw both the papers produced in Martin's room: it was in the beginning of April that he faw them, and before the meeting at Chalk-farm was held.—They were not then dated. Martin told him that he wrote thefe refolutions for the Chalk-farm meeting; and read them feveral times over in the room while the witnefs was prefent. He faid that he had put plenty of Cayenne in them, and if they would follow his advice, there would be a plenty of warm work before the month was out. His wife faw the papers, and Mr. Gay, Mr. Tourle, &c. fome other perfons heard the declarations of Martin, refpecting his having prepared the refolutions.

Mr. Gibbs crofs-examined this witnefs. He faid, that he was formerly a grocer; that he had once a difference with Mr. Martin about the room which he occupied in the King's Bench prifon, but that he never had ufed any expreffions of refentment againft Martin on that account.

Ann Evans faid, fhe is the wife of the former witnefs, and ufed to attend him while he was confined in the King's Bench prifon. (One of the papers was produced.) She had feen it in Mr. Martin's poffeffion, at her hufband's room in the prifon. Remembers Martin reading that paper, and in the courfe of fome converfation that paffed, his remarking that it was not lawful to take up arms againft the King.

Martin continued—that he had drawn up the refolutions to be fubmitted to the Chalk-farm meeting; that they were warm, for he had put plenty of cayenne into them, and if they took his advice there would be hot work.

The witnefs remembers Pearce brought fome of the printed refolutions that had been entered into at Chalk-farm (which were not the fame as thofe which were found in the poffeffion of Martin.)

The Attorney General remarked, that Pearce was the sub-secretary to the London Corresponding Society.

The witness proceeded.—Pearce, at the time he brought them to Martin, in the King's Bench prison, said, that he had a number more, but that he had given the greater part of them away among the men at a coachmaker's in Long-acre; that Hardy had plenty of them, and if he wanted any more he would bring them to him.

Mr. Gibbs cross-examined this Lady. She said, that the resofolutions were for the meeting of the society to have been held at a dancing-room in Store-street, Tottenham-court road. She had very frequenly read the paper. (This was the meeting which was adjourned to Chalk-farm.)

Thomas Tourle said, that he was a prisoner in the King's Bench at the time Martin was confined for debt there, and he became acquainted with him. He never saw the papers produced, but heard Martin say, three or four days before the meeting at Chalk-farm, that he had prepared resolutions for that meeting, which were warm; and if they would follow his advice there would be hot work. He knew Mr. Gay, who was a prisoner in the King's Bench.

The Attorney-General then put in the paper, which was read.

" At a General Meeting of the London Corresponding Society, held at   on Monday the 14th day of April, 1794.

" Citizen ——— in the Chair.

" Resolved, That all sovereign, legislative, and judicial powers are the Rights of the People; and though the People have delegated those their original powers to others, in trust for the benefit of the community, yet the rights themselves are reserved by the people, and cannot be absolutely parted with by the people to those persons who are employed to conduct the business of the State.

" Resolved, That the Constitution of England is held by the King, Lords, and Commons, and other Officers appointed by the People, in trust, for the benefit of the People; and though these trustees may regulate and improve the Constitution, yet they cannot alter or subvert it without committing treason against the nation.

" Resolved, That Magna Charta, or the Great Charter of the Liberties of England, made in the reign of King John; the Petition of Rights, assented to by Parliament in the reign of King Charles the First; and the several laws made at and in consequence of the glorious Revolution in the year 1688, are declaratory of those parts of the Constitution of England which are in and by them respectively declared.

Resolved, That the office of King of England was not instituted by the people merely as an office of profit and honour to the King, but he was so appointed as chief trustee and guardian of the Constitution and Rights of the People; and that important and laborious personal duties are annexed to the regal office, the objects of which

are,

are, to promote the good of the people, and preserve their rights in full vigour from innovation and corruption.

"Resolved, That it is the duty of the King to preserve the Constitution of England and the Rights of the People against every incroachment; and, in order to enforce that duty, the following oath is required to be taken by every King on his accession to the throne of Great Britain; to wit, the Archbishop or Bishop shall say—Will you solemnly promise and swear to govern the people of this kingdom of England, and the dominions thereto belonging, according to the statutes in Parliament agreed on, and the laws and customs of the same?"

"The King or Queen shall say, "I solemnly promise so to do."

"Archbishop or Bishop. "Will you, to your power, cause law and justice, in mercy, to be executed in all your judgments?"

"Answer. "I will."

"After this, the King, or Queen, laying his or her hand on the holy gospels, shall say, "The things which I have before promised, "I will perform and keep; so help me God;" and then shall kiss the book.

"Resolved, That his present Majesty, King George the Third, on his accession to the throne of these realms, did solemnly take the said oath.

"Resolved, That the constitutional rights of the people have been violated, and that it is the duty of the people, in the present alarming crisis, to assemble and enquire into the innovations or infringements which have been made upon the rights of the people, and how far the declarations of the Constitution, as they were uttered at the aforesaid Revolution, remain in force, and which of them have been violated, and by whom; and also whether such innovations, infringements, or violations, have been committed from the negligence or corruption of those who have been entrusted with the government of the state.

"Resolved, That this society do invite the people to meet in their respective neighbourhoods, to elect one or more person or persons as delegates, to meet in a Convention, to be held on the   day of   next, at such place as shall be appointed by the society; and that the delegates so elected do forthwith transmit to the secretary of this society, No. 9, Piccadilly, London, the vouchers of their several elections, in order that the place of meeting may be duly notified to them.

"Resolved, That it is the right and bounden duty of the people to punish all traitors against the nation, and that the following words are not a part of the oath of allegiance: to wit, "I declare "that it is not lawful, upon any pretence whatever, to take arms against the King."

John Edwards was sworn, and a hand-bill produced to him.

He was asked if he had ever seen such papers?—He said that he had seen one of those bills handed about at the division meeting of the

the London Corresponding Society, No. 11, held at Mr. Scotney's, on Snow-hill.

This bill was put in and read. The following is a copy of it.

"The Ins tell us we are in danger of an invasion from the French.

"The Outs tell us that we are in danger from the Hessians and Hanoverians.

"In either case we should arm ourselves.—Get arms, and learn how to use them."

William Middleton, one of the sheriffs officers of the county of Edinburgh, said, that, on the evening of the 15th of May last, he found in the house of Robert Orrock. Smith, in Edinburgh, thirty-three pike-blades, finished and unfinished. They were only the blades. On the same day he found, in the house of Robert Watt, who was lately executed at Edinburgh, twelve pike or spear-heads, finished. At a second search, in the same house, he found two other pike-heads, similar to those found on the first search, two battle-axes, and one shaft-pole.

Here an objection was taken by Mr. Gibbs, who contended, that, as these pikes were found after the prisoner was in custody, the circumstance could in no way apply to him, and was not therefore admissible evidence. His objection was over-ruled.

The examination of the witness proceeded.—He, in the first instance, went to search Watt's house for the goods of a bankrupt, which were suspected to have been secreted therein; in a closet or press in the dining-room, which was locked up, he found the pikes, on the first search, and in the lower part of the house he found the rest. These were delivered by him into the care of a Sheriff Clarke.

Joseph Edwards was called up again; he begged to explain to the Court, in a more distinct way, a part of the evidence which he had given on Friday, and which might have been misunderstood by the Court and Jury, respecting the proposed meeting in Green-arbour-lane, in consequence of a letter from Sheffield; he wished it to be understood that no meeting took place.

The Attorney General was proceeding to examine the witness on this point, when the Lord President interrupted him, and said, that it was a mere explanation of the witness of what had been given in evidence by him, arising, as it appeared to him, from a good motive, lest it should be misconstrued; and that therefore he did not think it right that the Counsel for the Crown should proceed to examine him, which would admit of a cross-examination, and thus there would be no end to the examination of the witnesses.

The Attorney-General said, that many questions might have been put to the witness, if his evidence had differed from what it originally was, which, if the witness was permitted to amend that evidence, and he was precluded from the possibility of again examining him, could not be put.

The

The Lord President admitted that it was so, and that the witness might have opportunities of refreshing his memory and amending his evidence, by the accounts in the newspapers; for it had lately become a practice to print such reports of the proceedings of a court of justice, as the industry of the persons attending for that purpose could produce, and in some cases he thought this practice inconvenient.

William Lockhart, sheriff-clerk-depute of Edinburgh, said, that he went with Middleton to the house of Watt, and was present at the finding of the pike-blades, the battle-axes, and one shaft-handle.

A box was produced, containing the pike-blades and battle-axes.

Mr. *James Clerk*, sheriff-depute of the county of Edinburgh, said, that the box produced, together with it's contents, was in his custody from the time the pikes were found until the trials at Edinburgh. One Scot, who was supposed to be implicated in the guilt of Watt, had absconded.

Lockhart was again called up, and said that he produced the box and it's contents on the late trials at Edinburgh, and from that time, until the present, it has been in his possession, and no one has opened it.

The box was then opened, and it contained the weapons which the witness stated to have been found at Edinburgh. The pike-blades, as well as the battle-axes, screwed into the pole which was found; and an iron handle was produced, which was found with them, contrived to fit the screw of the battle-axe, so as to render it fit for use without the pole.

Mr. *Gay* was proved to have been a member of the Society for Constitutional Information, by the minutes of that Society, which were read, and by which it appeared that he was proposed by Mr. J. H. Tooke, and seconded by Mr. Bonney. Mr. Gay was not called.

The Attorney General informed the Court, at one o'clock, that he had closed the evidence on the part of the Crown.

PRISONER'S DEFENCE.

The Hon. Thomas Erskine.—" Before I proceed to the discharge of that duty to which my situation this day calls me, I desire to return my thanks to the Court, for having adjourned their proceedings to an hour which has afforded me an opportunity to take that necessary refreshment which nature demanded, as well as to you, Gentlemen of the Jury, for the very polite manner in which you assented to an adjournment so essential to my accommodation, and to my being at all qualified for the task in which I am now engaged. Before I proceed to the case, as it regards the law and the evidence, I wish to follow the liberal example that has been set by the Attorney General, in his opening speech, in putting aside every thing collateral to the question. But first, both in the name of the prisoner for whom I stand, and for myself, I desire to subscribe to all that eulogium pronounced by the Attorney General on the constitution of this country, as handed down to us by our ancestors, the result of their superior wisdom and virtue, and entitled to the esteem and veneration of all posterity. But having premised this, the genuine expression of feelings, I trust not less sincere than those which dictated the panegyric of the Attorney General, What, I will ask, entitles the constitution to this eulogium? What renders it the object of our love and reverence? I will not now speak of the right which it affords to it's subjects, of making their own laws, but of the equal protection afforded to all, and the security provided for the impartial administration of justice. The Attorney General seemed to lay great stress on the anarchy and confusion of France, on which he descanted at length. Into that subject I will not at present enter; I neither will enquire into the causes by which they were first produced, nor the circumstances from which they have proceeded to such an extent. But what is it that the French have chiefly to deplore? They are at present under the dominion of a barbarous necessity, in consequence of which no man's life, liberty, or property is secure, or at his own disposal for a moment. The first instant that a charge of incivism, federalism, or moderantism, is brought against him, the sentence of the Revolutionary Tribunal follows—quick as the thunderbolt pursues the flash, and he is doomed to behold his friends and family no more. Such is the comparative state of England and France; and what is the inference we ought to draw with respect to the present case? If the prosecution be indeed intended to avert from this country the horrors of that anarchy, under which France at present labours; if it be intended to secure the continuance of those blessings which it enjoys under it's admirable constitution, let not the prisoner suffer from the execution of barbarous laws barbarously enforced, or from the well-meaning enthusiasm of those, who, sincerely attached to the constitution, are desirous to ensure it's preservation at any price. For in former instances in the history of this country, where we have to lament the sacrifice of innocent persons under legal pretexts, I am apt to think that we ought rather to condemn the mistaken zeal than the barbarous ferocity of the age. It is necessary then that you, Gentlemen of the Jury, should guard against this source of delusion and injustice; it is necessary that in the decision which you are called to give, you should stand on the strict and unequivocal letter of the law. It would not be enough that the prisoner should appear to you to have been rash, foolish, or even wicked—the last of which it will be impossible to support by any colour of evidence—for I trust I shall be able to vindicate his conduct, which, in the present instance, is of little consequence. It must be proved to your satisfaction, that he has offended against that statute under which he is indicted. He holds his life from the law, and by it he demands to be tried. This fair trial I ask; first, from the Court—I ask it more emphatically from the Jury—but lastly, and chiefly, I implore it of him in whose hands are all the issues of life, whose just and merciful eye expands itself over all the transactions of mankind, without whom not a sparrow falleth to the ground, at whose command nations rise and fall, and are regenerated. I implore it of God himself, that he will fill your minds with the spirit of justice and of truth, that you may be able to find your way through the labyrinth of matter laid before you; a labyrinth in which no man's life was ever before involved in the whole history of British trial, nor indeed the universal annals of human justice or injustice."

Mr. Erskine then proceeded to the indictment. The first charge of the indictment was, "that the prisoners maliciously, traitorously, and with force of arms, did amongst themselves and other false traitors, to the jurors unknown, conspire, compass, and imagine to excite insurrection, rebellion and war against the King, and to subvert the Legislature, Rule and Government of the kingdom, and to depose the King from the Royal State, Title, Power and Government of the kingdom, and to bring and put our said Lord the King to death." 'Gentlemen of the Jury,' said Mr. Erskine, ' you have been extremely good in taking down the evidence; allow me now to request you to attend to the form and substance of the charge. The whole treason lies in the last member of the charge, viz.—" And to bring and put our said Lord the King to death." The indictment then goes on to charge the overt acts.—" And to fulfil, perfect, and bring to effect, their most evil and wicked treason, and treasonable compassing and imaginations aforesaid, viz.--to bring and put the King to death, they met, conspired, consulted and agreed among themselves and other traitors to the Jurors unknown, to cause and procure a Convention and meeting of divers subjects to be assembled within the kingdom, with intent and in order that the persons so assembled, and at such Convention and Meeting should traitorously, without and in defiance of the authority, and against the will of Parliament, subvert and alter, and cause to be subverted and altered, the Legislature, Rule and Government of the Country, and depose, and cause to be deposed, our Lord the King, from his Royal State, Title, Power and Government thereof." This is the overt act—That the

X   Prisoner

Prisoner conspired the death of the King, and that in pursuance of this intention, he did all the acts charged in the indictment, provided arms, and concerted the plan of a Convention. And here two things occur for consideration, which are absolutely necessary in order to establish the guilt of the Prisoner under this charge. First, it is necessary to prove that he actually did the things which are charged in the indictment. Secondly, that he did them with intention, and in pursuance of the object of compassing the King's death. Was this Convention, by which he proposed to put down the King, to supersede the functions of the Legislature, and usurp to itself all the authority of the State? A man cannot be guilty of the overt act, without first conceiving the intention. It is the intention which at the time passes through his mind, that alone attaches guilt to the act. And if you are satisfied with respect to the guilty intention, you are then to consider whether the overt act is of a nature which amounts to the description of that charged in the indictment. And here I would earnestly implore the attention of the Court and of the Attorney General, to what the law is. It is not my attention, on the present occasion, to offer any thing of my own. It is only my wish to make you masters of the authorities. Nor is it necessary that I should bring forward my own authority for the purpose of defending the prisoner, and answering the arguments of my honourable friend the Attorney General—for my honourable friend I have often called, and still will continue to call him. He has not had recourse to barbarous precedents nor bloody murders committed under pretext of law; he has not brought forward the excesses of a rude and sanguinary age, or the legal sophistry of corrupt and profligate Judges—He has rested on grave and venerable authorities, though mistaken in my opinion with respect to the deductions which he has drawn from them. That mistake I ascribe neither to the defect of his understanding or his heart; I have too high an esteem for the enlargement of the one, and the integrity of the other. On those very authorities which he has brought forward, I also mean to rest; and I am persuaded that if there is any difference among them, it will be found only to arise from a mere tripping of expression. And first, I must advert to the constructive Treason of deposing the King. And here I must remark, that I stand in a fearful and delicate situation; it is necessary therefore that I should occupy a large ground, as not only the life of the Prisoner at the bar is at stake, but the lives of many, who are behind, involved in the same question, and dependent upon the same issue.

As trial was nothing more than the application of the facts disclosed in evidence, to a rule of human action or conduct, the breach and violation of which constitutes the charge, the preliminary discussion must be (Mr. Erskine continued) what was the

law,

law, and what the breach of it, which the prisoner was called upon to answer. To do this, as it became him, upon so solemn and awful an occasion, he must resort to the history of the country, the records of the law, and the authoritative writings of the most learned men upon the subject of High Treason. In doing this, it was not his desire, as he had said, to press upon the Court any theories or opinions of his own, but to extract, by legal reasoning, from those unerring sources—the law of the land upon the subject.

As to the crime of High Treason at common law, before the statute of the 25th Edward III. upon which the Indictment, and every Indictment for High Treason, must now be framed, little was necessary to be said concerning it; he should therefore dismiss the consideration of the common law on the subject of treason, with the observation of that great, excellent, and most learned person, whose memory would last as long as law or constitution remained to Englishmen, Lord Chief Justice Hale, who says, "That at common law there was a great latitude used in raising offences to the crime and punishment of treason, by way of interpretation and arbitrary construction, which brought in great uncertainty and confusion. Thus accroaching (*i. e.* encroaching on royal powers, was an usual charge of treason anciently, though a very uncertain charge, so that no man could tell what it was, or what defence to make to it." He then proceeds to state various instances of vexation and cruelty, and concludes with this observation, "By these and the like instances that might be given, it appears how arbitrary and uncertain the law of treason was before the statute of the 25th of Edward III. whereby it came to pass, that almost every offence that was, or seemed to be, a breach of the faith and allegiance due to the King, was by construction and consequence, and interpretation, raised into the offence of High Treason." To remedy these grievous abuses, by which every faction in it's turn sacrificed it's enemies by arbitrary executions, founded upon constructive treason, mak... ncient England like modern France, the wise and venerable ... of King Edward III. was made, whose excellent and benevo... nt object was to make treason certain. Lord Coke called the parliament who passed this statute, *Parliamentum Benedictum*; and the like honour was given to it by the different statutes which, from time to time, brought back treason to it's standard, " all agreeing in magnifying and extolling this blessed statute." As no Judge ever did or could deny that this statute was enacted to give, by it's letter, all certainty and precision to the crime of treason, and to prevent the arbitrary constructions by Judges, which had disfigured and dishonoured the ancient law, and brought, to use Hale's language, "insecurity upon both King and People;" it might be affirmed that this celebrated statute would little have deserved the panegyrics bestowed upon it, if it had not, in it's enacting letter, which professed to remove doubts, and to ascertain the law with precision, made use of expressions well known and ascertained; and it would be seen how cautiously it did so. The two great objects of the statute were to guard, 1st, the natural life of the King—and 2d, his executive power and authority. So important was it considered to save the kingdom from the confusion into which it must be thrown by cutting off the life of the first magistrate, that it made the *intention* to kill the King equivalent to the *act* of killing him; guarding the pre-eminent life of the sovereign by sanctions superior to the ordinary laws, which guarded even the state itself; and therefore, though a compassing the death of the King, Queen or Prince, was made High Treason, without the accomplishment of the purpose, yet a compassing to murder the Chancellor and Judges, whose lives, as the King's representatives, were also guarded by the statute, was not made treason. To compass their deaths, when sitting in judgment, was not made equivalent to the act of killing them; no, nor even the *compassing* to subvert the King's political authority by war and rebellion. The statute not having substituted the *intention* for the *act* in that branch, leaving the security of the King's natural person and life, and that of his Queen and Prince, the only exceptions to the ordinary rules of judgment and law. In order to prevent arbitrary constructions of this severe but arbitrary law, and to guard the subject from the uncertainty of judicial constructions of treason, it cautiously sought for an expression well known and understood in the ancient law, viz. *compassing the death*—the words are, " when a man doth compass or imagine the death of our Lord the King."

Mr. Erskine said, as he wished cautiously in this part of his address to avoid every observation or opinion of his own, he would resort to the explanation of this expression by the celebrated Judge Forster. " The antient writers, (says Forster) in treating of felonious homicides, considered the felonious intention, manifested by plain fact, in the same light, in point of guilt, as homicide itself. The rule was, *voluntas reputatur pro facto*, and while this rule prevailed, the nature of the offence was expressed by the term *compassing the death*. This rule has been long laid aside as too rigorous in the case of common persons; but in the case of the King, Queen, and Prince, the statute of treason has with great propriety retained it in it's full extent and rigour, and in describing the offence has likewise retained the antient mode of expression. When a man doth compass or imagine the death of our Lord the King, &c. and thereof be upon sufficient proof

provablement

provablement attainted of open deed by people of his condition, the words of the statute descriptive of the offence, must therefore be strictly pursued in every indictment for this species of Treason; it must charge that the Defendant did traitorously compass and imagine the King's death, and then go on and charge the several acts made use of by the Prisoner to effectuate his traitorous purpose, for the compassing the King's death is the Treason, and the overt acts as the means made use of to effectuate the intentions and imaginations of the heart, and, therefore, in the case of the regicides, the indictment charged that they did traitorously compass and imagine the death of the King, and the cutting off the head was laid as the overt act, and the person who was supposed to have given the mortal stroke was convicted on the same indictment." This instance of the regicides, selected by Forster to illustrate that the traitorous purpose was the crime, was very striking and remarkable. Although the King was actually put to death, the homicide was not charged, but the traitorous purpose; and the then Chief Baron, in his speech to the Grand Jury, said, " These persons are to be proceeded with according to the laws of the land, and I shall speak nothing to you but what are the words of the law. By the statute of Edw. III. it is made High Treason to compass and imagine the death of the King. In no case else, imagination or compassing, without an actual effect, is punishable by law."—He then speaks of the sacred life of the King, and speaking of the Treason says, " The Treason consists in the wicked imagination, which is not apparent. But when this poison swells out of the heart and breaks forth into action, in that case it is High Treason. Then what is an overt act of an imagination or compassing the King's death? truly it is any thing which shews what the imagination of the heart is." After shewing that the noble and sublime spirit of humanity, which pervades and supports the whole system of our jurisprudence, ever awake to interfere in protection of our imperfect natures, would not suffer the ancient law, with respect to private persons, to remain, he said, that for ages past the death of the private man had been held necessary to the completion of the felony; but as Forster truly observed in the passage he had just read, this rule, too rigorous in the case of the subject, the statute of Treason retained in the case of the King, and retained also the very expression. The Sovereign's life was made to remain an exception, and the *voluntas pro facto*, the will for the deed, remained the rule; and therefore, said Forster, the statute meaning to retain the law, which was before general, retained the expression. The statute did not, in it's first branch, make a new law in it's principle or expression, but retained the old one applicable to subjects. It followed inevitably from
thence,

thence, that within the letter and meaning of the statute nothing could be a compassing of the death of the King, that would not, in ancient times, have been felony in the case of a subject. The opinion of Judge Forster was confirmed by that of Lord Coke, by that great prerogative lawyer, whose infamous prostitution in the case of Lord Strafford would tarnish his name to all posterity; but still his opinions, as a critic and a commentator, made him a proper authority for him to use. Lord Coke, in his Commentary upon the words of the statute, which he did with that precision and technical nicety which, though not calculated to please the ear, were so valuable in a book of science, when he comes to the words " doth compass," says, " Let us see first what the compassing of the death of a subject was before the making of this statute, when *voluntas reputabatur pro facto*." Thus falling in with the opinion of Judge Forster.

He then stated Lord Coke's definition of the expression of common law, which went to shew that the compassing the death of the King, not only by the plain common sense of the expression, but by looking back to the common law, from whence, for centuries back, the expression was admitted to have been borrowed; it was clear that a probable speculative consequence must not be confounded with an intention, since the overt act must be laid directly to shew the traitorous purpose of the heart. Notwithstanding the benevolent precision of this statute, it was lamentable to see the departures from it, which mark and disfigure our history; but, at the same time, it should be a theme of consolation to Englishmen to reflect, that as often as in arbitrary and wicked times, it was invaded by Parliaments and Judges, the justice of better Judges and better Parliaments brought the law back to the ancient standard; these invading statutes and judgments, and their repeals, were indeed decisive of the true construction of the statute. The statute of the 25th Edw. III. had expresly directed that nothing should be declared to be Treasons, but cases within it's enacting letter; yet Lord Hale says, " that things were so carried by parties and factions in the succeeding reign of Richard II. that the statute was but little observed. But as this or that party got the better, so the crime of High Treason was in a manner arbitrarily imposed or adjudged, which by various vicissitudes and revolutions mischiefed all parties first and last, and left a great unsettledness and unquietness in the minds of the people, and was one of the occasions of the unhappiness of the King." Mr. Erskine shewed, in order, the various statutes which had altered and impaired the statute of Edw. III. The statute of the 21st of Richard II. which Lord Hale says " was a snare for the people, insomuch that the statute of the 1st Henry IV.

IV. which repealed it, recited that no man knew how he ought to behave himself, to do, speak, or say, for doubt of such pains of Treason, and therefore wholly to remove the prejudice which might come to the King's subjects, the statute 1st Henry IV. chap. x. was made, which brought back Treason to the standard of the 25th of Edward III." Now what did this statute of Richard II. which produced so much mischief? It only went beyond the statute of Edward III. by the loose construction of compassing to depose the King, and raising people, and riding to make war. Levying force to imprison or depose the King, was already and properly Treason; but this statute of Richard II. enlarged only the crime of compassing; making it extend to a compassing to imprison or depose, and making that equal to an actual levying of war; and this extension was reprobated, stigmatized, and repealed by the statute of 1st of Henry IV. and "so little effect," says Mr. Justice Blackstone, "have over-violent laws to prevent any crime, that within two years after this new law of Treason respecting imprisonment and deposing, this very Prince was both deposed and murdered." And thus were swept away at once the whole load of frivolous, extravagant, and ridiculous treasons, by which the subject was harrassed in the execution of justice, by venal wretches, of whom it might be said, in the words of the satirist, that you

Destroy his fib and sophistry in vain—
The creature's at his dirty work again.

Mr. Erskine then went on to the next departure of the statute in the 1st and 2d of Philip and Mary, which made a compassing to levy war, if manifested by printing, writing, or overt act, High Treason. This shewed that a compassing to levy war was not considered to have been treason within the Act of Edw. III. which required an actual levying of war. If compassing to levy war had been considered as compassing of the King's death, it would have been unnecessary to declare it treason by this act. The first branch of the statute of Edward III. made it High Treason to compass or imagine the King's death; but the second branch of the statute required an actual levying of war necessary to constitute treason. The law made the natural life of the King so much more sacred than his executive authority, that to imagine his death was treason, but there must be a positive attack made upon his executive authority by the levying of war, to constitute the other. What was it that was meant to be restored by the statute of the 1st of Mary? The letter of the 25th of Edward III. or the judicial construction of it? Clearly it was the letter that was to be restored. He wished nothing to be taken, he said, from any unauthorised opinion of his own; but he wished to

bottom

bottom himself upon the authority of the great Judges whose opinions had been pressed erroneously into the service against them. He said erroneously, because it would be seen that their declarations were reconcileable. The writings of those great Judges were thickly sown with warnings to Judges to avoid constructive treason. Lord Coke says, that " the statute of the 1st of Mary speaks a strong language against constructive treasons, when it says, it was declared by the whole Parliament, that laws justly made for the preservation of the whole common-wealth, without extreme punishment, are more often obeyed and kept, than laws and statutes made with great and extreme punishments, and in special laws and statutes so made, whereby not only the ignorant and rude unlearned people, but also learned and expert men minding honesty, are oftentimes snapped and snared."

" There must be a compassing or imagination—for an act done *per infortunium*, without *compassing, intent*, or *imagination*, is not within this act, as it appeareth by the express words thereof.

Et actus non facit reum nisi mens sit rea.

" This compassing, intent, or imagination, though secret, is to be tried by the Peers, and to be discovered by circumstances, precedent, concomitant and subsequent." The Lord Justice of Scotland, said Mr. Erskine, differed from this statute in what he said at Perth, " that very honest men were guilty of Treason without knowing it." In this statute of Mary, Lord Coke goes on to say that two things are to be observed, 1. That the word expressed in the statute of Mary excludes all implications or inferences whatsoever. 2. That no former attainder, judgment, &c. &c. other than such as are specified and expressed in the statute of Edward III. are to be followed or drawn into example, for the words be plain and direct. And further, on commenting on the word *proveablement*, he says, " In this branch, it is to be observed, the word proveablement, *proveably*, i. e. upon direct and manifest proof, not upon conjectural presumptions, or inferences, or strains of wit, but upon good and sufficient proof; and herein the adverb *proveably* hath a great force, and signifieth a *direct plain proof*, which word the Lords and Commons in Parliament did use, for that the offence of Treason was so heinous, and so heavily and severely punished, as none other the like; and therefore the offender must be *proveably* attainted, which words are as forcible as upon direct and manifest proof. Note, the word is not *probably*, for then *commune argumentum* (a common argument) might have served, but the word is proveably be attainted." Nothing could be so curiously and even tautologously laboured, as this commentary of Lord Coke upon this

single

single word in the statute; which manifestly shews that so far from it's being the spirit and principle of the law of England, to adopt rules of construction, and proof unusual in trials for other crimes, that on the contrary, the legislature did not even leave it to the Judges to apply the ordinary rules of legal proof to trials under it, but admonished them to do justice in that respect in the very body of the statute. Lord Hale's words were equally striking. He brings forward instances to shew "how necessary it was that there should be some known, fixed, settled, boundary for this great crime of treason, and of what great importance the statute of the 25th of Edward III. was in order to that end; how dangerous it was to depart from the letter of that statute, and to multiply and enhance crimes into treason by ambiguous and general words, such as accroaching royal power, subverting fundamental laws, and the like; how dangerous it was by construction and analogy to make treasons, when the letter of the law has not done it, for such a method admits of no limits or bounds, but runs as far and as wide as the wit and invention of accusers, and the detestation of persons accused, will carry men." Surely the admonition of this supreminent Judge, ought to sink deep into the heart of every Judge, and of every Jury who were called to administer justice, under an accusation upon this statute. The great man seems to have had a bird's eye of the present trial; he seems to have anticipated the horrors of such a confused, heterogeneous mass of papers as were now brought before a Jury; where no specific overt-act directly expressive of an intention to compass the King's death was laid, no precise point of a man's life specified—but where four days had been necessary to the mere accumulation of the mass—where a speech of nine hours was required to explain the charge—and a whole life of treasons was to be collected from inferences, speculations, and tendencies, that no man could touch with his understanding, nor treasure in his memory.

The words of Mr. Justice Forster in his discourse upon treason were no less emphatical. After commenting upon writings and words when used as evidence of treason, he says, "I have considered the question of words and writings supposed to be treason the more largely, not only because of the diversity of opinions concerning it, but likewise for the great importance of the point, and the extreme danger of multiplying treasons upon slight occasions."

The next and the great question to be considered was, how the doctrines of these great lawyers who had, thus inveighed against constructive treasons were reconcileable with the positions to be

* X found

found in their works, which had been cited and relied on by the Attorney General. In order to difcufs the matter with precifion, they muft advert to the language of the paffages cited, in doing which they would find that none of thefe great authors had faid, that compaffing to change the laws by force, was treafon in the abftract, or that even compaffing to levy war againft the King was treafon in the abftract; or that compaffing to imprifon the King, until he yielded to particular demands, was treafon in the abftract; but only that any of thefe acts might be laid as overt-acts of compaffing the King's death; that they were acts that might be legally fubmitted to the Jury, as the means made ufe of to effectuate the purpofe charged in the indictment, viz. the compaffing the death of the King, and might therefore be legally charged upon the record, as overt-acts of that treafon: the ftatute required that the compaffing the death, which was the crime, fhould be manifefted by overt-act; the overt-act, therefore, muft be laid in the indictment. What might be an overt-act was matter of law for the Judges, but whether, when fo laid, it was fufficient to eftablifh the traitorous purpofe, was matter of fact for the Jury.

This diftinction was not peculiar to treafon, but pervaded the whole law of England. What facts were evidence from whence any matter in iffue might be legitimately inferred, was matter of law; but whether any given facts, which were legally relevant to prove the matter which they were adduced to eftablifh, were fufficient in any particular inftance, depended upon the conclufion which the Jury fhould draw from the facts fimply, or from the whole evidence upon the trial of the iffue. Mr. Erfkine illuftrated this by a recent cafe, relative to bills of exchange, which came before the Houfe of Lords. When the queftion was agitated in the fhape of a demurrer to evidence, it was decided by the Houfe of Lords, that the conclufion to be drawn from relevant and admiffible evidence, to prove any matter in iffue criminal or civil, could not, by demurrer to evidence, or by any other procefs, be withdrawn from a Jury to the Judges; the province of the Judges being to judge of the law, and confequently of the irrelevancy and inadmiffibility of evidence as a branch of law, but that it belonged to the Jury alone in each particular cafe to draw the particular conclufions from relevant and admiffible evidence. This diftinction would at once explain all the feeming contradiction in the books concerning overt-acts of treafon; particularly in the treafon of compaffing the King's death. The charge of compaffing being a charge of intention, which, without a manifeftation by conduct, no human tribunal could try; the ftatute required that the intention

tion to cut off the Sovereign should be manifested by overt-acts, and as a prisoner charged with an intention could have no means of knowing how to defend himself, when an intention was the crime, without notice of the facts from whence such intention was to be imputed to him, it was the practice to state, upon the face of the indictment, the overt-act, as the means taken to effectuate his purpose; and by the statute 7th William III. no evidence shall be admitted or given of any overt-act, that was not expressly laid in the indictment. In order to confirm these doctrines, he would make his appeal to every record and authority in the law of England. In the first place, so far were the overt-act of compassing to depose, for compassing to imprison, or compassing to change the laws by force or intimidation, or any other compassing short of the direct compassing the death of the King, capable of being made High Treason, that the indictment must charge that the prisoner did traitorously compass the death of the King; and the overt-act can be put upon the record in no other way than as the means by which the existence of that traitorous pupose was to be put for the consideration of the Jury. He quoted Lord Coke in his 3d Institute, 11 and 12, to prove that this was his opinion. The contemplation, purpose, and contrivance must be found to exist, without which, says Lord Coke, there can be no compassing. Lord Coke's doctrine was so implicitly followed by Lord Hale and Forster, as far as related to this part of the subject, that it was almost unnecessary to advert to their works, but as he wished to stand upon authority in every stage, he would refer to them.

He then quoted from Lord Hale's P. C. page 107, stating that the overt-act must be laid down so far as to enable the imagining to be brought to trial by human judicatures. As long as the English Constitution preserved to a Jury the legal cognizance of facts, we had the best security for the preservation of the subject. There was a misconception in this particular, that produced the innumerable controversies upon the Trial of Libels, and which were at last happily quietted by the late Act of Parliament. But in the case of a libel it must be allowed there was some plausibility, in the judicial usurpation, whereas applied to Treason there was none. In the case of Treason, the purpose of the mind was, the crime charged; the overt act was only alledged to be an act done in pursuance of that intention; which made it shocking alike to common sense and to conscience to say, that because the Jury gave credit to the overt act as a matter of history, that they must therefore find the traitorous purpose.

He then enumerated Lord Hale's inflances, which had been held to be fufficient overt acts of compaffing. "When men confpire the death of the King and thereupon provide weapons, &c. or fend letters for the execution thereof, this is an overt act within the ftatute. If men confpire to imprifon the King by force and a ftrong hand, until he has yielded to certain demands, and for that purpofe gather company, or write letters, that is an overt act to prove the compaffing the King's death, as was held in Lord Cobham's cafe by all the Judges." In this fentence Lord Hale did not depart from that precifion which fo eminently diftinguifhes all his writings; he did not fay that if men confpire to imprifon the King, that was High Treafon; no, nor even an overt act of High Treafon; but to prevent the poffibility of confounding the Treafon with matter which might be legally charged as relevant, he faid, this is an overt act, to prove the compaffing the King's death, and as if by this mode of expreffion he had not done enough to keep the idea afunder, and from abundant regard for the rights and liberties of the fubject, he immediately adds, " But then there muft be an overt act to prove that confpiracy, and then that overt act to prove fuch defign is an overt-act to prove the compaffing of the death of the King." The language of the fentence laboured on the ear from the exceffive caution of the writer; afraid that his readers fhould jump too faft to the conclufion, upon a fubject of fuch awful moment, he pulls him back after he has read that a confpiracy to imprifon the King is an overt act, to prove the compaffing his death, and fays to him, " But recollect that there muft be an overt act to prove in the firft place the confpiracy to imprifon the King, and even then that propofition, that intention to imprifon fo manifefted, by the overt act, is but in it's turn an overt act to prove the compaffing or intention to deftroy the King." He fays too, the detention muft be forcible, and he proceeds to reprobate a conftructive compulfion upon the King independently of actual reftraint. Lord Hale goes on to diftinguifh, between a conftructive levying of war againft the King's Executive Authority from confpiracies to levy war upon his perfon; and declares that though it might be *prima facia* good upon an indictment when barely laid as a levying war againft the King, yet it would fail when it appeared in evidence to be no more than a levying war by conftruction and interpretation. The mind of the Prifoner, which it was the object of the trial to lay open would be fhut and concealed from the Jury, whenever

ever the death of the Sovereign was fought by circuitous means, instead of a direct and murderous machination. It was curious to compare Lord Coke's speech to the Jury as Attorney General against Lord Essex, with the writings which he had left as monuments to posterity of the law upon this momentous subject. But it was loss of time to consider the argument of an Attorney General, who could so dishonour himself and degrade his profession, as Lord Coke, to his eternal infamy, did in the case of Sir Walter Raleigh. His Honourable and Learned Friend, the present Attorney General, would, by his candid proceeding in the opening of this cause, go down to posterity with a purer character, though he might not have written so many books as this great, base, and degraded man. It was fit, nevertheless, for the present argument to observe, that in the case of Lord Essex, Lord Coke expressly treated High Treason as a crime of intention. What was the rule with regard to penal statutes of every description? The rule notoriously was to adhere rigidly to the letter. Judge Forster says it may be laid down as a general rule that indictments grounded on penal statutes, especially the most penal, must pursue the statute so as to bring the party precisely within it. It was needless to say that if the benignity of the law required this precision in the indictment, the proof must be correspondingly precise; for otherwise the subject would derive no benefit from the strictness of the indictment. If a defendant could be convicted by evidence amounting to a breach of the real or supposed spirit of the statute only, then the strictness of the indictment would be no protection of the Prisoner, but would be a direct violation of the first principles of criminal and civil justice. He illustrated this by referring to many different cases. In Mary Mitchell's case, Judge Forster says, " Although a case is brought within the *reason* of a penal statute, and within the mischief to be prevented, yet if it does not come within the unequivocal letter, the benignity of the law interferes." He referred also to Gibbon's case, and those of John Howard and John Bell, for illustrations of the same doctrine.

Having maintained the argument by the letter of the statute itself, the authoritative writings whose works were for ever referred to by the officers of the Crown in state prosecutions, the next stage in the argument was to examine whether these authorities had been acted upon. He meant to maintain that in every case which was considered as a precedent, the same construction had been put upon an overt-act, and that no overt-acts had been regarded but such as went directly and not constructively as an attack on the person of the King. The first cases that deserved attention after England had her present Constitution, were the trials on the assassination plot against King William. The trials of Sir John Frend, Sir William Parkyns, and others, before Lord Chief Justice Holt; nothing in these trials went against the principles which he had been endeavouring to establish. The charges against Sir John Frend were unequivocal; the overt-acts relied on were, sending Mr. Charnock into France

France to King James, to desire him to persuade the French King, to send forces over to Great Britain, to levy war and depose King William. The next overt-act was—preparing men to be levied, to form a corps to assist in the restoration of the Pretender, and the expulsion of King William, of which Sir John Frend was to be Colonel. In this case the proof was either to be wholly discredited, or it went directly home to a legal overt-act of the compassing the death of the King upon the principles which he had laid down. It was not a speculative tendency to his death, but was a consequence so direct and immediate, that he who pursued the act, might be justly convicted of the intention, for if the plot had succeeded, and James had been restored, King William must have been necessarily attainted and executed by the forms of English law. Observing in the gestures of the Counsel for the Crown, their hesitation as to this proposition, he repeated the fact, and said, that indisputably the restored King might, and inevitably must have brought King William as an usurper before a Tribunal like the present, either at the Old Bailey, or wherever else it should have been appointed. No man who engaged in that plot could be reasonably supposed not to have foreseen, and to have intended the King's death. Lord Holt's summing up did not go beyond this admitted principle. " The Treason," said he, " that is mentioned in the indictment, is conspiring, compassing and imagining the death of the King. To prove the conspiracy and design of the King's death, two principal overt-acts are insisted on." He did not consider the overt-act of conspiracy to be the Treason, but evidence to prove the compassing. He then sums up the evidence for and against the Prisoner, and leaves the intention to the Jury as matter of fact. Afterwards he comes to answer the Prisoner's objection in point of law. " There is another thing," said Lord Chief Justice Holt, " he did insist upon. The statute of Edward III. contains divers species of Treason. One is compassing and imagining the death of the King; another is the levying war: Now," says he, (Frend), " here is no war actually levied, and a bare conspiracy to levy war does not come within the law against Treasons," To pause here a little, said Mr. Erskine, Frend's argument was this :—Whatever my intention might be; whatever my object by levying war might have been; whatever my design; however the destruction of the King might have been effected by my conspiracy if it had gone on; and however it might have been my intention that it should, it is not Treason within the 25th of Edward III. To which Lord Holt's reply was;—" If there be only a conspiracy to levy war, it is not Treason; it is only a substantive Treason; it is not Treason in the abstract; but if the design and conspiracy be either to kill the King, or to depose him or imprison him, or put any force or personal restraint upon him by force; and the way of effecting these purposes is, by levying a war, there the conspiracy and consultation to levy war for that purpose is High Treason, though no war be levied; for such consultation and

conspiracy

conspiracy is an overt-act proving the compassing the death of the King." If Holt had meant to lay down that such a conspiracy to levy war in order to depose the King, without the further intention to kill him, was in itself High Treason, he would have stopped here; but that great lawyer went on to qualify his proposition by saying, that such conspiracy was an overt-act proving the compassing; that is, a conspiracy to depose the King was evidence of an intention to destroy his life. He then goes on:—" There may be a war levied without any design upon the King's person, which if actually levied is High Treason, though purposing and designing such a levying of war is not so." Thus, as for example, if persons do assemble themselves to act with force in opposition to some law, and hope thereby to get it repealed, this is a levying war and treason, though the purposing and designing is not so—So when they endeavour in great numbers, with great force, to make reformation of their own heads without pursuing the methods of the law, that is a levying war, but the purpose and designing is not so; so that the objection he makes is of no force. Here again we have a prophetic glance at the present trial: for the whole volume before the Jury went to no more than to accuse them of the design of making reformation of their own heads, and he concludes by again leaving the matter to the Jury. Lord Holt, therefore, in this Address to the Jury, did not say that if a man conspired to do an act which act might produce a given consequence, and which consequence, again building construction on construction, and consequence on consequence, might lead to the King's death—was an overt-act of compassing. But he put the conspiracy directly, with reference to the point before him, as an immediate and direct conspiracy to depose the King, and to set up another. Compare this doctrine with the case before us. Let the Jury but turn their eyes to the mass on the table of the Court. He did not mean to accuse the law officers of the Crown, but let them reflect on the sort of circumstances that had been amassed and brought together in order to affect the Prisoner at the bar. Could any man, whatever had been his attention—whatever were his powers of discrimination, he defied him to develope the intention, gilt and end of the heap before him. There was consequence added to consequence—there was speculation upon speculation—the Prisoner was to be led from this to that—the desire of enlightening his fellow citizens was to produce a desire of reform of certain grievances—the desire of reform was to lead them to Republicanism—this was to lead them to arming and violence—and in some future time, this was to produce a change in the frame of our Government, and this change was to affect the King's dignity, and finally this was to be taken as an overt-act of compassing his death.—If it were not unfit to introduce any thing ludicrous upon so solemn an occasion, he should say that all this reminded him of the story in every child's gilt book, of " Here was the bull, that tossed the dog, that worried the cat, and so on, 'till you get to the house that Jack built.

built.—Good God! in this land of security and justice, were the lives of men to be put upon such hazards? Was it in England—was it in the year 1794, that such a trial was brought into a Court of Criminal Justice?—He knew that he might stop even here, and leave the life of the prisoner confidently to the sense and conscience of the Jury, for he had marked their unwearied attention, their discriminating judgment, and he would so leave the case, if he were not anxious for the prisoner's honour, as well as his life. Let them try him by this doctrine of Lord Holt: He told the Jury, in answer to a legal objection from the prisoner, that a conspiracy to levy war was not treason, but that a conspiracy to levy it, for the purpose charged in the indictment, was an overt-act, and it certainly was relevant evidence to prove the intention; for if the conspiracy was palpable and direct to dethrone King William, the design of King William's death was an inference not of law from the act, but of reason and fact. Frend might have said that the intention was to send King William back to Holland, to resume his station of Stadtholder, but who would have believed him? If the fact was proved that he intended to depose the King, and inrroduce King James, they must have found the compassing of his death as an inference. The other cases of Parkyns, Layer, &c. he did not enumerate, though they all served to confirm his doctrine; but he had already so far exhausted himself, and had still so much to go through, that he must depart from his original intention of passing through all the cases *seriatim*.

He referred to the case of Lord George Gordon, and he should not be afraid of the Solicitor of the Treasury, if he were to act in this way. If he was to come to the House of Commons with ten thousand men, for the purpose of having a turnpike bill repealed, and they actually did nothing but appear there, that would not be Treason. He was now brought to that part of the speech of the Attorney General which referred to a more humble authority than any he had yet mentioned, he meant a part of his own speech on this trial, just mentioned,—that of Lord George Gordon: The Attorney General had stated Mr. Erskine's own proposition on that part of that trial, as if it was against the prisoner at the Bar in the present case; it should be remembered that Lord George Gordon was not indicted for compassing the death of the King, and Lord Mansfield said so on the trial, in which Mr. Justice Buller concurred, that the record on that trial, did not contain a charge against the defendant for compassing the death of the King—Lord Mansfield told the Jury upon that trial.

" The Prisoner at the bar is indicted for that species of High Treason, which is called levying war against the King, and therefore it is necessary you should first be informed what is in law a levying war against the King, so as to constitute the crime of High Treason, within the statute of Edward III.; and perhaps according to the legal signification of the term before that statute. There were two kinds of levying war:—One

against

against the person of the King, to imprison, to dethrone, or to kill him, or to make him change measures, or remove Counsellors: —the other, which is said to be *levied against the Majesty of the King*, or, in other words, against him in his regal capacity. In the present case, it does not rest upon an implication that they hoped by opposition to a law to get it repealed, but the prosecution proceeds upon the direct ground, that the object was by force and violence, to compel the legislature to repeal a law; and therefore, without any doubt I tell you the joint opinion of us all, that, if this multitude assembled with intent, by acts of force and violence, to compel the legislature to repeal a law, it is High Treason."

Such were the words of the venerable Earl of Mansfield on that trial. Now he would take the liberty, as the Attorney General had alluded to it, of quoting his own words upon the same trial. This was the sentence alluded to by the Attorney General:

" *To encompass or imagine the death of the King*, such imagination, or purpose of the mind, visible only to its great author, being manifested by some open act; an institution obviously directed, not only to the security of his natural person, but to the stability of the government; the life of the Prince being so interwoven with the Constitution of the state, that an attempt to destroy the one, is justly held to be a rebellious conspiracy against the other."

This was true, the destruction of the King lead to the destruction of the State; but did the converse of this doctrine follow of course, as the Attorney General seemed to insist upon? That to compass or intend any alteration in the other branches of the Legislature was compassing the King's death. The charge of compassing or imagining the death of the King was the inference of reason from overt-acts; but did it ever enter into the mind of man, that the intention was matter of law? Certainly not, for it was a fact to be determined by a Jury, and by them only; it was the inference of their reason from the facts, and not the inference of law.

What the fate of the Prisoner would be, Mr. Erskine said, he knew not; he was confident in leaving it to men of honour, diligence and attention, who would be guided by the evidence under the rule of the law, which governed this case, of real evidence in the cause. What they had heard of in the proceeding of the Secret Committees of the two Houses of Parliament, under Number A, or Number B, or Appendix C. and as to the evidence that was offered, he hardly knew where he stood when he examined it in a court of justice: One man heard another say something, but he took no notice of it, though employed as a spy for the purpose; another took some notes, but did not hear all that was said; a third heard something, somewhere of arms, and so on, but nothing of all this in the Prisoner's hearing. He would maintain, without fear of contradiction, that if any excess had been committed, the Spies of Government had proved that they provoked it all. Did he really believe that the Prisoner was guilty he would have taken a very
different

different course; but believing him to be really innocent, he would defend him to the utmost of his power.

The Societies and the Prisoner at the Bar, as a Member of one of them, were charged with having formed a plan to subvert the established Government of the Country, as the means of carrying into effect their traiterous purpose against the Life of the King. The charge was not, that they had conspired to assemble the Convention which met at Edinburgh, but that they had conspired to assemble another Convention which never did meet. All the extraordinary evidence they had heard, and the most extraordinary the greater part of was ever heard in a Court of Justice, went to prove the intention with which this second Convention was to be held. Whether a Reform of Parliament was a measure likely to produce all the good that some expected from it, or all the mischief that others apprehended, the discussion was, in the case of his Client, neither necessary nor proper. It was sufficient to examine whether all that had been said, or written, or printed, in the proceedings of the Societies, on the necessity of Reform, for every article of whose conduct the Prisoner, in the idea of his Prosecutors ought to be amenable, was said *bona fide*, with honest intention, and in the sincere belief of its being true, or resorted to as a mere stalking horse, behind which to prepare the shafts of treason, and take aim at the life of the King. He was ready to confess that, if the same defects in the Representation of the People in Parliament had not been noticed in any former period, had never occurred to persons in much higher stations, and, as far as motives of self-interest could attach men to any system, to persons who had a much more important stake in the Constitution of the Country, he might have been led to suspect that the intention of these Societies was not exactly what they professed. Happily, however, this was not the case. That the Representation of the People in Parliament was defective, that many and great abuses had crept into it, and that the health and longevity of the Constitution depended upon the correction of those abuses, was a doctrine supported by many and high authorities. On maintaining this doctrine, the great Lord Chatham built the fame and glory of his life, and bequeathed it to his son, who raised upon it his own fame and fortune. If the Counsel for the prosecution had chosen to carry their evidence so far back, they would have found that the Society for Constitutional Information, owed its birth to Mr. Pitt and the Duke of Richmond, whose plan of Parliamentary Reform was Universal Suffrage and Annual Elections: and although he thought, with those whose political opinions he had been accustomed to consider with more respect, that this would not be an improvement, yet he could not imagine that they, who originally promulgated or strenuously supported it, had in contemplation the subversion of the Government, much less were compassing the Death of the King. The Duke of Richmond was a man of great fortune, of the highest rank, and it was not to be imagined

gined, that by contending for Universal Suffrage and Annual Election, he meant to subvert the Government, and strip himself of his own honours. The Duke of Richmond was not only a man of high rank, but well known to be a man of extensive reading and deep reflection. The plan he proposed as the only adequate plan for the Reform of Parliament, was not the offspring of rashness or folly, but of information and reflection. The Duke of Richmond said what he (Mr. Erskine) should be ready on all occasions to say—and he cared not how many of such miserable spies as had been brought forward to give evidence on this trial, were present to take down his words, or, as was more commonly their practice, to report what they thought fit to understand by his words, without taking them down—that if the representation of the People in Parliament was not reformed, if the abuses that had crept into it were not corrected, abuse accumulating upon abuse, must inevitably lead to a Revolution. The Duke of Richmond published his plan in 1782. The plan was addressed to Colonel Sharman, and proposed appointing Delegates by Assemblies of the People, no matter whether styled Constitutional or Corresponding, or any other Societies, to meet in a general Convention. The terms, Delegates and Convention were therefore, no new inventions, no imitations of a French Model, but the natural growth of our own soil. When the Convention met at Edinburgh, although many imprudent speeches were made in it, speeches which he had no inclination, and which the defence of his Client certainly did not call upon him to justify, the declared intention of those who composed it, was to obtain what they, following high, and unsuspecting authorities, were taught to believe the unalienable Right of the People. A free and fair Representation in the Commons House of Parliament was the unalienable Right of the People. He did not mean to state this as a right to be recognised in a Court of justice, in opposition to positive law, by which Courts of Justice could alone be guided; but as a right not of new imagination, sanctioned by the most unimpeachable authorities, and in prosecuting which by legal means no man incurred either guilt or censure. On this right was founded the right of his Majesty to the Throne, as he himself had maintained in Parliament, in opposition to the then newly adopted tenets of Mr. Burke—" Of Mr. Burke," said Mr. Erskine, " I speak not to blame. He possesses a mind enriched with the greatest variety of knowledge, the finest imagination, the most powerful and fascinating eloquence, the most extensive acquaintance with the history of the British Constitution. He is now suffering under a domestic misfortune, which every man who sympathizes in the feelings of another, must deplore. I allude not to his change of political opinion as a fault: that change, I think, is to be liberally interpreted. I speak not here to blame any man, I speak to recommend Charity among men, for the opinions of one another, to concilliate all hearts in favour of our common Country, and by a fair, clear and unprejudiced application of the Laws of that Country, to

induce

induce all to pursue the common interest, unterrified by armed Associations on the one hand, or Courts of Justice on the other." The Counsel for the Prosecution must prove the intention charged in the indictment, and that satisfactorily—not by proof of surmise and conjecture. To illustrate this he quoted the passage in Chief Justice Eyre's charge to the Grand Jury, " Whether this be a veil under which Treason is concealed, &c."—He had no doubt but that when this humane language was held, the Judge was unacquainted with the whole of the case; but it was sufficient to shew that on the surface of it his Client, and those with whom he was implicated, were not traitors. He next quoted a passage from Holt, importing that forced or strained constructions are not to be put upon men's words or actions, but that the intention of them is to be tried and made out by clear and palpable evidence. Now let the intentions of the Prisoner and his Associates be tried by this criterion. Were they the first to take up the doctrines now charged upon them as proofs of a treasonable purpose?

The first witness from Sheffield said that he acted upon these doctrines as the Duke of Richmond had done, whom he never imagined to have any intention of subverting the Government, or compassing the death of the King. He did not mean to say that one man's having committed a crime with impunity would justify another in committing a like offence; but that if one man had circulated particular opinions, without ever being accused or even suspected of evil intention, the circulation of the same opinions by other men was not to be held as evidence of evil intention. To whom did the Duke of Richmond transmit and recommend his plan? To Societies provided with half a dozen pikes? No; to Colonel Sharman, at the head of 10,000 men, armed and in military array: to men not commissioned by the King: to the Volunteers of Ireland, to whose exertions it was owing that his Majesty now enjoyed the Crown of Ireland. These men, so armed and arrayed, held a Convention, not secretly, but in the face of day. By the authority of the King? No. By the authority of the Lord Lieutenant? No. By the authority of circular Letters; and so far was this from being stigmatized as Treason, that their demands were complied with—wisely and properly complied with—for to grant the People their Rights was the surest way to harmonize their minds and attach their affections to the Government. Of all the Witnesses called on the part of the prosecution, was there a man, except the Spies, who said that their intention was any other than a Reform of Parliament by legal and Constitutional means? If the Spies were not to be believed, in contradiction to all the other Witnesses, the Court and the Jury were mis-spending their time; they might close the proceedings at once, and go home. All but the Spies said, that they would have renounced the Societies with indignation, if they had believed there was any intention of deposing or killing the King. How could the poor Prisoner at the Bar hate the King, from whom

it

it was impossible he could ever have received an injury? Was not the character of his Majesty such as to conciliate the love and affection of his subjects? Did he not confide so much in that affection as daily to ride abroad among them, without the parade of guards or attendants?—Where, then, was the ground of this black suspicion, as unworthy of the King, as unmerited by his People. The minds of the men who composed those obnoxious Societies were irritated into intemperance by the representations of those who were now his Majesty's Ministers, of the abuses flowing from the decay of Representation and the consequent corruption of Parliament; and, if the Prisoner at the Bar should be hanged, while the Duke of Richmond was called to a seat in the Cabinet, he should say—

"—————————— Plate sin with gold,
" And the strong lance of Justice hurtless breaks;
" Arm it in rags, a pigmy straw doth pierce it."

He should say, that, with respect to the protection of known law, we were in as bad a state as the People of France, where there was now no law: but there too, he had no doubt, the People would yet claim and obtain law, as the most valuable of their rights. In 1782, during the disastrous period of a War, pursued with as ill success as the principles upon which it was undertaken were bad; when increase of taxes and decline of commerce had generated discontent in every corner of the Country, and turned the minds of men to no mild scrutiny of the defects of Government, the Duke of Richmond's plan of Reform was published, and Conventions were held, which even arrogated the controul of the expenditure of public money, a function which had ever been understood to belong exclusively to Parliament. Here was a direct usurpation of the authority of Parliament which his Clients were charged only with intending.— " Let us hear," said Mr. Erskine, " Mr. Burke, on the nature and character of the House of Commons, not with regard to its legal form and power, but to its spirit, and to the purposes it is meant to answer in the Constitution. The House of Commons was supposed originally to be *no part of the standing Government of this Country*; but was considered as a *controul* issuing immediately from the people, and speedily to be resolved into the mass from whence it arose. In this respect it was in the higher part of Government what juries are in the lower. The capacity of a Magistrate being transitory, and that of a Citizen permanent.—(Citizen! It would be as dangerous now to mention the word *Citizen*, as to mention the word pikes.)—The latter capacity, it was hoped would of course preponderate in all discussions, not only between the people, and the fleeting authority of the House of Commons itself. It was It was hoped that being of a middle nature between subject and government, they would feel with a more tender and nearer interest, every thing that concerned the people, than the other remoter and more permanent parts of the legiflature. Whatever alteration time and the neceffary accommodation of bufinefs may have introduced, *this character can never be fuftained, unlefs the Houfe of Commons fhall be made to bear the ftamp of the actual difpofitions of the People at large.* It would (among public misfortunes) be an evil more natural and tolerable, that the Houfe of Commons fhould be infected with every epidemical phrenzy of the people, as this would indicate fome confanguinity, fome fympathy of nature with their conftituents, than that they fhould in all cafes be wholly untouched by the opinions and feelings of the people out of doors. *By this want of fympathy they would ceafe to be an Houfe of Commons."* Mr. Burke goes on to ftate, that " The virtue, fpirit, and effence of the Houfe of Commons confifts *in its being the exprefs image of the feelings of the nation.* It was not inftituted to be a controul *upon* the People, as of late it has been taught, by a doctrine of the moft pernicious tendency, but as a controul *for* the People." Thus we fee that the true intent of the Houfe of Commons is, not to act as a controul upon the People ; the King and the Houfe of Lords are the conftitutional controul, and the Commons the voice and organ of the People. But how are they this organ, if they are not chofen by the People, which they now notoriously are not. To be convinced of this, it is only neceffary to look at the Report of the Society of the Friends of the People, which they offered to fubftantiate by evidence at the Bar of the Houfe of Commons, and which to this hour ftands uncontroverted. Let us hear Mr. Burke on the Houfe of Commons as it is now conftituted. " An addreffing Houfe of Commons and a petitioning Nation; an Houfe of Commons full of confidence, when the nation is plunged in defpair; in the utmoft harmony with Minifters, whom the People regard with the utmoft abhorrence; who vote thanks, when the public opinion calls upon them for impeachments; who are eager to grant when the general voice demands account; *who in all difputes between the People and Adminiftration, prefume againft the People; who punifh their diforders, but refufe even to enquire into the provocations to them; this is an unnatural, a monftrous ftate of things in this Conftitution.*

" Such an Affembly may be a great, wife, awful Senate; but it is not to any popular purpofe an Houfe of Commons." This, he fays, in his Thoughts on the Caufe of the Prefent Difcontents, coolly, foberly and deliberately written during the American war; and the word *prefent* will as well apply to this time as to that. In another part of the fame publication he fays—" It muft always be the wifh of an unconftitutional Statefman, that an Houfe of Commons who are entirely dependent upon him, fhould have every Right of the People entirely dependent upon their pleafure. For it was foon difcovered that the forms of a free, and the ends of an arbitrary Government, were things not altogether incompatible.—The power of the Crown, almoft dead and rotten as Prerogative, has grown up a-new, with much more ftrength and far lefs odium,

under

under the name of Influence. An influence which operated without noise and violence; which converted the very antagonist into the instrument of power; which contained in itself a perpetual principle of growth and renovation: and which the distresses and the prosperity of the Country equally tended to augment, was an admirable substitute for a Prerogative, that being only the offspring of antiquated prejudices, had moulded in its original stamina irresistible principles of decay and dissolution."—" Parliament was indeed the great object of all these politics, the end at which they aimed, as well as the instrument by which they were to operate. But before Parliament could be made subservient to a system, by which it was to be degraded from the dignity of a national council, into a mere member of the Court, it must be greatly changed from its original character."—Remark that Mr. Burke here says, not the House of Commons, but Parliament. Who does this? Not a poor shoe-maker, like the Prisoner at the bar, but a Member of the House of Commons, a man well versed both in political and philological distinctions: yet it is evident that he means the House of Commons, and therefore it is an abuse of words to say that when the word Parliament occurs in the proceedings of the Societies, any thing is meant by it but the House of Commons. So far is the Prisoner from being conscious of evil intention, so far from imagining he is engaged in a conspiracy to subvert the Constitution, that he writes a letter to the most eminent and able defender of the Constitution, a Member of Parliament and a Privy Counsellor (Mr. Fox), desiring him to present the Petition of the Society to the House of Commons. The answer to that letter, although stating that Mr. Fox is an avowed enemy to Universal Suffrage, he preserves among his papers, and it has been read to you as evidence in support of the prosecution. He writes also to the Society of the Friends of the People, whose sole object he knows to be a Reform of the Representation in the Commons' House of Parliament. They also return an answer, never once suspecting that the object of the Corresponding Society is any thing but a Reform of Parliament, although they disapprove of their mode of pursuing that object. Then come the Crown Lawyers, and say, we understand better what is meant by these letters than those who write them, or those to whom they are written; you say they mean only Parliamentary Reform, we, the interpreters of your most secret thoughts, tell you that they mean subverting the whole frame of the Government, and destroying the King. Mr. Erskine again referred to a passage from Mr. Burke, importing that Ministers had made a lodgment in Parliament, that by laying hold of Parliament itself they had the power of obtaining their object in all cases, and upon all occasions. The proposition contained in this passage was unqualified; it was not restricted to this or that occasion, but extended to all occasions; it asserted that the controul of the people over the Executive Power was wholly and absolutely lost. Not so, said the Defendants; they said nothing was lost but the controul of the People in the House of Commons. Would any man stand up and say he disbelieved this?—If he did, nobody would believe him. The Counsel for the Prosecution contended, that to attack the Parliament was to attack the King, because the King was an essential part of Parliament. By no means.—Who, in talking of Parliament, in common acceptation, was supposed to mean the King? When these Societies attacked what they thought the abuses of Parliament, they meant what those who went before them had meant—the abuses in the representation, which might all be corrected without trenching in the least on the natural or political existence of the King. But, it was said, they talked of reforming Parliament by exciting the People.—Mr. Burke had said before them, that no remedy for the distemper of Parliament could be expected to be begun in Parliament; and that the People must be excited to meet in Counties and in Corporations, and make out, if they could, lists of those who voted, and on what side; in short, that, to obtain any correction of the abuses in the House of Commons, the impulse must come from the People. After a petition for Reform, in 1780, had been rejected, the Duke of Richmond wrote in a manner much stronger than those who were now accused of conspiring to lay hold of the Parliament by violence—He wrote, that the less Reform had been tried and failed; that not one proselyte had been gained; that the weight of corruption was such as to bear down every thing; that he had no hopes of Reform from the House of Commons; that Reform must come from the People themselves; and that they ought to meet more numerously than ever to claim their undeniable rights, Universal Sufferage and Annual Elections. How were the People to assert these rights after Parliament had refused to grant them? In this manner, the persons now under prosecution had done, and professed to do—not by rebellion, but by collecting and bringing before Parliament, the weight and influence of collective opinion. It was said that this war against the State had amounted to Rebellion—The assertion was unfounded—What was the State? The State was the Body of the People, with their Sovereign at their head; nothing was Rebellion that had not for its object the destruction or enslaving of the People and their Sovereign so connected, and he trusted he should never hear again that the People all meeting, must mean to depose the King—that the King stood only supported by the few who called themselves the King's friends, and branded all others with the name of Democrats, or Jacobins, or whatever else was the nickname of the day. It was clear from the beginning to the end, that the Societies with which the Prisoner was connected spoke only of the Representation in the House of Commons; and he would maintain as they did, that they had a right to do so; and he knew that if the People were so met, they would be for the continuance of the Crown. It was their inheritance—what a dangerous principle it would be for to lay down, that if the People were collected together, the necessary consequence must be the destruction of the King? The King's protection stood on the love of the People collectively, not on the adherence of

this

this or that description of men, and to say otherwise was a libel both on King and People. He was sorry to hear any man called a traitor for talking of the Rights of Man. The Duke of Richmond had long since said that they were the foundation of all legitimate government. Because men professing, but abusing the same sentiments, had destroyed every thing in France, it ought not to be fastened upon the Prisoner, that he, professing to claim the Rights of Man, meant also to destroy every thing in England. Before going into the Duke of Richmond's definition of the Rights of Man, he would mention one more in his recollection, because it arose out of a discussion, in which it was his fortune to bear a part. In the debates upon the memorable India Bill, one of the most popular topics of declamation against it was, its being an attack upon the chartered Rights of Men. Mr. Burke took fire at the expression. He said he did not know what was meant by the chartered Rights of Men. He feared there was something in this more than was indicated by the affectation of the phrase. For what end, but the end of the moment, was the word *chartered* introduced, for the Rights of Mankind were founded in nature, and needed no charter to give them sanction. Chartered Rights he had always understood to be matter of compact, and to be forfeited by breach of compact; but the natural Rights of Man were sacred, and could neither be lawfully forfeited nor infringed. Let those who call themselves the champions of the authority of the Crown, take care that they do not pull down what they profess to support. Let them beware of weakening his Majesty's Rights, by the very means they adopted to confirm them. The ancient Kings of this country abused their government by cruel and infamous trials, by more cruel and infamous punishment, by packing Juries, by arbitrary imprisonments, by scandalous abuse of law, by depriving the People of arms; thus not only their Government but their persons became odious; they dreaded to assemble the People; and when King William issued his writs calling the People to meet, they did not meet; but had they met, the general consent of the people would have been given to his accession. He recognized their rights under a Law which all knew and all revered—the Bill of Rights—Rights which they always had; and here began the mischief in consequence of which the Court was now sitting. The denial of that proposition brought Mr. Paine into this country. But for this denial Mr. Paine never would have been an author amongst us. Why came Mr. Paine here as an author? To answer Mr. Burke, who denied the King's right to the Throne by denying the right of the People to alter the succession. The French had pulled down a system of corruption and tyranny, so enfeebled by its own inherent defects, that it was ready to fall of its own accord. Mr. Burke denied their right to do this. Mr Paine wrote an answer, and as a Republican, threw in much stuff about Monarchy, which had nothing to do with the main question. The first part of the Rights of Man was applicable only to France. But a book, called an Appeal from the New to the Old Whigs, applied it to the

Government

Government of this country. Mr. Paine arrived, and notwithstanding his first intentions, this attack exasperated his spirit, and he wrote a second part to his Rights of Man, in which he vindicated the Rights of the People in this or any other country to change their Government.

Mr. Erskine said he would vindicate, in presence of as many spies as could be collected, the Right of the People to oppose Despotic power, and to change the form of their government, when that form was radically and essentially bad. He had opposed, and would always oppose, the Right of Despots to prevent any People from forming a Government for themselves, of the sweet or bitter fruits of which they themselves must eat. If the People of France were to say to the People of England, " You shall have a Republican form of Government," the People of England would say, " No ; we have already chosen our form of Government, a mixed form, a limited Monarchy, which we approve, and if we did not, we would receive a form of Government from no power on Earth but our own." The People of England have a right to change their Government if they please ; they will not, if you use them well ; but it is to the denial of this principle all the calamities of these trials are to be imputed.

The Duke of Richmond's plan proceeded on the Rights of Man. His Grace, however, had not the merit of being the inventor. He adopted the ideas of Mr. Locke; who maintained the principle of " *Salus populi, suprema lex est,*"and so did Mr. Yorke, in his speech delivered on the Castle Hill, Sheffield. Mr. Yorke, indeed, had hardly the merit of adopting, for he recited what Locke had written almost verbatim. Mr. Erskine read the Duke of Richmond's Letter to the Sheriff of Sussex, in 1780, in which he observed there was much good sense, although he could not agree to the whole. It concluded with asserting " that the people have rights, know they have rights, and will assert and obtain them." How obtain them ? by peaceable means, which was all that the prisoner had attempted. If they libelled Government, if they resisted the Magistrate in the due execution of his duty, if they committed any legal offence, they were amenable to legal punishment. But when men were considering on Constitutional means of effecting a purpose, they could not be found guilty of the crime charged in the Indictment. Let no worse motives be imputed to the Prisoner than to so many others who had pursued the same object, much less the highest of all crimes, the crime of Treason. Suppose these Societies, which they never did, had resolved to petition Parliament no more. Was there no way for the people to bring about a Reform in Parliament by peaceable means ? The Attorney General seemed to think that Parliament was a part of the permanent Government, forgetting that it died a Constitutional death at certain periods, and that there was no necessity for reviving it in the same form. A voter had a right to say, " I will vote for no Parliament that is disposed to

resi

resist my rights; I will vote for none who will not call us, the People, their Constituents; I will vote for none who will reject our petitions; I will not arm a few individuals with power to collect taxes, to pass coercive laws, and to be used only against ourselves. Such are not the true House of Commons of Great Britain. I will oppose such an House of Commons, not by tumult and insurrection, but by concurring in the appointment of Delegates to consider how my rights may be supported." Such language the People of this country had a right to hold; and how were they to act upon it? They might petition the King. They might give weight to their Petition by shewing that it had the sanction of the public opinion. To collect this opinion they might say, " We will not assemble in numbers, for that might give rise to tumult; but we will assemble in our respective neighbourhoods, and appoint Delegates with instructions to confer with other Delegates; and thus without danger or inconvenience, we shall collect the public sentiment, and carry it to that place where we know it will be treated with respect. In this way we shall obtain our imprescriptable Rights." This they must do, because a Court of Justice could not give them their imprescriptable Rights, consistently with the administration of the law; but a Court of Justice could do that which it was called upon to do in this case; it would not on any presumption of evil intention punish any man for legal acts done in pursuit of these Rights. The Attorney General seemed to think that petitioning the King on the subject of Parliamentary Reform, was to ask him to do that which his coronation oath forbade him to do, and consequently could only mean to compel him by force. Mr. Erskine said, he did not understand what was meant by this, He never heard it argued that, but for the articles of Union with Scotland, the King might not alter the composition of the House of Commons, as far as depended on calling in new places and persons to elect, without the consent of the House of Commons. This was the opinion of Mr. Locke, a man inferior to none his country ever produced, except Sir Isaac Newton.

Mr. Erskine here quoted the opinion of Locke upon this subject, from his Treatise on Government, B. II. chap, xiii. sec. 157-158. This book was written in answer to the Jacobites, who denied the right of King William to the Throne; and when Dr. Sacheverell attempted to refute the doctrines it contained, by resorting to the exploded doctrines of Divine Hereditary Right and Non-resistance, he was impeached by the Commons, and found guilty by the Lords.

Mr. Erskine then proceeded to recapitulate the evidence, observing, that he had been obliged to omit many and important topics of general defence, in order to apply his attention to disembroiling the chaos which he had had no time to consider but by the indulgence given him by the Court and the Jury. The original Address of the Corresponding Society they would not have published, had they thought it criminal. They not only published it, but they sent it as

a circular

a circular letter by post, addressed to various persons, and even a copy to the Secretary of State. On the tremendous evidence adduced in this trial, he observed that a song found among Hardy's papers had been produced against him, without the shadow of proof that it had been written, published, or even approved by him. He had received it, as many things were received by men of all descriptions in this town, without knowing whence it came. It had been perhaps dropt down his area. If such evidence were held sufficient to affect a man's life, he (Mr. Erskine), who received and read papers of all sorts, had probably now in his house evidence sufficient to hang him and his whole family. The Address of the Society was founded on the Duke of Richmond's letter to Colonel Sharman, containing a plan, upon which men of high rank sat as Delegates in the city of London, with Aldermen of the city of London. A little time before the Convention met at Edinburgh, a Convention of Delegates from the Counties of Scotland met, of which the Chief Baron of his Majesty's Exchequer in Scotland was Chairman, and the Lord Advocate, the Dean of Faculty, and Sir Thomas Dundas, now Lord Dundas, sat as Members. An application had been previously made to Parliament, for a Reform in the mode of electing Members for the counties, and rejected. What did this meeting of Delegates according to their own advertisement? They met for the purpose of altering and amending the Law; they agreed upon certain heads, and resolved to send them, where? To Parliament?—No; but to the several counties in Scotland to collect opinions and signatures. Was this Meeting called treasonable?—No; it would have been called scandalous to impute treasonable motives to any man who attended it. The object of the Corresponding Society on the first piece of evidence, viz. their own Address, was Reform of Parliament, by legal means. Would the Jury impute to his Client, against whom not a contumelious word respecting government had been proved, the shocking crime of Treason for supporting a measure, sanctioned by so many and so recent authorities? Let them read the lines prefixed to the Address of the Corresponding Society, and see if they could find any thing in their subsequent proceedings to match them.

"On Virtue can alone my kingdom stand;
For, lost this social cement of mankind,
The greatest Empire by scarce felt degrees
Will moulder loose away, till, unsustained,
They prone at last to ruin rush,
Unblest by virtue, Government a league
Becomes, a circling junto of the great,
To rob by law; Religion mild, a yoke
To tame the stooping soul; a trick of state
To mark their rapine, and to share the prey.
What are without it senates, but a face

Of consultation deep, and reason free,
While the determined voice and heart are sold?
What boasted freedom but a sounding name?
And what election, but a market vile
Of slaves self-barter'd? Virtue! without thee
There is no ruling eye, no nerve in states;
War has no vigour, and no safety peace:
Even justice warps to party, laws oppress,
Their weak authority protects no more,
First broke the balance, and then scorns the sword.
Thus nations sink, society dissolves;
Rapine and guile, and violence break loose,
Confunding life, and turning life to gall;
Man hates the face of man, and Indian woods
Hide in their savage haunts no beast so fell."

Yet these Verses were written by Thomson, under the roof of Lord Littleton, under the protection of the Prince of Wales, who perhaps thought that the Rights of the People were the surest guarantee of his own Rights.—By a man who had studied and understood the British Constitution, who venerated liberty but loved order—by a man whose works had been the delight of a nation, and to whose memory a monument was now erecting. If the objects of the Societies were treasonable, then every man who had been a Member of any one of them was guilty of Treason, and he held his life as tenant at will of the Attorney General. Of the Convention either held or proposed, the Attorney General imputed the whole original sin to the London Corresponding Society. The contrary, however, was the fact. A Convention of Delegates from the Scot's counties had been held as above-mentioned at Edinburgh; and the Societies in Scotland, on the usual principle of national vanity, resolved to imitate the example. They agreed on a Convention of their own, and invited the London Societies to send Delegates to it. Some of them sent Delegates, whose instructions were that they should concur in all Constitutional acts for a Reform in the Representation of the People. Every man was bound by the acts of his agent within the limits of his agency; but if an agent, sent to buy horses, should think fit to steal horses or commit treason, his employer would be amenable neither for the Felony nor the Treason. By the same rule, no acts concurred in by those Delegates which were not within the letter of their instructions, could affect the Societies by which they were sent. Mr. Erskine arranged, and commented upon the whole of the evidence in a masterly manner, illustrating every objection he took to it by the most apposite and pointed remarks. He warned the Jury against giving their sanction to constructive Treasons, and repeated Dr. Johnson's remark on the acquittal of Lord George Gordon—" I hate Lord George Gordon, but I am glad he is acquitted, because I love my country, and love myself." He remarked with particular severity on the attempt to implicate Hardy in the charge of providing arms, on no better evidence than because a man at Sheffield had written a letter to him, offering to make pikes, and desiring him to forward another letter of the same tenour to Norwich; although it clearly appeared that Hardy had never read the letter addressed to himself to any body, nor forwarded the letter to Norwich; and on the still more atrocious attempt to implicate him in the business of Watt at Edinburgh, from the mere circumstance of Watt's having written a letter on the subject to Hardy, with whom he had never corresponded before, and from whom he had received no answer to his letter. If such evidence were to be tolerated, the most innocent, the most meritorious man living might be stript of his fortune, reputation, and life, by any ruffian who chose to address a treasonable letter to him, and get it conveyed into his house. If the witnesses for the Crown, not spies by profession, were worthy of credit, then the prisoner was innocent—if they were not, then the testimony of the spies, admitted on all hands to be insufficient of itself, was left totally destitute of support. One or other side of the alternative must be taken. It was impossible to say that the witnesses for the Crown were to be believed where their testimony made against the Prisoner, and disbelieved where it made for him. If the testimony of the Spies could be supported by other Witnesses, whose evidence would not prove at the same time that the Prisoner never harboured the treasonable intention imputed to him, why were they not produced?—For this reason only, that out of more than 40000 members of the several Societies, not one could be found. On the character of Spies, having no eloquence of his own, he would avail himself of the eloquence of a writer who had much (Mr. Burke).

" A mercenary Informer knows no distinction. Under such a system, the obnoxious people are slaves, not only to the Government, but they live at the mercy of every individual; they are at once the slaves of the whole community, and of every part of it; and the worst and most unmerciful men are those on whose goodness they most depend.

" In this situation men not only shrink from the frowns of a stern Magistrate; but are obliged to fly from their very species. The seeds of destruction are sown in civil intercourse and in social habitudes. The blood of wholesome kindred is infected.—Their tables and beds are surrounded with snares. All the means given by Providence to make life safe and comfortable, are perverted into instruments of terror and torment. This species of universal subserviency, that makes the very servant who waits behind your chair the arbiter of your life and fortune, has such a tendency to degrade and abase mankind, and to deprive them of that assured and liberal state of mind which alone can make us what we ought to be, that I vow to God I would sooner bring myself to put a man to immediate death for opinions I disliked, and so to get rid of the man and his
opinions

opinions at once, than to fret him with a feverish being, tainted with the jail-distemper of a contagious servitude, to keep him above ground, an animated mass of putrefaction, corrupted himself, and corrupting all about him."

My whole argument, therefore, says Mr. Erskine, asserts no more than this, That before the crime of compassing the King's death can be found *by you, the Jury*, whose province it is to judge of its existence—it must be believed *by you* to have existed in point of fact.

Before you can adjudge a FACT, you *must believe it*—Not suspect it, or imagine it, or fancy it—BUT BELIEVE IT—and it is impossible to impress the human mind with such a reasonable and certain belief, as is necessary to be impressed, before a christian man can adjudge his neighbour to the smallest penalty, much less to pains of death, without having such evidence as a reasonable mind will accept of, as the infallible test of truth. And what is that evidence?—Neither more or less than that which the constitution has established in the Courts for the general admission of justice, namely, that the evidence convinces the Jury beyond all reasonable doubt, that the criminal *intention* constituting the crime existed in the mind of the man upon trial, and was the main spring of his conduct. The Rules of Evidence, as they are settled by law, and adopted in its general administration, are not to be over-ruled, or tampered with. They are founded in the charities of Religion—in the philosophy of Nature—in the truths of History, and in the experience of common life. And whoever ventures rashly to depart from them, let him remember that it will be meted to him in the same measure, and both God and man will judge him accordingly.

Gentlemen, these are arguments addressed to your reasons and consciences, not to be shaken in upright minds by way of precedent, for no precedents can sanctify injustice;—If they could, every human right would long ago have been extinct upon the earth.

If the State Trials, in a bad hour, are to be searched for precedents, what murders may you not commit; what law of humanity may you not trample upon; what rule of justice may you not violate; and what maxim of wise policy may you not abrogate and confound?

If precedents in bad times are to be implicitly followed, why should we have heard any evidence at all? you might have convicted without any evidence, for many have been so convicted in this manner, murdered even by Acts of Parliament.

If precedents, in bad times, are to be followed, why should the Lords and Commons have investigated these charges, &c. and the Crown have put them into this course of judicial trial, since without such a trial, and even after an acquittal upon one, they might have attainted all their Prisoners by Act of Parliament?—They did so in the case of Lord Strafford.—There are precedents, therefore, for all such things:—But such precedents as could not for a moment survive the times of madness and distraction which gave them birth, and which, as soon as the spurs of the occasions were blunted, were repealed and execrated even by Parliaments; which, little as I may think of the present, are not to be compared with it.—Parliaments sitting in the darkness of former times—in the Night of Freedom, before the principles of Government were developed, and before the Constitution became fixed.

The last of these precedents, as I before stated to you, and all the proceedings upon it, were ordered to be taken off the file and burnt, to the intent that the same might no longer be visible in after ages; an order, dictated no doubt by a pious tenderness for National honour, and meant as a charitable covering for the crimes of our Fathers:—But it was a sin against posterity, it was a Treason against Society—for instead of commanding them to be burnt, they should rather have directed them to be blazoned in large letters upon the walls of our Courts of Justice, that like the characters decyphered by the Prophet of God to the Eastern tyrant, they might enlarge and blacken in your sights, to terrify you from acts of injustice.

In times when the whole habitable earth is in a state of change and fluctuation, when deserts are starting up into civilized Empires around you, and when men, no longer slaves to the prejudices of particular countries, much less to the abuses of particular Governments, enlist themselves like the citizens of an enlightened world into whatever communities shall best protect their civil liberties, it never can be for the advantage of this country to prove that the strict unextended letter of our law is no certain security to its inhabitants. On the contrary, when so dangerous a lure is held out to emigration, it will be found to be the wisest policy of Great Britain to set up her happy Constitution, the strict letter of her guardian laws, and the proud condition of equal freedom, which her highest and lowest subjects ought equally to enjoy. It will be her wisest policy to set up these first of human blessings against those charms of change and novelty which the varying condition of the world is hourly holding out, and which may deeply affect the population and prosperity of our country. In times when the subordination to authority is said to be every where but too little felt, it would be found to be the wisest policy of Great Britain to instil into the governed an almost superstitious reverence for the strict security of the laws, which from their equal administration can seldom work injustice, and which, from the reverence growing out of their mildness and antiquity, acquire a stability in the habits and affections of men far beyond the force of civil obligation; whereas severe penalties and arbitrary construction of laws intended for ease and protection, lay the foundations of alienation from Government, which, at all times is dangerous, but at this time is certain and sudden ruin. Cultivate the old maxim of

the

the Church, *sursum corda*; look to the hearts of all your subjects, and do not entertain so stupid an imagination as that in days like these, a country can be preserved by corrupting one half of the People to defame, bully, and persecute the other. At a time when England may be put to great difficulties to support herself, even when the whole nation draws together with one heart and accord, is it wise at such a time to set up Lawyers to tell us that every man who sees and feels, and is determined to assist in removing the corruptions which are the parents of these calamities, are traitors to the Sovereign, and plotters of his death? Gentlemen, if this doctrine is established by your verdict, you do not leave your Sovereign, the King, one half his subjects; and although you may, in the ordinary course of things, keep the peace in England upon these principles, by armed associations, and the terrors of legal tribunals, yet, if ever the independence of the Nation were assailed by foreign force, in one hour would desolation come upon you. Look to the fruit of these miserable factions and divisions in Brabant! If the late Emperor Joseph had given to his subjects fully, and at once, the *Joyeuse Entrée*, their ancient Constitution, derived from the good Duke of Burgundy, to obtain which, I remember the same movements as in this country for the Reform of Parliament, they would—I know what I say—it is not what I have heard or read of—I have seen the process of the thing of which I am speaking—they would have risen in a mass to maintain their own liberties, and their Prince's throne, thus interwoven together; and the French, like the Giants of Antiquity (and they are indeed the Giants of modern times), when they attempted Heaven, would have been rolled and trampled in the mire of their ambition. But instead of this concession in due time, the Prussian army marched into Brabant, and all was peace—but it was such a peace as there is in Vesuvius or Ætna before they vomit forth their lava, and roll their conflagrations over the devoted habitations of men! When the French approached, the fatal effects were seen of a Government of constraint and terror; the well-affected were dispirited, and the irritated were inflamed into fury. At that moment the Archduchess fled from Brussels, and the Duke of Saxe Teschen was sent to offer them the *Joyeuse Entrée*. But the season of concession was past away; and the Throne of Brabant has departed from the House of Austria—I fear, for ever! In the same way, a far more important and splendid Throne departed from his Majesty's illustrious House. I will not give you my own words; I will again refer to the almost divine and immortal oration of Mr. Burke:—

" For that service, for all service, whether of revenue, trade, or empire, my trust is in her interest in the British Constitution. My hold of the Colonies is in the close affection which grows from common names, from kindred blood, from similar privileges, and equal protection. As long as you have the wisdom to keep the sovereign authority of this country as the sanctuary of Liberty, the sacred temple consecrated to our common faith, wherever the chosen race and
sons

fons of England worship Freedom, they will turn their faces towards you. The more ardently they love Liberty, the more perfect will be their obedience. Slavery they can have any where.—It is a weed that grows in every soil.—They may have it from Spain; they may have it from Prussia: but, until you become lost to all feeling of your true interest and your national dignity, Freedom they can have from none but you. It is the spirit of the English Constitution which pervades, feeds, unites, invigorates, vivifies every part of the Empire, even down to the minutest Member. Is it not the same virtue which does every thing for us here in England? Do you imagine that it is the Land-tax Act which raises your Revenue; that it is the annual vote in the Committee of Supply which gives you your Army? or that it is the Mutiny Bill which inspires it with bravery and discipline? No! surely no! It is the love of the People—it is their attachment to their Government, from the sense of the deep stake they have in such a glorious institution, which gives you your army and your navy, and infuses into both that liberal obedience, without which your army would be a base rabble, and your navy nothing but rotten timber."—Such was the language of that sublime writer, whose opinions, if they had been followed, would have done more than saved you America; it would have saved you the affections and the admiration of mankind. Instead of this you were mad to persevere in that horrible contest, to procure the means of extending that corruption at home, over those whom Mr. Tooke is represented to have called the Skip Jack Nobility, and in so doing you lost the Colonies for ever.

My wish and my recommendation is not to conjure up a spirit among us to destroy ourselves, by bringing on the tyranny of a French tribunal, where an accusation is enough to bring its object to the guillotine. Let us keep to the old and venerable rules and laws of our forefathers; and let a Jury of the country feel the duty they owe the public, to themselves, to posterity, and to God, to preserve by law the life of a man who only asks it of them on the terms they would, in their turn, ask their own. I shall now conclude with a fervent wish and a fond hope, that it may please God, who guides the world, moulds governments at his will, and who governs us all in justice and in mercy; from whose care and bounty has arisen the prosperity and glory of this happy Island, to enlighten and direct your minds! To your care I now commit my client, without fear, being confident that you will do him justice.

WITNESSES CALLED IN DEFENCE.

The Court and Jury returned into Court at nine, and, after being called over, Mr. Erskine called

LORIMOND GODDARD.

Q. Are you a Member of the Corresponding Society?—A. Yes. I entered into it about two years since, and withdrew my name after Mr. Hardy was apprehended.

Q. Did

Q. Did you frequent the same Division?—A. Yes, frequently.

Q. What was his conduct?—A. The most orderly and peaceable. He even requested that no person would bring a stick, lest it might be construed into an offensive weapon.

Q. What was his object, as it appeared to you?—A. A Parliamentary Reform in the House of Commons.

Q. Did it appear to you that he wished to dethrone the King?—A. Certainly not.

Q. Did you ever hear him argue that the House of Peers was a useless body, and ought to be abolished?—A. No. His discourse, when he did speak, (which was seldom) was confined entirely to the means of reforming the House of Commons.

Q. What was his general character?—A. So far as I know or have heard, perfectly harmless and honest.

Cross-examined by the ATTORNEY-GENERAL.

Q. You say that you have frequently conversed with him on political subjects?—A. Yes; and, as I said before, I thought his sentiments were highly friendly to the principles of the Constitution.

Q. Was you at the meeting at the Globe?—A. Yes.

Q. Did you see the Resolutions entered into?—A. Yes, (the paper shewn) and the witness believed it was correct.

Q. Was you at the great meeting at the Crown and Anchor?—A. Yes.

Q. Did you not hear several songs at these meetings?—A. Yes, I have heard many songs after dinner, but I do not recollect the contents.

Q. Perhaps I may refresh your memory. Was there not one sung which began with the following words:

" Plant, plant the tree,
" Fair Freedom's tree,
" 'Midst blood and wounds and slaughter."

—A. No, I do not recollect any such words being sung; and if they were, you seem to be much better acquainted with the song than I am. (A laugh.)

COURT.—This levity is highly reprehensible, and, indeed, criminal. It is offending the dignity and solemnity of the Court. Officers, if you see any person guilty of such gross indecency, I direct you to take him into custody immediately. The Crier called silence.

Q. Was you at the meeting at Chalk Farm?—A. I was, and every thing was peaceably conducted.

Q. What was the intention of that meeting?—A. I understood it was to elect fresh Delegates; but the meeting was dispersed.

Q. Do you not know that a circular letter was sent by the prisoner into Scotland, and several parts of England, containing instructions for assembling a Convention at Edinburgh?—A. I have heard, but I never saw those instructions.

Q. Do you know the fact?—A. I know that Margarot and Gerald were deputed to be the Delegates from the Corresponding Society to the Convention, and therefore I cannot doubt the fact.

Q. Do you know Mr. Thelwall?—A. Yes.

Q. Then you have seen several of his Constitutional songs?—A. I have had several of them in my possession, but I cannot recollect the particular words of either of them.

Q. Did Mr. Hardy visit Margarot whilst on board the transport ship?—A. I have heard that he did, but it was after the visit had taken place.

Re-examined by Mr. GIBBS.

Q. You positively swear that during all your communication with the prisoner, you never heard or understood that his views extended beyond a Reform in the Commons House of Parliament?—A. I do positively swear so.

Q. What was that Reform?—A. I always understood it to be according to the plan laid down by the Duke of Richmond—annual elections and universal suffrage.

Francis Dowling, of New-street, Covent-Garden, examined by Mr. GIBBS.

Q. What are you?—A. I am a truss-maker.

Q. Was you a Member of the Society in question?—A. I was amongst the earliest Members, and belonged to Division, No. 2.

Q. You know Mr. Hardy, and what were his public principles?—A. As far as I could learn, simply to effect a Reform in the Representation in the House of Commons.

Q. Did he wish to effect this Reform by open force, or by overawing the Parliament?—A. By no means; his views, as far as I could learn, were to obtain the sense of the whole nation by means of a Convention, and if it should be found to be in favour of the measure, then to apply by petition to the three branches of the Legislature.

Q. Did it appear to you that he intended to abridge the King of his authority?—A. I never heard the most distant hint of such an intention.

Q. Or to abolish the House of Lords?—A. No, never.

Q. Do you know what character he bears?—A. I have always heard that he was a peaceable and orderly man, and rather inclined to a religious turn of mind.

Cross-examined by the ATTORNEY-GENERAL.

With respect to the Meetings and Resolutions at the Globe Tavern, Chalk Farm, &c. his answers were very similar to those given by the last witness, and therefore need no repetition.

Q. Do you know Franklow, of Lambeth Walk?—A. I do.

Q. Was not a Club formed at his house, called the Loyal Lambeth Association?—A. I have heard there was.

Q. Have

Q. Have you heard the members of this club exercised themselves with musquets?

A. I have heard so, but I do not know the fact.

Q. Have you ever seen a letter from Sheffield, ordering pikes to be made?

A. I never did.

Q. Why, did you not know Edwards, one of the delegates, and Hilliard?

A. Yes, but I never saw them have any pikes.

Q. Was you at Robins's coffee-house when Mr. Yorke took his leave?

A. I was not.

Q. Have you seen a hand-bill like this, beginning, "Speedily will be performed a Farce, or, G——'s Head in a Basket?" (the hand-bill shewn).

A. No, I never saw or heard of such a hand-bill until this time.

Q. Or this hand-bill? (the bill shewn) "The Inns tell us we are in danger from an invasion of the French.—The Outs tell us that we are in danger from the Hessians and Hanoverians. In either case, we should arm ourselves; get arms, and learn how to use them."

A. I never saw this bill.

Q. Have you not heard that a bill-sticker was employed to stick bills in the night?

A. I have heard that a person was to be paid for that purpose.

Q. You admit you were at Chalk Farm, do you know what were the resolutions entered into at that meeting?

A. I do not recollect.

Q. Did you vote for them?

A. Yes, I did.

Q. What did you vote for resolutions which you did not understand or hear?

A. I voted for them on account of the good opinion I entertained of the persons who drew them up and proposed them.

Q. Who were those persons?

A. I understood Martin, Thelwall, and Lovett.

Q. Did you see a paper purporting to recommend that no more petitions should be presented, as it would be useless?

A. No, I never saw such a paper.

Q. Alexander Wills examined by Mr. Erskine. This witness was a member of the Corresponding Society, and likewise of the Constitutional Society. He gave a similar testimony with the other witnesses of the views and drift of the prisoner Hardy and the other members of the society, that a parliamentary reform in the House of Commons was their sole object; that at such of their

their meetings as he had attended, he never heard any thing derogatory to the King, but on the contrary, the utmost respect and honour; that it was never intended to overawe parliament, but to obtain a reform through the King and Parliament.

Q. What character does the prisoner bear?
A. I always understood his character was without reproach.

Cross-examined by Mr. Bower.

Q. What are you?
A. A dancing-master.
Q. What impelled you to become a member?
A. I heard there was some clever persons belonging to it, and not having the honour of hearing the debates in the House of Commons, I thought I should hear some good speeches.

Mr. Bower questioned him respecting the Chalk Farm business, the resolutions, hand-bills, &c. all of which he was unacquainted with.

Q. Do you know any thing about hand-bills?
A. I recollect that a subscription was made for a bill-sticker who was imprisoned.
Q. What was his name?
A. I think it was Carter.

William Sabine, a member of the society, was next called.—This witness gave the same account of the principles of the Corresponding Society which all the other witnesses did.

Q. Did you ever see the prisoner produce a letter from Sheffield at any of the meetings, purporting to be an answer from that town respecting any orders for the manufactory of pikes?
A. No; the prisoner never produced such a letter to me, or to any other person in my presence.
Q. How long have you known Mr. Hardy, and what is his character?
A. I have known him twenty years; I never heard any otherwise than that he was an orderly, quiet, peaceable man, a good friend and a good neighbour, for any thing I ever heard.
Q. Is that his general character?
A. I always understood it was so.

Mr. Law cross-examined the evidence.

Q. What are you?
A. An independent man; I employ my property sometimes in the Stocks, sometimes in purchasing lands, &c. as it best suits me. A relative, named Hunter, introduced me into the society.
Q. Was you at the meeting the 2d of May, when Mr. Wharton was in the chair?
A. No. I never attended any meeting of the Constitutional Society.

Q. Was

Q. Was you at the anniverſary dinner at the Globe Tavern?
A. Yes, I was.
Q. Was you at the meeting at Chalk Farm?
A. Yes.
Q. Then you are acquainted with the reſolutions entered into at thoſe meetings?
A. I am not. I heard them read, but I did not attend to them.
Q. Why?
A. I have an habitual inattentiveneſs about me, and always had.
Q. Where did you go after the meeting at Chalk Farm?
A. I went with Mr. Lovett, the Chairman, and other members, to No. 3, in Compton-ſtreet, Soho, where we all ſupped.
Q. Have you ever ſeen the priſoner produce a letter from Sheffield, reſpecting pikes?
A. No, I never have.
Q. Did you hear any ſongs ſung at any of the dinners?
A. Yes, ſeveral.
Q. Of what tendency were they; were they ſeditious?
A. I do not recollect any thing about them.
Q. You ſtate yourſelf to be a man of property; pray was you ever in buſineſs?
A. Yes.
Q. What was it?
A. I cannot now exactly recollect.
Q. Try.—Upon the queſtion being repeatedly put, the priſoner ſaid he was a perfumer and hair-dreſſer, about twelve years ago.

Alexander Fraſer, examined by Mr. Gibbs.

Q. What are you, Sir?
A. A taylor. I became a member of the Correſponding Society in April 1793.
Q. While you was a member, what were the views of the ſociety?
A. Our only object, at leaſt as it appeared to me, was to obtain a Reform in the Houſe of Commons, by a full and fair repreſentation of the people of Great Britain in that Houſe.
Q. Did you at any time collect from the members that they entertained a project to effect a Reform by force of arms?
A. No, by no means whatever.
Q. How long have you known the priſoner; and what is his character?
A. I have known him many years, and I neither know nor ever heard but that his character was unblemiſhed, both as a tradeſman and a moral man.

Here were a few cross questions put, of no importance.

Thus far the evidence went to establish the views of the Society, and to wipe away any impression which might have been made on the charge of any design to attack the King or Constitution.

The next head consisted of evidence to the prisoner's character.

William Barkley.

Q. What are you?

A. I am a shoemaker.

Q. Do you know the prisoner at the bar, and what is his character?

A. I have known him thirty years. He lived as forman with me seven years; he has quitted me about three years. He was a faithful servant, and, as a man, I know him to be peaceable, quiet, and orderly.

Q. Are you a member?

A. No, I was never admitted into any political society.

The Rev. Mr. Oliver, a Dissenting Minister. I have known Mr. Hardy three or four years, during which time I have been intimate with him.

Q. Did you ever hear him speak about the societies to effect a parliamentary reform? A. I have several times heard him say, when the society has been the topic of discourse, that their object was to obtain a reform in a peaceable and legal way, upon the plan laid down by the Duke of Richmond and Mr. Pitt in the year 1782. I have seen the prisoner in his own house since the report of the committee was made to the House of Commons.

Lord President. I desire the witness will recollect himself.

"I beg your lordship's pardon, I feel myself in an error, but I assure his lordship that it was not an intentional error."

Lord President. I apprehend not. Go on. I believe it was in May or June when I saw him last; and he then in a conversation avowed the same views and principles, from which he had at no time varied in the course of many other conversations.

Q. Are you a member of the Corresponding or the Constitutional Society?

A. No, I have divine service to perform, and four sermons to deliver every Lord's day; I therefore cannot dedicate any time to study politics.

Q. What is the character of the prisoner?

A. I really and conscientiously believe that he is a man who fears God, honours the King, loves his fellow-creatures.

Danniel Steward, secretary to the committee of the Friends of the People, examined by Mr. Gibbs.

Q. Do

Q. Do you know the prisoner, Hardy?
A. Yes. I have seen him several years since, but never conversed with him until December 1792, which was in consequence of a letter sent by him to the society of the Friends of the People, to which I wrote an answer, under the directions of the committee, and carried it to the prisoner's house. From that time there arose an intimacy, and I used to call upon him three or four times in a week, and scarcely ever less than twice.

Q. What was your conversation respecting a reform?
A. Whenever we conversed, the prisoner always said, that the object was solely to reform the representation in the House of Commons. For that purpose he continued to inform the people at large of the bad state of representation, under the hopes of obtaining their signatures to petitions which were to be presented to each branch of the legislature, in order to obtain redress.

Q. Did you ever hear him say that it was his intention, or that of any other person, to obtain this reform by force?
A. Never; and from the implicit confidence he placed in me, I think it is hardly possible but I must have known it, if such had really been the case.

Q. Did you agree to the same plan with the prisoner?
A. No, we differed widely in our opinion, not on the necessity of bringing the measure about, but on the mode of effecting it. Hardy insisted that the Duke of Richmond's plan was the best, and that any thing short of that would be of no avail, as it would not be a radical cure for the corruption which had, from time to time, crept into the representation of the people; whereas, my opinion was contrary, as I thought that universal suffrage would be too extensive, and that an annual election was too short a period. I rather inclined to the Constitution established at the Revolution in 1788, with an extension to all taxable people who bore the burthens of the state.

Q. What is his character?
A. A harmless peaceable man, of sober conversation, amiable manners, and good morals.

John Carr, a very respectable schoolmaster. I have known the prisoner twenty years; he has always been a man of a remarkably peaceable disposition, and of the best character.

Three other witnesses gave the same kind of testimony.

John Stevenson, a coal-merchant. I have known him nine years; he was always peaceable, and as a moral man I do not know his superior.

Peter Macbean, a shoemaker. I have known the prisoner seventeen years, and he has always bore an amiable character, both civil and religious.

Cross

Cross-examined by Mr. Garrow:

Q. Are you a member of the Corresponding Society?

A. Yes, and was a member at it's first institution. I continued to be a member for two years, and used to attend the Division No. 8.

Q. Did you not subscribe for Mr. Paine's works?

A. No.

Q. Did the Division which you belonged to enter into a subscription for those works?

A. Not that I know of.

Q. Recollect. Did you never hear so?

A. No, I cannot charge my memory with any such circumstance.

Q. You say that you was one of the first members; where was it then held?

A. In Exeter Street.

Q. How many members had you, and who was in the chair?

A. Margarot was in the chair at the meeting which I attended; and I believe there were thirty or forty members present.

Q. Who drew up the original laws of the society?

A. I am not certain whether it was Mr. Margarot, or whether they were settled in a committee.

Alexander Gordon, a cordwainer, I have known the prisoner twenty years, during which time he has borne an excellent character for peaceable behaviour, honesty and industry.

John Boak, cabinet-maker.—I have known him ten years. He was, during that time, a peaceable, quiet honest man.

Cross examined by Mr. Bower.

Q. Was you a member of the society?

A. Yes; but I have quitted two years.

Matthew Dickey—I have known the prisoner five years, and have always understood him to bear an excellent character, particularly peaceably and orderly.

Mr. Gibbs—My Lord, we have not gone through half of the evidence for the prisoner; and as my learned friend, Mr. Erskine, has by his great exertions indured such fatigue, I trust the Court will indulge us with an adjournment.

Lord President. The Court is very desirous to make all the progress possible. This seems to be a duty both with respect to the Jury and the prisoner. I therefore hoped and expected that the evidence to character might have been finished to night, that the Attorney General might reply on Monday.

Mr. Erskine. If your Lordship should direct that we shall proceed, I apprehend that we shall enter into evidence which may be objected to. In that case, in my present exhausted state, I cannot possibly take that active part which may be necessary to support the evidence which I mean to bring forward. I therefore rely upon the

the candour of the Attorney General, and the indulgence of the Court to adjourn.

Sir John Scott gave his assent.

The Court at one o'clock yesterday morning adjourned to this morning at seven.

After the adjournment, a mistaken person, ran down to the gate, and called out, " An acquittal, an acquittal," upon which a numerous assemblage of people, assembled in the Old Bailey, burst into a loud huzza!

The court was struck very much; the avenues were cleared, and the people were quickly undeceived. In about three minutes, a still louder huzza was repeated, several times. The sheriffs were directed to enquire into the cause, and upon their return reported that Mr. Erskine had that moment entered into his carriage, and the populace had welcomed him with their gratulations.

Mr. Sheridan and Mr. Grey were likewise applauded. The populace proceeded to take out the horses from Mr. Erskine's carriage. He remonstrated with and earnestly desired them to desist, but in vain, for they effected their purpose, and drew him in his carriage to Serjeant's-Inn, with continued shouts of triumph. When he alighted, he addressed the great body of people, desiring them to be peaceable, and to return to their homes; not doubting but the laws of their country would protect innocence, and dispense equal justice to every man. The populace gave him three cheers, and departed quietly.

Monday, November 3.

The Court sat at half past eight in the morning, and proceeded on the evidence for the prisoner.

Mr. Erskine stated, that he meant to call a witness to prove, that a letter, which had been given in evidence on the part of the prosecution, written by one Davidson, who had resided at Sheffield, to the Secretary of the Norwich Patriotic Societies, and enclosed in another which was sent to Hardy, was found in Hardy's possession, unopened, at the time he was taken in custody.

That such was accordingly proved; and Chief Justice Eyre observed, that Hardy had no right to open the letter that was enclosed for the Secretary at Norwich; but what constituted the weight of the proof in favour of Hardy was, that he had not sent that letter to Norwich.

David Martin said, he was an engraver, and lived at Sheffield. He had resided there about twelve years, and carried on trade. He had become a member of the Sheffield Society within three months of it's commencement, and had continued to be a member till the time that Camage and others had been taken up by Government. He said, his object was to obtain a reform in the Commons House of Parliament, by legal and constitutional means; and

from

from all that he obferved, heard, and faw, in the courfe of his attendance on that fociety, he had no reafon to fuppofe their views were different from his. He had not the moft diftant idea that the fociety meant to attack the Government by an armed force. He was a member at the time that they fent a delegate to the Convention that affembled in Edinburgh. The object of the Sheffield fociety, in fending their delegate was, in order to co-operate with the other delegates from the different focieties, to produce the end he had already mentioned, namely, a Reform in Parliament. After the petition, figned by a few individuals, for a Parliamentary Reform, which had been prefented by Mr. Grey, had been rejected, they thought the general fentiments of the people, as far as they could be collected, would make an impreffion on the Houfe, and induce them in their juftice to grant the prayer of the petition. If he had imagined that thofe gentlemen, who had been delegated from different focieties, had been to conftitute a Convention at Edinburgh, for the purpofe of devifing the means by which the Parliament fhould be forced to grant a parliamentary Reform, he fhould not have continued a member of the fociety. He did not think it was the intention of the fociety to affect the King in his perfon, his ftate, rule, or government, in this kingdom. There was no intention to touch the Houfe of Lords. He was at Caftlehill when Mr. Yorke made a fpeech there.

On his crofs-examination, he faid, the perfons who principally managed the bufinefs of the fociety, where a committee. He knew a perfon of the name of Gales. He faid, he (the witnefs) was an affociated member of the London Conftitutional Society, in March 1792. He knew the proceedings of the Britifh Convention, which was held at Edinburgh, as they appeared in the Gazetteer. He did not altogether approve of the proceedings of the Convention, particularly that part relating to a fecret committee. They had no fecret Committee at Sheffield. He did not hear that a refolution had been voted at Caftle-hill, not to petition the Houfe of Commons. There was a great number of people affembled there, and he ftood at the outfide of them, and did not hear it; but, if he had heard it, he might perhaps have approved of it. He knew Mr. Yorke. He believed he was not a Sheffield man, but he did not know what brought him to Sheffield. He had frequently heard him, both in public and in private, though he could not fay he was very intimate with him, or that he entertained exactly the fame opinions on Parliamentary Reform. He could not recollect the fpecific differences between him and Mr. Yorke. He faid, he did not know who was the editor of the Patriot, though he had heard that it was Mr. Campbell Brown, their delegate to the Scottifh Convention. He thought Mr. Brown was a peaceable, well-difpofed man. Letters had occafionally paffed between their Society and the Society of Stockport, and he believed they were affociated for the fame peaceable purpofes with themfelves. He knew that a motion was made on Caftle-hill, to addrefs the Houfe of Commons;

mons; but he did not know it was made, by contrivance, to be negatived.

On re-examination, he said, that whatever Mr. Campbell might do, while he attended the British Convention at Edinburgh, the society gave him no power to act but by legal and constitutional means. He for one would not have consented to send him to Edinburgh, if he had conceived that he would have transgressed the bounds of the law. The proceedings at Castle-hill, and Mr. Yorke's speech were published, and the witness said he had read the speech after it was published.

Edward Oakes Examined.

He had been a member of the Corresponding Society of Sheffield since the year 1791. Their object was Parliamentary Reform by peaceable means, and no other; and it was with this view that they sent delegates to Scotland. They had no design whatever against the King, or the government of the Country. They had no idea of attacking it, and this he swore with a very solemn degree of earnestness. He never heard of any proposition for making pikes till they had been threatened and attacked by the opposite party, and complaints made of it in the society. Being asked what he meant by the opposite party? He said some individuals in the town, and not the Government or magistrates.

Cross Examined.

He did not know that the Sheffield Society was associated with that of London. Was present when they resolved not to petition Parliament any more, finding their former petitions had been rejected; but believes it was their intention to petition his Majesty. He did not know of the letter of the 14th of March 1792, respecting the Rights of Man, though he had entered the society in the year 1791. But to account for this, he said, that they entrusted the management of a great part of their affairs to their committee, who were not accustomed to read all their proceedings to the society at large.

[At this time one of the Sheriffs observing, or thinking that he observed some noise in the Students gallery, called to tell them that if they did not pay more attention to the Court, he would *turn them all out.* He said he had his eyes upon them for some time.

The Lord President. " Gentlemen this is not the first time that this has been remarked to me; and I expect from you an example to be shewn of good behaviour to others. If you do otherwise, you will disgrace yourselves, and greatly insult the Court.

The witness then read aloud the letter which was handed to him, mentioning their forming a correspondence with the London Constitutional Society, and also the letter from Hardy, which advises their distributing themselves into small divisions for the more convenient propagation of their principles. He never heard this letter communicated to the society, but cannot say that it had not been communicated, as he did not regularly attend at their meetings. Does not know Brown the delegate to the British Convention, and editor of the Patriot; but read several extracts from that publication, as inserted in the Sheffield Register.

He then read the resolutions of the Sheffield Society, offering thanks to Paine for his book of the Rights of Man, which he said, were circulated by them through the town and it's neighbourhood; but that was *before* the work had been declared to be a libel. He was asked, what was the usual number of the society? He said it amounted to some hundreds. Why then did they say in some of their publications, that their numbers exceeded 2,000? He said that mistake might easily be committed, as many persons attended the meetings who were not regularly admitted members. What were they to have done if Government attacked them? They would have submitted.

Daniel Stuart examined.

This witness who had been examined before, now produced a letter signed, *Aston*, Sheffield, 14th May, 1792. The Society of the Friends of the People had on the 26th of April published their declaration, and this letter from Aston, President of the Sheffield Society, contained a full approbation of it, and expressions of attachment to the Constitution; and proposed that the different Societies should send deputies to London to co-operate in obtaining a Parliamentary Reform. To this the Friends of the People returned a civil answer, encouraging them to proceed in the same principles of moderation, observing that Liberty was in little danger from it's open and avowed enemies, but may suffer much from the indiscretion of it's friends, which their dextrous opponents were careful to avail themselves of, &c. To this they had a reply from Mr. Aston, greatly approving of the answer he had received.

Mr. Erskine then read the declaration of the Friends of the People, which appeared at the time in all the newspapers, and observed that the Jury must perceive by the signatures annexed to it, that the subscribers, though they may possibly be deceived, could have no designs against the Constitution. He then read over the names of those Noblemen, Members of Parliament, and other Gentlemen, who signed the Declaration; and produced a smile in the Court, by the vivacity with which, on coming to the name of the Hon. Thomas Erskine, M. P. he said, "meaning me Gentlemen."

Mr. Stuart was then cross-examined by the Attorney-General. He said, that on the 24th of May, he took the letter in answer to that of Aston to Mr. Gray, at the House of Commons, to be signed by him as chairman, and sent it off by the post that evening. What was Mr. Aston? A tanner. Was it of his own fancy that he addressed him by the title of Esq. No, it was at the desire of the Committee. Did the Committee know Aston's situation in life? He believed not at that time. Did he not hear of Aston's letter of the 26th of May to the Constitutional Society in London, denouncing the moderation of the Friends of the People? No.

It was then observed, that as a letter takes two days in it's way to Sheffield by the post, this letter to the Constitutional Society of
the

the 24th of May must have been written on the same day on which he received the letter of the Friends of the People, dated 24th of the same month.

Did he know that the society of Sheffield had twelve members associated to the Constitutional Society of London? He did not.

A very respectable list of names had been read, subscribers to the declaration of the Friends of the People. How many of these had since left that Society? About a dozen. Were not some of that society members also of the Constitutional Society? Some of them were then mentioned, and amongst others, we think, Lord John Russel, Mr. Dudley North, Mr. Curwen, Dr. Towers, Mr. Cartwright, Mr. Thomson, Mr. Wharton, &c.

How long has Mr. Wharton been a member of your society? He belonged to it before I had any connection with it.

Do you not usually inquire into the description of people before you direct letters to them? We do.

Was Lord Daer a member of your society? He is.

Did you not know that he was a delegate to the Scotch Convention? Yes.

Does he still remain a member? He does.

Mr. Erskine. Lord Dare, one of the sons of Lord Selkirk, was known to be a delegate to the British Convention, and no motion has in consequence been made to expel him from the society. Is not that so, Mr. Stuart? It is.

The Attorney General pressing the witness with respect to the inconsistency of Aston sending letters of so different a complexion to the Friends of the People and the Society for Constitutional Information, apparently on the same day,

Mr. Erskine, in order to conclude an examination which appeared to him more tedious than interesting, asked Mr. Stuart, if he ever knew of a man changing from a monarchy-man to a republican in the interval of one post?

The Attorney-General said, that he had better ask him if he knew a man change from a reformer to a traitor in the same post.

The Lord President expressing his disapprobation of this kind of retort, the examination of Mr. Stuart was for the present closed.

Mr. Erskine expressed his astonishment, that his client should be debarred the benefit of evidence of this nature, which had never been withheld on any former occasion. One instance only excepted, the state trials did not furnish a precedent; and when he stated that the execrable Jeffries sat in judgment on that occasion, it would be superfluous to assign any further reasons. The measure of justice ought to be *the same in all countries, and to all persons.*

He said, that for some days past he saw an opposition brewing which was likely to bring on a debate, owing, in a great degree to the singular anamoly of the present case. He then went into arguments on the analogies of evidence. The Judges in the Court of King's Bench, on the argument in the case of Holt, determined that a publication in the year 1760 was no defence for a similar publication in the year 1794. This, however, as a fact was charged, did not bear upon the prefent cafe. Hardy's accufation was not grounded on any fact, but upon a criminal and treafonable intention of the mind. He had therefore a right to call evidence to his opinions and intentions.

The crime of Lord George Gordon refted principally upon his intention, and though the profecution was conducted by lawyers of great experience and ability, they fuffered him (Mr. Erfkine) to call nine or ten witneffes in, on the fubject of the difpofition of his mind.

The next cafe he cited was that of Lord Ruffel, accufed of compaffing the King's death, being fuffered to give the evidence of Dr. Barnet in favour of his affection to the government.

Forefeeing an oppofition on this ground, little time as he had for ftudy, he took care to be prepared upon this fubject with cafes from the ftate trials, where the accufed were admitted to build upon the minds of the Court and the Jury an intrinfic probability to operate in the way of character. This, however, was not character, though it would carry a greater conviction. For inftance, if a man was accufed on the oaths of nine or ten credible witneffes of ftealing a horfe, his character would not acquit him, becaufe it was more probable that a man of good general character may fteal a horfe, than that ten honeft men fhould falfely accufe him of it. Character was the flow wide-fpreading circle of opinion, produced by a man's general demeanor: for which reafon a witnefs to character was not afked, What does this man? or, What does that man fay of him? But, from *all* you know, what is your opinion of him?

Henry Cornifh, in the reign James II. accufed of compaffing the King's death, was fuffered to give evidence of his loyalty.

John Auften, in the 2d of William and Mary, was accufed of endeavouring to introduce popery, and was tried before Judge Holt; and that great lawyer did not oppofe his giving evidence to fhew his attachment to the proteftant religion.

Sir John Frend was accufed of compaffing the life of the Sovereign, and was allowed to give evidence to fhew that he expreffed his defire of living peaceably under the government, which, however, he did not like.

In all thefe cafes it was apparent that general character had nothing to do in thefe teftimonies; the character in fuch fituations which will operate as evidence muft be analogous to the offence.

In the 8th of William and Mary we find Cook admitted to give fimilar evidence on a fimilar charge.

Donelly, a waterman, belonging to Queen Anne, was found in the act of pulling down meeting-houfes, which by the ftatute is made conftructive treafon, and evidence was admitted of his converfation, to prove him friendly to government. He therefore afked no more now for Hardy, than what was granted to others in fimilar fituations before him; and even without this, he may ftand upon the rules of evidence.

Mr. Gibbs faid, it was laid down by Lord Hales, that an action in itfelf indifferent, may, by attending circumftances, be converted into an overt act of treason; and when the Crown had an opportunity of ransacking the whole of a man's life and conversation, he should at least have the means of rebutting that evidence by other evidence of his former conversation.

The Attorney-General replied to the arguments of the prisoner's Counsel. He said, that in the case of Holt, alluded to by Mr. Erskine, a new trial had been moved for by him, on the ground that Mr. Justice Wilson had refused to the Jury evidence which ought to have been adduced. Had any one heard the learned gentleman that day, he might have left the Court with an opinion unfavourable to the reputation of Courts of Justice. He hoped that, in the course of a trial affecting the life of the prisoner at the bar, and the life of every man in the country, the learned Counsel would decline making any observations on the difference between a poor shoemaker and a person of rank and fortune; or, if he would not decline them, he trusted he would have the goodness to state where, in the course of the present trial, he had seen any severe or improper conduct on the part of the prosecution. The law of England, like the care of Providence, protected alike the high and the low, the rich and the poor; and he consented that he might, from this moment, be considered a degraded and infamous man, if at any time, during the course of the prosecution, he should act, with respect to the prisoner at the bar, in any other manner than the law authorised. If he could be guilty of such a crime, he would merit the reproach and execrations of every good man, nay, he should deserve that death which the prisoner at the bar would most undoubtedly suffer, provided he was convicted.

When the declarations of Mr. Tooke, in the Constitutional Society, had been received in evidence, it was because what he had said there related to the business of the society directly, to the transactions in which both the societies were concerned. In the case of Lord George Gordon, his declarations were facts, and therefore they had been received in evidence. Any thing that Mr. Hardy had said in any of the societies, or any where else, respecting the concerns of the Societies, might be heard; but here was a gentleman (Mr. Daniel Stuart) who did not belong to any of the societies, and who only heard the sentiments of Mr. Hardy in private conversation. Such evidence could not be received. If it could be received in favour of the prisoner, it must also, by the rule of law, be received against him; and though, in the case of the prisoner at the bar, no further evidence could be given on the part of the Crown, it should be considered what this principle might lead to; he should consider it his duty to bring that species of evidence for the Crown, in any prosecution that he might have occasion to conduct.

The Solicitor-General said a few words. In allusion to one of the cases quoted by Mr. Erskine, he denied some points which that gentleman had asserted. Mr. Solicitor said he supposed he had not understood it.

Mr. Erskine. You certainly did not understand it.

This

This observation, made in a particular tone of voice, nettled Mr. Solicitor. He asserted he knew his duty in the civil and criminal law of the country as well as the learned gentleman did, and he was as determined to perform it. He then offered a few arguments against the admissibility of Mr. Stuart's evidence.

Mr. Erskine agreed with and submitted to the decision of the Court. He noticed the improper warmth of the Solicitor General, to whom he would have been the first to make a proper satisfaction if he had given offence. From the language that was sometimes made use of, even between himself and his learned friend, who were on terms of the most perfect intimacy and friendship, it might be seen how little confidence there was to be placed in words spoken in heat, whether they were uttered in a Court of Justice or a division of the London Corresponding Society, by Mr. Yorke or Mr. Solicitor-General.

The President of the Commission interupted Mr. Erskine. He mentioned the situation of the Jury, who were suffering by every moment's unnecessary delay.

Mr. Stuart was then asked, by permission of the Court, whether Mr. Hardy ever mentioned to him the plan of reform he meant to pursue?

Mr. Stuart said, he had always adhered strictly and strongly to the plan proposed by the Duke of Richmond.

Q. Have you had frequent opportunities of conversing with the prisoner?

A. Very frequent. I never was very much in public company with him; he supped with me one night along with another gentleman; we had a long conversation on the subject of parliamentary reform, and the only point on which we differed was the propriety of universal suffrage.

Q. What is your opinion of the prisoner's character for sincerity and truth?

A. I always thought him to be a civil, honest, good man.

Mr. Ferguson and Mr. Andrew Stirling were next called, to prove the transactions that took place at a meeting held in Scotland, for the reform of the Scotch boroughs. This evidence was objected to by one of the Crown lawyers.

The Attorney-General had no objection to consent that it might be read.

The President. But the Court has an objection to it. The transactions to which these gentlemen are called to speak have no manner of connection with the facts alledged against the prisoner at the bar. Evidence relative to the Irish associations had been received, because the witnesses had spoken with regard to them, and sworn that the reform they intended was the same with that proposed by the Duke of Richmond.

William Towsnap said he was a member of the Society at Sheffield, very nearly from the first to the last; the only object they had in view, was a reform in the House of Commons; and the way they intended to bring it about was by petition. They
pro-

proceeded on the plan of the Duke of Richmond; that was the idea that he formed of the bufinefs; he had no idea that the object of the fociety was different from his own; from the knowledge he had of the fociety, he believed they had the fame ends in view that he had, that he folemnly believed to be the general object of their fociety. If he had the leaft idea that they intended to fubvert the authority of Government, he fhould not have belonged to them, or if he difcovered it fince he became a member, he would have withdrawn himfelf. He always underftood from what was faid in their fociety, that delegates where chofen in order to inform the minds of the people, and to draw up fuch papers to be prefented to Government as they thought the moft conducive to bring about a reform in Parliament; Mr. Brown, their delegate, had no other authority. He faid with regard to the party who oppofed them at Sheffield, he faw people affemble together, and heard them threaten to affault and infult the fociety; and he heard of an inflammatory letter by one Ruffel. With regard to the pikes, he faid he was almoft an entire ftranger to that bufinefs; if it had been the object of the fociety to provide arms, he muft have heard of it, for he was in the committee, and it was a queftion never agitated in the committee, to provide arms againft the Government; he never heard of fuch a thing, either before or fince. He had no idea, for his own part, of any thing but a reform in the Commons Houfe of Parliament, and he really thought and hoped that was the view of the fociety. They had the object of the Duke of Richmond in view, and that was ftated from time to time in the fociety, and a number of his letters to Colonel Sharman had been diftributed among them for the fole purpofe of informing the fociety itfelf of the principles on which they went, and they appeared to him to adhere to the object ftrictly.

On his crofs-examination he faid, he had continued in the fociety for two or three years. That it was their object all along to petition. That he was at Caftle-hill, at Sheffield, at the time of the meeting there; the propofition for petition Parliament was negatived; there was a very large concourfe of people, but he could not fay exactly what was done, for he could not get near enough to hear what was going forward; he might fee an account of the proceedings afterwards in Gale's paper, he believed the queftion for petitioning Parliament again was carried in the negative; he did not hear any voice in the affirmative, and he had not heard of a fingle individual who had withdrawn himfelf, in confequence of the negative to petitioning Parliament. He had fome recollection that the proceedings of the Convention were approved of by their Society. He did not know that the queftion at Caftle-hill was put for the purpofe of being negatived;

tived; that was a matter which he could not speak of. After that propofition was negatived, it was faid to be intended to petition his Majefty. With regard to Mr. Yorke, he faid he had feen him at Sheffield, but never fpoke to him; he did not know of any pikes being prepared under the direction of Yorke. He faid he had heard that Davidfon had written a letter to Hardy after he had been taken up. He had heard of thofe defending themfelves againft what they called the oppofition party.

Being examined again by Mr. Erfkine, he faid if their had been a propofition for arming he muft have heard of it; there could not be any propofition of that kind; he muft have known it if they had any idea of arming; they muft have had a great number indeed of them. The petition that was negatived at the meeting at Caftle-hill, was the petition of the people of Sheffield. They never negatived the idea of prefenting a petition to Parliament, that might be agreed on by the delegates of the Convention.

Edward Smith, cutler, in Sheffield, faid he was a member of the fociety ever fince the year 1791, up to the time when this bufinefs happened; the object of the fociety was to obtain a Parliamentary reform upon the plan of the Duke of Richmond and Mr. Pitt. They had perufed the Duke of Richmond's letter to Colonel Sharman, and that contained their object for every thing. When they talked of the Rights of Man, he underftood equal reprefentation in Parliament; they did not mean any thing about France. If other people's object had been different from his, and he had know it, he would not have been in the fociety a fingle day. He never heard it in the fociety as a thing intended to attack the King or any of his prerogatives; but much the other way. They never wanted to touch the Crown. Their objects were the glorious advantages we obtained in 1688; but he never heard that their object was to be accomplifhed by force. He never heard of arms until a paper was thrown out in the ftreets, and what was publifhed in the Courant, calling upon the people of Sheffield to deftroy thofe whofe opinions were different from themfelves; it was that which produced the arms among fome of the fociety. The party who oppofed the fociety, when any good news arrived from the Continent, came out and fired piftols in the ftreet, and one of them fired at his window; the fociety did not affemble to damp their joy, or ever gave them any offence of any kind; notwithftanding all this the fociety never regularly armed; if they had wifhed it they might have had 10,000 pikes in one day. They never had any idea but that of purfuing their means by peaceable and orderly proceedings, according to the law of the land. He did not exactly know what fome men might mean by calling him a Democrat, but he underftood that it

ment

meant a perſon who wanted to overturn the Houſe of Commons. They never had any idea of touching their Sovereign in any ſhape.

Croſs-examined.

Mr. Garrow in the croſs-examination availed himſelf much of the deplorable ignorance of this old man. Though he had no muſket or pike for his own defence, he applied to no magiſtrate for protection againſt the threats and ill uſage of his perſecutors, nor did he make any application to that effect to the Secretary of State. He acknowledged, though rather reluctantly, that his ſociety had diſtributed hand-bills, exhorting the people in the ſame words as thoſe of the other bill of which he complained, to arm for the protection of their property. Of the plan about which he was ſo ſanguine an advocate, he appeared to have very little conception. The Duke of Richmond's plan, he ſaid, was a free repreſentation, and Mr. Pitt's plan was, that " every man ſhould have his voice." Being aſked if he had not a cheap edition of Tom Paine's book of the Rights of Man? Aye! ſaid he, and I have ſeen the other too. You of courſe thought it a very excellent book? Aye, that I did. I liked it very well. Were there not many thouſands of that work circulated amongſt the cutlers by a ſubſcription of the Society? That and ſome few other books were circulated by ſubſcription. This ſubſcription was only amongſt a few friends.

The Counſel then read the paſſage againſt heritable thrones, where the people were repreſented as flocks and herds, and aſked the witneſs if that was a paſſage very favourable to Kings? He anſwered, that he believed Paine was no great friend to Kings, but that neither he nor his Society ever minded theſe paſſages about Kings: All they wiſhed was a Parliamentary Reform. Several other paſſages were read, to which the anſwers were ſo ſtupid, that we ſhall not tire our readers with them.

He was at the Meeting at Caſtle-hill: did not know that the motion for petitioning Parliament was only put that it may be negatived; the queſtion was carried by a ſhew of hands: did not know that the motion was ſeconded, or that any other hand was held up for it but that of the perſons who made it. He was alſo at the celebration of the Faſt Day, and never heard that his Society had ſent any Addreſs to France. Theſe witneſſes having ſo frequently repeated, that their object was a Reform in Parliament, according to the Duke of Richmond's plan, Mr. Erſkine thought it would be proper to give that plan in evidence, and the next witneſs called was

D d

His

His Grace of Richmond.

Mr. Erskine handing him a copy of the letter to Col. Sharman, "Will your Grace do me the honour to state whether that be a copy of the letter which you addressed to Mr. Sharman in the year 1780?"

Duke of Richmond. "It is extremely difficult for me to tell whether the paper now put into my hand is the same as the letter I wrote to Mr. Sharman or not. I know that there was a mutilated edition of it published at the time."

Mr. Erskine. "Will your Grace have the goodness to look over it, and ascertain whether it be a genuine copy or not."

The Duke proceeding to look over it, the Lord President asked, whether he would wish to retire while he read it in another room.

The Duke said, "I believe I may spare Mr. Erskine some trouble, by giving him a correct copy which I have brought in my pocket."

This was immediately agreed to, and the letter to Col. Sharman, which had been in Court, was read by the Clerk of the Arraigns, while Mr. Garrow and others looked over the Duke's copy, both of which exactly agreed.

His Grace then ascertained that to be the letter which he addressed to Col. Sharman.

Mr. Erskine wishing Col. Sharman's letter to be read, asked the Duke of Richmond whether that letter was not written in answer to one from Col. Sharman after the resolutions taken by the Irish Volunteers, assembled at Lisburne? And whether Col. Sharman's letter and his were not bound up and published together?

The Duke replied, that he wrote the letter in answer to one from Col. Sharman, and they were bound together in the same manner in which they now appeared.

The Attorney General objected to reading Col. Sharman's letter, as the Duke of Richmond's only was referred to in the evidence before the Court.

Mr. Erskine said he was ready to argue that point, but as it was not very material, he would neither exhaust his strength, of which he retained but very little, nor occupy unnecessarily the time of the Court.

After the Duke of Richmond's letter was read, Mr. Erskine offered a piece of evidence on the part of the prisoner, which was opposed by Mr. Attorney General. Mr. Erskine wished to produce witnesses to prove what they had heard the prisoner at the bar declare in conversation, with respect to a Reform of Parliament, and what his sentiments were with regard to a Convention of the People, &c. After a very learned argument, Mr.

Erskine

Erskine and Mr. Gibbs on the one hand, and the Attorney General and Solicitor General on the other,

Chief Justice Eyre said, the Court went a certain way with Mr. Erskine. Nothing was so clear as that all declarations that applied to the facts of the case, were evidence against the prisoner, though not evidence for him. It was presumed that no man would declare any thing against himself that was not true. That was the general rule; but if the question here was as his Lordship thought it was, what were the political speculative opinions which the prisoner at the bar entertained touching a Reform of Parliament; his Lordship was of opinion that that might very well be learned and discovered by the conversations which he had held at any time, or at any place. If his declarations were meant to apply to a disavowal of the particular charge made against him, as for instance, if he had said to some friend, when there was a plan for holding a Convention, that it did not mean to affect the King and the Government, such a declaration could not be given in evidence in favour of the prisoner, though it would be evidence against him, because it was supposed he would not have made such a declaration unless it were true.

Of the Duke of Richmond's excellent composition, the following extracts are most important with respect to the prisoner's defence:

"Sir,

"I have been honoured with a letter from Belfast, dated the 19th July last, written in the name of the Committee of Correspondence, appointed by the delegates of forty-five volunteer corps, assembled at Lisburn on the 1st of the same month, for taking preparatory steps to forward their intention on the subject of a more equal Representation of the People in Parliament," and signed by their secretary, Henry Joy, jun. Esq.

"In this letter, after shewing the corrupt state of the boroughs in Ireland, the general opinion of the people that the constitution can be restored to it's antient purity and vigour by no other means than a Parliamentary Reform, and informing me of the steps which have been taken, and are taking by the volunteers, in determining to procure this desirable object, the committee is pleased to request my sentiments and advice as to the best, most elegible, and most practicable mode of destroying, restraining, or counteracting this hydra of corruption, borough influence, in order to lay my opinion before the Provincial Assembly of Delegates, which is to be held at Dungannon on the 8th of September next.

"The subject of a Parliamentary Reform is that which of all others, in my opinion, most deserves the attention of the public, as I conceive it would include every other advantage which a nation can wish; and I have no hesitation in saying, that from every consideration which I have been able to give to this great question,

question, that for many years has occupied my mind, and from every day's experience, to the present hour, I am more and more convinced, that the restoring the right of voting universally to every man, not incapacitated by nature for want of reason, or by law for the commission of crimes, together with annual elections, is the only reform that can be effectual and permanent. I am further convinced, that it is the only reform that is practicable.

"All other plans that are of a palliative nature have been found insufficient to interest and animate the great body of the people, from whose earnestness alone any reform can be expected. A long exclusion from any share in the legislature of their country has rendered the great mass of the people indifferent whether the monopoly that subsists continues in the hands of a more or less extended company; or whether it is divided by them into shares of somewhat more or less just proportions. The public feels itself unconcerned in these contests, except as to the oppressions it endures, and the exactions it suffers, which it knows must continue so long as the people remain deprived of all controul over their representatives.

"The lesser reform has been attempted with every possible advantage in it's favour; not only from the zealous support of the advocates for a more effectual one, but from the assistance of men of great weight, both in and out of power. But with all these temperaments and helps it has failed. Not one proselyte has been gained from corruption, nor has the least ray of hope been held out from any quarter, that the House of Commons was inclined to adopt any other mode of reform. The weight of corruption has crushed this more gentle, as it would have defeated any more efficacious plan in the same circumstances. From that quarter therefore, I have nothing to hope. It is from the people at large that I expect any good. And I am convinced that the only way to make them feel that they are really concerned in the business is to contend for their full, clear, and indisputable Rights of Universal Representation. The more extensive plan, at the same time that it's operation is more complete, depends on a more effectual support, that of the people.

"I am also persuaded that if the scheme for additional county members had proceeded any further, infinite difficulties would have arisen in adjusting it. Neither the Yorkshire Committee nor Mr. Pitt have given the detail of their plan. A just repartition would have been a most intricate task, for where different interests are separately represented, the proportion is not very easy to ascertain. The doubt you state concerning this mode of reform appears to me well founded; a few great families might divide a county between them, and chuse the members by a house list, like East-India Directors. Another difficulty, from the increase of the number of members, which might render the house more tumultuous than deliberate, has it's weight. But the greatest objection, in my opinion, to this and to every other narrow and contracted plan of reform is, that it proceeds upon the same bad principle as the

abuse

abuse it pretends to rectify; it is still partial and unequal; a vast majority of the community is still left unrepresented; and it's most essential concerns, life, liberty, and property, continue in the absolute disposal of those whom they do not chuse, and over whom they have no controul. In the arrangement of plans of this kind, there is no leading principle to determine that the addition ought to be one hundred and fifty, or two hundred; that the allotment should be according to the population, property, or taxes paid in each county; that any supposed proportion between the landed and trading interest is the just one, and that the division of County and City members will correspond with this proportion when found. All is a sea, without any compass to enable us to distinguish the safe from the dangerous course.

" But in the more liberal and great plan of universal representation, a clear and distinct principle at once appears that cannot lead us wrong. Not conveniency, but right; if it is not a maxim of our constitution, that a British subject is to be governed only by laws to which he has consented by himself or his representative, we should instantly abandon the error; but if it is the essential of freedom, founded on the eternal principles of justice and wisdom, and our unalienable birth-right, we should not hesitate in asserting it. Let us then but determine to act on this broad principle of giving to every man his own, and we shall immediately get rid of all the perplexities to which the narrow notions of partiality and exclusion must ever be subject.

" In the digesting a plan upon this noble foundation, we shall not find any difficulty that the most common understanding and pains will not easily surmount.

" The present number of members in the House of Commons is preserved, so that all apprehension from too numerous an assembly ceases.

" An account of the whole number of males of age in the kingdom is, to be taken and divided by the number of members to be sent, which will find the quota of electors to chuse one member; from the best acounts I can now get, it will be about two thousand six hundred; these are to be formed into districts or boroughs from the most contiguous parishes; and by having all the elections throughout the kingdom in one and the same day, and taken in each parish, all fear of riot and tumult vanishes.

" The great expence of elections, which arises chiefly from the cost of conveying electors to the place of poll, and entertaining them there and on the road, will be no more when every man will vote in his own parish. Bribery must intirely cease; in a single Borough it would be difficult, on so many as to have any effect, impossible. The numbers to be bought would be infinitely too great for any purse. Besides, annual Parliaments, by their frequency and by their shortness, would doubtless operate in preventing corruption.

" The vast expence of petitions to Parliament on account of
illegal

illegal returns would be reduced almoſt to nothing. The points on which theſe conteſts generally turn, are the qualifications of the electors under the numberleſs reſtrictions the preſent laws have impoſed, which require the attendance of witneſſes, the production of records, and are ſubject to infinite diſpute. But when no other qualifications ſhould be neceſſary but that of being a a Britiſh ſubject, and of age, there can be but little left to contend upon as to the right of electors to vote.

But there is another ſort of objection, againſt which no proviſion can be made, as it is merely imaginary. It is feared by ſome that the influence of poverty and riches will give to the Ariſtocracy ſo great a lead in theſe elections, as to place the whole government in their hands. Others again dread, that when paupers and the loweſt orders of the People ſhall have an equal vote with the firſt commoner in the kingdom, we ſhall fall into all the confuſion of a democratic republic. The contrariety of theſe two apprehenſions might of itſelf be a ſufficient proof that neither extreme will take place. It is true that the pooreſt man in the kingdom will have an equal vote with the firſt, for the choice of a perſon to whom he entruſts his all; and I think he ought to have that equal degree of ſecurity againſt oppreſſion.

Another ſubject of apprehenſion is, that the principle of allowing to every man an equal right to vote tends to equality in other reſpects, and to level property. To me it ſeems to have a direct contrary tendency.

The protection of property appears to me one of the moſt eſſential ends of ſociety; and, ſo far from injuring it by this plan, I conceive it to be the only means of preſerving it; for the preſent ſyſtem is haſtening with great ſtrides to *perfect equality in univerſal poverty.*

It has been ſaid, that this plan of extending the right of voting to every individual creates much uneaſineſs in the minds of quiet and well diſpoſed perſons: and that if paupers, vagabonds, and perſons of no property were left out, there would be no objection to extend it to all houſeholders and perſons paying taxes, and that the fairer diviſion into diſtricts might take place. My anſwer is, that I know of no man, let him be ever ſo poor, who in his conſumption of food, and uſe of raiment, does not pay taxes; and that I would wiſh to encourage an enthuſiaſm for his country in the breaſt of every ſubject, by giving him his juſt ſhare in it's government. I readily admit, that ſuch an alteration would be a vaſt improvement; but I muſt prefer the adhering rigidly to a ſelf-evident principle, eſpecially when attended with no inconvenience in the execution, that I can foreſee. Beſides, we ſhould again fall into the difficulties of drawing the line of ſeparation, and into the diſputes about qualifications.

For my part, I agree in opinion with thoſe who are for reſtoring to all parts of the ſtate their juſt rights at the ſame time; to do it generally, not partially, is what I muſt contend for. At the ſame time

time, I admit I am not for restoring the negative of the crown. My reason is, that it appears to me preposterous that the will of one man should for ever obstruct every regulation which all the rest of the nation may think necessary. I object to it, as I would to any other prerogative to the crown, or privilege of the Lords or People, that are not founded on reason.

But I agree, that if the House of Commons was reduced to it's natural dependence on the people alone, and the present system of making it the exclusive part of government was continued, we should approach to a pure democracy more than our constitution warrants, or than I wish to see. I am not for a democratic, any more than for an aristocratic, or monarchic government, solely; I am for that admirable mixture of three, that our inimitable and comprehensive constitution has established; I wish to see the executive part of government revert to where the constitution has originally placed it, in the hands of the crown, to be carried on by it's ministers; those ministers under the controul of Parliament; and Parliament under the controul of the people. I would not have Parliament made, as it daily is, a party concerned in every act of state, whereby it becomes the executive for which it is not calculated, and loses it's superintending and controuling power, which is the main end of it's institution. For when the two Houses are previously pledged by addresses, votes, and resolutions, it becomes extremely difficult for them afterwards to censure measures in which they have been so deeply engaged by acts of their own. Another great inconvenience arises from Parliament's taking so much of the executive of government on itself, which is, the excessive length of the sessions; an evil which of late had greatly increased. Now that parliament is engaged in every detail in order to screen the minister, it never can finish it's business till the middle of the summer, when the independent country gentleman, tired of a long attendance and hot weather in town, is retired to his private business in the country, and that of the public left to be settled in thin houses by a few dependants of the minister. A short session of two or three months would be sufficient to examine the expenditure of former grants, to make new ones, to redress grievances, and pass such general laws as circumstances might require. The inconveniency and expence to a private member of parliament in attending his duty would then be trifling; and, instead of forty commoners, and three peers, to form a quorum to decide the greatest matters of state, the attendance of two thirds of each body, which would give respect to their proceedings, might and ought to be required. I am also free to own my opinion, that when the House of Lords shall be effectually prevented from having any influence in the House of Commons, as I think it must by this bill, it should at the same time recover it's equal rights in every respect with the House of Commons as a co-ordinate branch of legislature. These sentiments are, I think, consonant to the idea so well expressed in your letter to the volunteer army of the province of Ulster,

Ulster, " to restore to the crown it's original splendor, to Nobility it's ancient privileges, and to the Nation at large it's inherent rights."

A clerk of the House of Lords then attended with a journal of the proceedings dated the 8th of February 1780. It contained a motion of the Earl of Shelburne for a committee of those who were not placemen, pensioners, &c. to consider of the expenditure of the public revenue, and the means we had of defraying these expences. The motion was made in consequence of a petition couched in very strong language; and the motion was negatived. A protest was then entered in, which after describing the expences of the war to be so great as to exceed the patience which may be expected in the people to bear the additional taxes, to which they would give, said that their resource must then be in pensions, sinecures, and useless places. It asserted the right of the people to associate in bodies for the attainment of their reasonable demands, as associations proclaimed more loudly the voice of the nation than the remonstrances of individuals, &c.

This address was signed by that venerable constitutional lawyer Earl Camden, together with the illustrious names of Richmond, Portland, Devonshire, Grafton, Shelburne, Rockingham, Fitzwilliam, Tankerville, &c. &c. This protest was acknowledged by the Duke of Richmond, and Mr. Erskine said it supported and maintained all those proceedings which were now brought against Hardy as charges of High Treason.

A. Stirling identified the minutes of the Scotch Borough convention.

Mr. Ferguson was called.

Mr. Erskine said that much stress had been laid on the circumstance of the societies having adopted French phrases, particularly the terms Convention and Delegates; he had called this gentleman to prove that he was a delegate to a convention of respectable gentlemen in Scotland at the same time that the British convention were assembled in Edinburgh.

Chief Justice Eyre. I object to such evidence, as being quite irrelevant; it would lead to a history entirely unconnected with the cause.

Joseph Strutt was then called. He had belonged to a society instituted for the purpose of obtaining a reform in parliament.

Mr. Erskine asked him, had the society any other object?

A. No.

Q. Did it meditate any thing against the other two branches of the legislature?—A. It certainly did not. Since the rejection of the petition to the House of Commons, I believe the society has not assembled more than once.

Mr. Erskine proposed next to give in evidence the resolutions of the Association at the Thatched House Tavern in 1789.

The Lord President. What would you say if we were of opinion that these associations amounted o High Treason?

Mr.

Mr. Erskine. My Lord, I can hardly conceive it possible that some of the greatest characters in the kingdom, and some of the greatest favourites of the King, should have been guilty of High Treason.

- President. We know nothing of the circumstances of those associations.

Mr. Erskine said, he was ready to state them to his Lordship. He was however over-ruled.

Richard Brinsley Sheridan, Esq. was the next witness for the prisoner.

Mr. Erskine stated to the Court, that he called this gentleman to prove that Hardy had offered all his papers to be laid before parliament in the year 1793.

Question to Mr. Sheridan. Did you ever see the prisoner?
A. Yes.
Q. At what time?
A. The first time was in the month of March 1793. I'll state, as shortly as possible, how the circumstance happened. I had given notice in the House of Commons of a motion for a Committee of that House, to enquire into the seditious practices that were said to exist in several societies in this metropolis.

Q. Was the Scotch Convention sitting at that time?
A. I do not perfectly recollect. Having given the notice, I thought it was my duty to collect all the information possible on the subject. I was rather unbelieving with respect to what I had heard of the extent to which seditious practices were carried in those societies. By the advice of a gentleman of my acquaintance, I sent for Mr. Hardy. He immediately came to me. I shewed him the book which was circulated among the Members of the two Houses of Parliament, giving an account of the proceedings of those societies. He observed, that, in many things, government had received very correct intelligence, particularly with respect to the number of the divisions, and the places of their assembling; but he complained that their objects and principles had been greatly misstated and misrepresented.

Q. Did he, Sir, declare what their real object was?
A. He declared that their whole object was to obtain, by peaceable means, a parliamentary reform, on the plan of the Duke of Richmond. Upon my interrogating him, (I do not mean that I considered him under any obligation to answer) he told me the societies did not meet at the same places where they used to assemble. As they consisted chiefly of persons who could not afford to spend much, the keepers of public houses had been easily induced to dismiss them. I asked Mr. Hardy if the societies continued to meet any where. He answered, yes; and he

E e   had

had no objection to give me a list of the private houses where they had held their meetings. I took down the names of several of these places.

Q. Have you the paper now?

A. I believe I have lost it. I had it in my hand the day I made the motion in the House of Commons. Mr. Hardy offered me a sight of all the books, papers, and correspondence of the society; and he requested that, if I thought proper, I would make the contents of them known in parliament. When he understood the nature of the motion I intended to make, he expressed a most eager and ardent wish that the committee might be appointed, and that an enquiry into the affairs and conduct of the societies might be instituted.

Q. Was this offer voluntary, or did he conceive that he was bound to make it to you as a Member of Parliament or a Magistrate?

A. The offer was voluntary, and, as I believed, arising from a sincere wish that the motion I intended to make should be successful; that is, that a Committee of Enquiry might be instituted.

Cross-examined by the Attorney General.

Q. Did Mr. Hardy ever shew you any book, journal, or books?

A. Mr. Hardy did not shew me any journal, or book or books. He offered generally to give me all the information respecting the society he could. He said they had been greatly calumniated by the publications of government.

Q. Are you, Sir, a Member of the Society for Constitutional Information? A. Mr. Attorney, I hardly know whether I am, or not; I have not formally withdrawn my name from the books, but I have not attended the society since the year 1793; I should suppose I am a Member.

Mr. Francis was next called.

Q. Do you know the prisoner?

A. I do; but I never saw him more than once. On or before the 3d of May, 1793, Mr. Hardy sent to me, requesting me to present to the House of Commons a Petition for a Parliamentary Reform; and that I would permit Mr. Margarot and two of the Delegates whose names I forget, to come to my house on the subject;—they came, and, as the form of the petition seemed perfectly respectful, I told them I would present it; informing them, at the same time, that I was perfectly adverse to it's prayer. Hardy appeared to me to be a remarkable quiet, temperate man. I was surprised at the readiness of their arguments in defence of universal suffrage. Margarot said I need not be surprised, for they had learnt these arguments from the Duke of Richmond. I mentioned that

I thought

I thought it would have been better to leave the mode of redress, as in other cases, to the wisdom of Parliament. They said, they were sorry they had not known my objections sooner; but it was then impossible to alter the petition, as the names were subscribed, and there would not be time enough to prepare a new petition before the 6th of May, when Mr. Grey was to make his motion.

They all shewed remarkable readiness to hear reasonable arguments and objections.

On cross-examination, Mr. Francis said, the Delegates shewed great anxiety about the fate of their petition. They had forwarded it to Mr. Fox, who had refused to present it. Now they adhered to their original approbation of universal suffrage; they never said that they would accept of nothing less than universal suffrage. The letter of thanks sent by the London Corresponding Society to Mr. Francis, with that Gentleman's answer, were read. He said, he thought they were much misled, but he did not believe that they had any other objects than those which they professed.

Lord Lauderdale was next examined. He said, he had received a letter from the Society of the Friends of the People in the suburbs of Edinburgh, requesting to become a delegate to the Scotch Convention. He had seen Skirving, who had urged him to accept the offer. He said, that his (Lord Lauderdale's) coming among them would prevent them from committing those irregularities and informalities, which they might otherwise fall into; he heard nothing among them injurious to the Crown or the House of Lords. Their language was, to acquire, by peaceable means, a thorough Reform in Parliament.

The evidence on both sides being concluded,

Mr. Gibbs rose for the prisoner, but was so agitated as to be obliged to sit down in order to recover himself. After some minutes he proceeded—That he needed not state the anxiety of mind which he felt on the present occasion. He now rose, sinking under the weight of a cause in which the mighty abilities of his honourable and learned friend had almost sunk. It was not because he had any wish to spare himself; he was not desirous to withhold either his strength or abilities. Such as they were, they had been exerted to the utmost; he would defend the prisoner if his strength was equal to the task of conducting the defence; but he confessed himself unable to comprehend the vast mass of evidence which had been brought forward. On his part, no industry had been wanting, during the period of interval allowed by the Court. But he begged to advert to the particular and unprecedented circumstances of the present case. The Attorney General, in his opening speech, took up a space of nine hours—a circumstance unheard of in the annals of history—no speech, upon any occasion, had perhaps ever extended to so great a length. Yet to suppose that he had stated the case at greater length than was necessary, or had brought forward evidence which was not connected with the subject, would be to suppose that he intended to puzzle and harrass the counsel, and to confound and perplex the Jury. His learned friend, Mr. Erskine, himself, was unable to comprehend that immense and complicated mass of evidence; indeed it was impossible for any counsel so to comprehend it, as to be able to make a fair defence. First, he would state what was the law, which was to be found in the indictment, and in the statute of treason, as it applies to that indictment. The first charge of the indictment was that of compassing the King's death, and the overt act charged was that of concerting the plan of a convention, with a view to depose the King in order that they might afterwards destroy him. It was not necessary to state the other overt acts, because their tendency was the same. The facts stated against the prisoner were these:—first, that he had an intention of mind to destroy the King; secondly, that, in pursuance of that intention, he did the acts pursued in the indictment. His learned friend had argued very ably on the statute of Edward III. on which the present indictment was founded. The first treason in the Statute, and the first charge in the indictment, was compassing the King's death. In the present case, the form of the indictment and the statute went hand in hand. When he recollected that his learned friend (Mr. Erskine) had already so fully and ably stated what was the law of the case, he was sure the Jury would regret that it was at all necessary for him to go over the same ground. Lord Coke had very forcibly commented on the statute of Edward III. and what he had said on the subject shewed how exceedingly careful an English Jury ought to be, not to extend the statute beyond it's proper limits. (He then read an extract from Lord Coke's Institutes.) This passage contained an exhortation to all Juries, not to find their verdict guilty, without plain, direct, and manifest proof. Such was the proof which the legislature required in cases of treason, and such was the proof which the Jury were bound to require in the present instance. In proof of his assertion, he referred to the proceedings on the trial of Lord Russel for High Treason.

The doctrine delivered on that occasion he supposed to be law, because it had been alluded to from the Bench in the course of the present trial.

The indictment charged Lord Russel with conspiring to seize the King's guards, in order to destroy his Majesty. The evidence on the case went to prove the existence of such a conspiracy. Yet my Lord Chief Justice Pemberton, in his charge to the Jury, said to them, "You are to find whether, upon the whole matter, any design has been entertained against the King's life." Yet no man would complain that the proceedings on that trial were not sufficiently severe.

What made this proceeding on this occasion the more remarkable was, on the same morning some persons had been tried for being engaged in the Rye-House plot, and the distinction was taken in Court, that these persons stood in a different situation from that of Lord Russel, having been directly engaged in a plot to murder the King.

Such

Such was the charge of Lord Chief Juftice Pemberton, though the friends of Lord Ruffel complained that he was feverely dealt with, he left it to the Jury to find upon the whole matter before them. The Jury found their verdict guilty; and furely, when it was proved to them that a plot was in agitation to feize upon the King's guards, who were entrufted with the immediate protection of his perfon, they might reafonably enough form the conclufion that his life was aimed at. Yet when Lord Ruffel was brought up to receive fentence, and heard the indictment read, he ftarted back upon hearing the charge of compaffing the King's death, and was proceeding to ftate that the overt act by no means came under that defcription, when he was anfwered by the Recorder, that fuch a remark might, with propriety, have previoufly been made to the Jury, but that they had now found upon the whole matter, and that all fuch objections were too late. It was evident, therefore, that the point for the Jury, in all fuch cafes, was to confider whether the overt act charged in the fubfequent part of the indictment amounted to the treafon charged in the former part.

Having ftated what was the law of the cafe, he now came more particularly to confider what was charged againft the prifoner. It was ftated in the indictment, that he had concerted to call a Convention, in order to overthrow the Government, and depofe the King. It was allowed on all hands that he had agreed to call a Convention, but that the object of the propofed Convention was fuch as was charged in the indictment, the Counfel for the Prifoner could by no means admit. In order to prove that fuch was indeed the object, it would be neceffary for the profecution for the Crown to fhew, firft, that no Convention had in any inftance been called, except for treafonable purpofes—and fecondly, that this Convention was really called for the purpofe of depofing the King, and thereby compaffing his death. We on the other hand contend, that this Convention was in itfelf legal, and called for lawful purpofes. The prifoner believed that corruption had made great ftrides in the Britifh Conftitution, and that confiderable abufes had crept into the original frame of the Government. He was of opinion that it was neceffary, in order to reftore the Conftitution to it's purity, that thefe abufes fhould be redreffed; and at the fame time he had found, that every petition of individuals, demanding a remedy, had been peremptorily, not to fay contumelioufly, rejected. In this fituation, he thought that the only way to collect the voice of the people, and to convey it to Parliament with due effect, would be to call a Convention. All this was contended by the profecution for the Crown to be mere pretext. " You did not," fay they to the prifoner, " think that there exifted abufes in the Conftitution which might be remedied by calling a Convention; you talked of redreffing it's abufes by the very means you intended fhould effect it's fubverfion." But before a Jury be induced to give credit to a charge of this nature, it muft firft be made out by plain, direct, and manifeft proof.

There

There are two points which the prosecution for the Crown have laboured: first, to prove that there existed in the kingdom a general conspiracy of different societies; and, secondly, that the prisoner was concerned in the plots of all these societies. Both of these they thought necessary for the purpose of making out the guilt of the prisoner. They have therefore brought evidence of every thing that has been declared or done in all these societies, and which they contend proceeded from a design to depose the King, in order afterwards to destroy him; and in the whole of this plot they affirm that the prisoner was engaged. By this means the Counsel for the prisoner are laid under considerable hardship. It became impossible distinctly to state what part of the proof did or did not immediately affect the prisoner. Even his honourable friend, with all his abilities, had not been able to discriminate with respect to the complicated proof that had been brought forward. Sometimes evidence was produced of what had been done in one society, then of what had been done in another; nay, the actions and expressions of different individuals were brought together, in order to load the prisoner with the accumulated guilt of high treason.

Had the Counsel for the prosecution first brought forward the general proof of the existence of a conspiracy in the country, and, secondly, the particular proof as it affected the prisoner, the difficulty would then have been obviated. As the evidence has been brought forward, it has become impossible properly to discriminate between it's several parts, in conducting the defence. It was not his business to say whether some of the circumstances that had come out in evidence were criminal, or not; but he defied his learned friend to prove that any of these amounted to an overt act of high treason. He would not contend that there might not be some instances of improper or indecent conduct to be found in the transactions of those societies; but these, it is to be considered, proceeded from a rash or irritated mind. All that made for the prisoner ought to be taken into consideration, as well as what made against him. If it was alledged that the reform proposed to be obtained by holding a Convention was merely a pretext, the uniform tenor of the papers that had been produced proved that it was really his object.

Another charge brought against the societies was their introduction of French terms. But this was a charge which would have no weight; for when it had that day been attempted to prove that the terms Convention and Delegates, on which so much stress had been laid, were not adopted from the example of the French, but were English terms, in common use, the evidence was rejected by the Bench as immaterial, and not at all fit to be taken into consideration by the Jury. No inference, therefore, was to be drawn, that this alledged introduction of French terms implied by any means an adoption of French ideas.

Another charge was, that they approved of the French revolution. It was natural for them to approve of that revolution, because they were Englishmen, and because they were freemen. It

was

was natural for them to rejoice that a nation so long held in the most abject slavery, were at last likely to participate in that freedom which was the glory and the boast of Englishmen. But it was said that they continued to approve of the French revolution, after it had been disgraced by the most sanguinary excesses. Was it therefore to be inferred that they approved of those excesses, or wished a similar conduct to be pursued in this country? They might approve of the original revolution, as restoring freedom to a great nation, and at the same time lament those acts of cruelty by which it had been afterwards tarnished. At any rate, it was by no means to be inferred that they conceived that a similar revolution ought to take place in this country. Here the same necessity did not exist; they had not the same grounds of complaint from an overbearing Nobility, and an arbitrary Monarch. Even if, from a misguided zeal for freedom, they had approved of the worst acts of the French revolution, they were not to be set down as traitors to the free constitution of this country. But it was alledged that they had gone so far as to wish for an union with France; and what good subject would not wish for such an union? Enough surely had been experienced of the calamities of war to render such an union desirable, if it could honourably be effected. They might be mistaken in their politics, but they were not therefore to be branded as guilty in their intentions.

Another charge brought against them was, that they had passed a resolution to insert in the books of the society the speeches of Roland and Kersaint—a resolution which, by the bye, was never carried into effect. And what was the mighty guilt attached to such a resolution, which, at most, could only have afforded to the members an opportunity of being acquainted with the sentiments of the leading men in France. But how did a charge of this nature apply to the prisoner, a poor shoemaker, who could not be supposed to understand French, or be a reader of the Moniteur, in which these speeches were originally inserted? If they approved of the reasons for putting to death the King of France, were they to be supposed to entertain the same sentiments with respect to the King of England? What was the state of the case? The King of France had accepted of a Constitution which he was charged with having violated, and under which he suffered. The King of England never violated that Constitution by which he holds his Crown: he reigns less by the terror of his authority, than the influence of his virtues: he has nothing to fear for his security, while he lives in the hearts of his subjects.

But it has been said that they must have meant to have recourse to force, because they had resolved in future not to petition Parliament. It appeared to him that such a resolution necessarily preceded the measure of calling a Convention. If the petitions of individuals had been successful in order to procure a reform, there would have been no necessity for calling a Convention. It was because these petitions had been rejected that they therefore
though

thought a Convention would give greater effect to their request, and procure that redress which had been refused to their former applications. The protest of the venerable Lord Camden had been that day read in Court, from which, among other things, it appeared that after petitions had been rejected, the voice of a Convention was a Legal and Constitutional mode of conveying the sense of the people to the ear of Parliament. A good deal of stress had been laid on the proceedings of the Scotch Convention, particularly the resolution to resist the passing of a particular act by the Legislature. But to conspire to procure the repeal of an act already passed does not amount to High Treason: therefore the act of conspiring to resist an act that is not at all in existence, cannot surely constitute that crime. The Prisoner was only interested in the proceedings of the Scotch Convention, so far as the Delegates had acted under the authority and agreeably to the instructions of the Society to which it belonged.

The proceedings of that Convention he was not interested to defend:—they were such as he highly disapproved. But it did not appear to him that the Prisoner ought to be affected by proceedings, in which, in the first instance, he had no share. They were attempted to be fixed upon the society to which he belonged, in consequence of the subsequent publications. But they were then irritated at the fate of their Delegates—a fate which, from high legal authority, had been admitted to be severe; some allowance was to be made for what was done in the moment of irritation, and an English Jury would not be extreme to mark expressions rashly and hastily uttered. But he had legal authority to prove, that no act of the Scotch Convention amounted to High Treason; some of the Delegates to that Convention had been tried for a misdemeanour, and found guilty upon the same evidence which had been brought in the present instance to establish the charge of High Treason. But if the acts of the Delegates did not amount to Treason, much less could the concerts to bring about the Convention come under that description. He now came to the parole evidence brought to prove that the direct object of the Prisoner, and all the Societies, by calling a Convention, was to depose the King, in order that they might afterwards destroy him. The first witnesses were those from Sheffield, Camage and Broomhead, who were called to shew that means had actually been taken to support the Convention by force against the whole armed body of the Government. They proved indeed that some pikes had been prepared—but in what circumstances? They were made by a party, because they had every reason to apprehend an attack from those who differed with them in sentiment; inflammatory hand-bills had been circulated, in order to excite the populace against them; a musket had been

fired

fired into one of their houses. In such a situation, it was both their right and their duty to provide against an illegal attack. Neither the legality, nor the necessity of arming themselves, could in such a case be disputed. He here referred to the case of Dr. Priestley, who would have been justified in resisting the mob who destroyed his house—of Mr. Walker, of Manchester, who had experienced the effects of the same lawless fury—and, lastly, of the Mayor of Nottingham, who in defending his house, killed two of the rioters by whom he was attacked. But how was this charge of providing arms attempted to be fixed on the Prisoner? Because he, forsooth, was a member of a society which had corresponded with the Sheffield Society, and had received a letter on the subject of arms. This letter he does not answer, he does not even so much as communicate it's contents, except to one person, who asks him where he must apply in order to procure a pike; he does not send a letter which it incloses according to the directions; in short, he takes no step which can imply the smallest approbation of the proposal contained in that latter. Had he taken any step, it would not have failed to have appeared in evidence, surrounded as he has been for three years by a host of spies, who were continually at his elbow, who watched his every motion, and caught up every expression that fell from his lips. Was this evidence of such a nature as could convince any reasonable mind that the Prisoner intended to resist all the military force and armed associations of Great Britain? What were the means provided for this purpose? About three dozen of pikes, an order for sixty muskets, and somewhat less than half a dozen French case-knives. Such was the facility of arming themselves, that it had been stated in evidence, that in Sheffield they might have provided themselves with ten thousand pikes in one day. If they had the will, it appeared then that they had the means; but though they had begun to arm in 1792, or in the beginning of 1793, they had made no further progress in arming than he had just now had occasion to mention. Mr. Gibbs then proceeded to examine the circumstances of Hardy having recommended Williams, who was his customer, to the sale of a few muskets, and the armed Association of Franklow. This Association, he would not contend whether it was proper or improper, but it was at least open and avowed; Franklow appeared publicly in his uniform, and his cartridge-box lay exposed to view in his shop. Franklow was an old dabbler in military matters, and might chuse, when armed Associations were the fashion of the day, to have one of his own. He remembered himself once to have been in arms, and to have acted as Lieutenant, under his friend, Mr. Erskine, in 1780. Good God! exclaimed Mr. Gibbs, if such evidence be admitted to convict a man of High Treason, who can possibly be safe for a moment? Or, what sentence can we expect from the

Judge

Judge of the Univerſe, in the great day of retribution, if we can be ſatisfied upon ſuch proofs to condemn a fellow-creature? The next witneſs was Goſling, one of that infamous race of men who having no means of ſupport of their own, endeavour to pick up a livelihood by inſinuating themſelves into the confidence of others, in order that they might betray their ſecrets to Government. He would not ſay that the evidence of ſuch perſons, where it was corroborated with other teſtimony, ought not to be admitted, but it ought always to be received with extreme caution. In his chief examination, he had his ſtory quite ready and preciſe, but in his croſs-examination, he was abaſhed, confounded, and unable to reply even to the ſimpleſt queſtions. Some part of his evidence carried with it it's own contradiction. He ſtated that a man had gone about the country to tamper with the ſoldiers; that with ſome he had ſucceeded, but that many had reſiſted. If ſuch had been the caſe, could not theſe ſoldiers eaſily have been produced in evidence, and in the anxiety which had been ſhewn to procure proof from all quarters, would ſuch material witneſſes have been omitted? Another witneſs of the ſame ſort was Lynam; he ſpoke from notes, which, in many inſtances, were incorrect, and though taken for the expreſs purpoſe of being given in evidence, are all vague and general. He, forſooth, had not attended to particulars, he had only gathered the general ſtrain of the converſation, and in order to fix any particular imputation of criminality, he was obliged to have recourſe to his recollection. To the evidence given by ſuch a witneſs, no degree of credit was due. He next came to the evidence of Mr. Groves, upon which he commented at ſome length. This man appeared, by the ſubſequent teſtimony of Green, to have been guilty of perjury; and by his own croſs-examination, of a voluntary ſuppreſſion of the truth, in order to keep back evidence that might have been favourable to the Priſoner. Such were the arts to which this infamous Spy had recourſe, in order to enhance the value of his own evidence to his employers, and poiſon the courſe of juſtice. Yet even from his teſtimony, corroborated by that of the other witneſſes, it appeared, that the only object of theſe Societies was a Reform in the Repreſentation of the People, to be obtained by legal and peaceable means, and that they had not the ſmalleſt intention of interfering either with the dignity of the Peers or the authority of the Crown. An attempt had been made to fix upon the Priſoner the guilt of the man lately executed in Edinburgh—likewiſe a Spy of Miniſters, who having overvalued his ſervices, was diſmiſſed, and in attempting to make a plot, which might entitle him to a reward from Government, the expence of the lives of innocent or deluded men, was caught in his own ſnare, and hanged as he richly deſerved—

a perſon

a perſon too with whom Hardy, the priſoner, had no correſpondence, and whom it could not even be proved, that he knew by name. A queſtion had been put to the witneſſes whether they thought that theſe Societies intended to purſue their object by peaceable and orderly means. This was intended to throw duſt into the eyes of the Jury; it was not the queſtion how far the means were in themſelves peaceable and orderly, but whether they went to depoſe and ultimately to deſtroy the King. If one act did not clearly amount to High Treaſon, all the acts brought out in evidence could not by any fair conſtruction of the law of England amount to that crime. Though the whole Court were full of offenſive matter—though the evidence went to prove innumerable libels and miſdemeanors, ſtill the Jury, laying aſide all conſiderations of politics, and attending only to facts, were bound only to find a verdict guilty upon the plain, direct and manifeſt proof of the crime of High Treaſon. Miſerable as the evidence was with reſpect to the ſubject of arms, yet without it nothing could have been done in making out the charges of the indictment. It was proof of ſuch a nature as would even weaken the force of a ſtrong caſe, and the preſent caſe would certainly have been much ſtronger, if no ſuch charge had been introduced. The overt-act, he apprehended, was the reſolution to call a Convention, the words of which he read; yet ſurrounded as they had been by Spies, not one proof had been brought to connect this calling of a Convention with any preparation of armed force, or to ſhew that they intended to proceed to the object in any other way than by the peaceable means of diſcuſſion. Yet if they could not prove that this reſolution to call a Convention, was connected with a determination to ſupport it by armed force, they proved nothing to the purpoſe.

One curious circumſtance he could not but remark, that the counſel for the proſecution ſeemed much better acquainted with the evidence for the defence, than even the counſel for the priſoner:—for inſtance, when a Mr. Stevens was called, they aſked whether it was Mr. Stevens of Rathbone-place, or Mr. Stevens of the Minories. If there was, therefore, any deficiency of proof on the part of the proſecution, it did not at leaſt ariſe from any want of care in providing witneſſes, nor could it be ſuppoſed that there remained any thing behind which could have been brought forward to advantage. Yet there was hardly one act which had been brought forward in evidence which had been made public at the time by the ſocieties themſelves—ſo far were they from being conſcious of any illegal conduct or treaſonable intentions. Of the evidence called for the priſoners, two were particularly entitled to attention.

He referred to the evidence of Mr. Sheridan and Mr. Francis, as proof that the priſoner could have no evil intention. To Mr. Sheridan he had offered the inſpection of all his papers without reſerve. Mr. Francis he had aſked to preſent a Petition to the Houſe

House of Commons, praying for univerſal ſuffrage and annual election; reaſoned upon the ſubject, and profeſſed his adherence to the Duke of Richmond's principles. On being told that it was informal in a petition complaining of a grievance, to inſiſt upon a ſpecific remedy, he had profeſſed his readineſs to adopt any form, but ſtill maintained that univerſal ſuffrage and annual elections was the only adequate remedy. Surely this was the conduct of a man, who, however erroneous he might be in his opinions, was himſelf ſincere in the belief that they were well founded. The counſel for the Crown wiſhed the Jury to believe, that all this was only pretext on the part of the priſoner to cover treaſonable deſigns. Let the Jury examine how this ſtood. The priſoner and thoſe with whom he acted, thought the Repreſentation of the People defective, and the Houſe of Commons in conſequence corrupt. They were perſuaded alſo that a majority of the people held the ſame opinion—he did not ſay ſo, but they thought ſo—and therefore wiſhed to appoint a meeting of delegates, by which they might aſcertain beyond diſpute that this was the opinion of the people, and concert the means of giving it effect. What ſaid the Duke of Richmond? That all attempts to obtain Reform from the Parliament itſelf, with every incidental help and advantage, were overborne by the corruption of Parliament; that not a ſingle proſelyte had been gained from corruption; and that the only remaining hope of Reform was from the people.—What was the remedy he expected to come from the People for this corruption of Parliament? Univerſal ſuffrage and annual elections. Now it was objected to the priſoner, that his own complaint of the corruption of Parliament, was all a pretext. What colour was there for this, when twenty witneſſes had depoſed, and almoſt any number might have been produced, that both he and they adopted the opinion of the Duke of Richmond? The priſoner thought a Convention of delegates the beſt mode of obtaining a Reform. The Duke of Richmond publiſhed that he expected no Reform but from the people at large. When the Duke of Richmond ſaid this, how was a plain man, like the priſoner, to underſtand it? The fair conſtruction was, that he thought the collected ſenſe of the people at large, communicated to Parliament, would not be diſregarded, as the petitions of comparative ſmall bodies had been, and that thus by Conſtitutional means, the reform he thought neceſſary would be effected. If this, which was the probable interpretation of his views, were but barely poſſible, ſurely, ſurely, the Jury would not prefer the harſher to the more lenient conſtruction.

It was a maxim of law, that in all doubtful caſes they were to incline to innocence, and that acts, of themſelves indifferent, were in every caſe to be taken in the moſt favourable ſenſe. He referred to a motion for a committee to enquire into certain abuſes made by Lord Shelburne, in the Houſe of Lords, during the American War. This motion, although negatived by the majority in point of numbers, might be ſaid to have been ſupported

by

by the majority in point of character and talents. Among the supporters of it were the venerable Earl Camden, a man who surely understood the law and the constitution of his country; Marquis of Rockingham, Duke of Portland, Earl Fitzwilliam, &c. They not only supported it, but thought it their duty to hand down their reasons for doing so, in a protest. The second reason in this protest was, that a great majority of the people, as appeared by the Resolutions of numerous associations, were desirous of such an enquiry. They added, that although some persons were alarmed at those associations, the sole object of them was to make the whole body of the Representatives of the People acquainted with the wishes of the whole body of their constituents. This too was the object of the prisoner. The Protest went on to state the impossibility of rejecting the petitions of the collective body of the people. If Lord Camden and the illustrious characters who signed that protest said so; if they held it to be impossible to reject the petitions of the collective body of the people, surely a man like the prisoner, who followed great authorities rather than thought for himself, might be allowed to say so too, without being suspected of evil intention. "It is admitted," said the protest, "that the House of Commons may vote as they please, but it is hoped that so wise a body will never, by rejecting the petitions of a majority of the people, put to hazard the question whether they have not betrayed their trust." This he read to shew, that in the opinion of great constitutional lawyers, of eminent statesmen, of unimpeachable characters, associations of the people to watch the conduct of parliament, were not only innocent but commendable. If all this was true, what offence had the prisoner committed? He defied any man to shew, from the evidence produced on the part of the prosecution, that the prisoner had taken any step for acting by force. To conclude that his intentions were treasonable when nothing appeared against him, but acts which the law admitted to be innocent, and which great authorities had held to be laudable, would neither be charitable, nor befitting the character of an English Jury. Suppose the Duke of Richmond could descend from his high station, and become the advocate of the prisoner:—he would say, "His sins are mine, if he was misled, I misled him. But it will be said that harsh resolutions were passed in the societies of which the prisoner was a member—Granted.— The prisoner was an ignorant man compared with those whose plans he followed, and when the ultimate end, and the means of effecting it were so clearly the same, a little indiscretion on his part might be excused. I, with all the advantages of rank and knowledge, with connections to support me in the attempt, or to comfort in case of failure, prepared this plan. He, with none of these advantages, followed the example I had given him. You will say that he has gone farther, than I did. Perhaps he may; but he had less information and greater provocation." If the Duke of Richmond were to feel for a moment, that the life of the prisoner was in danger, his blood must curdle with horror; he must shudder at
the

the very idea of guilt being imputed to the prisoner for the very same opinions and principles, that had been thought commendable in himself. None of the evidence that was not brought personally home to the prisoner, ought to have any weight, except as it went to prove the general charge of a plot, and this would exclude nine-tenths of the whole. The prisoner had co-operated in a plan for assembling a convention, but by no part of the evidence was there a shadow of proof, that he ever meant to employ force. He was aware of separating the evidence on these heads, he had attempted it, but from the immense mass, and not having in his possession one third of the papers read, he had found it impossible. It was proved, and indeed admitted, that for two years the prisoner had never been without a spy at his elbow. He had been watched in the societies. He had been watched in the moments of unsuspecting intercourse with his private friends, in the moments of familiar and unguarded conversation. Was it not singular, if he really harboured in his mind such purposes as were imputed to him, that in such a length of time, not a single expression of disrespect to the King or the House of Lords, had ever dropped from his lips; not an unguarded word about employing force upon any occasion had escaped him? No matter who else had meditated employing force; if the prisoner had not, he was innocent. No word of his, no casual expression to this effect, was attempted to be proved. No man, however cunning, could have kept such a watch over his secret thoughts. It was not in human nature to act; it was not in human credulity to believe. If he had been a man of dissolute life, his rushing hastily into any scene of guilt might not have been improbable. But such a character had been given of him, as, of any man in his station of life, had never been given in a court of justice:—Friends, neighbours, employers, the clergy-man of whose congregation he was one—all concurred in declaring him religious, sober, industrious, mild in his temper, exemplary in his general conduct, and worthy of any trust. The clergyman said, that he had conversed intimately with him upon political subjects, for the express purpose of discovering his real intentions, and was persuaded that they were what he professed them to be. Many of the witnesses to his character, did not belong to the same societies, nor entertain the same political sentiments; yet they all concurred in stating his character to be irreproachable, and some of them had known him for twenty years. This was one of the cases in which character ought more particularly to avail, for the Jury were to try and pronounce upon the act of the prisoner's mind; and unless they were convinced that he meant to overturn the Government, as the means of effecting the death of the King, they must acquit him."

Chief Justice Eyre. "Prisoner, you applied to the Court for counsel, and counsel were assigned you. They have now concluded what they have to say in your defence. You are at full liberty to offer a defence for yourself. If you have any thing to say, this is the proper time."

Prisoner.

Prisoner. "I am perfectly satisfied with the defence my counsel have made for me, and wish to add nothing to it."

The Court adjourned for an hour, and being resumed,

The Solicitor General, Sir John Mitford, rose to reply, and in some degree to sum up. After some compliments to his learned friends on the able defence they had made for the prisoner, he said he must first notice what had been said to the Jury on the policy of their verdict. They were to decide on the evidence before them, and the law as it affected that evidence, without regard to political circumstances. Trial by Jury was not only the great protection of the State and of every individual who lived under it, but that controul over the administration of justice by the executive power, which the people had kept in their own hands—that which the tyranny of Cromwell could not subdue, and which was the first to shake James II. on his throne. In ordinary cases the State could be in no danger from the verdict of a Jury. In some cases it might —but even this consideration they were to lay aside. No important fact, at least none that could shake the main points of the charge, had been disputed by the prisoner. His Counsel, with great judgment, had forborne to touch upon the strongest facts. To attack the parole evidence, was indeed impossible, for numerous as were the witnesses by which it was supported, they knew it might have been supported by almost any number more. Much of what they had said tended rather to accuse the Duke of Richmond, and another of his Majesty's ministers, than to exculpate the prisoner. All this the Jury were entirely to pass by, and attend only to the evidence, as it applied to the prisoner. He should therefore take a short view of the law of the case; but first make a few remarks on the evidence, as it applied to the prisoner's intention. The Attorney General, in his opening, did not impute evil intention to all the persons who were members of those societies. He knew that a system of fraud and deception had pervaded the whole, by which the few had imposed upon the many. If this had been doubtful before, it was now clear. The whole of the Sheffield evidence went to shew that the members of the society there followed their leaders implicitly, and adopted whatever they thought fit to propose. In this manner inattentive and unsuspecting men, without any evil intention of their own, might be led by the evil intention of others, to the most violent and guilty extremes. Why, instead of witnesses who knew the prisoner but by general character, were not persons called who had been parties to the more secret transactions of the societies, or who at least had continued members till the time of his being taken into custody? It was only in the latter part of the business that the evil intention became clearly manifest. He denied that equal credit was to be given to the witnesses for the Crown, when their evidence made in favour of the prisoner, and when it made against him. The Jury would consider that the testimony even of honest men might be affected by a particular bias of mind, and judge of it accordingly. The people of Sheffield had been imposed upon, when they thought of

providing

providing themselves with arms. They were told by the designing few, that the Aristocrats, as they were called, were going to attack them, and that they were entitled by the Bill of Rights to provide arms for their own defence. But these arms, when provided for defence, might have been employed, on some new suggestion of the leaders for offence. They said they had been insulted and threatened by the Church and King Clubs. These clubs had very possibly done unjustifiable things; but their orator, Mr. Yorke, who, by the accounts they gave of him, was not a man destitute of information, when he told them they had a right to arm for their own defence, did not tell them they had a right to apply to the civil magistrate for defence. A plan had been once on foot for making 10,000 pikes, in Sheffield, in one day. When this was done, Mr. Yorke might have proposed what he had before hinted, viz. marching to London, rather than be trampled upon, as he said they were, and there acting like the Marseillois, who had transacted things not of the most agreeable nature at Paris. At Sheffield, a petition to the House of Commons had been prepared, couched in such terms as they knew must cause it to be rejected. Was this a *bona fide* transaction, or a pretext to cover the further proceedings they intended, and which were, perhaps, prepared before the petition? It was therefore clear that a system had been pursued, which absolved from any heinous degree of guilt, the greater part of those who had been drawn in to support it. Some of them said, they wanted only to bring back the House of Commons to what it was in the Revolution. The only alterations in the House of Commons since the Revolution were the Septennial Act, and some acts excluding contractors from sitting in it, and certain persons supposed to be under the immediate influence of the Executive Government from voting at elections, so that the House of Commons might truly be said to have been improved since the Revolution, instead of having gone to decay; such were the delusions practised upon the many by the few. The great majority being thus absolved from any high degree of guilt, though certainly not exempt from blame, the guilt of the few who deluded was the greater. Among these, the prisoner at the bar was deeply implicated by the evidence. He could not say, that he took no part in preparing the business to be transacted, or that he voted heedlessly and implicitly for whatever was proposed. A Secret Committee had been appointed; this committee was dissolved, but with powers to the members to elect a new committee, the names of the members composing which, were not even to be known by the society. Here was a thing unexampled in any state, for a little state this society was, and therefore dangerous. If their intentions were honest, why such secrecy in the prime directors of all their movements? Why not act openly, as they had done before? Speculative opinions on government, or on any other subject, were allowed in this country, unless hurtful in the manner of circulating them. Such a check must exist in every government, as no government could stand against constant attempts to disturb the opinions. All governments

vernments muſt be adminiſtered by a few in compariſon of the many, and how was the ſubmiſſion of the many to the few to be ſecured but by the force of opinion? Even the members of the Conſtituent Aſſembly of France, when they had framed, as they imagined, a free government for their county, thought that ſpeculative opinions were not to be left entirely without reſtraint, and the laſt legacy they left to their ſucceſſors was a decree againſt the clubs, connected by aſſociation and affiliation. The decree had never been executed, and ſince, the country had been under the direction of thoſe very clubs. The priſoner could not plead that he was a man deluded. He ſigned all the papers, and to him all the letters were addreſſed. He was privy to all the proceedings of the Secret Committee, and perhaps carried on a correſpondence of his own, which he never communicated to the committee. His connection with Tooke, Margarot and Skirving, appeared very myſterious. None but the priſoner, Margarot and Skirving, ſeemed to have known any thing in the firſt inſtance of the intention to ſend delegates to the convention at Edinburgh.

The Solicitor General then entered into a long and elaborate argument on the law of treaſon, which he read from his notes.

He proceeded to maintain, that a convention in any State, being a convention of the whole people, muſt neceſſarily become a Sovereign Power, and therefore that the King muſt ſubmit to it or be in danger, and it mattered not that the parties did not intend to depoſe him for life; for to depoſe him for one day, or for one hour, was the ſame thing in point of law as that of depoſing him for life; and the ſteps the priſoner had been engaged in led neceſſarily to that end, and therefore it was clearly treaſon. He then gave a hiſtory of the Revolution in France by the Convention; he ſaid, that the moment the French deprived the King of his power of negativing the proceedings of the aſſembly, he was then depoſed. He then gave an account of all the addreſſes preſented from the ſocieties of this Country to the National Convention, and the anſwer which the Preſident gave to them. He began with "Generous Rebublicans." This, he ſaid, was clearly underſtood by the preſident of the French Convention to mean, that theſe perſons wiſhed to eſtabliſh a Republican form of Government in this Country, and he had no doubt they did. The acts they did on this occaſion, he ſaid, he had no doubt whatever to be treaſon. He ſaid he would now proceed to another head of the ſubject.

Lord Chief Juſtice Eyre here ſaid, Mr. Solicitor General, if you have come to the end of this head, we had better adjourn: for no human powers would be able to go on, ſo as to take up the matter after you have done. We ſhall loſe no time then by ſtopping here for to night.

It was half paſt twelve o'clock.—Adjourned to eight next morning.

Tuesday, November 4.

The Solicitor General resumed his speech of the night before by observing, that he had already informed the Gentlemen of the Jury what idea he had of the persons engaged in the transaction which at present occupied the attention of the Court, and how far the Prisoner at the bar was implicated in the business, in the character of an agent to the characters concerned. He had stated the law on the transaction, law that had the sanction of from four to five hundred years continuance.—He had, when he left off on that night, arrived at the period when the society addressed the Convention of France. This address irrefragably shewed their objects, and he said, should be deeply impressed on the minds of the Gentlemen of the Jury. It shewed the object of the society, and how they meant to accomplish their views, by assembling a National Convention; if any thing was wanting to shew that this was their object, he had only to advert to the address presented at the bar of the National Convention, by Mr. Frost and Mr. Barlow, and the answer given to the address by the President. There was no doubt, he said, in his mind of the views of the prisoner, which were the destruction of the Established Government, by means of assembling the people, and of establishing in it's room a government founded on the Rights of Man, on that broad basis that would give every man a share of the government of the country.

He would not disguise but that there were abuses in our government; nay, he would suppose, abominable abuses, and, if the season were proper, he would himself bring such forward, if he thought it necessary. For whatever situation a man may hold in the state, either in a civil or political point of view, he certainly would exchange it for liberty; for neither riches nor honour could compensate for the loss of that which was so dear to Englishmen.

In his observations, he said, that he would naturally recur to the affairs of France, and requested if he should advert to any paper not given in evidence, that he may stand corrected by his learned friends. He next took a view of the letter from Stockport, dated November 3, 1792, in page 32, of the Second Report. He said that this letter proved that the objects of the societies were to establish a constitution agreeable to the Rights of Man. They stile themselves Friends of Universal Peace and the Rights of Man. The very terms begot a suspicion that they were not friends to the present constitution. They attributed, he knew, all wars to Monarchies; and their favourite idea was, that a Representative Government would secure universal peace, when nothing but the wishes and the interests of the people should be considered. Such an enthusiasm hovered over this notion, that it resembled that of the Fifth Monarchy-men, who rose in an insurrection for a kingdom of the Saints in the reign of Charles II. Nay, so thoroughly were they persuaded of the sanctity of their purposes, that many of them persisted filled in their last moments to aver, that if they were deceived, they had been deceived by *heaven*.

In people thus warmed by enthusiasm, no matter for what object, the most dreadful effects might spring up; politics might lead as far as religion. How, if they should fancy ardently a community of property? Should we be able to stifle so dangerous an enthusiasm? The letter proves, that the London Corresponding Society endeavoured to prevail upon all the other Reforming Societies, to address the National Convention of France. The prisoner had said, in their situation, signatures were the best supplies, and names in great numbers would be more serviceable to them than money. It is sufficiently obvious, that this society thought the French cause, *their* cause: they offer them their aid and assistance, express the utmost friendship, and their great satisfaction at the extinction of treacherous royalty. They congratulate them upon their glorious victory; and what victory, Gentlemen, do they term so? The 10th of August. No answer has been heard, nor observation ventured upon this address—the silence on the other side is conviction that they cannot repel it. However they go on to say, " if ever our ministers should lead this country to join the league of execrable despots combined against you, we will stand forward at the hazard of our lives."—thus meaning to compel or resist the measures of Government, if they should affect those they are pleased to term Defenders of Liberty.

The letter from Norwich, upon which observation has been made, as it was necessary to observe upon something, is dated November 11, 1792. It is addressed to the London Corresponding Society, and expresses admiration of their well adopted plan of reformation of the state. They desire to send three of their members to be incorporated with that society. With respect to this plan, it was pretended to be that of the Duke of Richmond. This I think a wild one; if I remember, it proposed to elect, by about 2600 voters, a House of Commons of 500 members. But the Duke of Richmond never thought of equal citizenship, and a share in the election of the executive government. The Sheffield declaration meant the Duke of Richmond's plan only, and accordingly soon found out that they must abide by the conduct of the Friends of the people, whose object was a moderate reform. The letter declared that they would have nothing to do with the Society for Constitutional Information on account of their idea, that they meant to go the length of all Paine's plans. It is thought that we press hard upon the defendants, when we depend on this approbation of Paine. It is, however, probable the Norwich Society understood the thing as we have stated it, and would have been contented with the Duke of Richmond's plan; however they ask of the London Corresponding Society, whether their plan be to rip up monarchy, and plant democracy in it's stead.

If this Society had only had in view the framing anew the composition of Parliament, they could have had no reason to demur at answering explicitly and directly. Lynam's testimony is here distinct and clear; whatever may be said about his being a spy, it stands uncontradicted and must be received. There would have been no occasion for deliberation—they would have answered it at once simply and indignantly, as being suspected of a design so abhorrent from their true object, a Reform by legal and constitutional means.

However, on the 28th of November, they do answer. In the Address the word Gentlemen is scratched out for Fellow Citizens. There can be no question that there is nothing criminal in the use of the term Citizen, unless it is with some peculiar view; but it is here meant to discriminate between the Citizen of a Government founded on the right of equal Citizenship, and the subject of Governments originating in conquest, or the progress of faction usurping upon the people. It has been asserted by Paine, that we have our Constitution from William the Norman—nothing can be farther from the truth; if you refer to the history of the country, you will find that he altered only the Aristocratic part, and that the Saxon Laws remained in full force, particularly in the administration of that justice, which secures the liberties of the people. The fact is, they determined to be Fellow-Citizens; that is, in plain terms, Fellow-Kings. The answer refers to their Addresses, upon which no comment has been made, and it was stated that if numbers of people united themselves, the reform would make itself—their difference is stated to be trifling—that is, between ripping up Monarchy and Reform of Representation. They advise a division into numerous small bodies, and that each of these should send a Delegate. They publish and recommend books for the instruction of weak members, by which are meant such as had not attained the requisite pitch of enthusiasm.

But what answer do they make to the query about ripping up Monarchy? " Let no disputes concerning monarchy, democracy, or religion molest us, let us set them entirely aside, and leave to a Parliament, fairly and freely elected by the people, the task of reforming all grievances." But it must necessarily be a pure democracy they meant, by alluding to a Parliament so chosen—" New Reforms were expected in a Parliament uncorrupted by a Minister."

But you have been told the Prisoner never talked of these objects. What does this prove, but that he practised himself the lesson he taught to others, and left their rights to be restored by this Parliament; however, this is declared, " that they are not so sanguine as to imagine they will be restored by the spontane-
ous

ours confent of thofe who have robbed them fo long of them. This affertion implies a degree of force in the means they fhould adopt to procure them. You may judge of a man by the focieties he is admitted to, and of the objects of men by their opinions. Let me afk you whether, if the Roman Catholics or Papifts (they make a diftinction, I believe) had fought to form a Convention, would you not have been warranted in inferring that religion was their object? The modern French are to the full as intolerant as the ancient Papifts, and there is the fame obligation on the confcience in politics as religion. If they hold their's the true government, and proclaim it unlawful to have any other, it will be to the full as mifchievous. Applying this intolerance to government is alfo new, and muft unfettle every eftablifhed ftate in the world. If our focieties will confider no government legal but fuch as is eftablifhed in France, and recommended by Paine, can they aim at any thing fhort of the deftruction of the Englifh government? If they get power to make a Reform, their principles lead them, and they muft neceffarily do the *whole*. They do not declare thefe merely as opinions, they fay they will *act* upon them—they refolve they will make it a Republic—they have declared how they will effect it—it is a confpiracy. They propofe that their Convention fhall be addreffed by the French as the Government of the country.

The Revolution in France fprung from fmall beginnings; but great has been the fimilarity, as far as our Societies have proceeded. The different effects may be found in the refpective governments of the country. France had been governed by a defpotifm the moft tyrannic and oppreffive: every body felt this, and at the voice of excitement, to redrefs their wrongs, the fpirit, the opinion of the people, by which alone Governments fubfift, failed all at once. The very circumftances attending the Affembly of the States General, made it obvious that there muft be a Revolution.

The Government by the Conftitution of this country had long been an object of attachment with all it's faults and all it's imperfections. We have been told all this is prejudice—moft of our opinions are fo. They flow out of education and habit, and a veneration without examination for a ftate of things from which our anceftors have recorded their beft bleffings to arife. Thefe are falutary prejudices. And here is the difference between the man of education and the man without learning, that the one examines the caufes of prejudice, and fpeculates upon the importance of defect confidered as working up from the temper and conftitution of our nature; the other receives them merely becaufe his father has tranfmitted them to him.

The

The great majority of the people cannot, with any suitable profit to themselves, apply to the confideration of governments—if they prefer any, it is either taken upon content, or becaufe they believe it to have produced happinefs greater than that of other governments. Few men are competent to difcern and confider how the alteration of the parts of a fyftem affect the whole. The firft attempt to deftroy a goverment, therefore, is to overturn the prejudice by which it is fupported. Such was the practice of the States General of France in the year 1789, and fuch is now the conduct of their imitators. I do not call them imitators merely becaufe they adopt certain terms—fuch as convention, (committee, I believe, is not French, they had it from us) but becaufe they know thefe men have deftroyed the conftitution of 1791, at the head of which was the King, and certainly as a free government this was nearly what they pretend here to require. Paine was perfectly aware of the force of this opinion which fecures States, and therefore he fets out with calling himfelf a Citizen of the World— When a man is fo, he becomes, in a degree, an enemy to his own country. All the endearing ties and dependencies that fpring from family, that extend to neighbourhood, and are bounded by the country which gave us birth, vanifh, and we learn to difmifs the feelings which produce the character of the father, the friend, and the patriots.

He opens the 2d part of his Rights of Man with declaring, " if we had a bafis on which to ftand, we might raife the world." —Thus applying to politics what had been faid of mechanics. The propagation of his principles would be that ftanding place. He fays, alluding to the expreffions ufed in France upon the 10th of Auguft, " that revolutions may be confidered now as the order of the day—their dangers were before them, and the principles and advantages were known and feen." Pamphlets were written for the purpofe of inducing the people to fubvert this government, by Paine, Barlow, &c. and to deftroy the two parts, the King and the Houfe of Lords, which, Counfel fay, the prifoner meant to retain. They declared we had no conftitution—how were they to reform what did not exift?

Nothing can furpafs the eafe with which revolutions may be excited, when the opinion of the people is deftroyed—an ancient writer fays, that, " he that goeth about to perfuade the people to remedy defects, fhall never walk in fafety, fince no man can remedy them all;" and many fuch are perhaps irremediable on account of the prejudices which have grown up with the people.

They knew that there muft be fome head in all governments, and they obferved the operations of the Jacobin Club and it's 44,000 affiliated focieties; that, in fact, it had given law to all France, and dictated to the convention—Their object therefore was union, and the Jacobin Club their model. One of thefe focieties, that for conftitutional information, had been originally compofed of men of character and talents, however fome of them might have been foured by difcontent at difappointed hopes. By degrees perfons crept in with bolder views, and more dangerous principles—the

original

original members left the society.—Sixteen or seventeen persons usually guided the society, among whom (a constant attendant) was Mr. Horne Tooke. However, this was not even then such a one as could be considered as any thing like the Jacobin Club. Mr. Sheridan had been a member, although he had not attended for several years. However, as they left the names of the original members standing in the books, it was not perceived that they had seceded.

It was, however, necessary to their designs to have some other society as subordinate, and, in consequence, Hardy and some others framed the London Corresponding Society. Hardy seems to be the leader; at all events in the character of secretary, he sanctions all the measures by signing them. He becomes also a member of the society for constitutional information. They were to form divisions—a committee of delegates, these a committee of correspondence, which became the committee of secrecy, and thus their proceedings were intimately combined.

They have declared by three publications, as they did in the Norwich letter, their resolutions to resist all oppressions, insinuating that this government is an oppressive one—only calling an act one of oppression, they declared they had a right to resist it. They declare that they have a right to share in the election of the executive government, not merely a right to choose their representatives, as in the Duke of Richmond's plan. They then declare the people not represented—they say they would have all partial privileges abolished. This latter applies to the peerage as much as any thing. Add to this their right to a share in the choice of the executive servants, and the amount is an wholly elective Parliament.

Another circumstance extremely singular is the proposal of tests to those inclined to become members—this precluded discussion of the objects—a man to be admitted must first profess himself of opinion that,

1. The present Representation of the People was inadequate and delusive.
2. That every Adult ought to have a vote for his Representation.
3. That he would promote a fair and free Representation, by all *legal* and *justifiable* means.

To understand this, we must remark, what they had determined to consider illegal, and justifiable means may then be interpreted by any. The design was thus to govern by a tyranny of these clubs.

In the next set of resolutions, the terms welfare of these Kingdoms are omitted, and the word Kingdom altered to Country in several places. Aware that the great majority of the people were not with them, they resolve,

That no majority can deprive the minority of their rights, and when they attempt it resistance becomes a right. These are understood of civil rights; and they explain them to be " Equality of voice to make laws, and equality of choice in the perfons to adminifter them."—Gentlemen, does the fpirit of the Britifh Conftitution permit this? It was ufually thought a ftrong thing to fay, that the majority had a right to alter the conftitution of a country;—individuals might be found whofe habits and occupations made the exifting government agreeable to them, their right to fuch a one was only vacated by the irrefiftible plea of neceffity.

If two men were floating upon a plank in the fea, and the plank would bear with fafety only one, the law fanctioned the ftronger pufhing the weaker off into the ocean—(the dreadful alternative forces thefe tears from me). They have taken a refolution to rebel againft every government not founded on their principles, and yet we are to be told that they have a perfect reverence for the government of this country. Their refolution of 6th Auguft flows from thefe principles, and other pretences are only veils to cover their defigns. They begin their addrefs with an extract from Thomfon, extremely well read, as his habits lead him to do, by Mr. Erfkine. The fentiments were not objectionable, but it was the view with which they were quoted that made the offence. Any and every good book might be fo proftituted, and in this view no one had fuffered more than the Bible.

We are told then that an *alarm'd* Ariftocracy had already made preparations to counteract their plans, (that Ariftocracy which they meant not to injure) but that they demanded the attention of the people to the vitiated ftate of the Britifh government. Great attempts, by the way, are always made to excite the *poor*. Paine's works are written upon that principle. The great end attainable by the whole nation was an equal reprefentation of the great body of the people.

It is obvious that a refolution had been formed to fubvert the government, and that the reform was a mere pretence. They were told this repeatedly. They continued to think in fecret, that if they could gain annually elected Parliaments, all the reft would follow. Some things particularly ftrike in their addrefs:—they will retrench the wafte in the revenue; wafte, therefore, *had* taken place. "The People's Parliament would reftore lands improperly granted by the Crown to the People." The whole landed property might, upon fuch pretences, be refumed; half the Crown lands being held by grants from the Crown, which cannot be traced, are cultivated and improved by men who would thus be plundered of their property.

This is precifely what was done in France, this was their grand injuftice, and this was a fecond time held out to delude the people. That particular baits were held out for the poor will be allowed; when the regulation refpecting Spitalfields is remembered. Other reforms were expected to take place when this Parliament fhould be held. Their object certainly was to exclude a Houfe of Lords, although the conftitution they fometimes affect to reverence exifts only by a middle power. This power was terribly decreafed by civil wars between the Houfes of York and Lancafter—moft of the

great

great families were destroyed, or scattered, or attainted.—When the Seventh Henry ascended the throne, there were only thirty Peers, and in consequence, there was not that stand made that would otherwise have checked the ambition of that monarch and his son. From this defect flowed the subsequent ascendancy of the Commons in the reign of Charles I.—And that Monarch lost his head, because the barrier which would have restrained the spirit of the Commons was no more.

That our Societies intended to *depose* the King is clear from all their plans centring in a republic—this is an evident act of High Treason. I must state to you a very artful proceeding, which has not been attended to—as the Society for *Constitutional Information* met on a Friday, that which was called the *Corresponding* met the evening before. All violent resolutions were to originate in the latter, or the country societies, and then be brought and submitted to the sanction of the elder club.

The letter from Sheffield, 15th October 1792, says, " It will be vain for the friends of reform to contend with their tremendous host of enemies, without mutual support—we clearly see that Scotland will take the lead of this country—there is a necessity for constant Correspondence—France by this means became united, and we ought not to lose sight of it." How can Government subsist with such bodies in the midst of it? Government is a Corporation; but these societies are distinct Corporations that act like States. The India Company is a Corporation for the regulation of our Indian Estates, in subordination to the Government of the Country. But these clubs are bodies moving in regular action, subordinate to one principal club; like the States of America they have one Government for the whole. Such a scheme, *imperium in'imperio*, is inconsistent with any Government. This was the error in the French Constitution of 1791, as distinctly stated by M. Andre.—It was not an improper thing that such clubs should assemble, while they did not *act*; but if they acted no government could subsist.

In all these proceedings the Prisoner has borne a distinguished part; besides that as Secretary, he was privy to every thing. The letter of Hardy to Mr. Vaughan of the 9th April, shews that he had concerted how the people might be deluded. With respect to all or any of these transactions, that gentleman has never been called to explain any thing.

With respect to the rise of the Convention, this was it. There had been several Societies formed about the country; they solicited a correspondence with the London Society. Delegates met early in the year 1793, and adjourned until the month of November. They described themselves merely a Society of Delegates for the purpose of effecting a Parliamentary Reform. Skirving, by a letter dated May 25, 1793, speaks of his disposition towards the work, and requests leave to correspond with him upon the subject. On the 5th of October, Hardy writes to Skirving. He speaks of Muir and Palmer's

H h

Palmer's trials—and he says " the idea of a general Convention appears to Margarot and himself an excellent measure. He wishes Skirving would communicate his ideas to the Society, without any hint of the private correspondence; he makes no doubt the Society would agree to it, and insists upon the necessity of availing themselves of this opportunity, which once lost may never be recovered."

Then a letter from Skirving, in an official way, communicates to both Societies the plan of the Convention, and they agree to send Delegates to the Scotch Convention; Sheffield and Norwich sent Delegates also. These were instructions to the Delegates given and signed by the Prisoner:

1. That they shall obtain Annual Parliaments and Universal Suffrage by rational and lawful means.
2. Sheriffs and Juries were to be chosen by lot, and the Representatives to be paid by their Constituents—

And this without reflecting what mischiefs had sprung in France from the consequence of this payment. Illegal force was defined to be that which prohibited the meeting of Societies for Reform. Thus resistance was declared legal of the powers of the Crown, if necessary to the attainment of their ends. If resistance can be made lawful, they may vote attack lawful for superseding the necessity of resistance.

The resolutions of the Society for Constitutional Information were more moderate; however, all that was done by the others they approved, and one Resolution they sanction, namely the Seventh: Yet if delegates go beyond authority, it ought to disavow their acts; this is not their case; they approve and declare they will support them. It is fitting I should examine now what were the proceedings of this Convention. I shall not search into them all, though some few it is proper for me to notice: They call themselves the British Convention of the People; this was unnecessary and improper. If they meant but to petition Parliament for a Reform, to convey their celegated opinions, is at all times improper. The people delegating, not appearing, made it still more improper. But if they imposed upon the world as a Convention of the People, they attributed to themselves the title, in order to seize and employ the power. Persons, however, so delegated, thus imperfectly upon their own plan, could not pretend to represent the people, they were merely Delegates from a few Clubs.

Yorke indeed puts this matter beyond a doubt; for he expressly says, the British Convention splits upon a rock, because they had declared themselves too soon a Convention of the People; they should have obtained that sort of tacit acknowledgment of their proceedings from the people, which is the result of a publicity not discountenanced.

The States General of France, assembled on the 7th of June, 1789, by the authority of the King, declared themselves a National Assembly.

bly. The people, by various arts being used, supported them as their Convention, and from that time lodged there the sovereign powers of the State. The British Convention at Edinburgh ought to have addressed the public at large, and, if approved, then they might have assumed all the powers and authorities of such a body.

They dated their transactions the 1st year of the Convention one and indivisible; not to be separated until their objects should be accomplished. This very act was an act of High Treason, as the Attorney-General had correctly said in his place in the House of Commons. His learned friend Mr. Gibbs, when remarking upon the prosecution, had said, that these acts did not amount to High Treason on account of defective evidence, although they were seditious. The Courts of Scotland had been erroneously accused of rigour in the prosecutions there for sedition. The matter for examination was, whether the law of Scotland pointed at any distinct crime as sedition? If it did, as assuredly it does, it was highly proper they should be tried upon it. Sedition was anciently the law of England; however, now the distinction is merely whether the offence rank as misdemeanor, or reach up to High Treason. It appears that the reformers of Scotland corresponded with the prisoner, that they adopted their proceedings in this country.

Margarot says, the Societies in London are numerous—In Sheffield alone 50,000 people were associated, although it is well known that Society never contained more than 600 at most—Thus by exaggeration he gave them a consequence that did not belong to them, and in the result, imagining their numbers thus great, they adopted the character of a Convention of the People.

The principal thing they did in their new junction, was to make another and a new Union between Scotland and England. Whether this might be a wife measure may admit of some discussion—but they have assumed to break through by their own authority the Convention now existing. They appointed a Committee to draw up a plan of general Union—They issued tickets for admission, and voted themselves permanent. In the mode of their great model in France, they exercised the powers of a government, and received contributions—patriotic gifts—donations, &c. and in the formulary talked of taking the sense of the House.

That they meant to use force to effect their purpose was evident. The task of enlightening the Highlands must refer to arming. They were recommended to copy the Bill of Rights in the front of any of their declarations or pamphlets, to prevent improper constructions; but this was clearly meant to deceive. To what purpose else was that bill to be copied into their books, which some of them had called a Bill of Wrongs? But it told them it was lawful to assemble a Convention, and this was something; it would delude the people, as they had deluded one of the witnesses, Hill .who told you that he wanted only to restore the Constitution o !1688, when, except the triennial and septennial Bills, there had been no material changes.

He then alludged to the famous blank refolutions of November, 1793, when Citizen Brown difcuffed the Habeas Corpus Act; this man was the editor of the Patriot. Gerald addreffed them in an eloquent fpeech, and Margarot propofed the refolutions.

That the Convention had an undoubted right to difcufs all objects relative to their rights, and they declared before God and the world to follow the example of their brethren—and they will refift *fuperior* force 'that fhould ftrive to difperfe them. So that if any bill had been paffed then for the fufpenfion of the Habeas Corpus Act, they would have been in a ftate of rebellion. They were to have been ready to act, if an invafion of any foreign or internal enemy made it neceffary, and in that cafe the Secret Committee was to have been removed to fome other place of fecurity, he declared permanent, and act accordingly.

But what muft have been the nature of thefe proceedings, which could not bear the light of day, and were fo myfterioufly hid, from the eye of Government? They inftituted *Suppléans* of their Deputies—the Delegates were to hold themfelves always in readinefs to depart at an hour's notice, and the Secret Committee was to fix the place; if they fhould be difperfed by Government. They did refufe to difperfe—as Margarot communicated how he was dragged out of the chair. A Committee of Emergency was to fit not merely if they fhould be difperfed, but on account of any extraordinary meafure. In cafe of invafion they were to be affembled. Margarot ftates in his letter of Dec. 2, that they had done what could not be communicated. Seven Delegates could vote themfelves permanent, and 21 could act. Thus you fee they were provided againft whatever might happen. Papers were referred to as making part of a parcel they did not dare truft by the poft——thefe were to be read by Hardy to fuch Members of the Society as he fhould think proper to truft. Thefe cautions to Hardy are in private letters, to be communicated or not as he fhould judge of the fervour of the individual. The Prifoner was the active agent of their defigns, and intimately acquainted with all their proceedings. Have they, let me afk, the flighteft femblance of a defign to petition Parliament.

The picture of a Highlandman, properly dreffed with his broad fword and target, before their books, could only be meant to excite them to arms, it had certainly nothing to do with a peaceable petition to Parliament. There was a propofition to form a Commiffion of Obfervation to keep watch over the Britifh Parliament—this was negatived, and it was determined to requeft the London Correfponding Society to keep a clofe look out upon the proceedings of Parliament.

Touching the Reform of Parliament, their fincerity may be gueffed at from the obfervation of Margarot, that it was unneceffary to lop the branches when they intended . . . .

. (To cut down the tree is the only way in which the blank can be filled up.) They, no doubt, meant to avail themfelves of foreign

affiftance

assistance, if it could be had, or by their own force accomplish their objects.—In London, a variety of proceedings took place, for the purpose of procuring another Convention, in consequence of the dispersion of the British Convention in Scotland.

The first proposition that appears of this kind is in a letter from Hardy to Adams, dated 10th of January, 1794, to hint to him the Anniversary Dinner of the 20th January, 1794. In the mean time Margarot had communicated the circumstances of their situation, and incited them to spirited measures. Hardy answers that they were determined to act like the men they professed themselves—and he accordingly writes to the Norwich Society, Jan. 11, communicating what he has done. He adds, " Now is the time to do something worthy of men." Now while the Defenders of Freedom are South and East of the Channel, driving their enemies before them like chaff before the wind. He reports, that there were no hopes the people would generally join them, but the French would enable them to succeed. He adverts to a Meeting of the 20th January, as the time when something would be done.

The Solicitor referred to the proceedings of January 17, in the Constitutional Society: They allude to Judge Jefferies, and add that those who imitate his conduct deserve his fate—meaning that the persons in Scotland had experienced similar injustice: That the Convention merited the approbation of all *wife*; and the support of all *brave* men: the latter epithet marked their design. The time was fast approaching when power must oppose tyranny. The Solicitor observed, that such matters were not to be decided by a Jury, they appealed to the sword. They pass a resolution opposing all the acts of the Scotch Convention. In allusion to the transportations to Botany Bay; they add, Do you think we also shall not be treated as felons? Do you believe they will not send us after our brothers to Botany Bay? Their cause and ours are the same—We are at issue—We must oppose force to force—We must chuse freedom or slavery now.

You may ask what means they have taken to accomplish their objects? As to their means, they themselves explain them, not to petition the Parliament. " Who hopes to gather grapes from thorns, or figs from thistles? We must seek redress from our own laws, and not those of our enemies, plunderers, and oppressors—there is no other redress for a nation circumstanced as we are."

Can any man doubt that the act of proclaiming the Pretender would be treason? Is not the act of proclaiming a Representative Government the same? He referred to the election of Barrere and St. Andre, members of the Society for Constitutional Information. He remarked upon two of their toasts:

" Success to the arms of Britons, against whomsoever directed."

The other sentiment was only intelligible by referring to Barlow's letter to the Convention, in which he said that a King was good for nothing. The sentiment alludes to this,

"All that is good in every Constitution—but may we never have superstition enough to reverence any part that is good for nothing."

March 27, Hardy writes a letter to the Society for Constitutional Information, respecting measures to be taken in consequence of the moment being arrived. He declares that he looked to the speedy accomplishment of all his wishes—and these must be the annihilation of all ranks, of a King, of the Nobles—and the establishment of Representative Government. The Chalk Farm Meeting, and the arms, drew from the Solicitor some comment, though brief, and not in any new form.

He touched upon the evidence, and stated the candour of the Crown, in concealing nothing from the Jury—if defective or contradictory, it was then to make for the prisoner.

And now, Gentlemen of the Jury, said he, I have nothing more to offer—I have discharged, God knows! with much pain, the harsh duty reposed in me—You will now do your's—If your verdict shall discharge the prisoner, I know you will give it with joy; if the contrary, yet it must be given; the cup, although it be bitter, must not pass away from you. I have had a duty to perform beyond my strength and my abilities; I have discharged it faithfully, and satisfied my conscience.

It may here be proper to remark, at the close of the prosecution, that no men ever conducted themselves with more mildness and humanity, than the Counsel for the Crown. Mr. Attorney General was manly and dispassionate, firm and humane. Mr. Solicitor was so visibly affected, that he concluded quite suffused in tears.

The Lord Chief Justice rose and said, he had received a suggestion, that it might be desirable, in such a mass of evidence, to refresh the minds of the Jury by either reading over the written evidence, or repeating such parts of the parole as might he judged essential to the giving them as perfect a knowledge of the subject as could be had.

Mr. Attorney-General and Mr. Erskine, after consulting with the Prisoner, expressed their opinion that it was not expedient. His Lordship then said, that if there was any paper which he might omit in summing up, affecting either the prosecution or the defence, he begged they would remind him, and at their desire it should be immediately read. He added, that if the Jury pleased, they might now take their refreshment; after which he should begin and conclude the summing up of the evidence to them. He begged they would consider his time as theirs, and send for him, if he should not be present when they were refreshed, and he would instantly obey their pleasure.

Lord

Lord Chief Juſtice Eyre.—We are now in the 7th day of trial; it comes to me to ſum up this great and momentous Cauſe. If it is expected or wiſhed on the part of the Priſoner, or on the part of the Proſecution, that the whole of the written evidence ſhould be repeated to the Jury, I will do it. Or would it be ſatisfactory to every body, that parole evidence only ſhould be ſummed up to the Jury, and leave it to your recollection, Gentlemen, on the written evidence; then I ſhall ſum up the oral teſtimony, together with ſuch parts of the written evidence as in the courſe of ſumming up ſhall appear to me to be neceſſary to have recourſe to. If it is the wiſh of the Priſoner, or the Counſel for the Priſoner; or, if it is inſiſted upon on the part of the proſecution; but certainly, if deſired on the part of the Priſoner, I ſhall not at all regret the expence of my time, or of the bodily fatigue for me perſonally to go through. I would willingly ſpare the Jury as much as poſſible, becauſe their labour has been infinite. If I were to go through the whole of the written evidence, I am afraid it would only load them with an imperfect recollection of a maſs of evidence, which would make them the leſs able to comprehend or underſtand that part of the evidence which appears to me to be material.

Attorney-General—I cannot better conſult the public benefit than to leave the whole to the execution of that duty which reſides in the Court.

Mr. Erſkine—My Lord, if you pleaſe I will conſult with the Priſoner himſelf?—The Court conſenting, Mr. Erſkine went to the Priſoner at the Bar, and, having converſed with him, Mr. Erſkine returned, and ſaid that his client, confiding in the juſtice of the Court, had acquieſced in what his Lordſhip had ſtated.

The Chief Juſtice ſaid, as this was the caſe, he ſhould take that courſe, deſiring it to be underſtood, that if there was any thing that he ſhould not ſtate accurately, the Counſel for the Priſoner would be ſo good as to remind him of it. He wiſhed the Counſel on both ſides to underſtand this, and particularly the Counſel for the Priſoner. And that they ſhould put him in mind of any thing that was material, if he would happen to omit it.

The Court and Jury then withdrew for an hour for refreſhment.

Chief Juſtice Baron Eyre proceeded to ſum op the evidence.—Gentlemen of the Jury, this Priſoner ſtands indicted for High Treaſon, in compaſſing and imagining the King's death. The Indictment contains nine counts or overt-acts. Of theſe are, firſt—conſpiring to levy war againſt the King—ſecondly, preparing arms for that purpoſe. Three others are, firſt—conſpiring to ſubvert the Government—ſecondly, ſending letters, and preparing arms for that object. The four other overt-acts relate to the aſſembling of a Convention, the firſt of which is—concerting to call a Convention—the ſecond, publiſhing books, letters, and pamphlets, in order to induce his Majeſty's ſubjects to ſend Deputies to the ſame Convention

vention—the third, meeting, consulting, and deliberating how, when, and where this Convention was to be held—the fourth, the appointing Jeremiah Joyce, John Augustus Bonney, &c. to meet and co-operate towards the calling and assembling such Convention. You will attend only to the evidence necessary for establishing one of these acts; the general effect of the whole will come afterwards to be considered. The Chief Justice then went on to sum up the evidence in the order in which it had been brought forward; and began with adverting to the Witnesses from Sheffield, Camage, and Broomhead. In the course of his statement, he ordered the Clerk to read to the Jury the Address to the People, and the Petition to his Majesty, which had been voted on the Castle-hill. As to the general libellous tendency of the Address, he remarked that it was not very much to the purpose. There was one expression in the Petition which deserved to be remarked; mention is there made of "the impending storm," but what was the application to be given to this phrase, taken along with the date, was matter of fit consideration for the Jury. The whole of this printed paper had been very much relied on by both sides, and had received very different constructions from the Counsel for the Prosecution, and the Counsel for the Prisoner. Its importance arose not so much from the other extravagances which it contained, as from one Resolution, "That they would petition Parliament no more."

It was evident, therefore, that they meant to take some other course in order to obtain their object. What that other course was, it remained for the Jury, taking it in the chain of evidence along with the time at which the Societies had in agitation their plan of a Convention, to determine. The next witness to whom he adverted was Henry Alexander, whose testimony, from the manner in which it was given, was not entitled to much credit, and upon which indeed nothing material depended. All that could be gathered from him was, that he had been present at a meeting where Yorke, who was then on the eve of going abroad, talked extravagantly. Thomas Whitehall confirmed nothing. The testimony of the next witness, George Widdison, suggested one remark. This was the first witness who had talked of a Reform of Parliament, and stated his sentiments upon the subject, which he professed to have borrowed from those of the Duke of Richmond. And this ought to afford an important lesson to all men of rank and property, how they committed their sentiments to the public upon such subjects, since they there gave to others the power of dispersing them to an unlimited extent, and hazarded the mischief that might be produced by their falling into the hands of those who were either not qualified to understand them, or not disposed to draw from them proper conclusions. Henry Hill, who was next examined, among other things stated, that there were ten thousand persons present at the meeting on the Castle Hill, at Sheffield, who expressed their approbation of the proceedings which many of them could not hear, and this no doubt was the way in

which

which very frequently the approbation of so great a multitude was obtained to proceedings with which they were entirely unacquainted, or which, if they knew, they were not qualified to understand. The Witness knew not that the Motion for a Petition to Parliament had previously been agreed to be rejected by the Junto, which gives one an excellent idea of what sort of a thing a debate is conducted in such an assembly. John Edwards proved that he had received from Baxter that infamous paper "*The Guillotine*," which he ordered the Clerk to read. This, he said, was a most infamous and detestable paper. The allusion contained in it was too obvious to require to be pointed out. But whether it ought at all to be interwoven with the Indictment, or allowed to have any weight in the charges against the Prisoner, was for the Jury to consider. The Witness did not think that Hardy had ever seen the paper, or that if he had seen it, he would have approved of it's contents. One material circumstance which appeared from the evidence of this witness was, that Hardy had received the letter from Sheffield relative to the pikes, and had so far acted upon it as to have communicated to the witness the direction where he might furnish himself.

The next witness, Samuel Williams, spoke only to the subject of guns. He had given Hardy an order for boots and shoes, who in return had found customers for three or four of his guns; thus far the transaction was merely in the way of trade and mutual accommodation, and could reasonably fix no imputation upon Hardy.—But it appeared afterwards that Hardy had recommended him to Franklo's Association. The private and clandestine way in which this Association met to exercise, and the manner in which they shifted about from one place to another, warranted at least a suspicion, that they were conscious that they were engaged in no good purpose. From this recommendation, it was evident that the nature of this Association was not unknown to Hardy; but what were their designs; how far the Prisoner might be implicated in them, were questions fit for the consideration of the Jury. Edward Gosling had stated an expression to have taken place in the Society, which was certainly a very strong one, " that they would arm to support their Convention as the French had done." If the Convention, which it had been so much contended was to have met in a legal and peaceable manner, were to have been supported in their proceedings by an armed force, it gave indeed a new complexion to the business.—At the same time it was to be recollected what degree of credit was due to a witness of this sort, who was professedly employed as a spy, and whose character was by no means the most unexceptionable; were there not objections to his credit, his testimony would be very important indeed, as it would serve to mark a determined purpose against the King and his family. He had ascribed to Baxter, language so very imprudent, as could scarcely have been supposed to be used. His evidence was to be received with great caution. John Groves was a Witness, whose veracity was still more directly impeached. The Chief Justice ordered

ordered a letter from Stockport to be read, dated 5th January, 1794, the whole of which he affirmed to be inflammatory, but particularly the laſt paragraph. This was followed by reading a ſong full of ſeditious matter, which had been found among Hardy's papers. The Chief Juſtice obſerved that it had been very fairly taken notice of by the Counſel for the Priſoner, that he, being a Secretary of a Society, was expoſed to receive all ſorts of papers, and could not be reſponſible for their contents. The circumſtance of improper papers being found in his poſſeſſion, might only afford an indication of imprudence, and it remained for the Jury to determine how far that, taken in connection with other circumſtances, ought to attach a charge of criminality. The Chief Juſtice then proceeded to remark on the evidence of Lynam, and the evidence brought from Scotland, relative to the conſpiracy of Watt and Downie, from any ſhare in which he ſeemed to conſider the priſoner as completely exculpated. He then adverted to the papers found in the poſſeſſion of Martin and Thelwall, which, whether they were allowed to affect the Priſoner or not, proved at leaſt the exiſtence of very dangerous deſigns, and that the minds of ſome of thoſe with whom it was connected, were infected with a degree of violence, the probable effects of which he ſhuddered to contemplate, and with a wickedneſs which it was almoſt impoſſible to believe. He then went over the witneſſes that had been brought to prove the virtues of the private character, and the moderation of the political ſentiments of the Priſoner, ſhortly remarking on the evidence that had been given by each.

The Chief Juſtice having gone through all the Evidence, ſaid he ſhould be very glad to go on with what he had to ſay to the Jury on the ſubject, but as what he had to ſay muſt neceſſarily run into an inconvenient length both for them and for himſelf, and as he was ſo much exhauſted, he muſt trouble them to attend to-morrow, and then he hoped to be able, in a few hours, to diſmiſs them, requeſting their attendance at nine o'clock.

The Court then adjourned at half after eleven o'clock.

EIGHTH DAY—NOVEMBER 5.

THE Court ſat at nine o'clock, when Lord CHIEF JUSTICE EYRE proceeded in his charge as follows:

Gentlemen of the Jury,

Laſt night, at a late hour, I finiſhed the parole evidence and ſome of the written evidence that ſeemed to be more immediately connected with the parole evidence on both ſides, except that I did not ſtate to you the proteſt in the Houſe of Lords, which was read to you by the conſent of the Attorney-General, as evidence on the part of the priſoner. I did not ſtate it to you at that time, becauſe it did not appear to me from the nature of the caſe to be evidence. It is ſomething that has paſſed in the Parliamentary Hiſtory of this country,

try, from whence arguments might be drawn on the part of the prisoner, to evidence the purity and honesty of his intentions, and it is in that view only that I mention it.

Having thus finished the summing up of the evidence, I may say to you that this cause, which is a great and a momentous cause, between the King and the Prisoner at the bar, is at length brought to a point of conclusion; and it must be a satisfaction to the mind of every honest man, that this cause has been happily so conducted, and has been proceeded upon with so much patience and temper, as that your minds may have been sufficiently informed on the subject to enable you to discover its true merits, and to pronounce a verdict, which in the first place will be satisfactory to your own minds, and being satisfactory to your own minds, cannot but be satisfactory to the country.

Gentlemen, it is as much satisfaction to me, as I can feel in the exercise of so painful a duty, as that which has been cast upon me, that upon this occasion there is, I think, no possible chance of our being entangled in any difficulties in point of law. The verdict in this case will not proceed, and you will receive no directions from me that it ought to proceed on any technical grounds. The overt-act is in substance, that the prisoner at the bar, and those who have been concerned with him, conspired to depose the King, and to subvert the Monarchy; and this is charged, and always has been considered, an an overt-act of the Treason of compassing the death of the King. It is indeed an old presumption of law, acknowledged by the writers of the law, and particularly by those writers who have been cited as authorities by the Counsel on both sides, that he who conspires to depose the King, imagines the death of the King; and there is no question, whether the compassing or imagining the death of the King was the primary intent conceived in the mind, prior to the conspiracy to depose him, as if a conspiracy to depose him, must necessarily, from the nature of the thing, be subsequent to the conspiracy to compass and imagine. I say it is not to be put to you, that the compassing and imagining the death of the King is to be proved a conception in the mind, prior to the conception of deposing the King. The deposing of the King is evidence of a conspiracy to compass and imagine. It is a presumption of law only, because it is such a necessary and violent presumption of fact. Who can doubt that the natural person of the King is immediately attacked and attempted by him who attempts to depose him.

Gentlemen, I shall waste no time in the discussing of such questions. Many, many hours were spent at the bar in this discussion, but on the part of the prisoner it was manifest, that after the discussion, the fact broke down under them, and it became impossible for either of the Gentlemen to set his face distinctly to this proposition. I say no honest man ought to doubt whether he who conspires to depose the King, has compassed or imagined his death.

Gentlemen,

Gentlemen, you will therefore proceed to the examination of the facts, and I am most cordially disposed to agree with the Counsel for the Prisoner, that if he is this day to be convicted, that the proof must be clear and convincing. It must consist of convincing circumstances, the result of which shall leave no doubt in your minds.

Gentlemen, the short state of the question of fact may be stated thus: Whether the prisoner and the other persons have conspired to subvert the Monarchy, and whether they have set on foot the project of a Convention of the People in order to effect it.

Gentlemen, I have employed a part of that time, which was necessary enough for me to have devoted, in endeavouring to take such a review of the evidence of this cause, as might enable me to lay the questions of fact as they exist, between the King and the Prisoner at the bar, with some tolerable distinctions before you, that you might see where the matter hinged, and that you may apply your attention and consideration to the different points of the case. I do not know whether I shall succeed or not, but I do hope I shall be able to point out to you the leading features of this case in a way that may be of some use to you in forming your judgments.

I begin with stating to you, that I think it ought to be conceded to this prisoner upon the whole result of this evidence, that he had set out originally upon that which is called the Duke of Richmond's plan of the Reform of Parliament, that is, upon a plan to obtain annual Parliaments, and a Representation of the People in the Commons House of Parliament by universal suffrage; and I think it will be incumbent on those who sustain the prosecution, to satisfy you, that the prisoner and the other persons, who have been concerned with him, whether irritated by their own enthusiasm, or by the example of France, have departed from that plan, and have entered into a criminal pursuit of another object—another object—in the opinion of very wise men, not very far removed from that; and it is that consideration which has made the laboured promulgation of such opinions so dangerous to the community. The object I now allude to is, the substituting, in the room of an improvement of the Representation of the Commons House of Parliament, a pure Democracy; the establishment of a Government by a Representation of the People, only, or what may be expressed under the words—a full and free Representation of the People.

Gentlemen, there are parts of the evidence, and these will not be found to be extremely numerous, which will be fit to be submitted to your consideration, as grounds from whence the prosecutors have drawn the conclusion by which they are to support the treason which accompanied this departure from the original plan, and which shew, that these people have entered into criminal pursuits. The parts of the evidence to which I particularly refer you, are those passages in it which mark the conduct of these people in the course of the year 1792, prior to their addresses to the National Convention. When you have considered this, you have then to consider those addresses to
the

the National Convention, with the circumstances belonging to them. After you have cast an intelligent eye on that subject, you will then have to look at their subsequent conduct, down to the time of the dispersion of the British Convention in Scotland, in the latter end of the year 1793; and then you will have to consider and to form your judgment upon that project of a Convention, which was conceived, and proceeded to a certain extent, in the beginning of 1794.

Gentlemen, I think I may state to you, without troubling you with particular evidence, that it is clear, from the whole mass of the evidence which you have heard, that these popular societies had, in the beginning of the year 1792, so conducted themselves as to raise a question upon themselves and their conduct, some time before the addresses to the National Convention took place. You will recollect that it appeared from some of the papers that were read, that there was a Society, calling themselves, " The Friends of the People ;" consisting of men of rank and property, and of great distinction in the country, who had refused to correspond with the Constitutional Society. You will recollect that the same set of men had exhorted the Sheffield Society, with whom they were in Correspondence that year, and had exhorted them in vain, to make an explicit declaration of their attachment to the Government as by law established. Some of these popular Societies had gone so far, and particularly a Society at Stockport, as to put the question directly to the London Corresponding Society, by a letter addressed to the Prisoner now at the bar, to know what it was they meant, and particularly to know whether they meant to go on with the House of Lords? That Society intimated their doubts, whether, with the House of Lords, they could effectuate their plan of Reform; or whether with the Bishops, who made a part of the House of Lords, liberty of conscience, as they understood it, could never be satisfactorily established.

Another Society, in the same year, from Norwich, put the question more distinctly and clearly, but in a way which could not possibly be misunderstood, for they put this direct question, and to the Prisoner Hardy—Do you intend to rip up the Monarchy by the roots? It was in evidence, they suspected that this last letter was a snare intended for them. You will recollect Lynham's evidence to that effect. They were on their guard, and answered it and the other letter. To be sure, one might reasonably have expected, that men, who adopted the Duke of Richmond's plan, with sincerity of heart, and who meant not to go beyond his plan, would have, when so called upon, most distinctly avowed the extent of their plan, in terms which could admit of no equivocation or exception. They would have avowed their dutiful attachment to the King; they would have avowed their adherence to the Constitution of the government as by law established, in King, Lords, and Commons. They would have left no man to doubt, and particularly those persons who put the question to them, what their opinion was,

upon

upon that important point which was to govern the conduct of others—what the opinion was, that they really entertained.

Gentlemen, the answers to these two requisitions, I shall desire may be read, not that I think, in a case of this nature, much stress ought to be laid on particular expressions. God forbid that men's lives should depend on nice interpretations and constructions of words. I am against even a very strict interpretation of actions to the prejudice of any prisoner. But sometimes expressions are too strong, sometimes transactions are too explicit, to admit of any doubt, as to the real interpretation and meaning. Gentlemen, read the answers to these two requisitions, attend to them, and see what it is they do import, and particularly whether they do import any satisfactory and explicit avowal of attachment to the constitution of the country, as by law established, in King, Lords, and Commons.

[The two letters from Stockport and Norwich, were first read by Mr. Shelton, and then the answers given to them by the London Corresponding Society.]

Gentlemen, all the observations that are to be made in the particular expressions in these two answers, have been already made by me, and you will judge of their proper force, I have no occasion to repeat them. Such of them as strike your minds clearly and distinctly, are probably well founded. If it requires much niceness of critical enquiry to fix the meaning imputed to the words, I should advise you not to employ yourselves in that sort of criticism. I think you would only entangle yourselves; and you would not see the case in its great outlines, which I believe is the only way in which it can be seen truly. One observation only I shall make on the last letter, because it is immediately connected with the history of this transaction, namely, that in the last letter they inform the Society at Stockport, that they have resolved on addressing the French National Convention; and then follows this extraordinary passage *" Without entering into the probable effects of such a measure—effects which your Society will not fail* TO DISCOVER *we invite you to join us."* What were to be the probable effects of this measure, which these persons were to discover? And why did they not expressly avow to the Society the whole of their project, in terms that could admit of no equivocation or doubt? These are the only observations that I make on this letter. They state that they had resolved to address the National Convention, and they did in fact address it; and it is very apparent, in the evidence, that the Society to which Hardy belonged took a lead in that measure. They notify it not only to the Stockport Society, but also the other Societies with whom they were in intimate correspondence and connections. They transmitted that resolution to the Society for Constitutional Information. The Society for Constitutional Information declared their approbation of the intention of the London Corresponding Society to address the National Convention of France, and the result was, that the Society for Constitutional Information did not think fit to join them

in

in that particular address, but they also resolved to present an address of their own to the Convention of France, and they, in fact, did so. What their objects were in presenting that address, are only darkly alluded to in the letter of the Corresponding Society to the Society of Stockport; but whatever their objects might seem to be it is a fair observation upon their conduct, in fact, towards those two Societies, to whom they sent these two letters, and upon their conduct in thus presenting this address, namely, that if you could suppose that they had measures to keep with those Societies, the violence of some to check, the moderation of others to animate, or any other objects which made it necessary for them to keep measures with those Societies, was the answering every man in his own way, so as to lose none, and to increase the number of their followers. If you were disposed, therefore, to attribute the particular language of these answers to some such necessity, yet, in respect of their conduct to the National Convention of France, they appear to be perfectly volunteers; to have no measures to keep with any body, and to be therefore directly responsible for all the consequences that might follow from such addresses.

Gentlemen, I believe it may be necessary to trouble you with the reading of these addresses, because they, on the part of this prosecution, infer from those addresses this proposition—that they admit of no explanation whatever, that they are the conduct of determined Republicans, going out of their way to express their zeal in the cause of republicanism. Now you will hear these addresses read, and you will judge for yourselves how far they merit that imputation.

Mr. Shelton here read the Addresses, and also the following extract from the Resolutions of the British Convention:

" Resolved, That the following Declarations and Resolutions be inserted at the end of our minutes, viz.

" That this Convention, considering the calamitous consequences of any act of the Legislature which may tend to deprive the whole or any part of the people of their undoubted right to meet, either by themselves or by delegation, to discuss any matter relative to their common interest, whether of a public or private nature, and holding the same to be totally inconsistent with the first principals and safety of society, and also subversive of our known and acknowledged constitutional liberties, do hereby declare, before God and the world, that we shall follow the wholesome example of former times, by paying no regard to any act which shall militate against the Constitution of our country, and shall continue to assemble and consider of the best means by which we can accomplish a real Representation of the People, and Annual Election, until compelled to desist by superior force.

" And we do resolve, That the first notice given for the introduction

duction of a Convention Bill, or any Bill of a similar tendency to that passed in Ireland in the last Session of their Parliament:

"Or any Bill for the suspension of the Habeas Corpus Act, or the Act for preventing wrongous imprisonment, and against undue delays in trial in North Britain:

"Or in case of an invasion, or the admission of any foreign troops whatsoever into Great Britain or Ireland;

"All or any one of these calamitous circumstances shall be a signal to the several Delegates to repair to such place as the Secret Committee of this Convention shall appoint; and the first seven Members shall have power to declare the Sittings permanent, shall constitute a Convention, and twenty-one proceed to business.

"The Convention doth therefore resolve, that each Delegate, immediately on his return home, do convene his constituents, and explain to them the necessity of electing a Delegate or Delegates, and of establishing a fund, without delay, against any of these emergencies, for his or their expence; and that they do instruct the said Delegate or Delegates to hold themselves in readiness at one hour's warning."

Gentlemen, it appears from the evidence, that these addresses were presented by persons appointed from hence. The name of one of them is J. Frost. The language in which Frost presented them, you are in possession of, and the evidence has been laid before you. It will be proper that you should hear it read. *(Mr. Shelton read it.)* Such was the language, Gentlemen, in which the Addresses were presented to the National Convention in France. I forbear, at this time, to remark on the language and conduct of the persons employed to present these Addresses, except so far as that language is connected with the case of the prisoner, because, in any other view of it, it is not before you. But this language, though not held by the prisoner himself, nor by the persons who deputed Frost to deliver it, yet it will be found to affect them in some degree, because the language of the presentation of the address is transmitted by Frost to the Societies, and you will find an unqualified approbation of the conduct of Frost, after they had been informed in what language it had been presented, was given by the Society for Constitutional Information, of which Hardy was an associated member. One material observation that occurs upon it is, that it was publicly declared, till the National Convention of France had begun to act, there was little to be done here with respect to the views of these Popular Societies. Whether that goes any way towards warranting the idea of a new interpretation of the phrase, Representation of the People by universal Suffrage and annual Elections, arising out of the proceedings of the National Convention of France, or if not rising out of them, yet in consequence of the National Convention of France having exhibited that great scene on the theatre of the world, that their attempts were to be carried into execution, and they did, in fact, address it, is for your judgment.

The

"This presentation has expressed an expectation that felicitations might soon come over to a National Convention here. What then was the National Assembly which was to be established here in England, and which was to be felicitated by France, will be a material subject for your serious consideration.

" Gentlemen, I have stated to you that the only effect, in this case, which the language of the delegate who presented this address has, is in respect of the adoption of it by the prisoner, and by the persons concerned with him. It was truly observed, that if an agent be employed, it would be cruel to bind his principal to any thing in which he went, beyond the bounds of his agency. It would be cruel if the acts of an agent could be imputed to his principal, when that principal never approved of them: But if the principal does approve of them, there is no hardship in such imputation. There is no cruelty, or even impropriety, in construing the language and sentiments of the agent to be the language and sentiments of the principal. Now you will judge, whether those concerned to support this prosecution have, upon solid grounds, or otherwise, branded these proceedings with rank Republicanism; and with being a distinct avowal, that every one of those people was embarked in the cause of Republicanism. It is an extremely important point to settle; for the review of the former proceedings in this cause will undoubtedly have, and must have a very different complexion, as they are understood to be the proceedings of determined republicans, or, as they are understood to be, the proceedings of dutiful and loyal subjects to the King, zealously affected to the constitution of the country, as established in a King, Lords, and Commons. Men of the one description are entitled to a large, liberal, and candid interpretation of all their words and actions. Men of other principles must expect to have their language, sentiments, and conduct, referred to those principles.

" Gentlemen, the next head of enquiry for you will be, the transactions of these societies, subsequent to the presenting of those addresses, and prior to the conception of the present design of a National Convention in England, which is the immediate subject of this prosecution; and you will examine whether the persons who had taken this extraordinary step, which seems to have been uncalled for, and to have for it's principal object a demonstration of principle which actuated the address to the French Convention), whether the authors of it, and the persons concerned in it, have in any manner redeemed themselves by their subsequent conduct from the imputation which the presenting of that address has brought upon them. I stated to you, that as far as voting an unqualified approbation goes, they immediately adopted it, upon consideration, and after hearing their own agent's comments upon it.

" Every thing done by the British Convention is completely brought home to the societies, by the following unqualified approbation of their conduct.

"At a Meeting, 17th January, 1794.

"Resolved, That law ceases to be an object of obedience whenever it becomes an instrument of oppression.

"Resolved, That we recall to mind, with the deepest satisfaction, the merited fate of the infamous Jefferies, once Lord Chief Justice of England, who, at the æra of the glorious Revolution, for the many iniquitous sentences which he had passed, was torn to pieces by a brave and injured people.

Resolved, "That those who imitate his example deserve his fate.

"Resolved, That the Tweed, though it may divide countries, ought not, and does not make a separation between those principles of common severity, in which Englishmen and Scotchmen are equally interested; that injustice in Scotland is injustice in England; and that the safety of Englishmen is endangered, whenever their brethren of Scotland, for a conduct which entitles them to the approbation of all wise, and the support of all brave men, are sentenced to Botany Bay, a punishment hitherto inflicted only on felons.

"Resolved, That we see with regret, but we see without fear, that the period is fast approaching when the liberties of Britons must depend not upon reason, to which they have long appealed, nor on their powers of expressing it, but on their firm and undaunted resolution to oppose tyranny by the same means by which it is exercised.

"Resolved, That we approve of the conduct of the British Convention, who, though assailed by force, have not been answered by argument; and who, unlike the members of a certain assembly, have no interest distinct from the common body of the people."

"Gentlemen, as to the evidence of a project of a National Convention in England, the acts of these societies more immediately referable to that sentiment, and which have been laid before you on the part of the prosecution, consist chiefly of votes, and of the warm and unqualified approbation of the works of two celebrated writers, Thomas Paine and Joel Barlow, the first writing upon the Rights of Man, and the last on what was called the *privileged orders*. These works, whether the whole object of them was that way or no, I do not take upon myself to affirm, not being sufficient master of the whole extent of them; but they do in part most assuredly attack directly, and pointedly, the establishment of the monarchy of this country; and they do attack, more or less pointedly and directly, the establishment of that order in this country—the House of Lords. The societies not only approved of these works, but they dispersed them all over the country with a wonderful anxiety, and at a great expence. The prosecutors in this case have asked the question, why was this done? They say it is acting consistently, it is done by Republicans, who wish to subvert the monarchy, and to overturn the established orders; but if it

is

is done by dutiful subjects of the King, and persons attached to the Constitution of the country, what explanation can they give it? In the defence that was made for the prisoner, it was observed, that there was part of these works going to the general rights of men—going to such general rights as can exist in society without going into the particular establishments of particular countries. That to that part of those works there could be no objection, and that those parts might therefore be disseminated by honest men and good subjects. I do not know whether the observation is founded; but there is another observation—Was it not the duty of honest men and good subjects, who were disseminating those parts of these works as might serve to enlighten mankind on subjects on which they ought to be enlightened; was it not fit that those who circulated these works, should have taken some pains to separate the bad parts from the good, or at least given the public some caution that, in reading these works, they should make a separation; that when they were reading of the general rights of men, and found passages striking at the monarchy of this country, they should be careful not to imbibe prejudices against the monarchy; that when, reading observations on privileged orders, they should take care to remember, this was not intended to strike at the orders of this country, to which the public had a devoted attachment?

"Such would have been the conduct of good subjects. That this was not the conduct of these persons, is most apparent; and that they have had the effect of doing a great deal of mischief by alienating the minds of the King's subjects from his person and government, and from the constitution, is perfectly clear. How much of this effect these persons intended, I shall leave entirely for your consideration. Only thus much I think is clear, that there is nothing in those publications, which can serve to remove any prejudices which arise against the prisoner, and the persons concerned with him, from the addresses that were presented to the Convention of France.

"Gentlemen, another general feature in the transactions of those men is, the abundance of licentious observations scattered throughout their publications, and tending to produce the same effect—the alienation of the affections of the country from the King and Government. Grievances may and will exist in all governments, and that they may exist, in a greater or lesser degree, in this government, may be true; but dutiful and good subjects, who honestly mean the reform of these grievances, will take care, in their endeavours to procure this reform, not to hazard the overturning the government itself. It is here the transactions of the early part of the year 1793 commence, upon which the prosecutors rely as exciting a spirit of disaffection by which these men were actuated, and as evidence of the furthering of measures taken to prepare men's minds for some alteration in the Government of the country. It appears, that, in the course of the summer of that year, the idea of a National Convention, to be held in Scotland, originated; and they on the part of the prosecution, and certainly not without colour (how far it is diſtinctly proved you will judge)—they ſay, it originated with the priſoner at the bar, as they aſſert that a letter was written by the priſoner to Skirving, in Edinburgh, that recommended this meaſure that was to be taken by theſe popular ſocieties, ſending delegates to Edinburgh.

[Hardy's letter to Skirving, dated May 17, 1793, was here read.]

" The particular expreſſion upon which my finger is laid, is, " I wiſh you to begin there." Now you will read the anſwer which Skirving ſent to that letter, and you will attend to it, becauſe that anſwer is charged on the part of the proſecution to have a great deal of matter tending to explain the mechaniſm of the National Convention, and alſo what was to be it's great object. (Reads Skirving's letter, 25th of May, 1793.)

" Gentlemen, every part of this letter deſerves the moſt ſerious attention, with a view to this point, which I, juſt before the reading of the letter, ſtated to you; I think there is one paragraph in it which may acquire my reſtating to you. This letter ſays, " I have not a higher wiſh in the preſent exertions for reform, than to ſee the people univerſally, and regularly aſſociated, becauſe I am perſuaded that the preſent diſaſtrous engagements will iſſue in ruin, and the people then muſt provide for themſelves." What do theſe myſterious words mean? diſaſtrous engagements to end in ruin! If we underſtand this to relate to any political engagements in which this country was engaged, and might end ill, the people would not have to provide for themſelves, becauſe that would not diſſolve the government. What does he mean, therefore, when he talks of theſe diſaſtrous engagements; " and it would be unhappy when we ſhould be ready to act with unanimity, to be occupied about organization, without which however anarchy muſt enſue?"

" It is true, if the country was to be brought to ſuch a ſtate, that the government was to be deſtroyed, and another government to take place, if that was the moment of organization, it would be a very unhappy circumſtance, when we ſhould be ready to act with unanimity, to be occupied about organization, without which, however, anarchy muſt enſue.

" We will not need but to be prepared for the event, to ſtand and ſee the ſalvation of the Lord. Let us therefore take the hint, given us by our oppreſſors; let us begin in earneſt to make up our minds relative to the extent of reform which we ought to ſeek."

" The extent of reform which we ought to ſeek was diſtinct, and had been ſo a great while, for it was the Duke of Richmond's plan of reform.

" Be prepared to juſtify it, and to controvert objections, let us model the whole in the public mind, let us provide every stake and stay of the tabernacle which we would erect, so that when the tabernacles of oppression, in the palace of ambition, are broken down under the madness and folly of their supporters, we may then without anarchy and all dangerous delay, erect at once our tabernacle of righteousness, and may the Lord himself be in it."

"What does this mysterious man mean?—Does he mean that it is probable there may soon be a revolution in the government of this country; and in that case it would be fit some body of men should take upon themselves the powers of government; and to act upon it? Or does he only mean a reform in parliament would be found to be necessary, that people ought to know what it is they mean to ask, and in what manner they mean to ask it?

"Gentlemen, this is an exposition of this doctrine of a Convention, coming from a Briton, and immediately communicated to the prisoner at the bar; and in that respect has a direct application to him, and is of the utmost importance, to satisfy you, that he has not been surprised into any thing; but that, from the moment of the communication on the subject, he had an opportunity of weighing it.

"Now, there was another exposition of a National Convention, which the evidence affords, but I have not stated it to you particularly, but I shall now mention it, though, under the particular circumstances of this case, I do not think it ought to press much against the prisoner. I mean the speech of Barrere, on the subject of a National Convention, in which he takes a great deal of pains to shew, that it is a thing perfectly consistent with an established government; that a National Convention was the authority of the people by itself, which might lawfully have consisted with the established orders of the country. It was well observed on the part of the prisoner, that a people had a right to alter their government; and I agree to it as a general proposition; but it is improper to be urged in a Court of Justice, that is to proceed on the laws of the land as already established; and therefore, while we are administering those laws, to listen to such argument would tend to annihilate the whole system of justice. I now take notice that this exposition of a Convention can have no application to the present case. My reason for thinking to press the prisoner on the French exposition of National Convention, is, because it came over to this country in the Moniteur, to the Constitutional Society; but, though it was received, and ordered to be entered in their books, it does not appear it ever was translated into English; there was no evidence of it, and therefore it was extremely probable that the prisoner never had an opportunity of knowing Barrere's sentiments

ments on that subject: but it is otherwise with respect to the letter that was sent to himself. He had a full opportunity of weighing it; of asking for explanation; of rejecting any part of it; of contradicting it; or of correcting the ideas that were in it; and to take care that, if it was set on foot, it might not lead to any bad consequences.

"Gentlemen, on the 5th of October, of that year, the prisoner wrote a letter to Skirving, in answer to a letter of Skirving's, dated October 2, which letter is not in evidence. In this letter the prisoner speaks of himself and Mr. Margarot, and also of the plan of a Convention in Scotland: he recommends it to Skirving to write an official letter to his (Hardy's) society, to propose to them to send Delegates to that Convention; and in that letter he desires Skirving not to take notice that he had any communication with him. Here the prisoner Hardy appears quite in a new character. He was certainly not an inactive member of the society, independent of his being secretary of the society. Had he acted only as secretary, it might be said he might have been misled in a great many things. He might have written many things which he did not understand, or which he had not time to weigh; as a man might write whole sheets without having any idea of the sense after he had written them; it was therefore very much in his favour to consider the prisoner only as secretary. But here he certainly is a principal, and most extraordinarily so;—a principal acting with a great share of the spirit of intrigue and [duplicity, which totally changes the character of the man, as it appears from all the rest of the evidence in the cause.

This letter is written, and the delegates are appointed. They are very able men, viz. Margarot and Gerald. The Scottish Convention is held. They sat for fourteen days, and were then dispersed by authority. What was to have happened, if that Scottish Convention had not been dispersed, I can only conjecture; but in order to form any rational conjecture, it is necessary to attend to the general objects of that Convention. It is fit you should call back to your memory just the leading features of it. It is pressed on you, on behalf of the prisoner, that the meeting of the Delegates of these bodies was for this single object—to consider what was the best way of appealing to Parliament to procure a reform of Parliament.——With respect to that, you will recollect the transactions of that year, on the ground of an application to Parliament. There had been an application to Parliament, and the principal mover was Mr. Grey. Of the sincerity of the honourable mover for a Parliamentary Reform, I suppose no man will doubt; but on the sincerity of their application to Parliament on this evidence every man must doubt, because there are plans to arm, but there are no certain means of coming to an end. They sought a Parliamentary Reform, not as a measure of which they approved, but as they

thought

thought it might be useful by way of preparation for what they had in their minds, and to keep the public mind agitated on the subject; and therefore this oftensible purpose was not the only purpose of the Convention. When there was a motion made that a petition should be presented to Parliament, they put the order of the day upon it—they negatived it; and therefore, if that was their only object, the purpose of their meeting was at an end.

But laying that object aside, view this Convention as it was. You find it clearly imitating the manners of the National Convention of France; you hear of primary assemblies and sections. Committees are common to all, and therefore no stress ought to be laid on that.—You perceive this National Convention assuming to itself a formality that is very becoming where it is subject to no just exception; but in the place in which it appears, certainly very alarming. We find the Convention is constituted every day by solemn prayer: it is closed every day by solemn prayer. There was also a Committee of Finances, and other things of less consequence, though still deserving of consideration.

After the 10th day they assumed this title—"*The First Year of the British Convention.*" Recollect how closely that goes to the language of the National Convention of France. Say, what would have happened if that Convention had not been dispersed at the end of fourteen days. No man, I should think, could take upon himself to say, but if they continued to assume in the manner in which they began, and some interval had been permitted to them, it seems to me that I am warranted to say, from what did take place in France, that supposing in that time they had happened to get the public opinion, that body of men would have been the government of this country. They were however dispersed; and it would ill become me, in this place, to take notice of the consequence of that dispersion, except that occasion was taken to complain of this as a grievance; and most certainly the prisoner, and those who are connected with him in these societies, did take occasion from thence to irritate the public mind to as great a degree as it was possible to do, by the reflections that were made on these proceedings.

Gentlemen, the immediate consequence of the reflections which were dispersed on the subject of these proceedings, was the plan of adopting a British Convention, to be held in England; which leads us nearly to the point to which all the present enquiry is to have it's relation more or less. Now it deserves serious attention on your part, to the circumstances with which this new plan of Convention was introduced to the public notice, and by which it was recommended to the public attention, in order to enable you to judge, whether the object of it was that peaceable object which is insisted on the part of the prisoner, and really the bottom of the whole; or whether the object of it must have been to carry into effect a full and free representation of the people, but not in the Commons House of Parliament, in our Constitution. One should have apprehended, under any provocation, which these people
thought

thought they had felt, or which they really might feel, that they would have followed a very different course. As they were acquainted with the circumstances of the dispersion of the former Convention, and with all the objections that were made to that Convention; as they were determined to have another Convention, it was to be expected, that they at least would have taken care so to guard their language and proceedings, that it was impossible they could be misunderstood; to have expressed themselves clearly and distinctly on all occasions; to have explained the grounds of this Convention; to have conducted themselves with a decent moderation towards the government of the country, and towards it's proceedings. It might reasonably have been expected, that it would have made an express avowal of loyal sentiments, and an express disavowal of going any lengths which could be justly objected to; an express disavowal of going beyond the original object of parliamentary reform, as stated by the Duke of Richmond; and every thing that was inflammatory ought to have been most carefully avoided, in order to prevent their purpose being misunderstood; and as what was most material, in order to insure success to the measure itself. What was done you will see, and from that you will form your own conclusions. You will hear the paper relating to this business read, and you will mark it. I do not consider it as my business to make particular comments on it.

The different parts of the evidence will make a certain impression on your minds, and you will take care that they do not go too far.—I think the first great paper, (there are many which are connected with it) is the address of the 20th January, 1794, of the London Corresponding Society, at a general meeting held at the Globe tavern.

[*This Address to the People of Great Britain and Ireland was here read, as follows.*]

"Citizens,

"We find the nation involved in a war, by which, in the course of one campaign, immense numbers of our countrymen have been slaughtered, a vast expence has been incurred, our trade, commerce, and manufactures are almost destroyed, and many of our manufacturers and artists are ruined, and their families starving.

"To add to our affliction, we have reason to expect that other taxes will soon be added to the intolerable load of imposts and impositions with which we are already overwhelmed, for the purpose of defraying the expences which have been incurred in a fruitless crusade, to re-establish the odious despotism of France.

"When we contemplate the principles of this war, we confess ourselves to be unable to approve of it, as a measure either of justice or discretion;—and if we are to form our calculation of the result from what has already passed, we can only look forward to defeat, and the eternal disgrace of the British name.

"While

" While we are thus engaged in an expenfive and ruinous foreign war, our ftate at home is not lefs deplorable.

" We are every day told, by thofe perfons who are interefted in fupporting the Corruption Lift, and an innumerable hoft of Sinecure Placemen, that the Conftitution of England is the perfection of human wifdom; that our laws (we fhould rather fay, their laws) are the perfection of juftice; and that their adminiftration of thofe laws is fo impartial and fo ready, as to afford an equal remedy both to the rich and to the poor; by means of which we are faid to be placed in a ftate of abfolute freedom, and that our rights and liberties are fo well fecured to us as to render all invafion of them impoffible.

" When we afk how we enjoy thefe tranfcendent privileges, we are referred to Magna Charta, and the Bill of Rights; and the glorious Revolution, in the year 1688, is held out to us as the bulwark of Britifh liberty.

" Citizens,

" We have referred to Magna Charta, to the Bill of Rights, and to the Revolution, and we certainly do find that our anceftors did eftablifh wife and wholefome laws; but we as certainly find, that of the venerable Conftitution of our anceftors hardly a veftige remains.

" If we look to Ireland, we find that acknowledged privilege of the people, to meet for the fupport and protection of their rights and liberties, is attempted, by terror, to be taken away by a late infamous Act of Parliament; whilft titles of honour—no, but of difhonour—are lavifhed, and new fources of corruption opened, to gratify the greedy proftitution of thofe who are the inftruments of this oppreffion.

" In Scotland, the wicked hand of power has been impudently exerted without even the wretched formality of an Act of Parliament. Magiftrates have forcibly intruded into the peaceful and lawful meetings of freemen; and by force (not only without law, but againft law) have, under colour of magifterial office, interrupted their deliberations, and prevented their affociations.

" The wifdom and good conduct of the Britifh Convention at Edinburgh, has been fuch as to defy their bittereft enemies to name the law which they have broken; notwithftanding which, their papers have been feized, and made ufe of as evidence againft them, and many virtuous and meritorious individuals have been, as cruelly as unjuftly, for their virtuous actions, difgraced and deftroyed by infamous and illegal fentences of tranfportation. And thefe unjuft and wicked judgments have been executed with a rancour and malignity never before known in this land; our refpectable and beloved Fellow Citizens have been caft fettered into dungeons amongft felons in the Hulks, to which they were not fentenced.

" You may afk, perhaps, by what means fhall we feek redrefs?

"We answer, that men in a state of civilized society are bound to seek redress of the grievances from the laws, as long as any redress can be obtained by the laws. But our common Master whom we serve (whose law is a law of liberty, and whose service is perfect freedom) has taught us not to expect to gather grapes from thorns, nor figs from thistles. We must have redress from our own laws, and not from the laws of our plunderers, enemies, and oppressors.

"There is no redress for a Nation circumstanced as we are, but in a fair, free, and full Representation of the People."

Gentlemen, you have heard this paper read, and it expressly refers to a Convention; and it was certainly published at a time when the idea of a Convention was in the minds of the people. Now, with regard to that paper, you are to judge between the King and the prisoner, whether the object of that Convention was, merely to procure a free and full representation of the people in the Commons House of Parliament, and in the due course of law, and according to the constitution of the country, or whether that paper is to be understood as a manifesto, as a call to the people against the government, to direct the people's minds to the use that should be made of a Convention for the purpose of overturning the government.

Gentlemen, this happened on the 20th of January, 1794. They began in these two societies to consider how this Convention was to be brought about. The Constitutional Society had resolved it in terms which upon the face of them were open to some observations.

There was a committee of correspondence and co operation in order to produce this Convention, and to consider the means of doing it; but before I come to that, I shall take notice of a joint committee, who corrected, in some measure, the language of this proposed Convention. They made it more moderate; and it is fit that should be stated.

[The proposal for a Joint Committee of the two Societies was here read.]

The language of it is a Convention of the People, for the purpose of taking into consideration the proper method of obtaining a fair and full representation of the people. This is their object, as they think fit to express themselves upon consideration; and it would never be too late for them to have retracted any part of the rashness and violence of any former measure that they had taken; and therefore if you were warranted to suppose that the languague that had been formerly used was too violent, and the sentiments too extravagant, if they really meant to moderate and confine the objects of the Convention within it's just limits, they certainly ought to have it's full benefit. This is not accompanied with any useless declaration that it ought to be in the Commons House of Parliament, and still less that no attempt was meant against the King, and the jurisdiction and authority of the House of Lords.

The

The Attorney General. "Will not your Lordship also desire the application from the Corresponding Society, for a junction of the two societies, to be read. I consider it as extremely material."

Chief Justice Eyre. "It has already been repeatedly read in the course of the evidence; the proceedings have already extended to so great a length, that I do not, in the present stage, wish to trouble the Jury with any thing except what is absolutely necessary."

The paper being read, the chief Justice proceeded—

"You see, that here they adopt the comparatively moderate language of calling a Convention, for the purpose of taking into consideration the proper methods of obtaining a full and fair representation of the people. It certainly never was too late to have retracted any part of that rashness and violence of which they might have been guilty. If they, thinking that they had been too violent in their expressions, or extravagant in their sentiments, had come to this resolution with a view to remedy the fault of their former proceedings, that consideration would no doubt have it's due weight. But even in this resolution, we find no declaration that they sought only a reform in the House of Commons, and that they had no intention against the authority of the House of Lords, or the power of the Crown. But on the contrary, we find that on the 14th of April, the Corresponding Society published a declaration, and circulated it in different parts of the kingdom. This declaration is intended to prepare the minds of the people for the arrival of that violent crisis, in which a Convention must immediately be summoned, and in which they would necessarily be called upon to act. If instead, then, of intending to bring things back, or to remedy the effects of their former violence, we find them advancing in the same career, and hastening by the same means to the accomplishment of their object, what must be the conclusion. Instead of coming forward with a declaration of their loyalty to the throne, or their respect for the House of Lords, in order to do away the impression of their former proceedings, and remove all suspicion and ambiguity with respect to their future intentions, we find them coming forward with another Manifesto, this Manifesto comes forward in a still more questionable shape than the former, as it is intended to carry along with it the appearance of great force, and to shew that they are ready, if it shall be necessary, to act in support of their former resolutions. I allude to the proceedings that took place at Chalk Farm on the 14th of April, 1794. These proceedings commenced with reading a letter that had been sent by the Corresponding Society to the Friends of the People, and the answer, which it had received from that society.

They then came to their own resolutions."—He then desired the clerk to read the account of the proceedings at Chalk-farm, which is printed in the first report from the committee of secrecy.

[*The Resolutions read, were as follows.*]

" Resolved Unanimously,

" I. That this society have beheld with rising indignation, proportioned to the enormity of the evil, the late rapid advances of despotism in Britain; the invasion of public security, the contempt of popular opinion; and the violation of all those provisions of the constitution intended to protect the people against the encroachments of power and prerogative.

" II. That our abhorrence and detestation have been particularly called forth by the late arbitrary and flagitious proceedings of the Court of Justiciary in Scotland, where all the doctrines and practices of the Star Chamber, in the times of Charles the First, have been revived and aggravated; and where sentences have been pronounced, in open violation of all law and justice, which must strike deep into the heart of every man the melancholy conviction that Britons are no longer free.

" III. That the whole proceedings of the late British Convention of the People, at Edinburgh, are such as claim our approbation and applause.

" IV. That the conduct of citizens Margarot and Gerald in particular, by it's strict conformity with our wishes and instructions, and the ability. firmness, and disinterested patriotism which it so eminently displayed, has inspired an enthusiasm of zeal and attachment which no time can obliterate, and no persecution remove; and that we will preserve their names engraven on our hearts till we have an opportunity to redress their wrongs.

" IX. That the thanks of this meeting be given to Earl Stanhope, for his manly and patriotic conduct during the present Session of Parliament, &c.

After these resolutions had been read, he continued.—" One cannot hear this paper read without being astonished that men should be so blinded by enthusiasm, or any other affection, as not to see the consequences to which they exposed themselves by this violent conduct, and while they were passing these resolutions, they had the sword of the law hanging over their heads by a single thread. But it had been argued that the publicity of these proceedings implied a consciousness, on their part, that they were perfectly innocent and legal. What! did they not see something extremely criminal in publishing to 200,000 people (the number of copies of those resolutions, which they ordered to be printed) that the social compact between the English nation and their governor was to be considered as dissolved; and that the safety of the people was the supreme, and in cases of necessity, the only law? What could be implied by this resolution, but that they looked forward to the framing of another government to be erected on the ruins of the

present

present establishment? In their 8th and 10th resolutions, they glance, and that not in an indirect manner, to the House of Lords, as not intitled to the respect of the nation.

"The question still recurs. What did they mean to do by this proposed Covention? On the part of the prisoner, it is urged that they intended to meet in a legal and peaceable manner, in order to take into consideration the most proper method of procuring a fair and full representation of the People in the House of Commons. Whether this can be inferred, after all the steps they had previously taken, and all the addresses they had published to the nation, must remain for your decision. Another thing to be taken into consideration was what respected the society in Sheffield. This society was connected with the society for constitutional information, and the corresponding society in London. It was extremely numerous: the persons assembled at one time on the Castle-hill had been stated to amount to ten thousand. These came to certain resolutions, to which they were brought by one Yorke, not a native of Sheffield, but a member of the Corresponding Society of London, who had got down there, in what particular character does not appear. It is, however, some consolation to attend to the manner in which these resolutions were brought about. Though the names of a great number of persons, were signed to them, but few of these can be considered as having really assented to them in their minds, or adopted them as principles, upon which they were to act. And though ten thousand were stated to have been present, perhaps not above two hundred were concerned in planning and carrying these resolutions. The motion to petition Parliament was previously concerted to be overuled by the Junto of four. But what attached to the societies the criminality of these resolutions was their subsequent publications and promulgation. It has indeed been fairly put on the part of the prisoner, that the resolution that they would no longer petition Parliament, does not imply that they might not petition in a larger body, when they might think they would have a greater chance of a favourable reception. But what is the reason assigned on these Sheffield resolutions, why they were no longer to petition?—" Because they will not petition a body who are not their representatives." This is a reason, which must equally apply at all times against petitioning the House of Commons, while it continues on it's present footing. The nature then of the proposed convention is to be gathered from the language of those addresses. And from those it appears to have been intended to be a convention in order to concert the means of establishing a representative government of the people. There is one piece of parole evidence, which it is extremely material to attend to. It occurred in the examination of Lynam. He was present at a meeting of the society where Bell asked, "Whether it was intended to introduce the same laws into this country as in France?" Margarot answered, "No doubt;" all the others were silent. Hardy was present at this meeting. There is also parole evidence, so far as it goes, of a certain preparation of arms in order to support the convention. One witness, but not of the best credit, states that it was said that these arms were provided in order to defend the convention. On this head, however, the parole evidence cuts two ways, for different witnesses, from the societies contend that these arms were procured merely in order to defend themselves against illegal attack. Much has been insisted on the exhortations to peaceable and orderly conduct contained in the addresses, published with a view to the meeting of the Convention. But it is to be recollected that the character of such a Convention as was proposed, is perfectly consistent with inculcating peace and good order, as their object was in the measures which they should adopt with respect to the Government, to carry the public mind so forceably along with them as to render all resistance vain and useless.

The same Witness, undoubtedly not intitled to much credit, mentioned that it was always expected by the Society, that a struggle would be necessary in order to accomplish their object, and that they looked forward to an actual rising in the country. This would amount to conspiring to depose the King, by levying war in the kingdom—a clear overt-act of High Treason. And though the witness from whom it came was not entitled to much credit, yet so far as corroborated by the testimony of others, against whose character there is no objection, it is not without it's weight.

Gentlemen of the Jury,

I have given you the charge along with the evidence, in order that you may be able to ascertain the amount of the whole facts, and see how far they go to establish what is laid in the indictment. On the other hand, you are to attend with favour to the arguments urged, and the evidence brought forward, in behalf of the Prisoner, and to weigh well whatever makes for the defence. The written evidence against him has not been attempted to be disputed, nor can it indeed be controverted. From that evidence it appears, that the Prisoner was not merely a person who acted under the direction of others, and signed papers as Secretary, without adverting to their contents, or being able to comprehend their meaning, but that he was himself a principal in the transactions of those Societies, and a designer, promoter, and inventor of many of the proceedings which had come out in evidence. He cannot therefore set up a defence upon any ground of that sort. The Counsel for the Prisoner attempted to vindicate the temper and views of the Sheffield Society, on the ground of the letters which they had written to the Friends of the People. But if these are taken along with their letter, dated 26th of May, 1792, addressed to the Correspondiog Society, it will then

be

be perceived how far they were sincere in their first professions, or, if they really were sincere, how far they had afterwards adhered to them. The Prisoner's Counsel had also made several fair and weighty observations on the credit due to witnesses, who had introduced themselves into these Societies for the purpose of giving information of their proceedings, and of the subject-matter of their testimony, particularly as it related to the preparation of arms. I have no hesitation to admit, that if the question of criminallity depended solely on the proof, brought with respect to arms though there might be strong cause of suspicion, yet that would not be sufficient ground to impute to those Societies all that mischief, which might, in the present instance, be apprehended to arise from their designs. The Counsel for the defence state the Prisoner to be a plain, honest man, orderly in his demeanour, and moderate in his temper, having one great object strongly rivitted on his mind, namely, a Reform in the Commons House of Parliament, upon the principles of Universal Suffrage and Annual Elections. These principles, they contend, he borrowed from a work of the Duke of Richmond, in which they are inculcated, and that to carry these principles into effect all his measures were directed; that the very idea of a Convention is, taken from the same work of his Grace, which certainly contains a strong allusion to the People meeting in a body in order to procure the object which he there recommends. The Prisoner, they alledge, conceived that a Petition to Parliament, coming from a large body, would have more weight than Petitions from Individuals or smaller bodies, and that he had no intention to use a Convention for any other purpose than that which is above stated; that he had not the smallest idea, by means of that Convention, to interfere with the privileges of the House of Peers, or the power and dignity of the Crown. They contend, from the statement of the force, said to be prepared, that there could be no such intention as to overturn the Constitution; for if the means, as in all cases, are to be proportioned to the end, such an attempt, in the circumstances of these Societies, was not only highly improbable, but altogether impossible. They further argue, that if the Convention proposed to be assembled was of the same nature with the British Convention that had been already held at Edinburgh, it could not be treasonable, as some of the Delegates to that Convention had been tried and convicted only upon a charge of misdemeanour. If Treason, therefore, did not attach in the one instance, neither could it in the other; the crime of only concerting to hold a Convention, was certainly less than that of having actually held one; whatever, therefore, may be the inflammatory tendency of the papers, or whatever the violence of expressions adapted in them, still the

guilt

guilt of thofe Societies, cannot amount to High Treafon. The Prifoner has appealed to feveral members of the Societies with whom he was connected, for the foundnefs of his principles and of their own—their attachment to the eftablifhed branches of the Conftitution, and their intention to proceed towards their object in a legal and peaceable manner. A cloud of refpectable Witneffes have come forward to his private character—to teftify that he is a peaceable, fedate, orderly and religious man, having one great idea relative to a Reform of Parliament. It appears, alfo, from the evidence of Mr. Sheridan, that he made a propofition to him to give up all his papers and correfpondence for the infpection of a Committee of the Houfe of Commons—a circumftance, which would feem to imply a ftrong confcioufnefs of innocent intentions. Mr. Francis has ftated, that he waited on him with a Petition from his Society, addreffed to the Houfe of Commons on the fubject of a Parliamentary Reform, and mentions that his conduct on that occafion was fuch as was calculated, not only to imprefs him with a favourable opinion of his general character, but of the moderation of his political fentiments, and his intentions to follow them out in a peaceable manner. In alluding to the work of the Duke of Richmond, there is one circumftance which I forgot to mention. At the fame time, with that work there was brought forward in evidence by the Prifoner's Counfel, a copy of a Proteft, figned by feveral Noble Lords, and ftating the fame fentiments with refpect to the rights of the People to meet, and deliberate on certain objects. This paper, falling into the hands of an ignorant man and an enthufiaft, if ever it fell into the hands of a perfon of fuch a character, might, no doubt, have a tendency to miflead him, and difpofe him to the profecution of violent meafures. But thefe pieces of evidence applied only to one part of the cafe. It certainly never would be imputed to that Noble Perfon, the Duke of Richmond, and to the other Noble Lords, who figned the Proteft, that they intended, by the publication of their fentiments, to overturn the eftablifhed Government of the Country, and introduce in it's ftead a Democracy.

It never could be contended that their views went fo far as thofe which have been proved upon fome of the focieties. I conceded to the prifoner that he might, in the firft inftance, have fet out with a fincere profeffion of the Duke of Richmond's principles and a determined refolution to confine himfelf to the object of univerfal fuffrage, but whether he has not departed from thofe principles, and gone beyond that object, is to be made out from the evidence, and is matter for you to determine. The reply goes to impeach the credit due to the evidence from the members of the Sheffield Society. The characters of thofe members is in fome degree implicated with that of the prifoner; and it is to be confidered what degree

gree of weight ought to be given to the teſtimony of a man called upon to ſwear to his own loyalty, and the ſincerity of his attachment to the Conſtitution, more particularly if his conduct be ſuch as has been charged with reſpect to thoſe witneſſes, as to beget a ſuſpicion that he is actuated by very different ſentiments; in this caſe there is *proteſtatio contra factum*. His conduct is the reverſe of his ſentiments; and therefore juſtly affords ground for diſtruſt. The reply refers alſo to the written evidence as a proof of the duplicity of the priſoner. One inſtance of this is his conduct with reſpect to Mr. Francis, upon whom he waited, in order to requeſt him to preſent a petition of his ſociety for a Parliamentary Reform, and whom he induced to believe that he was really anxious to obtain that object, though from different papers it appeared that he had no ſincere deſire for that purpoſe, but was only deſirous, by bringing forward this petition, to agitate the public mind on the ſubject. Another remark on the reply goes directly to his character; that though he was deſcribed as a ſedate, moderate, religious man, it was evident that he was ſtrongly tinctured with enthuſiaſm; a circumſtance which, notwithſtanding the other parts of his conduct, makes it ſtill highly probable that he might be concerned in the attempts charged againſt him. And an inſtance was quoted in the caſe of the Fifth Monarchy Men, where a charge of High Treaſon might be founded againſt them on the expreſs ground of their religion. It is to be remarked, that the particular acts done by this man, are not contradicted by any of his own witneſſes.

They were certainly ſuch as are totally inconſiſtent with the idea of only effecting a Reform in the Commons-Houſe of Parliament; they are ſuch as are conſiſtent with the other idea of ſubverting the eſtabliſhed Conſtitution, by introducing in it's ſtead a repreſentative Government of the people.

" Gentlemen of the Jury,

" Upon all this ſtatement, you are now to exerciſe your own judgment, and in doing ſo, you will pay no more attention to what I have ſaid, except ſo far as it may be ſupported by the facts of the caſe, and lead you to the principal points of the evidence brought forward, both for the proſecution and for the priſoner. The Jury are in no caſe bound to attend to any opinion, except their own, in forming their deciſion on the general queſtion of guilt or innocence. Every verdict ought to be the Jury's own verdict, more particularly in a caſe of ſuch magnitude as the preſent, to which the eye of the public are turned, in order that the country may be ſatisfied that you, as you are bound by your oath, have made a true deliverance. I am ſorry to remark, that during the courſe of this trial, the dignity of a Court of Juſtice has, in conſequence of conduct that has taken place, both within and without doors, been in more inſtances than one, groſsly violated. What ſuch a conduct can mean, except from perſons who are deſirous to diſſolve all the ties of Government, and deſtroy all reverence for authority, I cannot poſſibly underſtand, and I truſt I ſhall not again witneſs a repetition of ſuch a conduct, either in this, or in any other caſe, in which the public juſtice may be called upon to determine.

"Gentlemen, you will now conſider of your verdict."

The Jury, before withdrawing, aſked for a copy of the Indictment.

Chief Juſtice Eyre. "I ſee no objection to letting you have a copy of the Indictment, although it is not quite regular, provided it be done by the conſent of the parties."

No objection was made; and a copy of the Indictment was handed to the Jury.

Chief Juſtice Eyre. "Gentlemen of the Jury, It is proper to inform you, that after you withdraw you can be allowed no refreſhment. If you wiſh for any refreſhment, now is the time to take it."

The Jury. "My Lord, we thank you, but we ſhall have occaſion for no refreſhment."

At half an hour paſt twelve o'clock, the Jury withdrew, and at half paſt three, returned a verdict of

NOT GUILTY.

The Lord Preſident then thanked the Jury for their diligent attendance on ſo long and arduous a trial; and gave directions that the priſoner be immediately diſcharged.

Mr. Hardy then thanked the Jury for the verdict they had given, both on behalf of himſelf, and of all his fellow-ſubjects.

The populace, who, notwithſtanding the wetneſs of the day, filled the ſtreets adjacent to the Court Houſe, received the news of his acquittal with the loudeſt acclamations of joy. And after he was diſcharged, they followed the coach which conveyed him to his lodgings, and taking the horſes from it, drew him through different parts of the town.

The Court adjourned to Monday ſe'nnight.

In pronouncing the verdict, the Foreman was ſo overcome that he was ſcarce audible, and literally fainted away.

Had Hardy been convicted, Englishmen must have heard the fatal tidings with compassion for the victim to the law—and alarmed, lest their enthusiastic attachment to the restoration of their Constitutional Rights might subject them to the same terrific fatality. Although we have been told that the enthusiast is criminal, and, therefore, deserving of punishment, yet, according to every principle of ethics or moral philosophy we have studied, we cannot abandon the idea, that neither civil, political, moral, or religious virtue could exist without enthusiasm. It is this which constitutes the flame and energy of every worthy action that distinguishes the statesman, soldier, lawyer and citizen. Had it not been for the enthusiastic attachment of Mr. Erskine and Mr. Gibbs, to the cause of national freedom, justice, and humanity, England might have had one of her champions fall beneath the vengeance of legal prosecution. What could withstand such a formidable mass of written and parole evidence, such a phalanx of the ablest crown prosecutors, but the enthusiasm of the counsel for the prisoner? convinced of his innocence and his political attachment to the King, and the Constitution, their electric favour illuminated the shrine of justice, and thus restored the patriot again to society.

The momentous acquittal of Mr. Hardy is a subject that will ever be equally dear to the feelings, and memorable in the recollection of every individual in the kingdom. When persons with the most ardent attachment to the constitution are liable to suffer the ignominy, and hazard of a prosecution for High Treason; how much are they to be congratulated in finding their innocence secure in the sanctuary of National Justice! However the servants of the crown are bound by their duty to their King and their Country, to exert every vigilance to preserve the community from the secret machinations or open outrages of the intriguing, ambitious, or disputate, yet the people have now the satisfaction of knowing they are secured from the errors of zeal for exemplary punishments.

END of Mr. HARDY'S TRIAL.

☞ The Court will meet at the Old Bailey, on Monday the 17th of November, to proceed on the Trial of another of the Prisoners charged with High Treason, when it is expected Mr. HORNE TOOKE will be put to the Bar.

The Readers is therefore requested to observe, that the FIRST PART of his Trial will be published on Tuesday the 18th of November.

www.ingramcontent.com/pod-product-compliance
Lightning Source LLC
Chambersburg PA
CBHW031934230426
43672CB00010B/1921